Global Governance

Global Governance

Drawing Insights from the Environmental Experience

edited by
Oran R. Young

The MIT Press
Cambridge, Massachusetts
London, England

This book was set in Sabon on the Poltype system by Doyle Graphics, Tullamore, Ireland.

Printed and bound in the United States of America.

Library of Congress Cataloging-in-Publication Data

Global governance : drawing insights from the environmental experience / edited by Oran R. Young.
  p. cm.
 Includes bibliographical references and index.
 ISBN 0-262-74020-6 (alk. paper). - - ISBN 0-262-24040-8 (alk. paper)
 1. Environmental policy -- International cooperation. 2. Natural resources -- International cooperation. 3. Social ecology- -International cooperation.
 GE170.G58   1997
 363.7'0526 -- dc21   97-22911
                                                 CIP

Contents

Acknowledgments

This book is a product of the research program of the Institute on International Environmental Governance (IIEG) based at Dartmouth College. IIEG, which is sponsored jointly by the Dickey Center for International Understanding, the Environmental Studies Program, and the Rockefeller Center for the Social Sciences, came into existence in 1993. Its mandate is to bring together the concerns of those interested in international issues, environmental issues, and issues of governance through the organization of major research projects, the publication of *International Environmental Affairs*, a quarterly journal, and the mounting of conferences, like the 1995 Dartmouth Conference on Governance in the Twenty-First Century, which produced the papers included in this volume. Financial support for this conference came from the Dickey Center and the John L. Steffens 21st Century Fund at Dartmouth and from the Rockefeller Brothers Fund in New York. Each of the authors benefited from the general discussion that took place at the conference and from the comments of other participants including: Mlada Bukovansky, Abram Chayes, Antonia Handler Chayes, Angela Cropper, Carol Goldburg, Genady Golubev, Yolanda Kakabadze, Peider Koenz, Gene Lyons, Francis Magilligan, Gail Osherenko, Kilaparti Ramakrishna, Daniel Sabsay, Adele Simmons, Monica Tennberg, and Alexander Wendt. Much of the credit for moving this volume through the various stages of the publication process goes to the staff of the IIEG and especially to Nicki Maynard, who serves as the institute's office manager.

Contributors

Thomas Bernauer is assistant professor of international relations at the Swiss Federal Institute of Technology.

Lee Botts is an environmental advocate and independent consultant who lives in the Indiana dunes at the south end of Lake Michigan.

Helmut Breitmeier is a research scholar and manager of the International Regimes Database located at the Technical University of Darmstadt.

Paul R. Muldoon is a staff lawyer at the Canadian Environmental Law Association.

M. J. Peterson is associate professor of political science at the University of Massachusetts, Amherst.

David Reed is director of the Macroeconomics for Sustainable Development Program at the World Wide Fund for Nature in Washington, D.C.

Olav Schram Stokke is senior research fellow of international environmental governance and research director at the Fridtjof Nansen Institute.

Marcia Valiante is professor of law at the University of Toronto.

Konrad Von Moltke is adjunct professor of environmental studies at Dartmouth College, visiting professor at the Institute for Environmental Studies of the Free University of Amsterdam, and senior fellow at the International Institute for Sustainable Development and at the World Wildlife Fund US.

Paul Wapner is associate professor in the School of International Service at the American University.

Oran R. Young is professor of environmental studies and director of the Institute on International Environmental Governance at Dartmouth College.

Introduction

1

Rights, Rules, and Resources in World Affairs

Oran R. Young

Every thoughtful observer knows we have entered a period of profound challenges to humankind's capacity to solve international and transnational governance problems. But few are aware that we are, at the same time, witnessing a steady stream of experiments with promising new approaches to solving problems of governance in these settings. The resultant innovations have emerged piecemeal as responses to specific problems, and many of them reflect developments that do not fit easily into our conventional view of international society as a decentralized system of sovereign states. As a result, we are much more conscious of the growing demand for governance in world affairs than of emergent innovative procedures to supply governance in this social context. Yet the new approaches are exciting not only as novel ways of addressing specific problems at the international and transnational levels but also as sources of insights into strategies for meeting demands for governance that have a broader or more generic interest (Young 1994a).

The Dartmouth Conference on International Governance in the Twenty-first Century, which met in Hanover during September 1995, attempted to assess the current state of knowledge regarding the new approaches to governance in world affairs in order to chart a course for future research in the field and to capture intellectual capital of value to policy makers dealing with specific problems of governance as we prepare to embark on the next millennium. This volume describes the principal substantive findings and analytic insights developed during the conference.

Innovative approaches to governance have had the greatest impact on issues pertaining to natural resources and the environment. Whereas the Cold War bred an intense desire to protect and preserve existing institutions in other issue areas, the concurrently emerging environmental agenda prompted a growing awareness of the need for new arrangements that would foster sustainable human/environment relations. An especially notable innovation is the growth of functionally specific regimes to deal with an array of matters, such as endangered plants and animals, migratory species, marine pollution, transboundary fluxes of airborne pollutants, hazardous wastes, ozone depletion, and climate change. Moreover, efforts to solve environmental problems both reflect and affect significant developments in the character of international society. Although states remain central players in natural resource and environmental issues, nonstate actors have made particularly striking advances both in the creation of environmental regimes and in efforts to make these regimes function effectively once they are in place (Princen and Finger 1994; Wapner 1996). Environmental concerns are clearly one significant force behind the rising interest in the idea of global civil society (Lipschutz 1996).

Dealing with environmental concerns has also brought to our attention the need to think more systematically about institutional linkages and about the ways in which individual regimes are embedded in larger institutional structures and impinge on one another in international society (Charnovitz 1995). Interest in the idea of global civil society does not suggest that international society is likely to undergo a sea change in the foreseeable future to some well-defined and coherent alternative to the familiar states system. But we now realize that we need a more sophisticated understanding of international society, one that emphasiizes the significance of new forms of governance in a setting in which states continue to serve as primary repositories of authority. We also realize that we can gain some insights by turning to the idea of global civil society and exploring the interactions between international society and global civil society likely to affect the future supply of governance in world affairs.

The 1995 Dartmouth Conference tackled the problem of governance through several distinct yet related approaches. Each part of this volume focuses on one distinct approach. Part I seeks to clarify the key concepts of global governance, starting with the now familiar idea of regimes and moving on to the emerging idea of global civil society. Part II explores the links between institutions and organizations, a rich topic that has been seriously misunderstood by many commentators on governance in world affairs. Part III examines one substantive issue area — fresh water — destined to loom larger and larger in world affairs (Gleick 1993). Part IV moves beyond the study of individual issue areas to consider linkages among emerging arrangements to deal with specific governance problems. The last chapter of the volume gathers together and assesses the insights regarding governance in world affairs developed by these four approaches.

In the substantive sections of this introductory chapter, I sketch out the main contours of the new perspective on governance that is arising among students of international relations, particularly in reference to natural resource and environmental issues. The first section addresses the idea of governance at the most general level; the second section turns to some conceptual issues that require attention in making the transition from generic ideas about governance to the specific settings of issues pertaining to natural resources and the environment at the international and transnational levels. The next three sections discuss the formation of environmental regimes, their effectiveness as determinants of collective outcomes in world affairs, and the processes through which these arrangements change over time. Two final sections provide a brief overview of the volume's individual chapters and set forth four general questions presented to the participants at the opening of the Dartmouth Conference. These questions also provide a framework for the conclusions set forth in the final chapter.

The Idea of Governance

Governance arises as a matter of public concern whenever the members of a social group find that they are interdependent: the actions of each individual member impinge on the welfare of the others. Interdependence gives rise to conflict when the efforts of individual actors to achieve their goals interfere with or thwart the efforts of others to pursue their own ends. It emerges as a basis for cooperation, however, when opportunities arise to enhance social welfare by acting to coordinate the activities of the individual members of the group. More generally, interdependence leads to interactive decision making and generates the potential for collective-action problems in the sense that individual actors, left to their own devices in an interdependent world, frequently suffer joint losses as a result of conflict or fail to reap joint gains due to an inability to cooperate (Olson 1965; Schelling 1978; Hardin 1982; Young 1989a). The higher the level of interdependence among the members of the group, moreover, the more pervasive and complex collective-action problems ordinarily become.

At the most general level, governance involves the establishment and operation of social institutions — in other words, sets of rules, decision-making procedures, and programmatic activities that serve to define social practices and to guide the interactions of those participating in these practices (North 1990). Social institutions may address a wide range of issues, from patterns of speech to the definition of gender roles. Politically significant institutions or regimes, however, are arrangements designed to resolve social conflicts, promote sustained cooperation in mixed-motive relationships, and, more generally, alleviate collective-action problems in a world of interdependent actors (Young 1994a). Governance, on this account, does not presuppose the need to create material entities or organizations of the sort we normally think of as governments to administer the social practices that arise to handle the function of governance (Ellickson 1991). The burden of proof may actually reside with those who maintain that the establishment of governments or more limited public authorities is necessary to achieve these ends because the operation of any government or organized public authority is costly, both in material terms (for example, the funds required to run public agencies) and in terms of more intangible values (for instance, the bureaucratic inefficiencies and the restrictions on individual liberties imposed by even the most enlightened of governments).

Approached in this way, the initially counterintuitive distinction between *governance* and *government*, as well as the growing interest in the idea of "governance without government," become clear (Rosenau and Czempiel 1992). The key issue in making such a distinction concerns the role that social institutions, rather than organizations or governments, can play in ameliorating or resolving collective-action problems currently rising to the top of the political agenda in a variety of settings. The general proposition that groups of interdependent actors can and often do succeed in handling the function of governance without resorting to the creation of governments in the conventional sense is now well established. The literature on arrangements governing the use of common property resources (CPRs) in small-scale stateless societies — growing rapidly as an opposing view to the intuitively appealing but empirically dubious notion of the "tragedy of the commons" — bears this out (Hardin 1968; McCay and Acheson 1987; Bromley 1992). Today, leading students of governance are busy pinning down the conditions under which "governance without government" can succeed, instead of prolonging unproductive debates about the need to establish centralized organizations to solve an array of collective-action problems (Ostrom 1990; McKean 1992).

In drawing a clear distinction between governance and government, we need not, however, abandon the idea that organized public authorities can and often do play important roles in coming to terms with governance problems arising in the world today. On the contrary, the distinction opens up a major new research agenda for students of governance (Young 1994a). What roles can organizations perform in establishing institutional arrangements designed to help groups avoid or alleviate collective-action problems? Under what conditions can the resultant institutions operate successfully without the aid of organizations to administer their provisions? When administrative arrangements are needed, how can we tailor organizations to the roles they are expected to play in connection with specific institutions? Answers to these questions will aid us in developing the intellectual capital needed to meet the challenges to our capacity to solve the problems of governance likely to arise in the foreseeable future.

International Environmental Regimes

Recent work on governance at the international and transnational levels centers on the study of *regimes*: social institutions that consist of agreed upon principles, norms, rules, decision-making procedures, and programs that govern the interactions of actors in specific issue areas (Levy, Young, and Zürn 1995). For the most part, the formal or official members of these regimes are states, although it is increasingly apparent not only that a variety of nonstate actors play influential roles in the formation and operation of international regimes but also that, in transnational concerns, there is nothing out of the ordinary about the emergence of influential regimes whose principal members are not states (Gereffi and Korzeniewicz 1994). Thus, state-organized regimes include the international trade regime that rests on the General Agreement on Tariffs and Trade (GATT), as well as the more recent agreement that establishes the World Trade Organization (WTO); the regime for Antarctica and the southern ocean comprising the several components of the Antarctic Treaty System, and the ozone regime consisting of the 1985 Vienna Convention together with the 1987 Montreal Protocol as amended in London in 1990 and in Copenhagen in 1992. An example of a nonstate regime, however, is the transnational regime that deals with issues relating to the supply of air transport and is administered by the nongovernmental International Air Transport Association (IATA). As these examples suggest, international and transnational regimes can and often do vary substantially in terms of membership, functional scope, geographical domain, degree of formalization, and stage of development. Yet most regimes rest on one or more (not necessarily legally binding) constitutive documents, and all successful regimes serve to enmesh their members in social practices that evolve over time and guide the behavior of a variety of actors in significant ways.

Approached in this way, environmental regimes that operate at the international and transnational levels — in contrast to the arrangements emerging in small-scale societies and national societies to govern human/environment relationships — are not about property rights in the ordinary sense of the term. In the case of international regimes, which constitute the principal focus of recent research in this field, an essential distinction is made between *imperium* and *dominium*. States — like other collective or corporate entities — can and often do become owners of land and natural resources. In some countries, the state holds title to the great majority of the land and its associated natural resources. Even in the United States, where the political culture emphasizes the virtues of private property, the federal government owns about one third of the country's land and its associated natural resources (Public Land Law Review Commission 1970; Brubaker 1984).

In their role as the principal members of international society, however, states are primarily concerned with the entitlements of political authority or, in other words, *sovereign rights* in contrast to the entitlements of ownership or *property rights*. By exercising sovereign rights (i.e., *imperium*), states can place restrictions on the activities of holders of property rights (i.e., *dominium*) and, in extreme cases, act to rearrange the bundles of rights available to property owners. Holders of property rights, however, have no such capacity to influence the exercise of sovereign rights, for the most part. It follows that international environmental regimes— such as those established under the provisions of the 1979 Convention on Long-Range Transboundary Air Pollution (LRTAP) and its subsequent protocols or the 1973 Convention on International Trade in Endangered Species of Wild Fauna and Flora (CITES)—are properly understood as systems of rights, rules, and relationships designed to bring order into the interactions of sovereign authorities rather than as systems of property rights intended to bring order into the interactions of property owners. Nevertheless, the similarities between environmental regimes in international society and property regimes in other social settings are sufficiently strong that comparing and contrasting these institutional arrangements in a systematic fashion can be illuminating (Young 1994b; Princen 1996).

Although it is obviously desirable to begin any analysis of a particular class of regimes with propositions aimed at the class as a whole, there are often good reasons to partition the universe of cases involving natural resources and the environment into several subgroups. Many criteria for grouping the cases are available, but none is objectively correct. In thinking about the formation and operation of international environmental regimes, however, I have found it particularly helpful to focus on the jurisdictional attributes of the problems at stake and, on this basis, to differentiate among international commons, shared natural resources, and transboundary externalities.

International commons are physical or biological systems that lie wholly or largely outside the jurisdiction of any individual member of international society but that are of interest to two or more of them — or their nationals — as valued resources. Examples of such systems of current interest include high seas fisheries, deep seabed minerals, the electromagnetic spectrum, the stratospheric ozone layer, the global climate system, the global hydrological system, and outer space (Brown et al. 1977). Three broad options are available to those concerned with the governance of international commons: (1) enclosure through the extension of national jurisdictions, (2) the creation of a supranational or world government, and (3) the introduction of codes of conduct analogous to common property arrangements in small-scale stateless societies. Although students of international relations have long focused their attention on the first two options, the idea of "governance without government" has stimulated a marked growth of interest in the third option.

Shared natural resources, by contrast, are physical or biological systems that extend into or across the jurisdictions of two or more members of international society. They may involve renewable resources (e.g., migratory stocks of wild animals or straddling stocks of fish), nonrenewable resources (e.g., pools of oil that underlie areas subject to the jurisdiction of two or more states), or complex ecosystems that transcend the boundaries of national jurisdictions (e.g., shared river basins and lake basins). As these examples suggest, there may be significant asymmetries among the states concerned with shared natural resources. The circumstances of upstream states differ from those of downstream states, for example, and fish stocks that are economically important to one state may be of little interest to others. In all cases, however, the fundamental problem in dealing with shared natural resources is how to establish joint management regimes or arrangements analogous to unitization schemes among property owners in domestic society (Bernauer 1994; Richardson 1988).

Transboundary externalities arise when activities occurring wholly within the jurisdiction of one state nevertheless produce (normally unintended) consequences that affect the welfare of those located in other jurisdictions. Classic cases involve tangible impacts, such as the acidification of Swedish lakes from transboundary fluxes of airborne pollutants, or the loss of biological diversity (which is of actual or potential value to people located everywhere) associated with the destruction of moist tropical forests in the Amazon basin. Transboundary externalities may also involve intangible concerns, however, as in the destruction of world heritage sites (for instance, the city of Dubrovnik) as a by-product of civil wars. As these examples suggest, transboundary externalities can and often do give rise to asymmetries between the victims and the perpetrators of environmental harms, which accounts for the widespread interest both in devising liability regimes that will cover the transboundary impacts of actions occurring within individual jurisdictions and in promulgating general rules or principles pertaining to such situations (for example, the "polluter pays" principle). Experience suggests that actual cases raise complex issues, such as the rights of outsiders to intervene in the domestic affairs of individual states or the benefits to victims of offering to assist perpetrators in changing their ways (Lyons and Mastanduno 1995).

Regime Formation

It is undoubtedly accurate to say that, in the past ten to fifteen years, students of international and transnational regimes have accorded top priority to the study of regime formation and, more specifically, to the search for reasons why regimes emerge to deal with some problems, such as trade in endangered species or ozone depletion, but not others, such as the treatment of forests of international significance or Arctic haze (Haggard and Simmons 1987; Rittberger 1990; Young and Osherenko 1993b). This research offers a broad range of perspectives on the forces at work in regime formation. But even in this brief account, it helps to define four distinct concerns central to the literature on regime formation: problem structure or the nature of the problem to be solved, the processes of regime formation, the stages of regime formation, and driving social forces.

One intuitively appealing argument suggests that the "properties of issues... (pre)determine the ways in which they are dealt with" (Rittberger and Zürn 1991: 171). This argument has generated an effort to introduce theoretically grounded distinctions among types of issues and to show the links between the type of issue under consideration and the prospects for success in efforts to form international or transnational regimes. Volker Rittberger and Michael Zürn, for example, claim that—from the perspective of regime formation—issues involving value conflicts will be harder to deal with than issues featuring conflicts of interests about relatively assessed goods; they also claim that both of these types of issues will be more difficult to handle than issues featuring conflicts of interest about absolutely assessed goods (Rittberger and Zürn 1991). Turning to game theory others suggest that coordination problems (that is, interactive relationships featuring at least one equilibrium outcome) will be easier to deal with than collaboration problems when it comes to the formation of regimes (A. Stein 1982; Martin 1992). Although intuitively appealing, this line of analysis often makes it difficult to characterize real-world problems in terms of distinctions of this sort, either because actual problems exhibit elements of several analytically different types of issues or because the participants have not sufficiently specified the problems to allow for clear categorization. Thus, game theory is a promising approach to the study of regime formation, but it has not yet made a major contribution to our efforts to explain successes and failures in the creation of international environmental regimes.

Another approach to regime formation focuses on processes rather than problem structure and features a distinction among spontaneous or self-generating regimes, imposed regimes, and negotiated regimes (Young 1989a). Although most regimes are sooner or later articulated in treaties, conventions, or other explicit agreements, there are cases in which such agreements are largely matters of codifying informal rights and rules that have evolved over time through a process of converging expectations or tacit bargaining (Downs and Rocke 1990; Rutherford 1994). Such regimes are appropriately regarded as *spontaneous regimes*. *Imposed regimes* arise in cases where a dominant actor (or a *hegemon* in the language of recent analyses of regime formation) plays the central role in the process of regime formation, either by coercing others into accepting its preferred institutional arrangements or by making it attractive for others to accede to its preferences (Keohane 1984). *Negoti-*

ated regimes, by contrast, are products of an explicit bargaining process in which a number of actors who possess significant, though not necessarily equal, bargaining strength reach agreement on the constitutive provisions of an institutional arrangement (Young 1989a). The process approach has proven quite helpful to those endeavoring to reconstruct and understand the specific processes involved in the formation of regimes, although it is now apparent that the distinctions between processes are analytic rather than concrete in nature because two or more processes may play some role in the same case of regime formation.

It now also seems helpful to subdivide the overall process of regime formation into at least three stages: agenda formation, negotiation, and operationalization (Young forthcoming). Recent studies have tended to concentrate on the negotiation stage of the process, which covers the period from the start of explicit bargaining over the terms of an agreement to the signing of the agreement itself. In the case of regime formation over climate change, for example, the negotiation stage began with the first meeting of the Intergovernmental Negotiating Committee on Climate Change (INC) in February 1991 and ended with the signing of the Framework Convention on Climate Change during the United Nations Conference on Environment and Development (UNCED) in June 1992 (Bodansky 1993). Agenda formation and operationalization bracket the central stage of negotiation. Agenda formation covers the steps by which an issue initially makes its way onto the international political agenda, is framed for purposes of consideration in international forums, and rises to a sufficiently prominent place on the international agenda to justify the expenditure of time and political capital required to move it to the negotiation stage (J. Stein 1989). Operationalization, however, encompasses the steps involved in moving from the negotiation of an agreement to the establishment of a regime—in other words, the movement from paper to practice (Mitchell 1994a). This stage includes not only ratification of the agreement but also setting up international machinery and the initiation of programmatic activities within the jurisdictions of individual members (Spector and Korula 1992). Although this line of analysis is a recent development, it is already clear that the distinction among stages crosscuts the distinction among processes so that different processes are more or less central during different stages of regime formation.

All this has given rise to a lively debate about the relative importance of various driving social forces in determining success and failure in efforts to form international regimes and in shaping the substantive content of emergent regimes. Recent studies of regime formation have directed attention to the exercise of power — for example, the role of hegemons (Keohane 1984; Snidal 1985); the impact of ideas — for instance, the significance of epistemic communities (Haas 1992); the interplay of interests — for example, the dynamics of institutional bargaining (Young 1989b, Young 1994a) and the impact of the broader sociopolitical context (Young and Osherenko 1993a). The debate about the relative weight of these driving forces as determinants of regime formation taps into larger debates about the roles of material conditions, cognitive factors, and interactive decision making as determinants of the course of human affairs. It is hardly surprising, under the circumstances, that we are nowhere near a definitive resolution of this debate. What is clear at this stage, however, is that different driving forces are more or less prominent in different cases of regime formation and, perhaps more importantly, that power, ideas, and interests often interact in complex ways as determinants of outcomes in specific cases of regime formation (Young and Osherenko 1993a).

Regime Effectiveness

Recently, those who study institutions have become increasingly concerned with whether and how regimes have an impact on the flow of collective outcomes at the international and transnational levels. Ultimately, the study of institutions in any social setting rests on the premise that some significant proportion of the variance in the collective outcomes occurring in that setting can be explained or accounted for in terms of the operation of institutions rather than in terms of other drivers, such as material conditions or ideas (Cox 1986). Although the premise that institutions are important in this way is generally accepted without debate among students of domestic societies, it remains debatable in the field of international relations, which has long been dominated by the views of realists and neorealists who tend to view institutions as epiphenomena that reflect deeper forces, such as the distribution of power in international society (Strange 1983). To meet this challenge, students of international environmental regimes and more generally of international or transnational institutions have now embarked on a rapidly growing research program that deals with the implementation of international accords, compliance with the provisions of regimes, and the behavioral impacts of international institutions (Chayes and Chayes 1995; Haas, Keohane, and Levy 1993; Jacobson and Weiss 1995; Levy, Osherenko, and Young 1991; Wettestad 1995). At this stage, the debate about regime effectiveness centers on four clusters of issues: the meaning of *effectiveness*, causal links between institutions and outcomes, behavioral pathways, and broader consequences.

Intuitively, it makes sense to regard international regimes as successful or effective when they serve to solve or alleviate the problems that motivate their founders to create them. As it turns out, however, empirically demonstrating effectiveness in this sense is extremely difficult, which has led to a variety of other perspectives that emphasize variables such as goal attainment, implementation and compliance, behavioral change, social learning, and the initiation of social practices (Young 1994a). Some relationship clearly exists among these different measures of effectiveness. Achieving the goal of a 30 percent reduction of sulfur dioxide emissions under LRTAP, for example, has something to do with solving the problems caused by transboundary fluxes of airborne pollutants. As this simple example makes clear, however, different measures of effectiveness can by no means serve as perfect substitutes for one another. Some analysts are equally, if not more, interested in evaluative considerations—such as the extent to which the outcomes produced by institutions are efficient, equitable, or sustainable—than in the question of whether or not regimes make a difference at all. It is evident that students of regime effectiveness have a sizable number of conceptual and methodological issues to resolve in coming to terms with the consequences of international institutions.

The issue of causal connections turns on the problem of separating spurious correlations from real linkages. In general, it is not sufficient to observe that after a regime was created, the problem that led to its creation subsequently subsided. Because both the problem and its apparent solution can be attributable to other causes, the danger of ending up with spurious correlations is great. Several analytic procedures have emerged as helpful devices in coming to terms with this problem, including natural experiments, thought experiments, and laboratory experiments. Sometimes, natural experiments can be conducted, for example, by finding situations that closely resemble each other, except with respect to the character of the institutional arrangements that are present, and then looking for systematic effects of the variance on the institutional dimension. With regard to thought experiments, attention has focused recently on the exploration of counterfactuals as well as on the use of process tracing and thick description as means of thinking systematically about counterfactuals (Fearon 1991; Biersteker 1993). Laboratory experiments or simulation exercises are often helpful sources of insights that can subsequently be recast as hypotheses to be tested through an examination of real-world cases (Axelrod 1984). None of these procedures can individually be counted on to yield decisive causal connections. Taken together, however, they can illuminate the linkages involved in many cases.

Useful as these techniques are for weeding out spurious relationships, they cannot substitute for exploring the behavioral pathways or causal mechanisms that link institutions to behavior and that ultimately determine the extent to which individual regimes succeed in solving the problems that motivate their creation. Among other things, an understanding of such behavioral pathways will prove invaluable to those charged with designing new institutional arrangements to deal with problems such as climate change and the loss of biological diversity. Two major studies have evolved from the attempt to understand behavioral pathways among students of international environmental regimes. One study concentrates on regime members as unitary actors and emphasizes the roles that institutions play in creating greater concern for relevant problems, improving the contractual environment among participants, and enhancing the capacity of individual members to implement the provisions of regimes (Haas, Keohane, and Levy 1993). A more wide-ranging study starts by spelling out a series of analytically distinct behavioral models and proceeds to investigate the extent to which these models can account for variance in the behavior of regime members in actual cases (Levy, Young, and Zürn 1995). Thus, regimes may be thought of as (1) utility modifiers, (2) enhancers of cooperation, (3) bestowers of authority, (4) learning facilitators, (5) role definers, and (6) agents of internal realignments. What differentiates these models most clearly from one another is the assumptions they make about the nature of the relevant actors and about the driving forces that affect their behavior.

Whether or not regimes prove effective in solving the problems that motivate their creation, international and transnational institutions can and often do produce consequences that extend beyond the issue areas in which they are located. These broader consequences may take the form of demonstration effects — that is, arrangements devised to deal with one issue are subsequently copied in other issue areas — or of cognitive effects — that is, efforts to solve one problem lead to the development of new ways of thinking that influence the analyses of other problems. At the same time, broader consequences may be more overtly political. Regimes can establish social practices whose operation alters the overall distribution of power among key actors over time or fosters developments that have important implications for international society as a whole (for example, the growing role of nonstate actors). For the most part, the broader effects are unintended and unforeseen by those who labor to create international regimes in the first place, which does nothing, however, to diminish their significance (Levy, Young, and Zürn 1995).

Regime Change

Once formed, international and transnational regimes rarely become static, unchanging institutional structures. On the contrary, they give rise to highly dynamic social practices that continually change over time. As the case of whales and whaling suggests, profound changes can follow shifts in the size and composition of a regime's membership. The case of ozone depletion illustrates how institutional change can stem from altered understandings of the nature of the problem to be solved. Or, to turn to the case of Antarctica, changes can involve a broadening of functional scope with the addition of new elements that enlarge the range of substantive issues a regime covers. These few examples are merely illustrative of the wide array of institutional changes that regularly occur in most regimes. Although regime change has received less attention from students of world affairs than issues relating to regime effectiveness and, especially, to regime formation, it is already clear that any systematic treatment of change in international and transnational institutions must deal with at least four concerns: types of change, forms of change, processes of change, and sources of change.

Institutional changes come in many varieties. At the simplest level, regimes may undergo changes that affect their functional scope, geographical domain, or membership. Many other types of change are common, however, and may occur in conjunction with these simple changes. Changes can lead to alterations in decision-making procedures, compliance mechanisms, or revenue sources. In other cases, organizations emerge to administer the provisions of regimes, although none existed in the original design of the arrangements in question. The recurrent debate about whether to create a standing organization to operate the Antarctic Treaty System centers on this type of change. Even more fundamentally, regimes may experience transformations of defining principles or norms, merge with other institutional arrangements to form new institutions, or cease to exist altogether. Some observers now ask whether international environmental regimes exhibit an identifiable life cycle, which features a process of growth toward maturity and subsequent decay. In real-world situations, of course, a number of these different types of change are apt to occur simultaneously so that characterizing the dynamics of any given regime can become a tricky business.

Regardless of type, institutional change may assume a number of different forms. Two central dichotomies help to organize our thoughts about the forms of change: change may be considered *endogenous* (developmental) or *exogenous* (environmental). Endogenous changes are those that take place as a result of the operation of a regime itself. The addition of new consultative parties to the Antarctic Treaty System as a result of explicit actions on the part of the Antarctic Treaty Consultative Meetings is a case in point. Exogenous changes, on the other hand, are the results of forces external to the regime itself (for example, major alterations in the character of a marine ecosystem due to changes in water temperatures). At the same time, institutional change may be *incremental* (gradual) or *discontinuous* (nonlinear). Although the distinction between them is sometimes arbitrary, incremental change takes place step-by-step (for example, the addition of new members to a regime one by one over a period of years), whereas discontinuous change involves a sharp break with the past (for example, a wholesale change in membership all at once). Combining these dichotomies yields a two-by-two table in which the cells represent incremental endogenous change, incremental exogenous change, discontinuous endogenous change, and discontinuous exogenous change. All four forms of change occur with considerable regularity in the realm of international environmental regimes, and any one of the four may affect any of the types of change identified in the preceding paragraph.

Several additional aspects of regime dynamics come into focus when we examine the processes of change. Changes may take the form of intentional (planned) alterations or unintentional or de facto alterations in institutional arrangements. To make matters more complex, some participants in a regime may ardently pursue some changes, while others vigorously oppose the changes in question. Consider the debate over the introduction of the so-called Revised Management Procedures for whaling or the negotiation of substantive protocols pertaining to the emission of greenhouse gases as cases in point (Victor and Salt 1994). Changes may also be made through procedures spelled out in the regime itself or through processes that are not recognized, much less accepted, as legitimate under the provisions of the relevant institution. Making the process more complex, regimes vary greatly both in the extent to which they prescribe procedures for changing their provisions and in the stringency of the relevant transformation rules in cases where they do set forth explicit procedures to be followed by those advocating change. What is more, real-world cases may turn out to be difficult to sort out with respect to these questions of process. Determined advocates of change typically pursue their goals through all available channels, both within the rules and outside the rules. Moreover, changes that are ultimately attributable to pressure brought to bear outside the confines of a regime itself are often ratified in due course through the use of formal procedures prescribed by the regime.

As these observations suggest, we should also ask questions about the sources of institutional change or about the driving forces that lead to alterations in international environmental regimes. Surprisingly little effort has been devoted so far to answering such questions. An early attempt on the part of Robert Keohane and Joseph Nye sought to explain institutional changes in terms of such factors as economic processes, overall power structure, issue structure, and international organizations (Keohane and Nye 1977). Although this analysis constituted a good beginning, it left much to be desired as a theory of institutional change. It overemphasized material conditions in contrast to shifting ideas or configurations of interests; reflected a preoccupation with power, which is common among students of politics but which is misplaced in the study of international and transnational regimes; and left no place for changes in the physical and biological systems with which social institutions interact and which are often highly dynamic in their own right. Understanding the driving forces, however, is critical to any effort to explain or predict patterns of change in international environmental regimes and is thus an area that deserves much more attention than it has received to date among students of governance in world affairs.

The Shape of Things to Come

The chapters that make up the four major parts of this volume are revised versions of papers prepared for discussion at the Dartmouth Conference on International Governance in the Twenty-first Century. They are organized in pairs, each of which represents a different strategy for gaining analytic purchase on the role of regimes (or, more broadly, social institutions) in meeting the current challenges of governance that have arisen in a variety of international and transnational settings. Taken together, the chapters offer both a broad and a precise assessment of the role of regimes in addressing problems of governance.

Chapters 2 and 3, by Olav Schram Stokke of the Fridtjof Nansen Institute in Oslo and Paul Wapner of the American University in

Washington, respectively, tackle the subject in broad, conceptual terms. Stokke offers a critical appraisal of the main body of work on international regimes created in the last two decades and concludes that this line of analysis remains a vital source of new ideas. Along the way, however, he suggests that we need to pay more attention to the role of nonstate actors in the creation and operation of regimes, as well as to the linkages between international regimes and the domestic political processes of their members. Wapner argues that global civil society has become a force to be reckoned with in thinking about governance in world affairs. He does not assert that international society is declining, but rather that global civil society is growing up alongside international society; this development provides a base not only for a variety of nonstate actors to play influential roles in responding to a wide range of governance problems in today's world but also for the emergence of transnational regimes in which states are not the primary players.

Chapters 4 and 5, by Helmut Breitmeier of the University of Darmstadt and M. J. Peterson of the University of Massachusetts at Amherst, respectively, examine the relationships between regimes and organizations as a means of generating insights into the processes involved in meeting the challenges of governance at the international and transnational levels. Recent students of international governance have drawn a clear distinction between regimes construed as social institutions and organizations treated as material entities that possess offices, budgets, personnel, and so forth. As the phrase "governance without government" suggests, these students have often deemphasized the role of international organizations in meeting the demand for governance in today's world. The distinction between institutions and organizations need not, however, lead to the conclusion that organizations are of little importance. As Breitmeier shows, international organizations frequently play vital roles in efforts to create regimes. Peterson demonstrates that organizations are often required to administer or operate regimes and that creating the right organizational arrangements is an important determinant of the effectiveness of international and transnational regimes.

Chapter 6, by Thomas Bernauer of the Swiss Federal Institute of Technology, and Chapter 7 by Marcia Valiante of the University of

Toronto, Paul Muldoon of the Canadian Environmental Law Association, and Lee Botts, a well-known environmental advocate, focus intensively on one substantive issue area: water and, more particularly, rivers and lakes treated as shared natural resources. This issue is profoundly important in the sense that issues relating to fresh water are destined to become critical to the capacity of a growing human population to survive and thrive on Earth in the future. Drawing on experience with longstanding arrangements, such as the set of institutions pertaining to the Rhine River and the regime articulated in the Great Lakes Water Quality Agreements of 1972 and 1978, the authors of both chapters make the case that institutional design matters when it comes to dealing with shared natural resources and that successful regimes are apt to combine top-down approaches to design with bottom-up developments featuring the emergence of communities of regime supporters.

Chapters 8 and 9, by David Reed of the World Wildlife Fund in Washington and Konrad von Moltke of Dartmouth College, address questions involving institutional linkages in general and, more specifically, the interface between regimes that deal with trade and the environment. These chapters offer the intriguing observation that although we often think of individual regimes as stand-alone arrangements, they are in fact almost always embedded in larger institutional structures. Moreover, the structure that has evolved in one issue area (e.g., trade) may differ fundamentally from the structure that has emerged in another issue area (e.g., the environment). When linkages emerge that cut across issue areas, therefore, clashes between different sets of institutional arrangements often instigate complications that cannot be ignored in efforts to solve problems of governance. Quite apart from their specific details, such complications are a major source of the difficulties that have surfaced in trade and environment regimes in recent years.

Chapter 10, which is based on the discussions that occurred during the Dartmouth Conference, provides a more general assessment of future prospects for "governance without government." Does this approach offer a basis for hope in responding to the challenges of governance that have overwhelmed conventional approaches in recent years? Should we expect regimes to arise in connection with some problems of governance, but not with others? Why are some regimes more effective as problem solvers than others, even though the causes of these differences are not apparent to casual observers? Do insights gleaned from the study of international regimes apply to the analysis of transnational regimes in which the principal players are nonstate actors?

Overarching Concerns

Four broad questions articulated at the opening session of the Dartmouth Conference became the central themes of the discussions at the conference. Taken together, the answers to these questions may determine whether regime analysis will give rise to a lasting and productive research program among students of world affairs.

1. Has regime analysis produced a distinctive conception of governance that directs attention to new ways of solving collective-action problems at the international and transnational levels? Most traditional accounts of problems of world order during this century have focused, first and foremost, on the need to create some sort of hierarchical, supranational structure and, to a somewhat lesser extent, on the attractions of extending national jurisdictions to enclose additional areas and resources (e.g., marine ecosystems) (Claude 1962; Suganami 1989). Much of the appeal of regime analysis arises from its claim to have articulated an alternative to these traditional and increasingly shopworn accounts. Regime analysis focuses on governance as a social function rather than on government as a collection of organizations; it thus opens up the prospect of horizontal structures — "governance without government" — as an alternative, or at least a supplement, to mainstream thinking about world order. The appeal of this line of reasoning is easy to understand, and it is not difficult to point to specific instances in which the idea of "governance without government" seems to work.

2. Are these successful cases outliers ultimately destined to appear as historical oddities, or are they harbingers of a new conception of governance destined to spread from a few initial applications to a growing collection of substantive problems and from strictly international arrangements to a growing array of transnational as well as international regimes? We may eventually conclude that regimes can

succeed as a means of supplying governance only when certain other more or less restrictive conditions are met. Just as the institutions associated with common property resources in small-scale societies may flourish, for example, only in situations characterized by the presence of a strong community (McKean 1992; Singleton and Taylor 1992; Ostrom 1992), the success of regimes at the international level may also depend on the presence of a vibrant international society (Dunne 1995) or some sort of global civil society (Lipschutz 1992). Similarly, success in creating and operating international and transnational regimes may depend on embedding specific arrangements in larger institutional structures rather than treating those arrangements as stand-alone institutions. It may require the presence of some specific technology or a particular distribution of the material bases of power among the members of specific regimes (Baldwin 1993b). The realization that success in the development of international and transnational regimes depends on the presence of a variety of social conditions need not cripple regime analysis, unless the probability of satisfying the relevant conditions becomes vanishingly small. But these observations do point to an important line of analysis that students of international and transnational governance need to pursue more systematically in the future.

3. Does the emergence of international regimes in a variety of issue areas have broader consequences for the future of international society in general? In recent years, students of regimes have devoted increasing attention to the issue of institutional effectiveness — in other words, to the question of whether regimes succeed in solving the problems that motivate their members to create them in the first place (Levy, Young, and Zürn 1995). Clearly, an increasing reliance on a network of regimes will also have significant consequences for international society as a whole and perhaps for global civil society as well. One particularly interesting question concerns the extent to which a focus on regimes carries with it a conservative bias regarding the future of international society (Choucri 1993). The main body of regime analysis assumes, for instance, that states will continue to be the most important, if not exclusive, members of regimes in the future; it also offers a vision of "governance without government" that may serve to reinforce the prevailing view of international society as a decentralized states system.

Exponents of more radical change in the nature of international society will likely find these assumptions objectionable. If, however, the concept of governance associated with regime analysis proves to be a successful vehicle for reforming the states systems — in other words, if it offers an effective means of solving a wide range of problems without abandoning the defining features of international society as we know it today — the resultant system of thought about regimes is likely to gain a large following among those striving to meet the growing demand for governance at the international and transnational levels.

4. Can we apply the experience gained from environmental issues to a broader range of governance problems that arise in international society or in global civil society? Many observers simply assume that problems of governance and, therefore, the requirements for solving them differ markedly from one issue area or functional realm to another. Security problems, for instance, are said to be matters of high politics in which power is the principal driving force. Economic issues turn on opportunities for reaping mutual gains and therefore generate incentives for cooperation, despite the fact that there is always room for conflict over the distribution of gains from trade. Human rights issues raise questions about the sovereign authority of individual states and run the risk of provoking hostile reactions to outside interference. How significant are these differences, however? Are they more fundamental than various analytical considerations that cut across functional realms, such as the distinctions between benign problems and malign problems, between coordination problems and collaboration problems, or between enforcement approaches and management approaches to eliciting compliance from regime members? The volume authors specifically draw on experience with environmental issues as a source of insights into governance in world affairs, but they also make a constant effort to determine whether these insights are generally applicable in seeking solutions to the varied challenges of governance that we can expect to encounter in the twenty-first century.

I

Concepts

2

Regimes as Governance Systems

Olav Schram Stokke

What has the now twenty-year-old scholarly debate on international regimes contributed to our understanding of global governance? This chapter focuses three general approaches to that question: (1) the concept of governance implied in regime theory; (2) changes in the research profile, including privileged themes and theoretical foci; and (3) the compatibility of that profile with the needs of policymakers and others to come to terms with current governance problems in world politics.

Within the larger, more liberal project in the study of international relations, which deals broadly with how a society of states can govern itself, regime theory has been especially oriented toward instrumental usefulness.[1] In other words, can past experience help us to deal better with situations in which the behavior of one member affects the welfare of another, and if so, how? Two common criticisms levied against regime analysis are that the concept itself is woolly and the theory basically conservative because of its focus on order, stability, and the centrality of states in managing world affairs. In this chapter, I show how those two criticisms are very closely tied to the policy-oriented ambition of regime analysis. The looseness of its conceptual basis has allowed or even encouraged theoretical heterogeneity, thus sensitizing analysis to a fairly wide range of mechanisms and processes related to international coordination. Moreover, the attention given to regime stability, especially in early contributions to regime analysis, reflects the sequential manner in which governance has been addressed in regime theory. Regime scholars have been cautious enough to split the larger question of governance into a number of smaller and more manageable ones—for example, singling out the international regime as one significant means of governance and then asking separate questions about its maintenance, change, and consequences.

Global Governance and International Regimes

The term *governance* derives from the Greek *kybernetes*, whch is etymologically linked to navigation and helmsmanship. When studying the phenomenon of governance internationally, scholars are quick to point out that the hierarchic connotations of the term can be misleading. Generally, governance can be understood as the establishment and operation of a set of rules of conduct that define practices, assign roles, and guide interaction so as to grapple with collective problems (Young 1994a: 3, 15). In post-Westphalian international affairs, those responsible for creating and operating such governance systems, or regimes, are also the ones to be governed: states, jealously guarding their sovereignty. This definition of governance can be maintained without necessarily agreeing with the conventional realist claim that the international realm is fundamentally different from the domestic one. Clearly, even within states, there can be pockets of substantial anarchy or a government unwilling or unable to enforce measures that will ensure security for its citizens; moreover, in the international realm, certain rules of conduct are widely perceived, often formalized, and sometimes enforced by states or collectives of states.

Thus, regime analysis tends to study governance through statist lenses, focusing on the creation and operation of rules in *international* affairs. The term *global governance*, on the other hand, encompasses not only those phenomena but also situations in which the creators and operators of rules are nonstate actors of various kinds, working within or across state boundaries. Rosenau (1995: 16–19) points out that a myriad of governance systems can be found at various levels; he also discerns a trend in world affairs in which authority is being relocated from the arena of state interaction to arenas where subnational, transnational, and sometimes even supranational actors play a significant role. Thus, students of global governance are rehearsing well-known themes from the early globalism and interdependence literature of the 1960s and

1970s, with perhaps a slight shift of empirical focus from transnational corporations with global reach to transnational environmental groups with global worries.[2]

Although regime analysis may have grown out of the same literature, its scope of concern remains narrower. The significance of subnational and transnational groups has always been acknowledged, both as agents and targets of governance efforts, but that acknowledgment has never shown up much in actual theorizing (Baldwin 1993a: 9). In practice, most regime theory has been in line with the methodological assumptions of structural realism that states can usefully be conceived of as unitary, rational actors and that opening the black box of domestic politics in an interactive rather than additive manner is not likely to be worth the costs involved. Although these assumptions ensure a simpler and more focused analysis, they also have two potentially troubling implications. First, unlike the study of global governance, regime analysis considers only processes related to international-level rules, implying that private regimes—in which the members are private organizations rather than states—have been given scarce systematic attention (Haufler 1993). Second, linkages between international regimes and transnational interaction have not been adequately explored,[3] including the question of whether mechanisms found to be relevant to international regime processes are likely to shape transnational ones as well. Today, these implications are finally being studied somewhat, especially in the analysis of regime consequences, but also increasingly in some accounts of how regimes are formed or maintained.

Another salient feature of regime analysis is its focus on explicitly delineated and separate *issue areas*. Governance, as conceived of in regime analysis, is clearly circumscribed spatially and functionally. This conception is compatible with the international law notion of regimes as systems of rules or regulations pertaining to various spatial objects of law, such as high seas areas, continental shelves, and territorial seas, as well as to various types of activities conducted there, such as fishing, navigation, or scientific research.[4] In regime analysis, issue specificity also reflects doubt—articulated strongly in the interdependence literature—concerning realist assumptions about cross-issue unity of agency and the fungibility of power capabilities (Keohane and Nye 1977). One advantage of an open attitude to these matters is that it allows us to theorize the conditions necessary for linkage of issues (Sebenius 1983) and to pose pointed questions about when issue boundaries can be crossed by certain actors and ideas or when such deliberate coupling will be difficult. Indeed, one of the presumed benefits of international institutions is that they may facilitate the productive linkage of various issues within a larger area of contention (Keohane and Martin 1995).

Some students of global governance, however, warn against the issue-area approach, arguing that it narrows the analysis of governance and tends to obscure the fact that regimes are linked by norms that come into play when two or more regimes overlap or conflict (Rosenau 1992: 9). Politically speaking, exaggerated issue orientation may serve to reproduce artificial boundaries between actors, ideas, and solutions. Environmental protection, for instance, is difficult to discuss adequately without delving deeply into other issue areas because relevant measures tend to affect actors engaged in various fields of economic production or military operation.[5] Likewise, as part of the current political reorganization of Central and Eastern Europe, a swarm of transboundary region-building efforts has been underway the past few years to generate or reawaken a wide range of political, cultural, and commercial ties across the old East-West divide (Stokke and Tunander 1994). The permissiveness of these processes in terms of issue scope reflects a desire to muster broad coalitions in support of the establishment and operation of such new arenas for cooperation.[6] On the other hand, although political processes may cut across issue boundaries, rules are still circumscribed, and, as Kratochwil (1993: 82) points out, the circumscription reflects a consensus established in a political process that itself is an integral part of regime analysis.

In summary, therefore, the concept of governance implied in regime analysis is narrower than the one intended by global governance. In terms of *locus*, regime theory has been largely preoccupied with inter-state relations, whereas global governance refers to the creation and operation of rules at other levels as well and to the involvement of subnational and transnational actors. As to *domain*, regime theory has taken over from international law and the interdependence school—an issue-area approach that students of global governance are now inclined to transcend. The concept of international regimes is not, however, incompatible with the concept of global governance; on the contrary, although they differ in emphasis, both concepts recognize the significance of nonstate actors and the relationships between issue areas.

The Contended Core of Regime Analysis

Regime analysis is certainly not a single compact body of thought. For one thing, considerable efforts have been invested in trying to reach a shared understanding among scholars about how to identify and differentiate among international regimes. Although most accept as a starting point Krasner's definition of regimes as "sets of implicit or explicit principles, norms, rules, and decision-making procedures around which actors' expectations converge in a given area of international relations", (1982: 186), this definition has been subject to protracted debate. On the one hand, slimliners prefer operational clarity and therefore explicitness and formality; on the other hand, fatliners emphasize the intersubjective nature of regimes and their embeddedness in practice. In particular, controversy has surrounded the question of "whether regimes are to be identified on the basis of *explicit rules and procedures*, or on the basis of *observed behavior*, from which rules, norms, principles, and procedures can be inferred" (Keohane 1993: 26–27). Today, the tendency is to emphasize explicit rules as the core of the concept,[7] but also to recognize that prescriptive status—that is, actors regularly referring to a rule when describing or evaluating behavior—can be achieved by other means than formal treaty making, as demonstrated by the rules that constitute customary international law. Another question is whether the rule also gives rise to a measure of rule-consistent behavior (Young 1991b). Krasner's slim definition of regimes excludes practices such as justification and behavioral adaptation from the concept proper, making them matters of empirical inquiry. As such, this definition comes closer to the definition of the term in international law, and it clearly becomes instrumental in splitting the more general question of how to achieve governance in a stateless society into a series of more specific questions.

The Main Puzzles of Regime Analysis

Three major themes can be identified in regime literature to date, although emphasis on any one theme has shifted over time. One theme concerns the *maintenance* of existing regimes, a phenomenon with several components. Many regime scholars have been struck by the robustness of international regimes, even in the face of considerable changes in the interest or power structures that presumably were important for their creation. This observation and the fact that governments continue to invest substantial resources in international regimes are often seen as evidence that regimes must be more than epiphenomena in world affairs (Young 1992; Keohane and Martin 1995). For instance, much scholarly fuel has been spent accounting for the continued significance of the postwar Bretton Woods institutions as arenas for interstate coordination of trade and finance, despite the declining willingness of their major architect and proponent, the United States, to support them with selectively biased market access and fixed exchange rates. How can we account for such robustness? Why do some international institutions grow stronger and more legitimate, whereas others shrink and fade? As we shall see, some accounts of regime robustness emphasize features of the regime itself, whereas others are largely concerned with various structural conditions in its environment.

Closer examination of regimes often discloses that such robustness does not necessarily imply stability. On the contrary, regimes typically change considerably over time: the number and composition of member states often change; the transparency of decision making may vary, for instance in the degree of openness to participation by nonstate actors; regulations may be sharpened or watered down; more intrusive compliance control mechanisms may be introduced; or new programmatic activities may be added to existing ones. Indeed, although institutional transformation is often a sine qua non for the continued political relevance of international regimes, it is nevertheless an aspect of regime maintenance that so far has been given comparatively little systematic attention in the literature.[8]

A second major theme in regime analysis is the *formation* of international institutions. Authors try to account for the success or failure of various efforts to create new regimes in the international domain, focusing on different types of factors. Are certain configurations of power necessary—for instance, one predominant actor promoting the regime project? What strategies of persuasion and what processes of realization mark successful attempts at regime creation? And what is the role of international organizations in the success or failure of regime formation? Again, a distinction can be made between accounts that emphasize certain features of the proposed regime—such as the stringency of rules or the intrusiveness of compliance mechanisms—and explanations that stress relationships and interactions between the players involved in the process of regime formation. Another distinction can be made between individualist accounts that emphasize purposive agency and sociological accounts that stress the embeddedness of regimes in practices and broader normative contexts (Kratochwil and Ruggie 1986), the latter suggesting a more restricted space for political engineering in such contexts.[9] Whereas the study of regime maintenance has tended to focus on certain economic institutions with considerable track records, much of the empirical research on regime formation has focused on the environmental arena, which is a fairly new and apparently fertile domain for international institution building.

A long-standing criticism of regime analysis is that it has been tardy in dealing with the third, and arguably very basic, theme of governance puzzles: regime *consequences*. Actually, this criticism is only partly accurate because much of the discussion on regime maintenance and formation has focused on the impacts of such regimes on the ability of states to coordinate behavior in mutually beneficial ways. Nevertheless, questions about regime consequences were not subjected to systematic empirical inquiry until the late 1980s, and we are still in an early phase of this work because a number of the early, transnational collaborative projects on regime consequences have only been recently completed or are approaching finalization.[10]

In line with the issue-specific and instrumental focus of most regime analysis, the limited and focused question of regime *effectiveness* has received the most attention so far, rather than the larger questions of what impacts regimes or clusters of regimes have on matters such as world order, international dominance, peaceful change, or the growing role of subnational and transnational actors in international negotiations. The issue-specific lens of regime analysis can be both a strength and a liability to empirical analysis: although it allows more focused causal accounts of regime impacts, it may also render the analysis myopic by obscuring how developments in one regime area are shaped by and affect governance in other functional areas.

Because regime effectiveness is currently the most dynamic field of regime analysis, it is worth delving somewhat deeper into its set of puzzles than those generated by the other two themes. Analysts vary in their conceptualizations of regime effectiveness (Bernauer 1995: 357), but all are interested in the performance of institutions.[11] Young and Levy (1996) relate regime effectiveness to the impacts a regime has on certain socially defined problems, whether economic, environmental, or some other type.[12] Because a regime is a social institution and works through social agents, it has probably affected the behavior of actors.[13] In addition to causation, however, which we shall return to later in the chapter, there is an element of evaluation in the concept of regime effectiveness. The key questions for evaluation are what kind of behavioral adaptation should qualify as relevant to effectiveness and how much adaptation should be required before the regime can be judged effective. For both of those questions, it might be tempting to resort to the goals expressed in basic documents or by actors who took part in their negotiation or are subject to the regime. Formal goal attainment, however, can be an unreliable yardstick of effectiveness. Frequently, the objectives and purposes defined in international agreements are too ambiguous or incomplete to offer much guidance. Even when goals are operationalized in specific behavioral prescriptions, it could be misleading to attribute effectiveness merely to compliance. Where these prescriptions are based on poor understanding of the issue area addressed, adherence to them may even generate consequences that counter the purpose of the regime.[14]

There is also the issue of hidden agendas. For instance, although nowhere stated explicitly in the convention text, among the major problems addressed by the marine living resources convention pertaining to the Antarctic was the perceived challenge from outside actors to the prominent decision-making position of the consultative parties in matters related to the region (Lagoni 1984). It is worth noting that even traditional means of treaty interpretation—as codified in Articles 31 and 32 of the Vienna Convention on the Law of Treaties—are not limited to the treaty text itself, but require that account be taken of the context and circumstances of a treaty conclusion, other relevant agreements between parties, their subsequent practice, and so on.

The focus on substantively defined problems rather than formally defined goals does not eliminate any of the difficulties of specifying the contents and origins of a standard of evaluation. Rather, it acknowledges the fact that formal goal attainment is insufficient and urges the analyst to proceed with a broader and more in-depth assessment of the socially defined purpose of the regime. Specification of the basic problems to be addressed is not always a straightforward matter: it may require prioritization; various actors may comprehend the problem in different ways; and changes may occur over time in their understanding of the problem. These dimensions should be incorporated in the evaluative standard, hence also allowing evaluations of the adaptability of the regime to a changing social environment.

In the rest of this chapter, I utilize the major analytic puzzles in offering a rough sketch of the developmental history of regime theory for the past two decades. I pay particular attention to two aspects of this development, both of which affect the relevance of regime theory to the emerging concern for global governance: first, I examine the *locus* of governance—that is, the level at which governance is studied, including the type of actors drawn into the analysis; and second, I discuss the *mechanisms* of governance—that is, the kind of intermediate causal processes invoked when regime analysts account for the creation and operation of international rules or the behavioral adaptation pursuant to such rules. The main thrust of my argument is that regime analysis is gradually taking a more inclusive approach in dealing with both the locus and mechanisms of governance, hence moving closer to the study of global governance.

The Productive Heterogeneity of Regime Analysis

In the evaluation of the distinctive contributions of regime theory, the bottom line is whether regime theory can address the various puzzles of governance more satisfactorily than some other approach. Although this is not the place for a focused comparative assessment, a few preliminary comments may show how regime analysis differs from an important precursor such as integration theory and from a major current competitor such as structural realism.

Regime analysis acquired many of its traits from the interdependence literature, including the blend of continuity and rejection stemming from integration theory.[15] Although regime analysis shares integration theory's strong concern with institutions and, increasingly, an emphasis on substate actors and transnational activities, it offers a far more pronounced articulation of agency and intentional pursuance of self-interest. Regime scholars have always assumed a cautious attitude toward agency-distant and apparently unidirectional phenomena such as incrementalism, spillover, and sense of community; they have sought more differentiated and conditional propositions about the origins and prospects of coordinated behavior.[16]

Put bluntly, regime theory sliced up and simplified parts of neofunctional integration theory in three moves. First, it lifted issue-specific, institutionalized cooperation out of the theoretical context of broader regional cooperation processes, thus dramatically increasing the number of cases to observe and compare simply because there are far more regimes than political regions. Second, it divorced itself from the notion that centralized decision making is the optimal response to situations of interdependence. Instead, regime analysis has tended to regard the appropriate division of labor between national governments and international organizations as a theoretical matter. Presumably, regime scholars argue, the division of labor depends more upon the issue area involved and the specific purpose of the institution in question than on some abstract stage reached in a process of unification. And third, by refocusing on institutions themselves, rather than the wider processes of which they are a part, regime analysis could inquire into the various ways in which regimes are significant to cooperation and discord among states. In short, regime analysis is less ambitious than integration theory in terms of how much it tries to deal with at a time, thus arguably rendering simpler and more tractable the analysis of the formation, maintenance, and consequences of international institutions.

Regime analysis's late arrival to the basic questions of whether and how regimes matter may have weakened its standing among some students of international relations. With one leg in integration theory and one in interdependence, regime analysis has always been criticized as being somewhat naive and ignorant of the hard realities of world affairs. The heaviest criticisms have been levied by proponents of structural realism, who tend to dismiss regimes as epiphenomena that merely reflect, but never transform, the underlying power relationships in an interstate system marked by anarchy.[17] For their part, Marxists have accused regime analysis of myopia—that is, of reifying phenomena that are simply superstructural responses to the needs of economic production.

Due to this external ridicule, self-justification has always been high up on the list of priorities for regime analysts. Indeed, few other theory traditions have spent as much energy in debating whether it really amounts to anything more than faddish up-to-datism or servile attendance to the political priorities of the day, with scanty prospects of offering new or lingering insights (Rochester 1986: 800). This debate may imply an exaggerated self-consciousness and perhaps some wasted energy, but it has led regime theorists to invest considerable energy in explicitly linking their propositions to larger bodies of theoretical work, especially the new institutionalism, both in its "thin" rational choice version and in the "thick" sociological one.[18] As a result, cumulativeness in the study of international governance has been enhanced, and regime scholars have been able to articulate clearly how their analysis differs from other approaches. Indeed, few contributors to regime analysis have any substantial quarrel with the realist claim that international affairs can usefully be portrayed as individual adaptation to a condition of anarchy, defined as absence of a central government. Nor will they deny the significance of power and interests in interstate relations, but they will add that the analysis of such relations often benefits from the inclusion of other facets of the situation. The most important difference between the average regime theorist and a structural realist is the weight the former places on international institutions. All regime analysts, but no realists, will argue that, despite anarchy, the presence and features of such institutions account for a substantial part of the variance in outcomes in international relations.

I previously noted that a slim definition of regimes was instrumental in splitting the broader question of how international governance occurs into a number of more manageable ones. The original "looseness" of the core concept, however, has ensured considerable theoretical diversity in regime analysis. Because the concept is so generous, it can include and study a wide range of real-life phenomena, which traditionally have been studied from a multitude of perspectives. Compared to other fields of inquiry, such as structural realism or neofunctional integration theory, regime theory has a far less restrictive set of assumptions and is therefore more permissive in terms of the kind of vocational training it takes to gain access to and contribute to the field. Lawyers, philosophers, sociologists, game theorists, new institutionalists, and even some heretical realists feel quite at home in regime discourse. Contributors to regime analysis have a common focus on political institutions but widely differing notions of what these institutions are, how they come about, how they change and how they affect political processes.

Although this chapter focuses on the policy-oriented, purposive aspect of regime analysis, some critical voices reprimand other regime analysts for failing to take into account the full consequences of the *social nature* of institutions (Kratochwil and Ruggie 1986). According to a number of sociologically inclined scholars, seeing regimes as "convergent expectations" clashes with the solipsistic, or self-contained, image of agency that is applied in mainstream regime theory. These critics complain, moreover, that exaggerated attention to the instrumental usefulness of regimes in solving certain problems obscures regimes' role in defining, interpreting, and justifying behavior (Kratochwil 1984), as well as in upholding some purposes, knowledges, and power relationships at the expense of others (Keeley 1990).

The alleged truncation of mainstream regime analysis is closely connected with its strong commitment to positivist canons, especially the requirement that theoretical implications be drawn with sufficient precision and close enough to intersubjective experience to allow empirical falsification. When applied to regimes, positivist canons tend to lead analysis away from those aspects of an institution that do not immediately translate into observable behavioral adaptation. For instance, they may veil the role of institutions in determining which issues or developments are singled out and framed as problems that require joint action. The main body of regime scholarship does not share, however, the skepticism of many sociological authors regarding the possibility or desirability of manipulating institutions in order to realize given goals: the generation of concrete policy advice on how to structure negotiations or institutions forms the very core of this tradition. Often inherent in such a pragmatic orientation is a preference for explanatory models that are simple and decision oriented rather than "thick" or context laden.[19] In other words, the *methodenstreit* between individualist and sociological contributions to regime theory also reflects somewhat different purposes; it also suggests changing emphasis on often competing criteria—parsimony and determinacy, on the one hand, and richness and empirical validity, on the other. The intellectual exchange between the two camps of regime analysis is currently on the rise.

The vocational and methodological diversity of regime analysis no doubt renders communication among regime analysts more difficult; it is clearly one of the reasons why so much intellectual energy has been spent on preliminary tasks such as concept definition and justification (Underdal 1995). But it also renders regime analysis more flexible than dogmatic notions addressing the puzzles of governance. In general, writers tend to be acutely aware of the partial and complementary nature of their contributions.

Mechanisms of Governance: The Functional Logic of Mainstream Regime Analysis

Regarding the puzzles of regime maintenance and change, the question of *hegemonic stability* is easily the most central nondebate in regime analysis. It is a nondebate because, since early in the 1980s, noone seems to have defended the thesis in its strong form—namely, that the robustness of regimes requires a predominant actor, prepared either to pay a disproportionate share of the costs of upholding the regime or to coerce others into behavioral conformity with it.[20] Yet almost every contributor to the regime literature has taken substantial pains to discuss the origins, merits, and especially shortcomings of hegemonic stability. Almost all conclude that there is every reason to distance oneself from the whole idea. This ritual—the continuous demolition of a thesis that nobody holds—might be seen as an expression of instrumentalist relief among mainstream regime theorists: had hegemonic power been necessary for the stability of international regimes, the policy lessons to be drawn from regime analysis would have been very limited in scope because hegemons are such a rare and threatened species in the international system. From this perspective, the role of the hegemonic stability thesis in regime analysis has been mainly to confirm that there is considerable leeway for human action and political determination in the maintenance and creation of international institutions.

The exaggerated focus on hegemonic stability in the literature has had the unfortunate impact of truncating the space devoted to the analysis of power. Clearly, the fact that regimes may emerge and survive without a dominant actor does not mean that power differentials are irrelevant to the creation, specification, and operation of rules among states. It would indeed be very surprising if superior access to financial, military, or research resources did not affect an actor's ability to influence the contents and form of a negotiated regime. Typically, such asymmetry allows for a whole menu of bargaining tactics—such as threats, promises, or side payments. On the other hand, in the hegemonic stability theory the relationship between power and the potential for institutionalized cooperation is sometimes more complex than assumed. For instance, rough symmetry among the actors involved—or at least "balanced asymmetry" in the sense that their strengths are in different areas—may in some situations facilitate efforts to coordinate behavior by reducing the suspicion and fears of being liable to exploitation as a result of a regime. Norway's relationship to Russia in the Arctic is a case in point. Its longstanding caution about deep institutionalized cooperation with this northeasterly neighbour receded only after the decline of the Soviet Union, which lessened the cumulative asymmetry in the region and also nudged Russia into becoming part of the broader-based collaborative institutions in the high north. Because a Norwegian rule of thumb in the Arctic has been to anchor eastward cooperation in multilateral Western solutions, those two changes removed an important barrier to deeper and more comprehensive cooperation in the Barents region.[21] Of course, such fear of domination comes as no surprise to structural realists sensitive to the efforts to counterbalance any concentration of power. In terms of institutional design, it merely suggests an awareness of how the membership composition of regimes may affect the level of perceived asymmetries among members.

The eagerness of mainstream regime scholars to repudiate the hegemonic stability thesis has stimulated the elaboration of a rationalist after-hegemony literature, which argues that regimes are maintained by their perceived usefulness in facilitating collaboration among self-interested actors (Keohane 1984). Here, the underlying logic is a functional one: various barriers to collective action are matched with efficient institutional remedies along the various dimensions of regimes. Reporting procedures, performance review mechanisms, and monitoring arrangements are all institutional measures that enhance transparency and reduce the risk of the actors' unilateral defection, thus increasing reciprocity and diminishing barriers to mutually beneficial cooperative behaviour in a range of collective situations (Martin 1992).

Rationalist regime analysis is extended to the puzzles of regime creation and consequences as well. Whether applying metaphors from games or from markets, economic models of regime formation portray regimes as rational institutional responses to collective suboptimality problems. Variation among cases, regarding both the likelihood that parties will succeed in establishing regimes and the particular institutional design they will opt for, is explained by differences in the interdependence situation, which is defined in terms of the configuration of preferences. According to Underdal (1987), it is more difficult to achieve a bargainer's surplus in situations that involve externalities or competition (as in the case of transboundary pollution or shared access to fish stocks) that it is in situations where cooperative gains are of a cost-effective type, involving synergy or contingency between the parties. In the former situation, the parties have a greater incentive to cheat on commitments, which may render them cautious and suspicious in the first place and dictate more intrusive monitoring or performance review arrangements in the second, thus making regime formation more difficult. Though it is not always done, power can be introduced in such a scheme by delimiting the set of integrative solutions, either directly through coercion or benevolence as in hegemonic stability theory, or indirectly as unequal ability to manage without cooperation.

Considerations such as these may also yield prescriptions regarding the membership and issue scope of international regimes—because both may affect the collective situation's complexity and malignness, including the ability to link issues and actors in order to enhance the size of the bargainers' surplus (Sebenius 1983).

Although stressing that regime formation is less a carefully designed response than a product of complex political interaction, rationalist regime analysis is also invoked by scholars usually identified with the sociological approach. In his influential article on the study of regimes and international organizations, John Ruggie (1975: 575) suggested that regime formation and institutional form are closely related to the prevailing collective situation—that is, the type and locus of policy interdependence characteristic of various issue areas over time.

Thus, the focus of the mechanism of governance implied in the rationalist core of regime analysis rests on how the incentive structure surrounding behaviour is affected by an existing or proposed regime.[22] In general, the existence of a regime may change calculations of cost and benefit for actors by providing rewards for those who comply with the rules, such as a green image abroad or at home, or by creating new costs for those who do not, such as political embarrassment. This change may affect both the attractiveness of a proposed regime—including the likelihood that it will be negotiated—and its effectiveness if the regime already exists. For instance, in discussions of the effectiveness of resource management regimes, attention is usually drawn to the adequacy of monitoring or sanctioning provisions. The underlying idea is that for a regime to have an impact, it must render noncompliance more costly or adherence more beneficial than they would have been without the regime. The indirect version of this mechanism may be just as relevant because entrance or adherence to the regime can be made easier, by rendering negotiations a regular rather than ad hoc exercise and by enhancing the flow of information and thus the confidence that others too are behaving cooperatively.[23]

We have seen that there is considerable heterogeneity among theorists of international regimes and that the rationalist core of this tradition is a contended one. Part of this contention is related to epistemology, as evidenced in the sociological critique of the positivist commitments of mainstream regime analysis, including its solipsistic conception of agency. Even some regime scholars who concur epistemologically with the rationalists, however, point to a broader and somewhat different set of causal processes than intentional adaptation to changing cost-benefit situations. In the next section, I show that regime analysis is currently being expanded by scholars who challenge the assumptions of rationalist regime theory by advocating a considerably "thicker", or more context-laden, approach. I organize the discussion around two such challenges. One seeks to expand the range of governance mechanisms available to regime analysis and questions the viability of discussing regimes only in terms of configurations of capabilities or preferences. The second challenge expands the conventional locus of governance implied in regime analysis by paying greater attention to subnational and transnational processes.

Questioning Configurations

The rationalist core of regime analysis tries to specify certain initial conditions necessary for regimes to emerge, survive, or affect behavior, in terms of configurations of preferences or capabilities among a group of states. Those conditions are then matched with certain proposed or existing attributes of the regime with an eye to whether the regime may help the group overcome collective-action problems. The beauty of this approach lies in its simplicity and in the plausibility of the basic assumption that states would rather be better off than worse off. In addressing regime puzzles, however, scholars more often recognize that this simplicity may hide situational complexities that are worth theorizing. Compact and elegant configurational theories are increasingly being complemented by models that alert the analyst to various factors related to the process of transforming such initial conditions to regime-relevant behavior and to the stability of the conditions themselves.

From Calculus to Causation

Explaining configurational approaches to regimes is a matter of calculus rather than causal process: if it is shown that a regime designed in a particular way is the best institutional response to a given collective situation, or to the presumed desires of a predominant actor, the formation and maintenance of the regime is considered explained.

However, when armed with tight analytical gems like this, analysts are vulnerable to three methodological missteps. One is the temptation to define the collective situation arbitrarily, for instance by being drawn without much discussion to certain well-known and particularly interesting game situations (Underdal 1987: 176), which can easily mislead the substantive analysis. A second misstep is to define the situation opportunistically by ascribing to the actors, without sufficient justification, those preferences that would predict the pattern of outcomes observed, which will reduce the explanation to description. A third misstep is to ignore the fact that, in the final analysis, these explanations are fundamentally intentional theories: in order to explain a regime this way, its conducive impacts must be recognized by actors who, galvanized by the prospects of those benefits, thereafter venture and succeed in creating or supporting the regime (Keohane and Martin 1995). Both the recognition of such benefits and its translation into cooperative behaviour are problematic processes.

In the study of regime effectiveness, causal awareness comes more naturally because the concept itself implies causation. Before claiming that the regime has caused a certain problem-related behavioral adaptation, we must demonstrate how such an impact has occurred and that, among the range of possible causes, the regime is the most plausible one.[24] Although we may believe that international regimes are important features of world affairs, the behavior of states and others is evidently affected by many other circumstances. In the realm of environmental protection, for instance, decisions to install purification equipment will often depend in part on the financial ability of the firms in question or on the availability of technological solutions at acceptable prices. It may even reflect adherence to a set of regimes other than the one under scrutiny. These other relevant processes must be charted when assessing the effectiveness of an international regime.

Needless to say, the need to consider the effect of other variables and to avoid spurious findings is no less acute in the analysis of regime formation and maintenance: it is typically dealt with through the use of comparative statics, which focus on shifts in configurations of preferences or capabilities. Similarly, the conventional way to render regime effectiveness plausible is to compare a situation before and after the establishment or change of a regime, or across policy areas that are similar in important ways but vary in terms of regime endowment. However, this approach is less helpful in supporting causal claims when there are many other ways, apart from the regime, to explain differences in outcomes. Also, when there are few similar units of analysis in such situations, it is very difficult to isolate the impact of the regime. Unfortunately, international regimes are rather few in number and tend to operate in highly complex and usually shifting circumstances.

In this type of situation, closer attention to the process may help to strengthen causal statements about international regimes and thus form a complementary approach to the control problem. Such an approach is often taken in single-case studies (Yin 1989). Evidence for a particular causal account is built by isolating the fine details of how an outcome came about through a sequence of events, each of which has a causal history less complex than the ultimate outcome and is thus easier to control (George and McKeown 1985). Although more costly in terms of research effort, this method encourages a richer and more nuanced account of the relationships between a regime and the states engaged in forming, operating, or implementing it. In some cases, it may also reveal tensions, contradictions, or shifts in the policies pursued by the various states over time, hence sensitizing the analysis to mechanisms other than rational maximization of fixed interests. For instance, environmental regimes tend to involve scientific activities that may generate new knowledge among members regarding the consequences of current behavior, thus affecting perceived interests in the matter (Young and Levy 1996). Or, as in the case of the ecosystemic objective developed in the Antarctic fisheries regime (Stokke 1996), regimes may help states to specify new goals different from previous ones, though not necessarily incompatible. Thus, this mode of analysis may bring out learning processes when practices associated with a regime cause states to redefine their priorities or modify their comprehension of the situation.

In general, therefore, more careful attention to the causal process may, for better or worse, cut the link of rationalist necessity in configurational analysis. As exemplified by the learning process, one point of departure from rationalist necessity is to problematize the fixity of actor preferences, which may be especially relevant when national interests are uncertain, internally contended, or themselves affected by the international negotiations. Quite often, assessment of the origin and robustness of state preferences over given regime options will involve the domestic level of politics (to be discussed later in the chapter). A second point of departure is to problematize the process of realizing the integrative potential defined by a given set of preferences. Both points, often in combination, are exploited in current regime literature on the significance of cognitive dynamics, institutional bargaining, and leadership in regime analysis.

The Problem of Realization
One criticism levied against configurational analysis is that it glosses over some important cognitive factors that may impede efforts to realize an integrative potential (Underdal 1983: 187). For instance, if actors are uncertain about the preferences of other states or about the range of solutions salient internal groups will accept, fear of exploitation or domestic controversy may render them cautious about making the commitment necessary to reach an agreement. It may also lead them to misperceive what an opponent is prepared to embrace and thus may encourage behavior that can complicate negotiations: for example, overly optimistic proposals may yield deadlock situations, or overly pessimistic disinterest may invite premature closure. Process-generated stakes, or costs associated with the way negotiations are performed, may be another impediment to the realization of a bargainer's surplus (Underdal 1983: 190). Two illustrations are offered by an ongoing dispute between two coastal states, Norway and Russia, and a long-distance fishing nation, Iceland, regarding access to Northeast Arctic cod in a pocket of international waters in the Barents Sea.[25] When a fleet of Icelandic fishing vessels turned up in this so-called Loophole in 1993, Norway and Russia were at first reluctant to negotiate the issue directly with Iceland because such negotiation would amount to recognizing Iceland as a legitimate party to management decisions in the region—a process-generated cost. As a result, although they fed on the same stock, coastal and noncoastal user states remained unable to coordinate their

management policies. When negotiations became inevitable later on, partly because the Icelanders did not bow to political pressure and partly because international law does not permit unilateral enforcement beyond two hundred miles, another type of process-generated stakes had become apparent: there is clear evidence that the prenegotiation hauteur of the coastal states infused the process with nationalist sentiments on all sides, thus enfeebling those domestic players who favor a cooperative approach in the negotiations. In general, as Sebenius (1992: 330) points out, strategies to reach distributive goals in a negotiation process may strangle efforts to reach even considerable integrative ones.

In elaborating on the model of institutional bargaining, Young (1989b) criticizes the tendency of some regime scholars to rely only on assessments of capabilities, preferences, and consequent acceptance zones. He notes that when states negotiate a new regime, overt power is usually employable only at prohibitive costs, and national interests tend to be highly unclear because a proposed regime will typically apply across a wide range of situations and over an extended period of time. The institutional bargaining model suggests that the configurational analysis is insufficient not only because preferences are difficult to specify but also because the configuration typically generates far more than one possible solution.

Students of institutional bargaining also point out that configurational analysis can be misleading because players quite often manage to cut deals even when the problems addressed involve considerable externalities and asymmetry. When accounting for this, Young (1989b) argues that a set of factors associated with the process itself can themselves decide how negotiations evolve, perhaps more so than configurations of preferences and capabilities. One such factor is the presence or availability of institutional *solutions* with certain properties that make them attractive to all sides—such as simplicity, previous application, apparent equity, or ready implementability. Another factor is the presence of leadership (Young 1991a), possibly entrepreneurial or intellectual, or of active participants who are able to pinpoint such solutions and rally support for their realization.[26] A third factor is situational: exogenous shocks may be important in putting pressure on policymakers to provide an agreement.

Basically, these various lines of realization theory render more pliable the analytical rigidity and apparent determinism of configurational analysis. According to this view, the structure of interest and power is less than determinate: regime formation and maintenance are seen as possible outcomes of fairly complex interactive processes with a number of pitfalls that are often related to cognitive matters and with certain shortcuts that actors may exploit in order to reach agreement.

The Force of Procedure

By demonstrating the potential of regimes to overcome collective-action problems, the rationalist core of regime analysis offers a cogent rebuttal of the view that such institutions cannot have an autonomous place in a world of power and self-interest. On the other hand, the determination to beat realism on its own homeground by largely accepting its portrait of the world system is not without costs. Among other things, it has led much regime analysis to neglect processes of legitimization in the creation and operation of international rules, or at least to truncate those processes by viewing them only as a matter of ensuring reasonably balanced gains.

In general, legitimacy depends on the extent to which those addressed by a rule see themselves as obliged by it and on whether that attitude of obligation is conditioned by the quality of the rules and not by the power that created and supports them.[27] Although Morgenthau (1978: 267) notes that "the great majority of the rules of international law are generally observed by all nations," clearly not all regimes, and certainly not all the rules of each regime, have the quality of inducing such obligation. Distinguishing legitimacy from justness, Franck (1990: 24, 38) defines legitimacy in the international domain as "a property of a rule or rule-making institution which itself exerts a pull towards compliance on those addressed normatively because those addressed believe that the rule or institution has come into being and operates in accordance with generally accepted principles of right process." He goes on to identify four features of a rule or institution that may uphold such a belief:[28] (1) pedigree, or historical track record; (2) determinacy—that is, the ability to balance the competing needs of clarity and flexibility, either textually or by remedial procedures; (3) coherence, or internal consistency and connectedness to principles underlying other rules; and (4) adherence, or vertical connectedness to a normative hierarchy, including secondary rules of lawful procedure. Let us examine how and the extent to which these presumably legitimizing features are addressed by students of international regimes.

Pedigree, which implies validation by durability and social practice, has been dealt with somewhat tangentially in all three subfields of the regime literature; it is rarely singled out as a key issue. Regarding the creation of rules, pedigree turns up in the analysis of spontaneous orders, seen as products of a large number of noncoordinated but sustained decisions about social behaviour (Young 1982). Game-theoretic versions have tried to show that such orders, exemplified by markets and language systems but presumably extendable to other types of coordination, may evolve even without as embryonic a level of community as shared norms of reciprocity (Axelrod 1984). Pedigree is also an issue in accounts of imposed orders, to the extent that regimes can be created by sustained unilateral practice by a dominant actor. One illustration of this is the significance of the U.S. postwar policy toward the evolving continental shelf regime (Andrassy 1970). Track record is also invoked in the institutional bargaining literature in that certain regime solutions are believed to stand out as particularly salient in international negotiations because they have been employed successfully in other areas.

Likewise, inertia or habit-driven behavior is sometimes invoked when explaining regime robustness over time and compliance with international norms (Rosenau 1986). A special version of this phenomenon is routinized behavior on the part of national bureaucracies; if the issue is not a matter of dispute among various domestic groups, the bureaucracies may tend to see international commitments as directive for everyday administrative decisions (Chayes and Chayes 1993: 179).

The second validating feature of a rule, determinacy, has been rather central in the regime literature because it hinges on the question of whether explicit and formal rules are essential to the effectiveness of international regimes. Remember that, early on, the focus on implicit and informal norms is one of the features that set regime analysis aside from parts of the international law or organization theory. The tendency has been to move toward a notion of regimes that more closely resembles the one used by international lawyers. This tendency does not, however, suggest any emerging consensus in the regime literature that formal rules are inherently superior to informal ones when it comes to the maintenance or effectiveness of international regimes. On the one hand, the process of hammering out formulations that all participants can ultimately agree to can be a way to ensure that the rule itself is based on well-considered understanding of national interests and goes no further than the real consensus (Chayes and Chayes 1993: 182). It may even serve as a transmission belt for ideas and solutions across state boundaries. Also, as Kratochwil (1993: 86–91) points out, formality will usually simplify the discovery and assessment of an alleged rule violation and permit a more focused discourse about it.

On the other hand, formal rules often come at a cost because stringent and unequivocal rules are generally harder to negotiate and have ratified than lenient and vague ones. Thus, in accordance with the law of the least ambitious program (Underdal 1980), insistence on clearcut, legally binding commitments tends to focus negotiations on the target area favored by the laggards rather than that favored by the leaders. Sand (1991) shows that there is a tendency today for governments negotiating international regimes to try to beat this bottom-line rule by relying on softer instruments such as guidelines, voluntary protocols, or resolutions and by diluting legally binding measures with loopholes and opting-out provisions. In general, implicit rules have the additional advantage of being more elastic than formalized ones and thus may be adapted more readily to differentiated or fluctuating levels of compliance. Moreover, in environmental regimes, programmatic activities like environmental monitoring, transfer of technology, or joint sponsorship of green investments can have greater effect than strict regulatory measures on the willingness or ability of regime members to mend their ways to alleviate joint problems.[29]

Both coherence and adherence, the two other features that presumably affect the legitimacy of rules, refer to linkages between international regimes, a phenomenon given relatively little attention in regime theory. Often, regime analysis proceeds as if a particular institution were a stand-alone regime—the creation, maintenance, or consequences of which can be discussed without sustained analysis of how secondary, adjacent, or overlapping regimes affect the process. This approach is often taken despite the fact that, from the outset, regime scholars have emphasized how the nature of a given regime is defined by its embeddedness in more general institutions or practices (Ruggie 1983) and how specific regimes are nested in more comprehensive ones (Aggarwal 1983). The role of the 1982 United Nations Law of the Sea Convention in guiding settlement of regional delimitation issues or establishment of joint resource management regimes is a case in point. Indeed, the focused-issue orientation of regime analysis makes it particularly well suited for the study of regime overlaps—that is, situations in which several regimes are in operation within the same issue area, but differ in terms of normative or programmatic contents. Such regime linkages can be supportive, as is largely the case for the cluster of regimes that make up the Antarctic Treaty System (Stokke and Vidas 1996b); but an overlapping regime can also be competitive or undermine the operation of another (Herr 1995).

A more systematic treatment of the issue of linkages between regimes may help provide a bridge between rationalist approaches to regime analysis, which tend to isolate and highlight the particular regime under discussion, and sociological approaches that emphasize the embeddedness of agency in a broader set of institutions.

The Significance of Form

Franck (1990: 38) notes that another avenue to obligation, besides legitimacy, is the perceived justness of regime contents; this point is exploited in parts of the regime literature as well. Young (1989a: 368) too holds that the perceived equity of a solution—when major parties and interest groups have a sense that their primary concerns have been treated fairly—is a more critical determinant than efficiency for successful efforts to create international rules.

Another illustration of the relationship between obligation and perception can be seen in the recent discussion about the significance of institutional form, particularly that of *multilateralism* (Ruggie 1992).[30] This term denotes institutions that have generalized rules and commitments: they do not differentiate among members as bilateral arrangements often do. The most-favoured-nation clause of the General

Agreement on Tariffs and Trade (GATT) is one example, and the indivisibility of the security guarantee in NATO is another. Although this institutional form entails some loss in flexibility for the members, proponents of multilateralism argue that the loss is more than made up for by the greater predictibility and perceived justness of such arrangements. Multilteralist institutions are thus rendered more persuasive and also more robust than other institutions when faced with changes in interests or power. A basic institutional design lesson emerging from this line of thought is to pay attention to whether principles and rules can be molded in terms that minimize plausible ascription to particularistic interests and that highlight coherence with universal and shared interests, even in cases where this may occur at the cost of short-term efficiency.[31]

In the case of environmental regimes, this lesson has implications not only for differentiating among regime members in terms of rights and obligations, but also for establishing any decision-making procedures. A regime feature often used to enhance the sense that rules are based on neutral premises, thus increasing the force of the participants' obligation, is to place scientific advisory bodies centrally in the decision-making process. Fisheries management regimes, for instance, tend to draw upon the authority of marine biological science an authority that is widely appreciated as a necessary tool for self-interested resource users and that is confirmed and strengthened by the centrality of scientific evidence in decisions on quotas or other regulative matters (Stokke, Anderson, and Mirovitskaya 1996). Such bodies tend to include, or at least be open to, scientists from all members regime. Their role in environmental regimes is often rather precarious. On the one hand, their advisory function requires that their activities are adapted to the needs defined by decision makers. At the same time, legitimacy also requires that such adaptation does not suppress the general perception that scientists are relatively independent and primarily guided by professional standards rather than considerations of political expediency.

The epistemic community literature does point out that scientific advisory bodies, and the network of experts associated with them, are not always impartial to the policy questions at hand.[32] The point here, however, is that in order to contribute to the obligation and hence the robustness and effectiveness of regimes, they must be seen as reasonably distanced from particularistic interests.

Configuration and Process in Regime Analysis

We have seen that the rationalist core of regime analysis is increasingly being complemented by approaches that in different ways are already complementing configurational accounts of regime formation, maintenance, and effectiveness with broader and more context-sensitive models. The turn to process has infused regime analysis with greater causal awareness and a clearer picture of the barriers to cooperation that originate in the negotiation process mediating between the collective situation, or problem structure, and regime developments. It has also encouraged regime analysis to address, although so far somewhat unsystematically, the relevance of a broader range of *causal mechanisms* beyond rational maximization of given interests when explaining regime developments: attention is now more oriented toward processes involving learning, obligation, and even domestic realignment among different groups interested in international regimes.

In many instances, several causal mechanisms may be simultaneously or consecutively at work. Indeed, the effectiveness principle of international law suggests that once complied with by relevant subjects—for reasons of either reward or punishment—the obligating force of a regime is enhanced. Similarly, evidence suggests that for social learning to take place as a consequence of a regime, the regime needs to be in operation for a certain period of time so that activities within it can accumulate a certain track record or so that domestic agencies have a chance to change their routines in response to new responsibilites that emanate from the regime.

It is worth keeping in mind also that causal mechanisms are quite general in nature and that no one-way street runs between their operation and the formation or effectiveness of a regime. In some cases, new incentives introduced by a regime may impede rather than promote the solution of the problem. For instance, if the regime leads to increased attention to an issue area, some actors may be tempted to emphasize the symbolic aspect of their participation more than they did before and to focus on the values signaled by their positions rather than on the instrumental effects. Giving in to this temptation may or may not be conducive to problem solving. As in the case of the International Whaling Commission, it may even play a role in redefining the problem.[33] Also, the prospect of a new regime may encourage forceful domestic alliances not only among groups concerned about the problem addressed by the regime, but also among those who fear the costs of future regulation. Hence, the observation that one or some of these mechanisms are at work does not necessarily mean that regime formation or effectiveness is enhanced.

The shift to process in regime analysis is not unproblematic. Propositions relating cognitive processes, leadership, saliency, and equity to the realization of cooperation sometimes tend to balance on the verge of circularity: depending on how such propositions are specified and operationalized, it may be very difficult in given empirical contexts to distinguish them from their hypothesized impact. Moreover, if the propositions are empirically permissive, they can easily become overly robust to empirical scrutiny. For instance, which of a range of previously used or round-figure solutions shall be defined as salient? And couldn't certain solutions be salient and symbolically forceful but also politically untenable, such as the principle of a common heritage of mankind in the context of Antarctic politics? How important must a crisis or exogenous shock be before we may expect it to incite negotiators with a sense of urgency?

These questions are neither nitpicking nor devastating. They merely reflect the fact that the turn to process is a fairly recent phenomenon in regime theory. Moreover, the operationalization problems that they suggest are not necessarily more overwhelming than those problems that develop when specifying state preferences or capabilities in situations in which environmental problems and their remedies affect various domestic groups differently.

Questioning Statism

Today, regime scholars almost unanimously agree that the process approach to regime analysis, like the study of international relations more broadly, must enhance its account of how variations in domestic politics and nonstate actors affect international developments. Although widely shared, this view is by no means self-evident. Traditionally, the wider public has played a far more modest role in foreign than in domestic affairs: unfamiliarity is pervasive, the level of attention moderate, and the degree of inclusion of societal groups in the development of policy usually lower. Because it deals with the security of the state, foreign affairs continues to be seen as requiring a highly stable and consistent policy, which can be ensured only by centralization: thus the tendency to give the executive branch of government a relatively privileged position in the foreign policy area. However, one consequence of globalized markets and means of communication is that a number of vociferous societal actors increasingly see themselves as having high stakes in foreign policy decisions and, hence, seek some influence over them. This is true for both interest groups and promotional organizations, such as those that target environmental matters, disarmament, and so on.

In principle, regime theory has been critical of state centrism right from the outset. In 1975, when discussing how interdependence is related to institutions, Ruggie (564, 576) emphasized its locus—that is, how directly the interdependence situation is linked to the domestic policy pursuits of states. He pointed out that success or failure in attempts to establish regimes often depends on how existing institutions at the domestic level are affected. Despite Ruggie's assertions, this part of the research program on international regimes remained in slumber until the late 1980s (Keohane and Nye 1987: 753) and is yet to awake fully. One reason for this neglect is probably the sequential aesthetics that prevail in regime analysis. After all, the determination to ask more limited and pointed questions, one at a time, about international institutions and how they relate to cooperation was one of the ways regime theorists distinguished themselves from their neofunctionalist forerunners. Another reason is that the primary pressure on regime analysis has come from structural realists, who generally tend to downplay domestic processes, arguing that they are rendered unimportant by the anarchical nature of international relations.[34] Also, the rationalist models often used in regime analysis typically dismiss processes of preference formation and change, whether they occur at domestic or systemic levels.

One important challenge, then, is to combine the insights and generalizations based on the simplifying assumption that states are unitary rational actors with more sophisticated models of how the external behavior of states is shaped.[35] In effect, this combination would move regime theory in the direction of foreign policy analysis. Two main approaches may be distinguished in this literature.[36] A society-centered, sectional-interest approach focuses on efforts of subnational actors to influence state attitudes to various regime options. Here, attention rests on societal alignment patterns; it is a feature of many contemporary political issues that this kind of activity takes place not only domestically but also transnationally. Often, governments are interested in including nonstate actors in the political process in order to channel their expertise into the decision-making process or to reveal in a manageable way the relevant societal views, especially the views of those most strongly affected by a foreign policy decision. Instrumentally, this inclusion may heighten the decision makers' sensitivity to societal opposition and support. Moreover, because such inclusion may build commitment and loyalty, it may also facilitate subsequent implementation.[37] More generally, there is a promising link to be exploited between the study of regime effectiveness and the range of theories on implementation in the domestic domain.[38]

A state-centred, institutionalist approach focuses on both formal and informal aspects of the state apparatus when accounting for the domestic origins of foreign policy. Particular attention is given to the level of centralization, decision-making rules, and procedures, as well as to the norms regarding inclusion of societal groups in the formulation of foreign policy. These features may vary over time and issue areas, and there can be interesting interactions between domestic and international levels. In some cases, certain groups, such as scientists or nongovernmental organizations, enhance their domestic influence by virtue of expertise and contacts acquired through participation in international deliberations. The converse may also be true: the fact that a few key countries, such as the United States and Australia, permitted environmental organizations to participate in domestic preparations for meetings in the Antarctic Treaty System proved instrumental in their subsequent inclusion as observers in the international consultative process (Stokke and Vidas 1996b).

Including domestic politics in regime analysis is bound to affect the complexity of the investigation. The literature on epistemic communities is one attempt to relax actor unity assumptions while still retaining some control on the number of actors and institutions that become included in the analysis.

Epistemic Communities

Like theories of institutional bargaining, the epistemic community literature reflects a perceived need to complement grand, abstract structural theory with middle-range, context-bound behavioral propositions.[39] Whereas the former tries to specify a range of solutions, activities, and situations likely to promote agreement among a set of bargainers, however, epistemic community scholars narrow in on the significance of certain transnational networks of expertise.

There are several reasons why the epistemic community concept has such resonance for regime analysis. It is compatible with the tendency in environmental and resource management regimes to address complexity and uncertainty by establishing separate scientific or technical bodies. And it is a rather short step from observing the regularity of formal and informal problem-oriented contacts between scientists who participate in these bodies to accepting the general idea that those involved may gradually develop convergent views of how the problem should be approached. Of course, uncertainty and complexity are not confined to environmental issues, and when established policies are widely perceived as insufficient, policymakers in other issue areas, such as trade or monetary affairs, may also be expected to seek the comfort of experts to point themselves new directions or at least to legitimize preferred policy changes.

Also, although the role of experts and ideas is an old theme in the study of international affairs, the epistemic community notion treats it in an agency-sensitive way that resonates well with the individualist methodology of mainstream regime scholars: the focus is moved from intangible phenomena, such as whether knowledge is consensual, to the flesh-and-blood carriers of that knowledge who can be named and biographed. The change in focus has the additional advantage of placing empirical inquiries very close to the negotiation processes themselves—the person-to-person exchanges and the day-to-day developments—that serve to thicken the description and render the empirical account more persuasive.

Finally, although epistemic community scholars thematize the role of emerging knowledge and intersubjective meanings, they proceed from there in a manner largely in line with the mainstream methodological requirements in the subfield (Keohane 1988) by emphasizing, at least in principle, the need to identify community members and beliefs prior to investigating their influence on outcomes (P. Haas 1992b: 34). This emphasis resonates well with a major finding of epistemic community scholars that such communities are most successful if their policy projects make up some acceptable middle ground between more radical proposals. Hence, such scholars deliberately place themselves in the space between the regularity-seeking rationalists in international relations theory and the interpretation-oriented constructivists (Adler and Haas 1992: 368).

Conclusions: The Turn to Process in Regime Analysis

We may now revert to the question that prompted this article; namely, what can we learn about global governance by studying the literature on international regimes? It is important here to recall that the concept of governance implied in regime analysis is somewhat narrower than the one emerging in the study of global governance. Although regime analysts tend to arrange the political agenda into more or less distinct issue areas, each with its separate focal point and political logic, students of global governance emphasize that such boundaries are so often transcended by various actors, ideas, and mediating norms that the issue-area distinction itself becomes questionable.

Another difference in concepts of governance concerns the locus of governance. Whereas regime analysts typically highlight norm-based coordination among states and state bureaucracies, global governance scholars tend to highlight relationships between a range of subnational and transnational actors as well. This difference should not be over-stated, however. This chapter has demonstrated that regime analysis, like the study of global governance, is an offspring of the literature on globalism and interdependence from the 1970s. As such, it has always paid some homage to the need for opening up analysis to actors other than states. Perhaps because the theoretical diversity of regime analysis has sapped it of the energy required to seriously introduce yet another complicating dimension, regime analysis has long remained more or less as state oriented as the realism it had always criticized on that account. In recent years, however, although so far not very systematically or broadly, subnational and transnational actors are increasingly being thematized in regime analysis. For instance, the significance of transnational networks of experts for the formation and implementation of environmental regimes is being scrutinized. Similarly, the concept of leadership directs attention to both individuals and nongovernmental organizations who provide entrepreneurial or intellectual skills to negotiation processes. The focus on regime effectiveness is also beginning to link international regime analysis more tightly to the study of how commitments are being implemented in member states. More generally, much regime analysis now acknowledges that state preferences over a range of institutional options are seldom fixed and that assessment of the content and stability of national preferences often requires analysis of political access and coalition patterns among various subnational groups.

Nevertheless, scholars generally agree that regime analysis has traveled a very short road in incorporating insights about domestic political processes. But it is a road where the concerns of global governance scholars and students of international regimes can now meet. The same can be said about the treatment of inter-regime linkages in regime analysis. The study of global governance, therefore, highlights exactly those themes likely to receive the most attention from regime theorists in the years to come.

Pressure from structural realists has led regime scholars to spend much analytical fuel trying to substantiate the claim that anarchy and rational egoism combined do not necessarily render regimes irrelevant in the international domain. What I have termed the rationalist core of regime analysis has developed the role of regimes to enhance transparency and improve conditions for iterated decision making, thus helping states overcome barriers to collective action and enter into mutually beneficial policy coordination. The causal mechanism resorted to by rationalist scholars is straightforward maximation of interest. Their hardboiled assumptions and simple causal logic have made this strand of regime analysis a formidable contender to structural realists, especially because the latter typically pride themselves on exactly those two accounts.

In one recent trend, however, many regime analysts seek to complement such general, axiomatically based regime accounts by introducing more of the situational context when fleshing out theoretical propositions. They are less concerned with compactness and elegance and more eager to provide a rich set of tools for analyzing causal pathways and mechanisms. Those tools can be seen as partial theories, or theoretical modules, with limited scope of pretended validity. Although most process-oriented regime scholars embrace the rationalist assumption of purposive behaviour, many question the methodological wisdom of assuming that integrative preferences automatically translate into cooperative outcomes. For instance, they point to cognitive barriers and process-generated stakes that may influence efforts to establish or maintain rules at the international level. Or they argue that preferences can be very difficult to operationalize in the first place and that outcomes are typically affected by certain types of behavior, such as various kinds of leadership, or by certain ideas or normative and procedural solutions that attract the attention of negotiators because they are salient, equitable, or previously used. Others criticize the fixity of preferences often assumed in rationalist analysis; in agreement with epistemic community scholars, they point out that regime processes can support certain kinds of social learning that may substantially affect the compatibility of interest among actors. They also investigate how noncoerced compliance with rules may stem from a sense of obligation that has been affected by rule features such as pedigree, determinacy, and internal consistency or by the less understood ways in which rules link up to other issue regimes or to more general international rules and procedures.

It is interesting to note that students of cognitive dynamics, institutional bargaining, and epistemic communities delineate very similar scopes of validity. All tend to emphasize factually complex situations in which domestic political attention is low, diffuse, or in a state of flux or in which central decision makers find it difficult to identify clearly what their interests are. Such situations reduce the determinacy of analysis and alert the analyst to factors associated with the interactive process.

Consider also that these conditions are the same conditions that in 1976 led Ernst Haas and others to conclude that although integration theory—the leading institutionalist research program at the time—might be improved further to account better for the new world reality of turbulent complexity, it no longer appeared as a worthwhile investment of time and ingenuity. Today's process-oriented regime theorists are less baffled, largely because they have lowered their aspirations regarding the scope and determinacy of their theoretical propositions. Instead, they have invested their intellectual energy in elaborating a set of middle-range, probabilistic propositions related to certain types of activities and interactions that mediate between collective situations and cooperative outcomes.

A promising aspect of the broadening of regime analysis is that it may help to narrow the gap between mainstream, positivist approaches to international regimes and the wide range of sociologically inclined approaches that are generally critical of the rationalist portrait of agency as self-contained units with fixed preferences. In the past, the intellectual exchange between those two camps has been fairly limited (Keohane 1988; Stokke 1995b). This chapter has shown how a number of scholars who focused on the social nature of norms and practices now place greater emphasis than before on revealing the practical implications of their metatheoretical quarrels with mainstream regime scholars, through problem-oriented theoretical and empirical discussions of phenomena such as epistemic communities or institutional form.[40] Conversely, the turn to process allows a number of regime scholars who subscribe to notions of purposive agency and positivist methodology to define states as learners who are exploring a range of possibilities in a permissive international environment. Thus, process-oriented regime theory, which includes both realization and epistemic community scholars, has now engaged the mutually skeptical rationalist and constructivist regime camps in serious debate on issues that they have previously been reluctant to discuss: the origin and transformation of preferences or identities; the role of perception and how cognition is shaped by features of the situation and the behavior of others; and, in the case of environmental regimes, the role of interactive generation of scientific knowledge in international management.

The wide range of approaches to the main puzzles of regime analysis has not been inconsistent with a continued ambition to offer concrete guidance about the design of negotiations and institutions. As noted, the fact that theoretical competition in the field is unresolved has pushed contributors to greater awareness of the empirical scope of their propositions, thus rendering regime analysis more sensitive to the conditional and context-dependent nature of findings regarding the formation, maintenance, and effectiveness of regimes.

This nondogmatic heterogeneity of regime analysis explains why its contribution lies more in synthesizing or integrating ideas developed in other fields of inquiry for practical usage in given policy areas than in ingenious theoretical revelations. Like the study of international relations in general, regime analysis is a tradition with considerable deficit in its flow-of-ideas: it is an importing rather than an exporting tradition. An inherent danger in such a situation is to succumb to eclecticism— that is, to tie together bits and pieces of theoretical notions in arbitrary ways. It would not be accurate to say that regime theory has fallen into this trap. The tendency in regime theory that I have portrayed in this chapter, especially regarding regime formation but increasingly in regime effectiveness literature as well, is one of alertness to the latitude of possible causal pathways in which international regimes play a role, combined with a growing determination to look for conditions in which various causal mechanisms are most likely to be activated. This tendency is clearly a second way to avoid the arbitrariness and posthockery of eclecticism. Rather than abstracting away complexity, as structural realism does, or complaining that everything is now up for grabs, as integration theorists did, regime analysis can move toward more reasoned determinacy by utilizing current middle-range, context-sensitive theories with a sustained focus on when they are likely to be relevant and when they can be black boxed without serious harm to the validity of the analysis.

This utilization of various theories holds the promise that insights generated by regime analysis will become increasingly differentiated according to the specific conditions characteristic of the issue areas in question. At the same time, if systematized further, the focus on conditioned activation of a multitude of theoretical components could amount to a metatheoretical enterprise of substantial interest to the study of not only global governance, but other fields of human affairs as well.

3

Governance in Global Civil Society

Paul Wapner

This volume studies the dynamics of global environmental governance. It concentrates on institutions that arise, and that can be potentially created, to address transboundary environmental challenges. Its fundamental starting point is that, although environmental issues transcend national boundaries, the prospects for establishing a world government to address them are dim (if not undesirable); thus, one must look to mechanisms of governance whose authority emanates outside government to address issues such as ozone depletion, species extinction, and global warming. Most of the chapters in the book focus on the way states negotiate and implement agreements to protect the global environment; they study the formation, changing character, and compliance mechanisms of international regimes to understand the institutional matrix of contemporary transnational environmental protection. This chapter pursues a different line of inquiry, however. Rather than focus on the state system, it concentrates on global civil society—a related but separate sector of world collective life—and attempts to explain how actors within it establish mechanisms of global environmental governance.

Civil society is that domain of associational life situated above the individual and below the state. It is made up of complex networks based on interest, ideology, family, and cultural affinity through which people pursue various aims. Churches, unions, movements, political parties, and clubs of all sorts are examples of such networks, and the host of these together constitutes civil society. Although the concept arose in the analysis of domestic societies, it is beginning to make sense in the analysis of global affairs (Commission on Global Governance 1995;

Falk 1992; Lipschutz 1992). The interpenetration of markets and the globalization of advanced communication technologies, among other phenomena, are enhancing people's ability to organize voluntarily across state boundaries, and vast networks of relationships are spreading as a result. Churches, movements, political parties, and so forth now transcend national boundaries and foster transnational affiliations. Thus, an amorphous yet analytically distinct sphere is beginning to exist in which people can collectively express their aspirations and pursue joint enterprises independent of their association with a particular state and outside the direct purview of the state system. Global civil society, in short, is the domain that exists above the individual and below the state but also across state boundaries, where people voluntarily organize themselves to pursue various aims.

Although global civil society is fundamentally a set of relational networks, it also has a political dimension. Many of the organizations that arise within its domain—generally called nongovernmental organizations (NGOs)—can and do directly shape widespread behavior in matters of public concern and involvement. They try to influence the beliefs and actions of people throughout the world concerning their particular issue area. To be sure, they are not as successful as states in exerting such influence; as a number of studies demonstrate, however, their efforts are far from in vain (Sikkink 1993; Lipschutz 1992; Walker 1988), especially with regard to environmental issues (Stairs and Taylor 1992; Wapner 1995b; Princen and Finger 1994). This chapter provides a theoretical account of why and how NGO efforts in general and environmental NGO efforts in particular make a difference in world politics. By understanding NGOs as part of global civil society and theorizing about the political impact of this domain, the chapter explains how efforts undertaken outside the state system nonetheless shape world collective life or, put differently, govern world public affairs.

The first section of the chapter reviews the meaning of the term *civil society* at the domestic level. By tracing the evolution of the term's meaning and by reviewing one of the more plausible accounts of how such a realm actually emerged, this section aims to provide a conceptual grounding for understanding what civil society is at the global level. The second section outlines the meaning of the term *global civil society*. It draws an analogy between domestic and global collective life and describes the emergence and dynamics of a realm that fosters transnational activity above the individual and below the state. This description specifies the nature of NGOs and explains how they constitute global civil society. The third section explicates how global civil society participates in global governance—first, by providing a theoretical account of the political dimension of global civil society and, second, by illustrating the political dimension with a number of empirical examples. Global civil society participates in global governance in both an unintentional and a deliberate manner. This section mentions the unintentional dimension but focuses more specifically on NGOs' calculated efforts to politicize global civil society and to use it to create institutions of global governance. The final section presents a concise rendition of the overall argument and draws out a number of implications for both the study of world politics and the practical challenge of constructing institutions to address public goods problems.

Before proceeding, it is important to make one caveat. Although I articulate governance in global civil society in this chapter, my intention is not to claim that global civil society is somehow more important than the state system or that it will someday replace the state system as the main source of global governance. States remain the main actors in world affairs, and their cooperative efforts to establish regimes remain the essential building blocks of global governance in environmental and other issues. The idea is rather to provide a more comprehensive understanding of global governance. The governing capability of global civil society complements but does not replace that of the state system. This chapter, in other words, is not an exercise in what Ruggie calls "institutional substitutability" (Ruggie 1993b: 143). It is a matter of completing our understanding of the forces that govern world affairs.

Civil Society

The concept of civil society has a long history that has been well documented by a number of scholars (Seligman 1992; Cohen and Arato 1992; Kumar 1993). This history is almost wholly confined to reflection on domestic collective life, but it remains relevant to the conceptualization of global civil society. Indeed, to understand the meaning of civil society at the global level, it is useful to appreciate, at least in broad outline, some of the more important developments in the evolution of the concept's relevance at the domestic level.

To begin, it is worth noting that until roughly the eighteenth century the term *civil society*—from the Latin *societas civilas*—was synonymous with the state or political society (Kumar 1993: 376; Cohen and Arato 1992: 83ff.). Civil society referred to a community of citizens who regulated their relationships and settled disputes according to a system of law, which was in contrast to human relations at large. A lawful society enjoyed a "civilized" existence: civility, not barbarism, governed human affairs. Civil society, as such, demarcated a domain separate from the so-called "natural relations" existing in the "state of nature" outside the *polis*, republic, or well-ordered state (Cohen and Arato 1992: 86ff.).

Central to early notions of civil society is that the legal code, according to which citizens interacted with each other, was supported by a broader set of norms and values (*ethos*) that permeated society. Governance was not simply a matter of governmental statutes, but rather a more holistic system. Social mores complimented legal codes, and thus civil society denoted an all-encompassing social system.[1] Civil society was not simply differentiated from the "state of nature"; it was also distinguished from systems of government in which political rule operated through despotic decree, for example. In short, the idea of civil society originated in an attempt to articulate the experience of living as a citizen in a well-ordered community. Civil society denoted lawfulness, in both the legal and social senses, in contrast to the capriciousness of human communal life at large.

Starting in the eighteenth century, for reasons well outlined by others, the equation between political rule and society began to break down (Keane 1988). The state, a predominant form of political organization at the time, began to be seen as separate from society, which had a form and dynamic of its own. The thinker most closely associated with the distinction is Hegel,[2] who saw civil society as a domain above the family but below the state wherein free association takes place between individuals and corporate groups.[3] Civil society, as such, was an arena where people pursued their own aims in the course of everyday life and was therefore associated with particular needs, private interests, and often divisiveness. The state was analytically separate from but, in classic Hegelian form, mutually constitutive of civil society in that it possessed the quality of publicness or "legality". That is, it accentuated universalist rather than particularist principles and thus organized the energies of civil society to realize the general good. Hegel represents a turning point in the history of civil society insofar as he articulated the character of civil society in dialectical relation to the state, thereby enabling theorists to think about the two spheres as analytically distinct.[4]

Building upon Hegel's view, most modern and contemporary theorists understand civil society as distinct from the state, although the justification for the distinction and its meaning for collective life assume different emphases. Arguably the most significant trajectory of thought on the subject is the liberal one that sees civil society as a function of a market economy and a limited government, although eventually with enough institutionalization to constitute a realm of its own.

It is often pointed out that the rise of the modern bureaucratic state brought with it a system of rights that constituted human beings as legal entities, and it was these rights that established a domain of private, horizontal interaction (Blaney and Pasha 1993: 8 ff; Lewis 1992: 37; Perez-Diaz 1995). As the state established itself as a material object possessing military, police, juridical, and administrative power, citizens necessarily organized themselves in opposition to and independent from its prerogatives and directives. Civic associations directed their energies toward the state in increased participation, and an associational sphere developed in which commerce, common enterprise, social trust, and other horizontal experiences could be cultivated in their own right. The idea of civil society arose in this context insofar as the state itself often recognized and legitimized citizen interaction and partially because of the bonds and interests that developed as a result of such interaction. The liberal state acknowledged that citizens do in fact possess a certain degree of freedom from state authority and particular rights to hold the state accountable.[5]

The theoretical articulation of this notion of civil society finds its origins in the thought of writers such as Montesquieu, Tocqueville, Paine, Ferguson, and Smith. Concerned in part with the debilitating effects of despotism, each of these thinkers reflected upon the extent and character of state rule and possible ways of accentuating antidespotic tendencies (Seligman 1992; Keane 1988). Each tried, in his own way, to justify the significance of a domain free from state regulation wherein people could experience the quality of associational life and concomitantly form networks that would structurally obstruct the domineering tendency of state authority. Additionally, they supported such a domain because it would possess an innate rationality that could, contra Hegel, help realize the general good. The notion of civil society that emerged from this thought saw it as a sphere in which social groups could interact independent of the state—thus forming their own codes of conduct—yet could also influence the dynamics of the polity. Key to the existence of such a domain was the existence of the modern, liberal state.

The rise of civil society is also tied, in the liberal notion, to the emergence of a particular form of economic life, namely a market-driven economy based on private property. Private property and market relations generate a distinct domain that is autonomous from the state and, to a degree, from other social spheres.[6] Private property enables people to concentrate their productive energies on genuinely personal, self-interested enterprises and, in doing so, to create and mobilize significant, autonomous sources of wealth. The spread of market relations accentuates this ability as it creates extensive networks between producers and consumers that pull successive members of society into a privately coordinated mode of economic life.[7] Together, the rise of private property and the spread of market relations give way to a rich, commercial associational life independent of the state (Calhoun 1992: 15).

Civil society, from this perspective, is characterized by the quality of human experience and relations that arises from commercial interaction. A market system of exchange is based on individuals and their associations engaging in countless uncoerced contractual transactions. Sellers and buyers are on their own, as it were, to find each other, devise prices, and so forth. This model of interaction accentuates the autonomous quality of human interaction—in other words, the experience of individual prerogative. On the other hand, economic intercourse also generates certain understandings and mores among producers and consumers that facilitate exchange. The idea of commodification, for example— wherein people see all kinds of goods and services, previously outside the ambit of the market, as objects of exchange—or the practice of providing written receipts for economic transactions represent social codes associated with a market economy (Bellah 1991). Accordingly, civil society, involves both the freedom to buy and sell all kinds of goods as one sees fit and the proprieties that arise as a result. It describes, in other words, the social relations of individuals and associations as they jointly pursue personal economic interest.

This second component of the liberal notion of civil society is connected to the first in that the state plays a key role in the formal codification of private property and often sets the terms of market exchange. The so-called rights of property, articulated by Locke and others, emanate from government as does the legal obligation to respect contracts (Mardin 1995). Private property and market relations are not separate from but rather are wrapped up in and partially constituted by the liberal state. Taken together, the conjunction of a limited state that respects citizen rights and a market economy that allows people to engage privately in exchange forms the basis for the liberal idea of civil society and the structural foundation of a nonstate domain of collective life.

Horizontal interactions become "civil," according to the liberal account, when the intrasocietal norms or codes of conduct that arise from such interactions assume an implicit cordial character. This notion stems from the Scottish Enlightenment idea that manners, education, and the experience of so-called civilization encourage people to treat each other with a certain degree of decency and tolerance. It recognizes that people have certain sensibilities that can be both harnessed for the good of society and preserved for individual enrichment through widespread mutual respect. Although it originally depicted the gentility of the literati, civility has since become associated potentially with all types of sustained social interaction—economic, social, and cultural (Bryant

1995). When people associate with each other in a sustained manner, it is *as if* they are cultivating manners, undergoing a type of education, and exposing themselves to elements of civilization. As such, they develop an implicit sense of social trust and mutual regard that binds them into a type of "society."[8] Civility is the interiority of this society—the collective mind-set that can emerge when people are free to associate outside the purview of the state. Civility itself is not, however, the same thing as the specific procedures, values, or codes of conduct that emerge within civil society. The mutual tolerance and respect related to civility form the backdrop, as it were, against which particular mores develop.

The combination of a limited state, a market economy, and the emergence of civility constitutes the liberal, and one could say the most prevalent, notion of civil society. Civil society, as such, refers to collective interaction taking place above the individual and independent from the state and resulting in a sense of allegiance and societal norms. Thus, a central aspect of this notion of civil society is the constitution of a space for collective life outside the direct purview of the state and yet partially responsible for generating and defining social life.

The Emergence of Global Civil Society

Transposing the concept of civil society to the global level is fraught with difficulties. As many scholars point out, the idea of civil society evolved within the Western tradition of political thought, so it found its empirical mooring paradigmatically in the liberal regimes that arose in the West during the latter part of the seventeenth century and the early part of the eighteenth century. From this perspective, civil society today is said to exist only in those countries with a rich liberal tradition, a stable conjunction of limited government and private economic enterprise, and rich civil relations. In other words, civil society is historically specific or, at least, contextually dependent and thus impertinent to most settings. According to this line of thinking, it makes no sense to talk about civil society in, for instance, Africa (Lewis 1992), India (Blaney and Pasha 1993), China (Wank 1995), or even Poland (Seligman 1992). It makes even less sense to speak, then, of *global* civil society.

Although the historicity of civil society is important to keep in mind, the concept of a global civil society is nonetheless attractive when it becomes apparent that the same type of space as well as similar affections and relations that define civil society at the domestic level are prevalent at the global one. Human interaction throughout the world is not contained within the territorial borders of the state. People communicate, collaborate, and build relationships across national boundaries. In doing so, they establish modes of interaction and generate affiliations that constitute rich transnational networks. The interpenetration of markets, the intermeshing of symbolic meaning systems, and the propagation of transnational collective endeavors establish structures for human interaction and affection that operate above the individual, below the state, *and* across state boundaries. Although perhaps less coherent than domestic economic, social, and cultural networks, sustained cross-boundary practices generate a domain that exists unto itself. Due to such conceptual similarities, it therefore makes analytical sense to understand this domain as global civil society.

Although developed through reflection upon collective life at the domestic level, the liberal account partially explains the emergence of global civil society. Yes, parts of the world certainly lack the liberal experience, but elements of the global system clearly have the same effect as liberal socioeconomic and political structures.[9] At one level, there is a state system under which much collective life is organized and which has the trappings of a governmental structure that can foster transnational civil relations. Since at least the seventeenth century, the state system has expanded to include all parts of the world. All regions are under the jurisdiction of the state, even if individual territories do not enjoy national sovereignty. National governments recognize each other's authority and interact in the attempt to realize their individual aims and to address public goods problems. The state system represents a public authority of sorts, then, that establishes a modicum of governmental presence at the global level. To be sure, the governance involved is only partial, continually contested, and often ineffective because states often fail to cooperate or honor their commitments; nonetheless, the state system does provide a structural component to global governance.

Although certainly not liberal in character, the state system recognizes, legitimizes, and encourages transnational citizen and corporate interaction. For example, as Thomson and Krasner (1989) point out, the state plays a key role in stabilizing property rights that make possible increased transnational economic interaction. The state possesses a developed legal apparatus that can enforce property rights, which include contractual arrangements, and this apparatus protects one's right to sell commodities and one's prerogative to do so through voluntary, rather than coerced, types of exchange. The state system correspondingly extends and ensures these rights across state boundaries, thus fostering transnational economic enterprise. At a more general level, the state provides resources that enable all kinds of transnational activity. International regimes, for instance, lay the groundwork for transnational economic, cultural, and social networks. They set the terms of much transnational practice, thus lowering transaction costs for all actors. One indicator of this is the profusion of transnational associations that emerged in tandem with the expansion of the state system. According to John Boli and George Thomas, the presence of nonstate actors "jumped to a far higher level than ever before at exactly the time that the nation-state form was adopted or imposed on practically all the remaining land mass of the world" (1995: 18). Such transnational associations expanded in the interstices of interstate activities, often taking advantage of the resources states devote to their own interactions. Finally, the state system has done much to acknowledge formally the rights and practices of nonstate actors. The United Nations, for example, officially recognizes thousands of organizations that operate transnationally, as do other international governing bodies such as the Antarctic Treaty System (Clark 1994; Gordenker and Weiss 1995; Conca 1995). Although not reducible to the state system, global civil society is partially a product of that system. Private and voluntary enterprises can and do arise transnationally partially because the state system supports them.

The second feature of the global system that fosters civil society is the degree to which an integrated world market continues to extend itself to all areas of the world. Many regions have possessed market economies for centuries, but now a globalized marketplace offers an arena where individuals and corporations produce, transport, and sell products and services the world over. The globalization of markets extends the experience of private economic activity because it circumscribes a domain that crosses national boundaries, a domain where people can interact free from complete governmental penetration.

The nonstate quality of globalization is partly indicated by the rise of multinational corporations (MNCs)—businesses that undertake production, sales, and investment within many countries and across national boundaries. Such firms have existed for centuries in some form, but their sheer quantity and extent have grown tremendously in recent decades (Kennedy 1993: 50). What marks MNCs is their quasi detachment from the particular interests and values of their country of origin. Although they start and initially grow in a particular country, they often jump its borders when labor costs, regulations, or tax conditions within it disfavor their operations. MNCs function transnationally.

A globalized market is not the same thing as a national economy based on private property and organized according to the market. Free markets do not exist everywhere, and smooth, integrative connections do not exist between separate free market systems. Nonetheless, a thin, if not heterogeneous, economic system spans the globe and is primarily animated by market relations based on private property. This economic system, like the globalized state system, provides a component of the structural preconditions for global civil society: it allows individuals and corporate bodies to experience free association across national boundaries, and it provides the ground for individual and corporate action based on prerogative rather than coercion or necessity. Considered along with the state system, the global economy sculpts a transnational sector of global life in which allegiances, solidarities, and codes of conduct can arise.

Although the state system and the global economy provide a space for global civil society, as a phenomenon the society's existence rests on the activities of certain actors that actually constitute it. Nongovernmental organizations—including international scientific bodies, MNCs, transnational political activist groups, religious associations, and all other voluntary affiliations that organize themselves or at least project their energies across national boundaries—instantiate global civil society.

Their activities actually establish horizontal transnational networks. If, for some unimaginable reason, they stopped operating, the potential for global civil society would still exist, but the actual phenomenon would not.

The term NGO, to be sure, is unwieldy insofar as it represents a vast diversity of actors.[10] The term is relevant in the context of global civil society, however, because it is the diversity that needs to be emphasized. Global civil society is not populated simply by politically progressive organizations that concentrate on issues such as human rights, environmental protection, and peace issues, as many analysts implicitly suggest.[11] Rather, it includes all organizations that operate across state boundaries. DuPont is as much an actor in global civil society as the Catholic Church; the transnational group Aryan Nations is as much a part of it as Greenpeace. What links these groups together is that they are not tied to the territoriality of the state. They can focus on issues and pursue aims free from the task of preserving and enhancing the welfare of a given, geographically situated population. Following James Rosenau's lead, one could call them "sovereignty-free" actors (Rosenau 1990).[12]

For many scholars, the term NGO is a misnomer with regard to global civil society because it lumps together businesses that operate for profit and organizations that seek social, cultural, or political goals. This criticism is part of a larger argument about whether the economy should be part of civil society (and thus global civil society).[13] The two types of associations—for profit businesses and nonprofit organizations—are said to operate according to different logics, and only the latter are said to be consistent with global civil society. On the one hand, businesses operate in a purely instrumental fashion, seeking, profit above all. They are motivated by individual self-interest and therefore not by the formation of allegiances that arise when people associate for less instrumental and seemingly unselfish reasons (Korten 1990: 96–97; see generally, Cohen and Arato 1992: 75 ff.). Noncommercial associations, on the other hand, fundamentally involve allegiances. They are about people joining together to express some felt concern and working together to win broader societal appeal for that concern. To be sure, noncommercial NGOs constantly aim to win resources for self-preservation and for constituencies on whose behalf they often operate, but this is not their raison d'etre. The communicative dimension of their activities—which involves self-understanding as well as intercourse with others regarding the group's concern—is central to the attainment of their goals. For thinkers who subscribe to this distinction, the genuine actors of global civil society include only the voluntary, nonprofit, or independent sector of world affairs.[14] Businesses are part of a different quarter of collective life.

The definition of global civil society expressed in this chapter does not recognize the distinction between commercial and noncommercial NGOs. Minimal allegiances and a rich body of norms do, in fact, develop in the process of economic exchange even if the associations are not formed with such an intention. Through business interaction, people begin to care about others and to establish modes of conduct that orient their activities. The business of business, in other words, spills over into the broader social domain that contributes to social sensibility; it is thus partly responsible for the "civility" of global civil society.

Global Civil Society and Governance

As a domain of transnational collective life, global civil society is not necessarily political; therefore, its contribution to global governance can be obscure. If global civil society operates simply as a sphere in which private individuals and groups engage in activities that affect only themselves—for example, international chess clubs—the political component is quite hidden.[15] Global civil society, however, is much more than this. Like its domestic counterpart, it supports activities that shape widespread behavior and influence the way public issues are addressed. As such, it plays a role in governing the world polity. To appreciate this, it is useful to delineate the role civil society plays in governing domestic affairs and then to apply that analysis to global civil society.

Remember that, in its classical form, the idea of civil society (*societas civilas*) denoted a system of rule within a given community. It designated a domain in which laws regulated relationships among and helped settle disputes between citizens. In this context, law was not simply directive but also social: norms, mores, and values were consistent with and embodied in the legal codes of society. The social order was conceived as an all-encompassing domain animated by a system of rules and norms as well as by legal edicts.

Although the term civil society eventually came to mean a distinct sphere within a social order—a domain above the individual but below the state—it never lost its political character. That is, it not only designated an unofficial domain within collective life, but also contributed to the overall quality of the polity. Although separate from the state, civil society has an element of political agency to it. It partially governs public affairs a role one sees most clearly in the attempt by scholars to articulate the exact relationship between the state and civil society.

According to Gramsci (1985: 181–182), the distinction between the state and civil society is fundamentally analytic. In certain contexts, for instance, the state and civil society are practically indistinguishable insofar as both operate according to a unified ideology. For Gramsci this means that by presenting its own interests as universal, a given class is capable of eliciting the consent of schools, churches, the press, councils, unions, and so forth as well as of the state. In these so-called hegemonic social orders, civil society is not subordinate to the state, nor is it superior to it. Rather, an integrated system of governance is at work, reinforcing itself through multiple institutions and organizations. The state and civil society represent two aspects of social order. The agency of civil society is recognized in this context insofar as it is essential to the unity and coherence of hegemonic social orders.

Such agency is also apparent in instances when the state and civil society are not integrated. At times, the state is captured by a given class that fails to define its interests universally and is therefore unable to win the consent of the organizations and institutions of civil society. In these cases, civil society does not disappear but plays a particular role in governing society and in, at least theoretically, transforming political rule. In their governing role, the norms, codes of conduct, and prevalent values of civil society organize and shape the everyday affairs of citizens insofar as such affairs are free from the dictates of the state. In their transformative role, the institutions of civil society can be successively enlisted in a counterhegemonic effort to shift the social foundations of power and eventually to topple the state. Schools, councils, the press, and other social bodies become organized to resist state ideological and cultural imperatives, in the process generating their own vision of social life—a situation Gramsci calls a "war of position." The presuppositions of such ideas is that certain modalities of power exist in civil society and that their activation and mobilization are potent forms of governance (see generally, Gramsci 1985: 210–278).

Although imprecise, Gramsci's insights are relevant at the global level. The global polity has a semblance of order constituted not simply by the state system but also by global civil society. In the same way that domestic civil society is always enacting order within a national polity, under both hegemonic and nonhegemonic settings, global civil society is always influencing the institutions of global life. This influence takes place in two ways. First, global civil society conditions world order in an unintentional and largely unfocused manner. Many, if not most, NGOs that populate global civil society eschew political affairs and pursue their transnational relations unaware of the political effects of their actions. Their activities in the aggregate, however, have public consequences insofar as they shape widespread understanding and behavior. That is, through the sheer multiplicity of NGOs, institutions that guide collective life are inadvertently born. To use postmodern language, the manifold force relations of global civil society create dominant discourses that consolidate and advance certain understandings and practices. Global civil society thus exerts influence on the world polity simply by existing.

The second way global civil society governs world order—a way more germane to the topic of this chapter—is through the deliberate efforts of politically motivated NGOs. A significant number of NGOs form for purely political reasons; they are part of transnational social movements whose aim is to advance particular normative agendas. The most obvious of these movements kinclude Amnesty International, Greenpeace, European Nuclear Disarmament, and Oxfam International; however, organizations such as Aryan Nations, World Anti-Communist League, and World Union of National Socialists must also be included. All of these organizations devote themselves exclusively to setting up institutions to guide behavior with regard to public issues, thus clearly indicating the social function of governance in global civil society.

The governing efforts of politically motivated NGOs can be seen in the way they directly pressure states to undertake specific actions, for example. Through lobbying, protest and other methods, they attempt to persuade state officials to adopt policy recommendations. They recognize that states are the main actors in world affairs and as such can most easily reach into and influence the lives of citizens. States, in other words, represent the quickest means for establishing effective institutions. NGOs expend tremendous effort trying to win the ear of states so that states will set up or remain in compliance with institutions that advance NGO aims. Examples of such activity abound.

Amnesty International and Human Rights Watch, for instance, constantly lobby states to promote stricter international standards for the protection of human rights. They define human rights in greater specificity and encourage states to identify and punish other violating states by publicizing specific cases of human rights abuses and organizing international censure. Such effort has had significant impact on the activity of states and on the further institutionalization of respect for human rights (see, for example, Forsythe 1989; Sikkink 1993; and Goldman 1993). Transnational environmental groups have made similar efforts with equal effect. Greenpeace and the Antarctic and Southern Oceans Coalition (ASOC), for instance, work to influence international negotiations concerning protection of the oceans and Antarctica. Greenpeace successfully convinced states to phase out industrial dumping in the North Sea and Northeast Atlantic as part of the London Dumping Convention—a policy recommendation initiated solely by Greenpeace itself (Stairs and Taylor 1992: 128). In the case of Antarctica, Greenpeace and ASOC orchestrated the defeat of the Convention on the Regulation of Antarctic Mineral Resources Activity (CRAMRA), which originally aimed to regulate mineral exploration on the continent; they also advanced the idea of and won support for the 1991 Environmental Protocol, which prohibits mineral exploration for at least fifty years and establishes a framework for preserving the continent as a world park (see Wapner 1996: 136–137; and Deihl 1991). In both cases, Greenpeace and ASOC pressured states to adopt certain policies that, through international cooperation, became institutionalized. Most importantly, although states ultimately institutionalized these policies, the initiation and articulation of them arose outside the state system, in global civil society.

NGOs also engage in global governance by mobilizing means of governance that operate independently of the state system. It is fair to say that they would prefer to work through the state system and enlist state capability in the construction of institutions. This route is often unavailable, however, in that many NGOs have little access to state officials—a situation prevalent in both democratic and nondemocratic settings. In these cases, therefore, NGOs make a strategic decision to identify and mobilize mechanisms of governance strewn throughout the nongovernmental sphere. Global civil society is not simply an arena from which NGOs emerge; it also serves as a terrain on which they carry out their political activities. Through sustained transnational interaction, social, economic, and cultural institutions guide widespread behavior. These socially constructed institutions change over time due to the evolving character of collective life. Knowing this, NGOs identify and manipulate such institutions in the service of their particular cause. In other words, they politicize the institutions of global civil society and *enlist them* as mechanisms of governance for their own purposes. To be sure, this practice is difficult and many times ineffective, and it some-times produces results that are difficult to assess. Nonetheless, to the degree that NGOs successfully shift the standards of good conduct, the economic incentives of certain actions, or fundamental understandings that animate particular widespread activities, it represents an important strategy for establishing institutions to govern widespread behavior.

For years, European Nuclear Disarmament (END) sought not only to influence European governments with regard to deployment of nuclear weapons but also to create what END members took to be more peaceful societies. The latter objective involved demystifying traditional understandings of one's supposed enemy, propagating expressions of nonviolence, and combating widespread faith in the infallibility of one's society (see Thompson 1990; for a more general overview, see Joseph 1993; and Galtung 1989). In such an instance, END attempted to bend social and cultural discourses about peace and war to support its objectives; it sought to reconfigure the existing ideational institutions to promote its goal of reducing the threat of nuclear war.[16] In a similar fashion, Friends of the Earth and a host of other national and international environmental groups have been working for years outside the domain of governments to reconfigure institutions that inform corporate practices. One of the more dramatic efforts along these lines is the establishment of the CERES Principles (referring to the Coalition for Environmentally Responsible Economies and formally the Valdez Principles), which specify a set of guidelines for corporate practices based on a code of conduct that would minimize corporate contribution to environmental degradation. To date, a number of Fortune 500 MNCs, including General Motors and Sun Company, are signatories to the CERES Principles, as are a large number of less prominent MNCs. The CERES Principles represent a new set of institutional constraints on companies and thus another instance of going outside the state system to institutionalize guidelines for widespread and transnational behavior (Ann-Zondorak 1991; Wapner 1996: 129–130). In both the END case and the CERES case, NGOs turned their gaze away from the state system and concentrated on other entities within global society to win support for and the instantiation of their goals. Both cases also illustrate an NGO effort to construct institutions out of the existing discourses and commonplace activities of global civil society.

Conclusion

Global governance has been one of the most perennial and daunting challenges in world history. Ever since the Stoics imagined a single world, organized by a set of common principles, thinkers and practitioners have worked to conceptualize and bring into reality mechanisms to coordinate the diverse activities of a complex, multifarious world. For some, this project meant establishing a world government to legislate common laws and policies. For others, it meant simply building institutions of common understanding and practice supported by sovereign entities below the level of a world government. Today, although some thinkers still advocate a world government, much more attention is being paid to the institutional authority that arises out of and is sustained by other entities. The latter emphasis has recently provided the justification for scholars of international relations to conceptualize "governance without government" (see, for example, Young 1994a; Rosenau and Czempiel 1992; Murphy 1994; and Commission on Global Governance 1995).

In this chapter I have tried to explain why global civil society, as a realm of collective life, must be included in the endeavor to understand and speculate about global governance. I have done this with an eye toward environmental issues in particular but have kept the discussion broad enough to make it relevant for all types of transboundary, public goods issues. Overall, I have argued that global civil society provides a terrain where actors can organize material and ideational resources to shift the institutional matrix that shapes widespread behavior. Institutions, as Oran Young reminds us, are "sets of rules of the game or codes of conduct that serve to define social practices, assign roles to the participants in these practices, and guide the interactions among occupants of these roles" (Young 1994a: 3). As such, they need not arise simply through the efforts of states but can emerge and be built by nonstate actors. To be sure, although such entities are less effective in establishing institutions, they can and do engage in such activity.

A number of scholars have documented the effectiveness of NGOs in establishing institutions (see, for example, Sikkink 1993; Princen and Finger 1994; Stairs and Taylor 1992; and Wapner 1996). They focus on NGO efforts to persuade national governments to pursue certain policy recommendations with regard to international negotiations and to work outside the state system to create norms, principles, and values that influence the thinking and behavior of individuals and collectives throughout the world. This chapter has presented a theoretical account of why such NGO efforts matter or, put differently, why such efforts actually establish specific institutions. By explaining the nature of global civil society and explicating its role in global governance, the chapter has analytically placed NGOs within a particular realm of collective life and has clarified why their activities within it have political effect.

The fundamental implication of the chapter is to remind scholars that when they try to understand the emergence and political quality of institutions, or when they attempt to construct international institutions for various purposes, they must remember that global civil society plays just as important a role as the state system. Too often, both scholars and practitioners focus attention solely on the state system to understand or speculate about the institutional character of world order. The chapter implicitly urges them to expand their focus and take into account the influential power and therefore the relevance of global civil society.

At a theoretical level, the chapter broadens the boundaries of the so-called "political" in international relations by highlighting the effect that actors within global civil society have on the world polity. Scholars many times assume that transnational activities are simply of sociological or cultural interest. By explaining the degree of agency in global civil society, the chapter emphasizes the political dimension: in other words, it specifies the dimension of governance within global civil society.

II
Organizations

4

International Organizations and the Creation of Environmental Regimes

Helmut Breitmeier

International Organizations: For What?

Two opposing political views about the importance of international organizations have competed with each other in the past fifteen years.[1] The first view argues that international organizations should play a more prominent role in the international system because of growing interdependencies among states and rapidly changing international relations. The international public's increasing demands that environmental, economic, or security problems be approached through cooperation and managed by an international polity have produced the expectation that the United Nations (UN) system contribute to global or regional problem solving.[2] However, after the end of the East-West conflict, the wave of optimism that a strengthened UN system would facilitate the management of environmental and security conflicts lasted only a short time. The second competing political view combines a growing critique of alleged malfunctions of single international organizations, such as the United Nations Educational, Scientific and Cultural Organization (UNESCO), and a general skepticism among important member states of the UN system toward the future role of such organizations. The outstanding dues of important member states such as the United States are the result of disappointed expectations, which in turn have resulted in highly politicized international organizations and ineffective bureaucracies. In light of growing aggressive economic liberalism and of a general trend toward deregulation, state bureaucracies and international organizations are more and more under pressure to justify certain activities and to save costs. This chapter addresses two questions: (1) Can global environment-al governance be achieved without a minimum of global polity? and (2) What lessons can analysts of international relations draw from the roles played by international organizations in the formation of environmental regimes?

International Organizations and Governance

Despite the fears and criticisms of single nation states concerning the loss of sovereignty, the number of regional, intercontinental, and global intergovernmental organizations has risen to 266 in 1995 since the creation of the first international organizations in the second half of the nineteenth century.[3] Scientific analysis of the roles played by formal intergovernmental organizations in international relations experienced its peak in the 1950s and 1960s. Since then, the research community has given greater attention to social institutions or governance systems created for collective action and has devoted much more effort to the analysis of international regimes than to the role of formal international organizations in the international system (Kratochwil and Ruggie 1986: 761).

This chapter focuses on the role of classic intergovernmental organiz-ations as bureaucratic organizations created during regime formation (Keohane 1989: 3; Rittberger 1994: 25–26). Regime analysis has always been aware of the links between international regimes and international organizations. Many intergovernmental organizations represent the home of treaty bodies, such as the secretariats of international regimes (Sandford 1994). However, many regimes have no or only partial links with larger bureaucratic intergovernmental organizations and have thus developed their own independent bodies. Normally created *after* the formation of a regime in order to carry out management tasks, such regime bodies can be neglected by scholars as they focus on analyzing international organizations' role *during* regime formation.

Global Organizations: A Starting Point for Further Analysis

The activities of international organizations are not only a sufficient but also a necessary condition to explain the formation of environmental governance systems. Although international organizations play an important role during regime formation, they may not always inevitably promote the creation of governance systems. They can also play the role of laggards, and their activities can delay or prevent the formation of a regime.[4] Conflicts between economic and environmental interests can arise between international organizations themselves. The lively debate about the greening of the General Agreement on Tariffs and Trade (GATT) bears some potential for further conflicts between international environmental organizations and economic organizations.[5] Debates over better consideration of environmental interests within the North American Free Trade Agreement (NAFTA) led to the adoption of a supplementary NAFTA agreement on environmental cooperation (Sands 1995: 714).

This chapter analyzes the role played by international organizations in the regime formation process at the global level. It takes stock of two major developments in international environmental politics: the formation of the global regime to protect the stratospheric ozone layer and the current efforts to create a global climate change regime.[6] In comparison to regional organizations, organizations with global membership exhibit a far higher number of state actors and a higher degree of heterogeneity among these state actors with regard to their levels of economic development, their political systems, and their cultural values. The high level of interdependence among the members of the European Union (EU) or within the Organization for Economic Cooperation and Development (OECD) generally enhances the conditions for the creation of governance systems. Such interdependence does not always exist, however, because global international organizations operate in a world comprising different world regions with different degrees of regional interdependence.

Regional international organizations play an important role in the creation and management of regional governance systems. The United Nations Economic Commission for Europe (ECE) served as a forum for negotiating the Long-Range Transboundary Air Pollution (LRTAP) Convention and subsequent protocols (Levy 1993; Chossudovsky 1988). Some world regions such as Western Europe or North America developed a far higher degree of regional institutionalization between states in creating governance systems for environmental protection and for economic or security cooperation. Environmental regime formation within a supranational organization, such as the European Union, and the organization's role in the process of creating environmental governance systems are still open fields for further research.

International Organizations and the Anarchical International System

Regime literature most often assigns international organizations at best a complementary role in the creation of environmental governance systems. The different approaches of regime analysis deliberately or unconsciously imply that major causal explanations for successful or failed efforts to create a regime have to focus on the roles played by nation states and by nongovernmental actors.[7] So far, regime analysis acknowledges only that normative institutional factors, such as international organizations, or norms and rules "carry some explanatory weight" for regime formation. In general, it considers international organizations "as supportive rather than as prime causes of regime formation" (List and Rittberger 1992: 102–103). Most of the research dealing with the role of international organizations in environmental politics has mainly focused on describing how the environment has become a prominent issue in the work of international organizations.[8] Two recent major volumes on international regimes attribute to international organizations only an indirect role during regime formation, but they do not evaluate the organization's role during the different stages of the political process.[9] This chapter's discussion about the role of international organizations during regime formation forms part of a larger discussion about the relative importance attributed to state power as opposed to knowledge in international relations.

Power, Knowledge, and International Organizations

Neorealism considers anarchy—in which a "lack of order and of organization" prevails (Waltz 1979: 89)—as the ordering principle of international politics. Despite the growing number of international organizations, neorealism neglects their importance and considers outcomes in the international system as a consequence of the power distribution between single units (states) in a given structure. Its counterpart, the neo-institutionalist school, although accepting that international anarchy is a dominating principle of international relations, considers the creation of international regimes as a replacement for self-help strategies and as a structure of regulated anarchy in the international system (Rittberger 1990: 2). Both schools of thought consider power important, although realism considers power as the dominating variable, whereas neo-institutionalism considers power as just one important variable among others. The power-structural approach of regime formation regards international organizations at best as actors used by powerful states to transform their state interests into internationally agreed upon governance systems.

Approaches that partially rely on the tradition of functionalist theory consider international organizations at least as an arena for agenda setting and negotiation processes (Haas 1964). Growing attention has been given to the roles played by scientific, technical, or legal experts in regime formation. The main functions of epistemic communities— which can be described as transnational networks of groups with special expertise in the issue area—are to use knowledge and information as a power resource and to diffuse new ideas, both of which can lead decision makers to create new policies. The epistemic community concept is not as state centric as the power structural or the game theoretical approaches. It focuses more on the role single individuals play in changing the attitudes of political decision makers and of the public. It considers international organizations as an important arena for the activities of a transnational network of experts; Moreover, staff members of an organization may also be part of the epistemic community itself.[10] In practice, however, such homogeneous epistemic communities are exceptional cases. They can by no means be considered as important phenomena during each process of regime formation. The epistemic community concept focuses more on the role of individuals and does not comprehensively analyze the influence of international organizations' activities in the creation of international governance systems. It does not adequately consider the patterns of influence displayed by nongovernmental organizations during regime formation because it works more toward detecting the existence of an epistemic community. Future studies about nongovernmental actors may perhaps contribute more insights about interactions between international organizations and nongovernmental organizations during regime formation.

The Different Stages of Regime Formation

Until recently, regime analysis did not develop a clear understanding of the chronological sequence of the policy process on the international level.[11] It is still unable to explain whether international organizations are more influential during a single stage or nearly equally influential during all the different stages of the policy cycle. As the first stage of regime formation, agenda building is based on the assumption that a political system develops filters to separate important from unimportant issues.[12] A large number of issues compete for a position at the top of the global environmental agenda and for entrance into the decision-making process. At least three types of regulating factors are used to prioritize single issues. The first type consists of the activities of actors who serve as gatekeepers in the political system (Easton 1965: 88). Single international organizations or several organizations combined can act as gatekeepers for an issue. The second type refers to certain features of a single problem—for instance, its importance for societies.[13] The more important the problem is to a society, the more likely it will be placed at the top of the agenda. A third type includes the existence of cultural norms in an issue area. Strong environmental values or the sudden occurrence of external shocks or crises, such as tanker accidents, normally increase the likelihood that a problem will be considered important. The long-term evolution of environmental consciousness, for example, was a prerequisite for the growing attention paid to environmental problems on the international agenda.

The second stage of regime formation spans the full period of negotiations, from beginning to end. Sometimes global environmental negotiations take place under the auspices of an international organization, which finds itself confronted not only with the participation of a large number of states and nonstate actors, but also with having to maneuver between opposing negotiating blocs. The third stage—the operationalization stage—spans the period from signing an agreement to entry into force; it figures as part of the management of a regime and therefore is not considered in this chapter.[14] The analytical distinction between these three stages of regime formation marks a step forward in regime analysis.

International organizations are embedded in a framework of interactions among various actors in the international system. They are dependent, not autonomous, institutions (Jacobson 1984: 77–80). A consideration of their relationships with states and other nonstate actors, as well as their own interests, leads to the following questions: How great is their influence on the process of regime formation when it is compared to the influence of other actors? Do they act as an instrument of other actors, or do they use other actors to promote their own goals? Constraints on autonomous actions arise from the polity of international organizations. States directly influence the budgets, policies, programs, and administration of international organizations through regular conferences and assemblies; they also determine guidelines for the routines.[15] The growing participation of nongovernmental organizations (NGOs) in negotiation processes has strengthened their position as institutionalized opposition in the developments of diplomatic processes and as watchdogs for the societies in nation states. International organizations make use of nonstate actors (just as nonstate actors make use of them) to pursue their goals. Apart from pursuing their own goals, such organizations can form tacit coalitions with NGOs or states; they are also subject to increased lobbying from environmentalist NGOs and private interests groups, including multinational companies.

The Roles of International Organizations during Regime Formation
International organizations have never been merely technical and apolitical institutions, although it was one of their classic functions to find rather technical solutions to problems in transnational cooperation arising from different national technical standards and regulations.[16] The functions displayed by international organizations during regime formation can be described under three different headings. They provide informational functions, offer a forum for the articulation of interests and the aggregation of interest groups, and contribute to the development of normative statements and rules in the issue area.

Informational Functions   International organizations are very influential in improving the cognitive setting of an issue area and in translating to the international level any information gathered at the national level about the causes and consequences of a problem. Improving the cognitive setting, sometimes even just detecting a serious problem, can create favorable conditions for agenda setting or can stimulate the dynamics of deadlocked negotiations. Data gathering, analysis, exchange, and dissemination help set certain environmental issues at the top of the international agenda and certain bargaining processes in motion. Monitoring and scientific collaboration help produce new consensus knowledge about cause-and-effect linkages.[17] Close cooperation between international organizations, national research organizations, governmental bureaucracies, and nongovernmental organizations can enhance the flow of new consensual knowledge from knowledge producers to decision makers. International organizations can display ideational influence (Goldstein and Keohane 1993: 7–9). They can even possibly put forward new systems of thought or world views or promote cognitive convergence that encompasses not only new ideas about the causes of the problem but also prescriptions for appropriate solutions.

Articulation of Interests and Aggregation of Interest Groups
International organizations can serve as an arena for states and nonstate actors to make statements about the importance of a problem and about the kind of solutions they prefer. World conferences and smaller ad hoc conferences have often stimulated the formulation of state and nonstate attitudes with regard to problems such as desertification, water, AIDS, population, or energy. International conferences can produce new or renewed attention to agenda formation and can influence the dynamics of negotiations. Nonstate actors can use negotiations and international conferences as an opportunity to influence the political process outside actual negotiations, to build up political pressure, and to raise public awareness for the problem (Princen and Finger 1994; Stairs and Taylor 1992). More and more, states are considering nonstate actors as instruments, using them as advisors to their national delegations and in their efforts to build up domestic political support for their international

environmental policy. Nonstate actors themselves want to influence government attitudes at the international level.[18] International organizations, therefore, are an important arena for coalition building among states and nonstate actors. Political initiatives launched by states not only influence the behavior of other states, but also form part of a two-level game: on one level, national decision makers have to take into account the domestic repercussions of their international policies; and on another level, transnational coalitions among nonstate actors, international organizations, and certain states aim at influencing the domestic public of other states (Putnam 1988).

Normative Functions and Rule Making   International organizations provide important administrative services during agenda setting and negotiations. States can use them as an arena for developing norms in the issue area. Conference declarations, resolutions, reports, and other normative statements about the causes and effects of the problem and about common approaches for problem solving can motivate states to tackle the problem and to think about possible solutions. When negotiations take place under the auspices of international organizations, these organizations can provide secretarial support and draft the reports of the negotiation sessions. They can also influence rule making by contributing to draft texts of legal conventions and protocols between the different negotiation sessions, and they can help determine the content of such conventions by identifying areas that have to be dealt with and by presenting models about the effects of different options considered by the negotiators. They display an influential role as proponents of comprise when different state coalitions are not able to overcome differences regarding single parts of the legal agreement. Servants of an international organization can provide political guidance within negotiations and can play an influential informal role when they provide expert knowledge to national delegations and when they suggest compromising solutions. The chairman of the negotiations, an experienced chief executive officer, and other staff members of international organizations may serve as mediators between confrontational state negotiating positions; they can also act as "corridor" advisors to national delegations or pave the way for compromise in closed meetings. The head of an organization can use his or her public role to apply political pressure on those states opposed to regime formation.

Agenda Setting for Ozone Depletion and Climate Change

Ozone depletion was considered an important issue on the global agenda much earlier than was climate change. In 1970, initial debates about the possible destruction of stratospheric ozone began in the United States, when scientists assumed that nitrogen oxide emissions from high-flying supersonic aircraft would damage the ozone layer (Morrisette 1989: 801; Dotto and Schiff 1980: 90–119). In 1974, two natural scientists, Mario Molina and Sherwood Rowland, published for the first time the hypothesis about catalytic destruction of stratospheric ozone as a consequence of chlorine emissions. It took less than eight years for the issue to be considered so important that state representatives started negotiations.[19] The agenda-setting period for the ozone issue—from 1974 to January 1982—was shorter than the period for the climate change issue. At the end of the nineteenth century, the Swedish chemist Svante Arrhenius had already pointed to the possible relationship between the atmospheric concentration of carbon dioxide and the Earth's temperature. Scientific cooperation between states in the field of meteorology began in 1873 with the creation of the International Meteorological Organization (IMO) and was carried on by the World Meteorological Organization (WMO), founded in 1950. It was not until February 1991 that formal negotiations about the climate convention began, after the ozone issue had already passed through several stages of the regime formation process.

Several factors account for the difference between the shorter period of agenda setting of the ozone issue and the much longer process of agenda setting for the climate change issue. The greater complexity of the climate issue made it much more difficult to popularize and politicize the issue. In contrast, the possible impacts of spray can emissions on the ozone layer were easy to understand and could be explained to nearly everybody, although it wasn't even clear whether the hypothesis was valid. The international public considered the ozone layer a symbol of the survival of mankind because it is a protective layer against the possible increase of ultraviolet radiation. Individuals felt themselves threatened by the possible danger of increased skin cancer. Possible measures to protect the ozone layer were also far less expensive than the assumed cost to achieve long-term decarbonization of industrialized and developing countries. The climate problem benefited from the earlier politicization of ozone depletion, which created global awareness for other global environmental problems.

Informational Functions and Agenda Setting

WMO's and the United Nations Environment Program's (UNEP) functions in coordinating comprehensive global research programs provided a basis for agenda setting in both issue areas. Global research programs coordinated and partially carried out by international organizations paved the way for enhancing the cognitive setting in these issue areas. It was more cost effective for states to coordinate their research activities concerning the ozone layer, weather forecasting, and climate change within an international network than to carry out these tasks independently.

The International Geophysical Year in 1957 was the starting point for the creation of the Global Ozone Observing System, coordinated by WMO. As part of the Global Atmospheric Watch system (GAW), the Global Ozone Observing System includes more than 140 national stations measuring stratospheric ozone concentrations.[20] The detection of the chlorofluorocarbon (CFC) problem and the creation of UNEP in the mid-1970s were parallel developments. Starting as a very weak organization with limited funds, staff, and competencies, UNEP had to figure out new areas for its future work as well as to gain credibility and standing. It identified ozone depletion as one of the basic issues it would deal with. In April 1975, UNEP's Governing Council decided to create a program on the protection of the ozone layer, which already called for "an examination of the need and justification for recommending any national and international controls over the release of man-made chemicals" (UNEP 1989: 6).

Coordination of monitoring and information exchange are WMO's traditional tasks. Since 1963, it has coordinated the global World Weather Watch system implemented by its member states for the purpose of collection, exchange, and analysis of weather data. Following the rapid development of meteorological satellites and of automated observing systems in the 1970s, the system now comprises more than 9,500 observing stations on land, approximately 7,000 ship stations, as well as several hundred buoys, aircraft observations, and satellites in the Earth's orbit at a height of 800–1000 km and in the geostationary orbit (WMO 1990: 13–17). Global and regional meteorological centers process weather data for short-, middle-, and long-term weather forecasts and provide other services to national meteorological centers.

The Second World Climate Conference in 1990 paved the way for collecting further scientific knowledge about the climate system and the greenhouse problem. Under the newly created World Climate Research Program (WCRP), which is part of the larger World Climate Program (WCP), scientists could now intensify their research about climate, which they had already been carrying out under the former Global Atmospheric Research Program (GARP). In 1967, WMO and the International Council of Scientific Unions (ICSU) formally agreed to collaborate closely in carrying out GARP, and they continued this collaboration after WRCP was established. In addition to ICSU's role, other international organizations such as UNEP and UNESCO take part in implementing the WCP. Global and regional monitoring of environmental pollution was completed by WMO's Global Atmospheric Watch System, which is now part of the Global Climate Observing System established by the Second World Climate Conference in 1990.

Articulation of Interests and Aggregation of Interest Groups during Agenda Setting

Several international conferences and workshops initiated by and carried out under the auspices of international organizations contributed to the agenda setting of both the climate change and ozone depletion issues. The conferences provided an opportunity for states to articulate their concerns. In an international conference held in spring 1977 in Washington, UNEP brought together scientific experts to talk about the ozone issue. The conference agreed upon a World Action Plan on the Ozone Layer, which included twenty-one items considered important for further research. UNEP was given a broad coordinating and catalytic role to oversee the work carried out by international organizations and nongovernmental organizations in the issue area (UNEP 1989: 7). As a consequence of the Washington conference, UNEP's Governing Council agreed to establish the Coordinating Committee on the Ozone Layer (CCOL), which met annually until the mid-1980s to assess the knowledge available about the ozone issue and to publish figures on the global production of CFC-11 and CFC-12 (Rummel-Bulska 1986: 282). In these annual meetings, states could exchange their attitudes about possible regulations for CFCs. Participating multinational companies represented the interests of the CFC-producing and consuming industries.

Between 1979 and 1984 three National Academy of Sciences (NAS) reports played down the expected depletion of the ozone layer. As a consequence, global and domestic attention for the issue declined, especially in the United States. UNEP's continued interest in the issue area, however, prevented it from getting lost on the global agenda. In 1980, UNEP's Governing Council reemphasized the importance of the issue and called upon governments to reduce the use of CFCs. In 1981, it decided to establish the Ad Hoc Working Group of Legal and Technical Experts, which served as a negotiation body for the next years to develop the Vienna Convention (Brunnée 1988: 226–229). In the same year, it held a meeting in Montevideo where environmental law experts and senior government officials prepared the Montevideo Program, which served as a work program and influenced UNEP's legal activities in the following decade. Stratospheric ozone depletion was one of the main issues of the Montevideo Program (Sands 1995: 42).

Global attention for the climate issue was also intensified by the June 1988 Toronto Conference on the Changing Atmosphere, organized by Canada, the WMO, UNEP, and other organizations. For the first time, global perception was directed on a conference that linked the ozone depletion and climatic change issues. Nongovernmental organizations used a number of different climate conferences in the following years to raise public awareness of the issue and to put pressure on those states reluctant to agree that climate change was an important problem. These environmentalist groups shared UNEP's, WMO's, and concerned states' beliefs about the political salience of the problem.

Normative Functions and Agenda Setting

International conferences organized by international organizations served to formulate normative statements about the salience of the two problems. WMO organized the First World Climate Conference in 1979, at which several hundred scientists agreed that carbon dioxide plays a fundamental role in determining the temperature of the Earth's atmosphere and that "it appears plausible that an increased amount of carbon dioxide in the atmosphere can contribute to a gradual warming of the lower atmosphere".[21] Several climate workshops in the 1980s helped integrate scientific knowledge. Scientific experts dealt with the greenhouse problem at an initial workshop organized by UNEP, WMO, and ICSU in Villach, Austria, in September 1980. At the end of the second workshop in Villach in 1985, the participants concluded in their declaration that "as a result of the increasing concentrations of greenhouse gases, it is now believed that in the first half of the next century a rise of global mean temperature could occur which is greater than any in man's history" (ICSU, UNEP, and WMO 1986: 1). In fall 1987, two workshops in Villach and Bellagio dealt with scenarios concerning the temperature increase, rising sea levels, and the effects of climatic change; they also focused on strategies for mitigation and adaptation as well as political strategies for conflict management (WMO and UNEP 1988a). The global conference on the changing atmosphere in Toronto 1988 recommended that carbon dioxide emissions be reduced by approximately 20 percent of 1988 levels by the year 2005. This normative statement was the first globally formulated policy goal in this issue area (WMO and UNEP 1988b: 291–304). In the following years, the Toronto goal had a great influence on the political discussion of future policies in the issue area.

People began to believe more and more that climate anomalies such as the El Niño phenomenon, droughts, hot summers, storms, and hurricanes represented the harbingers of climate change. In November 1988, Mostafa Tolba, at that time UNEP's executive director, and G. O. P. Obasi, WMO's secretary general, opened the first session of the newly established Intergovernmental Panel on Climate Change (IPCC). WMO's executive council had determined that IPCC's objectives were to assess scientific information on climate change, the change's environmental and socioeconomic impacts, and the formulation of response strategies.[22] Since then, the IPCC has gained greater attention in the global debate about causes and effects of the problem and, in close collaboration with national research institutes, has contributed to greater consensus on the problem. When the United Nations General Assembly adopted the resolution in December 1988 that climate change "is a common concern of mankind," requiring "necessary and timely action... within a global framework," and reaffirmed its promise to provide all necessary support for IPCC's work, the climate issue was established on the global agenda and the prenegotiation phase began.[23]

Theoretical Approaches and Agenda Setting

Agenda setting is a process in which state actors, international organizations, and nonstate actors struggle to decide whether an issue deserves a prominent place on the political agenda. Although state actors do calculate the costs of possible measures in the issue area during agenda setting, this stage of regime formation is more a struggle about ideational hegemony in the issue area than it is a detailed discussion about political measures. Therefore, international organizations are important actors during this stage, and they have equal status with states in the debate about ideational hegemony. No doubt, they depend on the support of important states. On the other hand, states interested in putting issues on the global agenda are aware that international organizations are valuable partners to achieve their goals.

The Power-Structural Approach   Political action of a powerful state is an important variable in explaining agenda setting for the issue of ozone depletion. The United States very early politicized ozone depletion internationally. By 1975, it had already experienced a lively domestic CFC debate, and a consumer boycott had led to a temporary decrease in sales of CFC products. A 1976 NAS report supported the CFC hypothesis, and in 1977 the Environmental Protection Agency (EPA) announced a ban on "nonessential uses" of CFCs in spray cans. It was not until the end of the seventies, however, that the United States and other nation states could induce the European Community to take similar measures toward a ban on nonessential uses of aerosols.

On the other hand, the United States was quite reluctant to agree that climate change should be considered an important issue on the global environmental agenda. In this case, a coalition of European countries, the Alliance of Small Islands States, and some developing countries politicized the issue despite strong resistance from the United States. The process of agenda setting for climate change shows that agenda setting does not depend on the presence of a strong dominating state in the issue area. Smaller states formed a coalition and displayed "soft power" resources (Nye 1990)—that is, scientific facts about the causes and consequences of the problem—to the international public. As they were in the ozone layer issue, international organizations could be used as important forums to transfer concerns about the problem, to articulate common interests, and to develop first normative statements about the salience of the problem. UNEP and WMO were more than merely agents of state interests. UNEP helped the ozone issue to stay alive between 1979 and 1984, when the position of the opponents to the CFC hypothesis was strengthened.

The Knowledge-Based Approach   UNEP and WMO displayed gate-keeping roles in collaboration with states and nonstate actors. A tacit coalition comprising environmentalist nonstate actors, leader states interested in establishing global regimes, and international organizations translated scientific knowledge into political demands. One reason why transnational nonstate actors were more involved in agenda setting for climate change than they were in the ozone issue is that their influence on the international level had grown by the end of the 1980s. Scientific knowledge produced by the IPCC was immediately politicized, and the IPCC itself was a political actor in the global discussion. Putting the ozone issue on the agenda was one of UNEP's early successes. The activities of both organizations do not, however, account for why the climate issue appeared much later than the ozone issue on the global agenda. Together with activities of nonstate actors and nation states, UNEP's and WMO's activities were reinforcing during agenda setting. They quite effectively used several windows of opportunities—such as the detection of the Antarctic ozone hole, climate anomalies, and a political climate in Western industrialized countries that favored consideration of global issues—to politicize climate change.

Although core knowledge about the causes and effects of both problems were basic requirements, final scientific proof was not necessary for these issues to reach the top of the international agenda. International organizations were most influential when they displayed their informational functions in both issue areas. These functions were the basis for other political activities—such as organizing conferences and workshops to lobby for both issues—and for initiating normative statements in which state delegations or experts raised concerns about the problems and asked for joint international management. Therefore, international organizations seem to be especially important and successful in agenda setting if they take part in the technical work carried out in the issue area. The knowledge-based approach best explains the role of international organizations during agenda setting for both issue areas. Although they depended on the support of national bureaucracies, governments, and research institutions, they had leeway to display their own goals. The power-structural approach complements this explanation of agenda setting in these instances because strong nation states or state coalitions pushed the issues and supported the activities of international organizations.

International Organizations and Negotiations Concerned with Ozone Depletion and Climate Change

The ozone negotiations served as a precursor to the climate negotiations. As in other environmental issue areas, the framework convention approach was used for these negotiations. The Vienna Convention for the Protection of the Ozone Layer 1985 was a model for the Framework Convention on Climate Change (FCCC) in 1992, although both conventions were the result of weak compromise rather than of specific plans. They remained framework conventions only because states could not agree upon regulations about ozone-depleting substances and greenhouse gases. In both negotiation processes, strong conflicts between industrialized countries prevailed. North-South (i.e., northern hemisphere versus southern hemisphere) issues didn't play an important role in the negotiations for the ozone regime until 1987, whereas conflicts between industrialized and developing countries were an important feature of the climate negotiations from the very beginning.

The negotiation processes for the ozone and clmate issue regimes differ in their degree of complexity and in the number of states that participated in the negotiations during regime formation. First, the climate problem and the different options for conflict management in the issue area are much more complex than the phase-out of ozone-depleting substances. Second, CFC negotiations started with only two dozen regular state participants, whereas the climate negotiations started with more than one hundred state participants. Among international organizations, only WMO, the European Economic Community, and UNEP as the organizing organization were regular participants in the ozone negotiations until the Vienna Convention for the Protection of the Ozone Layer was adopted in 1985. The number of state participants and observers increased in the final negotiations for the Montreal Protocol on Substances that Deplete the Ozone Layer in 1987. However, most developing countries became directly involved with the negotiations only after the regime had already been created in 1987. In contrast to the early period of the ozone negotiations, the climate negotiations immediately had to cope with greater participation of international governmental and nongovernmental organizations.

Informational Functions and Negotiations

Scientific consensus did not occur until the formation of the ozone regime in 1987, and states kept negotiating even up to the second half of the nineties because of uncertainty about the causes and effects of the climate problem. However, both WMO and UNEP were able to influence negotiations by coordinating scientific research and presenting new scientific facts to decision makers. Although they had a significant influence on the ozone negotiations, they could not influence the climate negotiations in the same way. The move of the climate secretariat from Geneva to Bonn demonstrates that, for the majority of member states of the Framework Convention on Climate Change, the proximity of UNEP, WMO, IPCC and INC was not an important factor.

From 1988 to 1990, WMO and UNEP were active players during the prenegotiations about a climate change convention; also during this period, states organized several climate conferences in order to produce global awareness and to convince states such as the United States that negotiations about a global convention were necessary. Both organizations used IPCC's work to disseminate scientific knowledge about the causes and effects of climate change. Three working groups of the IPCC, which was jointly sponsored by WMO and UNEP, provided a report for discussion at the Second World Climate Conference. The report included scientific assessment of climate change, assessment of potential impacts, and formulation of response strategies. Approximately two hundred scientists were involved in preparing the report. An update of IPCCs report and a new report of the panel appeared in 1992 and 1996.

In 1990, under its chairman Bert Bolin, IPCC was at the peak of its influence and helped establish the Intergovernmental Negotiating Committee on Climate Change (INC). However, the decision made by states to establish a separate body apart from IPCC has led to a decrease of IPCC's influence on climate negotiations. For a couple of years, science could not maintain its dominant influence. Negotiations were more and more shaped by traditional conflicts about economic factors among industrialized countries and about North-South equity. Although their direct influence on climate negotiations has decreased since 1990 due to states' efforts to keep negotiations more independent of science, both organizations have nevertheless continued to assign high priority to the climate issue. Criticism of IPCC's size and cumbersomeness, however, neglects the fact that the committee itself is hardly responsible for the slow but ongoing progress in creating consensual knowledge about climate change.[24] The creation of consensual knowledge is a process that includes the work of a large number of research institutes from many countries, and due to the complexity of the climate issue area, achieving quick scientific consensus was unlikely.

A scientific article published in *Nature* in spring 1985 by a British research team showed for the first time a significant decrease of stratospheric ozone concentrations over Antarctica. In 1986 UNEP and WMO published a scientific assessment report about ozone depletion. Both organizations published similar reports in the following years, mainly in collaboration with several U.S. research agencies, which included recent measurements of ozone depletion and scenarios that showed long-term concentration of ozone-depleting substances. These reports mainly synthesize the work of the most prominent experts in the issue area, thus gaining high credibility both inside and outside the scientific community.

The United States has had strong interests in the issue area and, in close collaboraltion with UNEP, has intensified scientific research about ozone depletion. In 1986 UNEP and the U.S. EPA organized a series of workshops and made strong efforts to gain more information about the CFC production of single countries, about the impacts of ozone depletion, and about the options for control strategies. The workshops were a cornerstone in the U.S. strategy to determine the outcome of the ozone negotiations.

Articulation of Interests and Aggregation of Interest Groups in the Negotiations

UNEP provided the institutional home of the negotiations about ozone depletion, whereas negotiations about climate change took place in a separate body created by the United Nations General Assembly. UNEP offered administrative services, helped coordinate research and assess ozone modifications, and lobbied for precautionary action. The negotiations provided a forum for states to articulate their interests and for state coalitions among like-minded countries to emerge. When the U.S. rediscovered its interest in the issue, it was clear that UNEP, WMO, the United States, and other leader countries had the identical goal to phase out ozone-depleting substances. The United States formed a coalition with the Nordic countries, which had already submitted a proposal during the first negotiation session in 1982. This leader coalition, the so-called Toronto group, experienced strong opposition from the European Community. As the strongest laggards, Great Britain, France, and Italy were unable to determine their position until early 1987. When a strongly politicized international public put the European Community and its member states under severe pressure and single member countries no longer supported the community's laggard position, the negotiation process experienced a new dynamic.

When states agreed in March 1985 on the Vienna Convention, the U.S. delegate made clear that if CFC use continued to grow, some depletion of the ozone layer was likely to occur. The United States criticized as insufficient the European Communitys proposal of a production capacity cap, but it did not succeed in establishing a significant reduction of CFC use in aerosols.[25] When global negotiations resumed in December 1986, the United States had totally revised and significantly enlarged its negotiation goals and now called for a long-term scheduled reduction of 95 percent. Within a few years, the United States achieved its goals under the 1987 Montreal Protocol, and under the 1990 London and 1992 Copenhagen agreements.

The fundamental change in other countries' readiness to join the regime and in the European Community's position, which had experienced only a slight change in November 1986 in favor of a new proposal for a freeze of the most important CFCs, was the result of several reinforcing factors. UNEPs and WMOs activities during the negotiations were important, but these activities constituted only a single factor among others that led to regime formation. First, the strong engagement of the United States in the issue area, its political pressure on the European states, and its strong research activities contributed most to the formation of the ozone regime. Second, the CFC-producing industry redefined its economic interests. After DuPont, the biggest CFC-producing company in the United States, began to reinforce research on substitutes in 1986, it became clear to other multinational companies that the global CFC market would change and that the ability to produce substitutes was necessary to maintain market shares. Third, external shocks, such as the detection of the ozone hole over Antarctica, produced strong public pressure. Fourth, UNEP's and WMO's informational functions were important, and the United States quite easily used them when it rediscovered its interest in the issue area. The heads of both organizations, Tolba and Obasi, worked as interpreters of new scientific knowledge for the international public, translating it into political demands.

Both Tolba and Obasi played similar roles during the climate negotiations. From the outset of the climate negotiations it was clear that states and state coalitions would use other forums outside the INC to coordinate their attitudes in the negotiations.[26] Among industrialized countries traditional meetings such as the group of seven most-developed countries (G-7) and other organizations such as OECD and the European Union have become involved in the climate negotiations. Developing countries have discussed their positions within the group of

77 (G-77); the Alliance of Small Island States (AOSIS) countries has established its own network; and oil-producing states have normally met within the Organization of Petroleum Exporting Countries (OPEC). Therefore, in the process of climate negotiations not only do different states negotiate with each other, but other international organizations also serve as advocates for their member states. The European Union too makes statements in the negotiations for their member states. Apart from other factors, one reason for the much slower progress in achieving fixed targets and timetables for stabilizing and reducing certain greenhouse gases may be the global character of the negotiations from the outset. Global participation in the negotiations made it impossible to manage conflicts in the issue area with the same step-by-step approach used during regime formation for the ozone layer. Although industrialized countries agree that it is mainly their task to resolve the issue of fixed targets and timetables, the inclusion of developing countries in the negotiations has increased the number of conflicts. Lessons from other global negotiation processes show that such processes are rather lengthy and do not promote conflict management between industrialized countries (Sebenius 1991).

Normative Functions and Rule Making during the Negotiations

The ozone negotiations received administrative support from a secretariat provided by UNEP. From an organizational point of view, the INC works independently of UNEP and WMO, although the latter two organizations still contribute to the work of the climate negotiations. Several resolutions of the UN General Assembly provided the legal basis for INC's work up to the First Conference of the Parties held in Berlin in 1995. Behind the scenes of the ozone negotiations, Mostafa Tolba made efforts to convince states to agree on CFC reductions and to establish the ozone fund. He was an important mediator, helping to reconcile opposing interests and to promote compromise during the negotiations. Until 1995 the two chairmen of the INC also played important roles in developing compromise about text to be included in the climate convention and about decisions made by participants in the first conference of the parties to the convention. Servants of UNEP, WMO, and the INC not only provided traditional functions such as the dissemination of information to negotiating parties, but also produced conference reports, revised documents of the negotiations, and identified different options for solving single problems related to the regime. States asked them to collect information about possible solutions to problems, thus building on the expertise of both secretariats.

During the negotiation process for both the ozone and climate issues, UNEP and WMO heads made normative statements about the salience of the problems and expressed their concerns about the importance of regime building. At the conference of plenipotentiaries on the protection of the ozone layer held in Vienna in March 1985, UNEP's executive director expressed concern about increasing CFC use. The Chemical Manufacturers Association had reported "about a 7 percent increase in CFC-11 and CFC-12 in 1983 over 1982 levels, and both aerosols and non-aerosol use were seen to have increased during that period". At the Second World Climate Conference, Mostafa Tolba talked about climate change as a "threat potentially more catastrophic than any other threat in human history", although he was also aware of the existing scientific uncertainties mentioned in the IPCC's first assessment report.[27]

Tolba influenced the final stage of the ozone negotiations when he organized several informal meetings that brought together delegations from key participants in the negotiations to develop a draft for the Montreal Protocol on the basis of a text that he himself proposed. He was one of the proponents of a step-by-step approach for CFC regulation, starting with a freeze and followed by different steps to reduce use of a couple of the most important CFCs. He strongly resisted efforts by the European Community Commission to water down parts of the reduction scenario (Benedick 1991: 83–87). The first INC Chairman Jean Ripert played a similar role during the negotiations for the Framework Convention on Climate Change. A few months before the Rio summit in 1992, a group of key delegations met in Paris in April 1992 to develop a final draft for the climate convention. The delegations could not agree on a joint document and asked Jean Ripert to develop a chairman's text on the basis of different text proposals; this text was then discussed during the final INC meeting before the Rio summit. INC's second chairman, Raúl Estrada-Oyuela, conducted similar activities when states were preparing for and while they actually held the First Conference of the Parties.

Theoretical Approaches and Negotiations

International organizations had less influence during the negotiation stage in the two issue areas than they did during agenda setting. The struggle over ideational hegemony is still an important feature during the negotiation stage. However, states have a much more prominent role than international organizations during this stage, and considerations of costs, benefits or problems of domestic implementation are dominant. Therefore, international organizations normally can only build bridges between opposing national interests; they remain influential when they are able to act as mediators and producers of compromise. Furthermore, they still provide indispensable services by helping to improve the cognitive setting and providing administrative services for negotiators. UNEP was quite influential during the ozone negotiations because Tolba's efforts to reach compromise between the United States and Europe were successful. Although states are able to establish a negotiation process without a coordinating international organization, it is obvious that UNEP's and WMO's motivations and actions were crucial in producing global awareness and greater willingness among states to enter the negotiation phase.

The Power-Structural Approach   The United States had very strong interests in the ozone issue, and they were aware that they could best achieve their national goals by focusing on the established CFC negotiations. Without UNEP's lobbying for CFC reduction and leading a negotiation process, the danger existed that the United States would feel forced to achieve CFC reduction by self-help, which would have been more expensive than the route taken under the negotiations. Global negotiations allowed the United States to achieve their goal without sanctions. However, it is also unlikely that a more influential role by UNEP and WMO during the climate negotiations would have led to stronger provisions in the climate convention. The influence of international organizations during negotiations is therefore limited to the extent that nation states determine their own preferences, which can only partially be changed by the activities and influence of international organizations.

The United States allowed UNEP to play a very active political role because UNEP's activities strengthened their position. UNEP legitimized

U.S. goals by supporting its argument that CFC reduction is in the global interest and not just in the interest of the United States as well as its efforts to create equal conditions for all chemical manufacturers on the global CFC market following its domestic ban on nonessential CFC uses, which had disadvantaged its domestic chemical industry. UNEP and WMO displayed similar importance only at the outset of the climate negotiations. Nation states were able to confine UNEP's and WMO's influence, although both organizations continue to play active roles as providers of information and as coordinators of research in the field. Initially, environmentalist nonstate actors displayed lower interest in the CFC negotiations, but UNEP's activities stimulated the environmentalists to intensify their actions. The climate negotiations were thus confronted with a large number of nonstate and media observers. Although technically observers, they maintained the pressure on nation states to produce concrete results. However, a large number of economic interest groups also lobbied quite effectively for their goals and supported laggard states in their efforts to avoid concrete targets and timetables for the reduction of greenhouse gas emissions. The power-structural approach provides an important explanatory power for the negotiation stage. However, it traditionally neglects international organizations. The political process in the issue area of ozone depletion shows that international organizations *can* influence the outcomes of the negotiations, help to overcome deadlock between states, and produce new dynamics in the negotiation process. UNEP was not just an agent of the United States in the CFC negotiations; rather, it pursued its own interest to establish a regime in the issue area.

The Knowledge-Based Approach   States opposed to any regulatory measures on greenhouse gases used scientific uncertainty as an argument for their reluctance to agree to any specific targets and timetables for greenhouse gas reductions. European states used the same argument to support their laggard role in the CFC negotiations until 1987. Both WMO and UNEP were effective in enhancing scientific knowledge about the causes and consequences of stratospheric ozone depletion. They received support especially from the United States, which intensified its national research activities after the detection of the Antarctic ozone hole in 1985. UNEP's and WMO's activities went hand in hand with research activities from leader states and from the scientific community to achieve reductions of ozone-depleting substances. Although the degree of effectiveness displayed by international organizations is only of minor interest in the ozone issue negotiations, which were a success, the question remains whether UNEP, WMO, and the UN system as a whole could have been more effective during the climate negotiations. First of all, weak commitments made in the climate convention were the result of antagonist state positions in the issue area. The negotiation efforts of international organizations reach their limits when states cannot reconcile their differing interests. One of the weaknesses displayed by international organizations during regime formation was IPCC's inability to link its work more closely with INC's work. However, this inability does not stem from IPCC's intention to maintain scientific independence, but from INC consideration of itself as rather independent from IPCC.[28] Finally, even the United States changed its position about the need for fixed targets and timetables. As a consequence of a new IPCC consensus report, the U.S. administration agreed for the first time in 1996 that binding targets to reduce greenhouse gases will be necessary.[29]

The role of knowledge matters in explaining the outcomes of negotiations among states in both issue areas.[30] The European Community changed its mind only as a consequence of strong U.S. pressure to agree on CFC regulations. Although final scientific proof about cause-and-effect relationships in the issue area was not available until the Montreal Protocol was approved, a growing body of knowledge made Molina's and Rowland's hypothesis about catalytic ozone depletion more and more likely. Stronger scientific consensus on the causes and effects of climate change may therefore also provide a stimulus for the ongoing climate negotiations. New scientific knowledge can influence the dynamics of negotiations, thus serving as an important contextual factor for explaining outcomes of negotiations.

Environmental Governance without a Minimum of Global Polity?

Can global environmental governance be achieved without a minimum of global polity? This study focuses on how international organizations are important for regime formation. UNEP, WMO, and the UN General

Assembly displayed leadership roles during the different stages of regime building in both the ozone issue and the climate issue. Due to their informational functions in both issue areas, UNEP and WMO were able to be activists for agenda building and to make important contributions that helped establish negotiations. This study also addressed the question of the relative importance, during regime formation, of international organizations in comparison to other actors. UNEP and WMO depended on the readiness of states to tolerate or approve their actions in the issue area. Without tacit approval from states, it would have been difficult for UNEP to play an advocacy role for the creation of the ozone regime. Moreover, the climate negotiations show that states can succeed in limiting the influence of international organizations. With a growing number of new nonstate actors participating in regime formation, international organizations have to deal with new allies as well as new opponents of regime formation. The creation of a global public, the growth in the importance of mass media, and an increased interest in global environmental issues are providing new opportunities for international organizations to present their programmatic activities and to lobby for their own goals.

This study also shows that research will get better insights on the roles of international organizations during regime formation if it distinguishes between the different stages of the policy cycle. This study came to the conclusion that UNEP and WMO had more leeway during agenda setting than during the negotiations, at which point states took over the initiative. UNEP did, however, remain a very active player during the ozone negotiations, and its executive director helped the different state coalitions to reach compromise on several important issues.

Historical case study research about international organizations could be complemented by a counterfactual analysis that asks whether it would have been possible to achieve cooperation without international organizations. Would the absence of international organizations during regime formation have resulted in slowing down or in speeding up the accomplishment of cooperation, and would the result of the process of regime formation have been better or worse?[31] Further comparisons of processes of regime formation that do or do not involve active international organizations could help us to determine the extent to which regime formation depends on the roles played by international organizations.

Regime research should attempt to answer the following question: In comparison to other approaches, how important are explanations that focus on the role of international organizations in regime building?[32] If research devotes more attention to the analysis of international organizations, it will be possible to generate better insights about the kind of international organizations we need to achieve and maintain global governance. In addition, does an increasing demand for the creation of international regimes strengthen the role of international organizations? The current debate about reforming the United Nations may lead to more effective organizations. One should not overemphasize the role of international organizations, but it is obvious that various theoretical approaches have not adequately considered their roles during regime formation. It may be that better consideration of their role will lead their critics to moderate their criticism and will create a political climate in which states at least pay their membership dues in time.

5

International Organizations and the Implementation of Environmental Regimes

M. J. Peterson

International regimes, including those that address environmental concerns, can best be understood as the products of policy processes with distinct, though interconnected, phases of agenda setting, problem definition, policy selection, policy implementation, and policy evaluation (Kingdon 1995). This chapter focuses on the implementation and evaluation phases of regime operation and outlines how intergovernmental organizations can best help increase the effectiveness of international environmental regimes.

Although the European Union demonstrates how supranational organizations can promote environmental protection (Haglund 1991; Liberatore 1991; McCormick 1995), this chapter focuses on how the more common "league of states" is established to foster cooperation among member governments rather than to coordinate a regional integration project. It assumes that such intergovernmental organizations have only modest material resources at their disposal and thus operate mainly as catalysts of other actors' activity; that rule making and rule modification involves bargaining among governments; and that implementation involves parallel action, decentralized compliance monitoring, and decentralized enforcement activity. These conditions mean that an intergovernmental organization is not an administrative agency acting for others but a process manager helping others concert their own activity more effectively.

Although regime effectiveness has several interrelated dimensions (see Young 1994a: 140–152), they can be grouped under two broad headings: *compliance effectiveness* and *result effectiveness*. Compliance effectiveness exists when the relevant actors obey regime prescriptions. Result effectiveness exists when the behaviors promoted by the regime produce real environmental improvement. These two dimensions of regime effectiveness are independent of each other, but satisfying both is necessary for environmental improvement: neither full compliance with low result effectiveness nor low compliance with high result effectiveness will yield the desired outcome. An intergovernmental organization managing an international regime must perform two distinct sets of tasks. It must work to increase compliance effectiveness by promoting desired behavior from the various types of actors whose conduct is addressed by or relevant to the regime, and it must work to increase result effectiveness by fostering the individual and collective ability to monitor environmental conditions, assess outcomes, and modify the regime when necessary to improve results.

In the abstract, intergovernmental organizations enjoy several advantages over individual governments or nonstate actors as regime managers. Their secretariats can be central and mutually acceptable aggregation, analysis, and dissemination points for information flowing in from member governments and nongovernmental sources; their plenaries and committees provide forums for inclusive discussions, exercises of peer pressure, and efforts to work out disputes; and their character as international organizations that draw participants from all affected countries permits them to endow activity with a political legitimacy of representing the "international community," which individual governments and nongovernmental organizations cannot do. This chapter seeks to illuminate the conditions under which intergovernmental organizations can act as effective regime process managers by examining their experience in managing regime implementation in the following issue areas: high seas fisheries, whaling, vessel-source pollution, widespread air pollution, the Antarctic, and outer space.

Increasing Compliance Effectiveness

Compliance with regime prescriptions results from a favorable alignment of actors' beliefs, interests, and capabilities. The first two are interrelated: actors perceive interests through the filter of their beliefs, and their material condition affects their receptivity to various ideas and competing policy proposals (see Hall 1989; E. Haas 1990; Odell 1982; Sikkink 1992; Goldstein and Keohane 1994). Capability involves acting in particular ways in order to produce particular outcomes ("power to") and to have influence or control over other actors ("power over"). Both abilities are relevant to regime implementation: a particularly strong actor may be able to create a result on its own no matter what others do, or an actor with little capability of its own may be able to influence others to adopt courses of action that yield an outcome different than what those actors would have produced without the influence.

The forms of compliance can be arrayed on a spectrum—with spontaneous compliance at one end, regime-enabled compliance in the middle, and induced compliance at the other end. Spontaneous compliance occurs when an actor aligns its conduct to regime prescriptions (or even goes beyond them) by its own volition and would do so even if the regime did not exist. Regime-enabled compliance occurs when a previously passive actor aligns its conduct with regime prescriptions because the existence of the regime removes one or more barriers to action. These barriers can include a low sense of urgency about the matter, lack of information, internal disagreement about the best policy approach, fear that unreciprocated action will lead to disadvantage, or the belief that acting alone will make no appreciable difference. Induced compliance occurs when an actor aligns its conduct with regime prescriptions only after others alter its perception of the situation by shaming, promising or providing rewards, or threatening or inflicting deprivations. Because the actor's initial beliefs and perceptions of material interest incline it toward inaction or violation, to bring it into compliance others need to send the clear message that the advantages of inaction or violation will be canceled.

The actors involved in an international regime can be divided into four broad categories: (1) leaders who believe strongly in the necessity for and correctness of regime prescriptions; (2) followers who have been persuaded to accept the prescriptions but are less intense about compliance; (3) laggards who are not fully persuaded but also not strongly opposed; and (4) resisters who remain strongly opposed either because they do not regard any prescriptions as warranted or because they prefer a different set of prescriptions. Leaders engage overwhelmingly in spontaneous compliance. Any lapses are due to slippages in bureaucratic routine or to temporary inability to influence the conduct of other actors within their control or jurisdiction; such lapses will be corrected once noticed. Followers engage mainly in regime-enabled compliance, but can also be relied upon to take corrective measures once lapses are identified. The pull of regime-enabled compliance on laggards is weaker; they are likely to need some measure of additional reinforcement, such as peer pressure or rewards. Resisters provide the toughest challenge; they engage in no spontaneous compliance, and the regime's existence exerts little pull either.

Inducing compliance involves solving all the familiar problems of rule enforcement: defining compliant and noncompliant behavior clearly enough that they can be distinguished, designing compliance monitoring systems able to identify the noncompliant, developing mechanisms for conduct assessment that permit the noncompliant an opportunity to explain their conduct, and providing adequate forms of peer pressure, opportunity constraint, reward, or deprivation. The decentralized nature of the international system complicates enforcement. Peer pressure, reward, and deprivation will be supplied only when other actors (primarily but not exclusively governments) have both the resources and the motivation to supply them, or when an international organization that defines its mission as ensuring regime success has ample resources. Enforcement of international environmental regimes suffers from two additional problems. First, most forms of environmental improvement are nonexcludable: even noncooperating actors will enjoy the benefits of improved air quality, a preserved ozone layer, avoidance of significant global warming, or conservation of natural resources. Second, exacting certain individualizable deprivations would be counterproductive. The traditional international practice of responding to the violation of an agreement with a proportionate counterviolation is inappropriate whenever such a counterviolation would increase the amount of environmental harm done (Koskenniemi 1992). Similarly, excluding a noncompliant actor from participation in an intergovernmental organization would insulate it from processes of information dissemination and peer pressure.

Intergovernmental Organizations and Voluntary Compliance

Both spontaneous and regime-enabled compliance involve actor internalization of the regime prescriptions. Intergovernmental organizations can assist in bringing about and maintaining such internalization in four ways: by helping to instill or reinforce favorable beliefs; by influencing actors' perceptions of interest; by improving actors' capacity to comply; and by preventing erosion of will by providing mechanisms for settling disputes.

Beliefs   Compliance is most deeply rooted when a regime attains what Oran Young (1994a: 147–149) calls "constitutive effectiveness" — a strong hold on actors through development of social practices and definitions of actor self-image ("identity") that promote compliance (see Wendt and Duvall 1989; Wendt 1992). In international environmental regimes, such effectiveness requires the inculcation of ideas and beliefs that promote concern for and care of the environment. Although some observers believe that the current international system prevents actors from making any needed attitude adjustments (e.g., Walker 1989; Redclift 1987), there has been enough shift in attitudes in the last twenty-five years to suggest that abandoning that approach would be premature.

The vast increase in international communications media offers many channels for disseminating and reiterating new environmental beliefs, but intergovernmental organizations can do much to focus and intensify the process. Although an intergovernmental organization's secretariat may on occasion become both the source and disseminator of new ideas, as was the United Nations' Economic Commission for Latin America under Raul Prebisch, more often they serve as network managers (Marin and Mayntz 1991; see also Shih 1989; Jonsson 1993; Kardam 1993) who encourage contacts, disseminate others' ideas, and promote discussions that lead to refinements of environmental understanding. They can serve as encouragers and occasionally, as in the case of United Nations Environment Program (UNEP), as promoters of advocacy coalitions (Sabatier 1988) for more environmentally sensitive problem definitions, policy proposals, and implementation programs.

Scientific knowledge is important in understanding the environment and legitimating policy to political and economic elites, so effective environmental advocacy coalitions need to include one or more scientific or technical epistemic communities (P. Haas 1989, 1992a). An environmental regime can, however, be maintained on a more general common belief system. Both the UN Committee on the Peaceful Uses of Outer Space and the Antarctic Treaty Consultative Parties operate within a belief system that stresses the importance of cooperation, conflict avoidance, peaceful activity, and mutual benefit, as well as environmental protection (Cristol 1982; Peterson 1988). To the extent that an environmental regime needs broad domestic support within countries, an exclusive focus on scientific knowledge may weaken the advocacy coalition by making it appear too remote from the needs and experiences of ordinary people (Tesh and Williams 1996).

Intergovernmental organizations vary considerably in their effectiveness as network managers. Some are more open than others to a wide array of nongovernmental actors. International Monetary Fund (IMF) still maintains contact with a narrow range of nonstate actors, as did the World Bank until a few years ago. Some, such as International Whaling Commission (IWC), have secretariats too small to provide effective network management. Government attitudes may impose additional constraints. Despite spreading democratization, governments vary considerably in their willingness to have nongovernmental actors in general (or sometimes particular sorts of nongovernmental actors) participate actively in the process of developing and disseminating common belief systems. This varied willingness showed clearly in the climate change negotiations when governments moved in 1990–91 to reassert control over the discussions (Shibata 1993: 27–28).

Interests   Both spontaneous and regime-enabled compliance mean that an actor regards compliance as being in its immediate interest. With some actors, beliefs may be strong enough to override immediate material calculations. For most, however, material calculations will affect their willingness to comply. Thus, intergovernmental organization efforts to foster longer-term changes in belief should be joined by efforts to increase actors' perceptions that compliance is in their interest even within the framework of their current beliefs. Success in such efforts requires matching arguments to actors' current calculations. Actors firmly wedded to a narrow or short-term view of interests will not be affected by appeals to broader or longer-term interest. Both the IWC and the international fisheries commissions active before 1976 devoted considerable energy to pointing out the advantages of conservation measures, only to be overridden by domestic influences concerned more with the short-term profitability of the fishing industry. In many cases, actors motivated by short-term considerations will begin to reconsider only when faced with a crisis (such as rapid decline of a fish stock) that clearly demonstrates the urgency of taking action. Intergovernmental organizations cannot create crises, but they can disseminate information about any crises and try to build on the momentum they inspire.

Regime managers faced with actors who operate on narrow and/or short-term definitions of interest can promote compliance by searching for opportunities to harness the actors' current interests to the cause of greater compliance. One opportunity is to make regime prescriptions as incentive compatible as possible. Efforts to regulate fisheries and whaling suffered because the most often used management measure—total allowable catch without suballocations by country or individual fishing boat—set up malign incentives. The rule encouraged each boat to catch as quickly as possible so that it would have a profitable haul before the total catch was reached and the season closed. Each boat owner invested in the most efficient fish-locating and catching gear available, thus unleashing a dynamic of competitive equipping that left no one better off and promoted considerable overinvestment in equipment. Overinvestment, in turn, increased fishers' resistance to regulations because they had to earn more to justify the higher investment.

In contrast, the success of the ozone layer regime has been aided by the fact that the ban on chlorofluorcarbons (CFCs) assures chemical companies of a market for the more expensive substitutes now in use (Oye and Maxwell 1994). Antiwhaling activists have sought to capture a similar dynamic by arguing that organizing whale-watching cruises would be more profitable than whale taking (Stoett 1995; 133). It is unlikely, however, that intergovernmental organizations would be able to rearrange incentives as intensely as national governments. It has been claimed, for instance, that the Swedish and Swiss governments increase compliance with water discharge regulations by requiring industrial plants to locate their water discharge outlets within one hundred meters upstream of their water intakes (Cohen and Stewart 1995; 228).

Intergovernmental organizations could work more toward devising rules that make compliance automatic. Compliance with the International Convention for the Prevention of Pollution from Ships (MARPOL) standards rose considerably when the "load-on-top" system, which required careful ballasting and deballasting of tankers, was replaced by a requirement for entirely separate ballast tanks never used to carry oil (Mitchell 1994a: 284–298). Intergovernmental or private bodies can also foster automaticity through standard setting (Raul and Hagen 1993: 53; Glenn 1995: 42). In developing product and processing standards for foods, the FAO-WHO Codex Alimentarius Commission can write those standards to promote the reduction or elimination of pollution. The International Standards Organization's 14,000 Series will address environmental aspects of business, and meeting the nine thousand standards on consistency of firm operations would ensure more even application of firms' own internal environmental standards.

Capacity Capacity to comply requires both resources that can be devoted to implementation and the skill to use them effectively. Resource transfers—whether in the form of finance, provision of physical equipment, or transfer of technology—involve commitments beyond the resources of most intergovernmental organizations other than the multilateral lending agencies. At best, intergovernmental organizations can serve as forums for agreeing on resource-transfer programs and as conduits for the money; they can also serve as forums for assessment of actual follow through.

A somewhat larger number of intergovernmental organizations do have the resources to help develop or improve the skill with which governments or other actors implement regime prescriptions. Yet only those with a local presence, such as the United Nations Development Program's (UNDP) Resident Representatives, can become a source of skill development because such presence is requisite to operating a successful program. Although some intergovernmental organizations do manage modest programs under which member governments lend each other experts or trainers, most intergovernmental organizations contribute most to capacity building by bringing together more and less experienced officials or experts from various countries to work together on common problems.

Capacity building by intergovernmental organizations has the longest history in fisheries issues. The scientific committees of the international fisheries commissions helped spread ideas about fisheries management and build contacts among fisheries managers and scientists in different countries. The UN Food and Agricultural Organization (FAO) and its regional fisheries commissions coordinated programs for increasing fisheries management capacity in developing countries. Since the early 1970s, however, capacity building has also been a staple of other environmental regimes (Kimball 1996). By spreading the assessment work among research stations in most participating countries, UNEP's Mediterranean program promoted considerable skills transfer (P. Haas 1990). The International Atomic Energy Agency (IAEA) is encouraging extensive contacts between nuclear engineers and power plant operators in the West and the countries of the former Soviet bloc so that the latter will learn and internalize the more exacting "nuclear safety culture" that characterizes Western operations (Connolly and List 1996). These collaborative arrangements not only raise skill levels, but also increase the political credibility of results because governments are given advice that is not merely the work of foreigners but that has support from their local experts. Wilbert Chapman's 1950 advice that the Inter-American Tropical Tuna Commission needed a multinational research staff "to gain the facts in conjunction with the Latinos so they will believe them" (quoted in Scheiber 1986: 465) is equally true today.

Intergovernmental organizations cannot do much to directly enhance the capacity of nonstate actors because of the political sensitivities involved in such an action. Here, private voluntary agencies and transnational social movements are far more important sources. When the efforts of such agencies and movements yield greater local awareness of and ability to influence decisions about environmental issues, they help promote better implementation of environmental regimes by creating in developing states the same public demands for improved environmental conditions that are a staple of politics in industrialized countries (Hurrell 1992).

Dispute Resolution   The implementation of any international environmental regime is likely to trigger disputes on such matters as whether a particular action should be defined as noncompliance, a particular actor is failing to comply, a noncompliant actor should be exempted from penalties because of special circumstances, or an individual government's unilateral enforcement efforts violate others' rights. Although a few unresolved questions may not impede implementation, an accumulation of them is likely to reduce the sense of mutual trust and common purpose needed to sustain high levels of spontaneous and regime-enabled compliance.

Providing facilities for dispute settlement is well within the resources of intergovernmental organizations. They can build on the long international traditions of formal settlement through adjudication or arbitration and of informal settlement through the use of existing institutions or the development of their own. As several commentators have observed, governments tend to avoid the most formal methods (Koskenniemi 1992; Chayes and Chayes 1995: 201–207), which has inspired considerable interest in elaborating new informal methods that rest on mediation and conciliation (Chayes and Chayes 1995; Kimball 1996).

Intergovernmental organizations should not, however, neglect the formal methods because they serve as important backups to the informal ones. First, some noncompliance is intentional and represents a conscious effort to exploit others' compliance for individual advantage (Downs, Rocke, and Barsoom 1996). Formal dispute-settlement processes can provide clear expressions of disapproval and the formal determination of noncompliance needed to legitimize deprivations. Second, the possibility of shifting to more formal procedures also protects informal dispute-settlement efforts from foot dragging. Establishing time limits on the submission and informal resolution of disputes is a common way of discouraging foot dragging. The Convention on International Liability for Damage Caused by Space Objects (Article XIV) requires that claimants notify launching states of accidents and claims within a year; it also permits either side to invoke the compulsory dispute-settlement procedures if a negotiated settlement has not been reached within a year of the complaint. The Madrid Protocol on Antarctic Environmental Protection (Article 20) and the Framework

Convention on Climate Change (Article 14) also stipulate a twelve-month deadline.

The ozone layer regime now incorporates closely related informal and formal dispute-settlement mechanisms that operate through a small intergovernmental implementation committee. Any participating government that believes another participating government is not meeting its obligations may communicate its views, together with corroborating information, to the Ozone Secretariat, which then sends those communications on to the named government for its response. When the response is received, the secretariat relays the statement and response to the implementation committee, which follows up on the matter and tries to promote an amicable settlement. If that effort fails, the committee can propose that the Meeting of the Parties formally declare that the named party is not in compliance and instruct it to take particular steps to bring itself into compliance. The meeting decides by a (nonunanimous) vote (Trask 1992: 1980–1981; Koskenniemi 1992), which not only keeps the named party from blocking a decision but also reveals the broad sentiment that it is failing to meet its obligations before it is formally and publicly criticized.

Intergovernmental Organizations and Induced Compliance
Though less desirable than spontaneous or regime-generated compliance, induced compliance is preferable to noncompliance. The meager resources of most intergovernmental organizations, however, confine them to facilitating roles in compliance monitoring, the application of peer pressure, and the provision of rewards or deprivations. These roles can be played well or poorly depending on the organization and the possibilities included in the regime.

Compliance Monitoring   Neither intergovernmental organizations serving as regime process managers nor anyone else can help induce compliance unless they know who is not complying. Thus, inducing compliance cannot occur without an effective compliance-monitoring system. Insistence on national sovereignty, however, has limited intergovernmental compliance monitoring to systems of government self-reporting. These systems can involve requests for several forms of information: (1) statistics showing the extent of government and private activity in the regulated field (e.g., fish-catch data submitted to FAO or CFC production, trade and consumption data sent to the Ozone Secretariat); (2) notification of adoption of national legislation and regulations that embody internationally agreed upon rules; (3) government investigations and actions addressing nonstate actor violations; or (4) actual or anticipated national programs and policies.

Almost all environmental self-reporting systems are ineffective because few governments bother to file reports (Sand 1992; U.S. General Accounting Office 1992). This sloth persists partly because governments seldom make an issue of nonreporting even when it is brought to their attention (Koskenniemi 1992; Chayes and Chayes 1995: 161), but even more because most reporting systems are so poorly designed.

An intergovernmental organization that desires to maximize the rate of reporting and enhance the usefulness of reports in assessing noncompliance can benefit considerably from some fairly simple steps. The first step, well within the resources of any intergovernmental organization, is to design and supply standard forms for reporting. The International Maritime Organization (IMO) was able to raise the fraction of member governments' reporting on action against ships that violate MARPOL regulations from 25 percent to somewhere between 33 percent and 49 percent by simply producing a standard form in 1985 (Mitchell 1994a: 132–133). Reporting will be taken more seriously if the organization aggregates and uses the information in general or in a country-by-country compliance review than if it files the information away. More ambitiously, the information might be made directly useful to participating governments or other actors. The fourteen European government parties that created the 1982 Memorandum of Understanding on Port State Control (MOU) agreed to inspect 25 percent of the foreign flag tankers entering their ports and to supply daily information about the results of inspections to a central office in France. Port authorities submit this information by computer network and in return can consult the constantly updated database for information about which ships have been inspected and which have been found deficient in any way. This information allows them to inspect more efficiently by selecting ships that have not been inspected recently or need to be rechecked to verify that a deficiency has been corrected (Mitchell 1994a: 135–136).

Using the information, particularly in the highly interactive mode of the MOU parties, requires intergovernmental organizations to become effective information managers and to take much more advantage of computer and information-transmission technologies. Wider use of information requires agreement on what information is needed and when; it may also involve some degree of compromise on what information will be disseminated publicly. For example, the MOU secretariat does not release information that would identify governments who fail to meet their obligation to inspect 25 percent of foreign flag tankers calling at their ports (Mitchell 1994a: 135–136). Similarly, information about production of CFCs is considered part of national "consumption" and is not broken down into production, imports, and exports, which would allow cross-checking individual government reports (Chayes and Chayes 1995: 191).

Even when reporting is fairly high, the value of data can be reduced by systematic errors. Chayes and Chayes (1995: 165–166) may be right that the low- to middle-ranking officials who prepare most reports have no real incentive to misreport because they need accurate information for their own work, but their concern for prestige or their desire to avoid embarrassment may lead to incomplete reports. Governments often depend on private actors for data, and those actors may have strong reasons to file inaccurate information. All fisheries regulation has been plagued by poor catch data because of the incentives to under report catch or to misreport the species of fish taken (Larkin 1977: 5); as suggested after revelations of massive Soviet under reporting of whale catches, the weakness of data can, in such extreme situations, discredit the population estimates used in management decisions (Stoett 1995: 132–133).

The weaknesses of self-reporting systems have encouraged interest in other forms of compliance monitoring. In some areas, governmental sources of information can be cross-checked against external sources. The 97 percent reporting rate on space launches (A. Young 1986: 295) partly reflects the existence of independent national tracking systems, at least two of which (the U.S. North American Air Defense Command and the U.K. Royal Aircraft Establishment) publish their own lists of launched objects. Greenpeace has provided pressure for fuller reporting of Antarctic activity by carrying out its own surveys of environmental practices at Antarctic research stations (Sabella 1993), and the Independent Tanker Owners Association (INTERTANKO), provides IMO with much more extensive information about the inadequacies of oil reception facilities than governments do because its members suffer the costs and inconveniences of the long waits in port (Mitchell 1994a: 130).

In a few cases, nonstate actors provide the bulk of information that intergovernmental organizations receive. The Convention on International Trade in Endangered Species of Wild Fauna and Flora (CITES) Secretariat depends almost entirely on the World Wildlife Fund's TRAFFIC network for information on noncompliance (Chayes and Chayes 1995: 164). Whether as supplements or as the main information source, such external reports are most useful when the providers can attain wide geographic coverage and their biases are either minor or sufficiently transparent that their information can be interpreted accordingly. The problem of bias is endemic because bias comes in so many forms, ranging from the obvious "cooking" of data to serve financial or other interests to the skewing of results by features or omissions of the assumptions that underlie reporting efforts. Intergovernmental organizations must thus develop not only good processes for receiving and disseminating information but also good processes for assessing biases and correcting accordingly (Kimball 1996: 139–148).

The weakness of most self-reporting systems has promoted the desire to develop centralized systems of compliance monitoring. These systems can be organized in either of two broad ways — as "police patrols" or as "fire alarms" (McCubbins and Schwartz 1984). In the "police patrol" model, agents of the central monitoring authority move around observing behavior and tagging violations as they see them; in the "fire alarm" model, agents are available at set locations and respond when summoned by a victim of or a witness to a violation. Intergovernmental organizations lack the resources to establish their own patrols. Yet they can promote greater levels of mutual monitoring by providing the transparency essential to effective mutual monitoring; they can also serve as alarm stations or encourage joint patrolling by national monitors.

Rules that promote transparency can be included in an environmental regime from the start, in which case the intergovernmental organization's task is to help ensure that transparency is maintained. Periodic compliance review sessions can, however, go further and explore whether new developments (such as domestic democratization or the great improvement of satellite-remote-sensing technology in the 1980s) permit the addition of new forms of transparency.

Intergovernmental organizations' potential as alarm stations remains limited by the long-established traditions that governments should state their concerns to each other directly rather than via a third party and that only the government whose domain or nationals is directly affected by a violation should raise a complaint. Thus, for instance, the MARPOL rule that governments notifying flag states of suspected violations should also inform the IMO secretariat has been largely ignored (Mitchell 1994a: 130). However, environmental regimes are beginning to escape some of these constraints. Both the Montreal Protocol on Substances that Deplete the Ozone Layer and the Madrid Protocol on Antarctic Environmental Protection allow any participating government to notify the secretariat of any noncompliant behavior it observes. The Convention on North Pacific Anadromous Stocks (Annex II) allows any two participating governments to initiate commission discussions about violations by ships or nationals of any other party.

The rise of environmental activism among the world's peoples suggests the possibility of opening up intergovernmental alarm systems to the participation of nonstate actors. Although the idea has occasionally been proposed (e.g., Susskind 1994: 114–117), it has not elicited any particular enthusiasm among governments. The tradition that nonstate actors should direct their information to the government that has territorial or other jurisdiction over the perpetrator remains very strong. Another possible alarm system is suggested by the World Bank Panel of Investigation; this system does not directly address government conduct, but it does permit complaints that work on a particular project is not conforming to the bank's policies. The spread of democracy, however, and the concomitant strengthening of domestic norms of government accountability to the citizenry mean that national channels for soliciting information about the conduct of government agencies and for correcting administrative laxity or abuse are becoming more acceptable and useful in many countries.

Joint patrol by national agents has aroused more interest among governments. This interest is most obvious in fisheries, where the older dichotomy of coastal state jurisdiction within national fishing zones and flag state jurisdiction outside them is being supplemented by more collaborative arrangements. Some new arrangements involve the exchange between countries of on-board observers; some involve regional coordination of enforcement within a series of national Exclusive Economic Zones (EEZs) (Mfodwo, Tsamenyi, and Blay 1989; Moore 1993); and some involve closer coastal and flag state cooperation on the high seas (e.g., the North Pacific Anadromous Stocks Convention, the FAO Agreement to Promote Compliance, and the Agreement on Straddling and Highly Migratory Stocks). However, joint patrolling arouses concern among nonstate actors that they will be subject to multiple and inconsistent monitoring. Intergovernmental organizations can do much to allay such fears by encouraging governments to adopt standard rules and verification routines and providing forums for discussion of problems that arise in carrying out the monitoring.

Peer Pressure   Some scholars have argued that the desire of governments to acquire and maintain a reputation as a "good" or "reliable" member of the international community provides significant leverage to induce compliance with international regimes (for example, see Chayes and Chayes 1991; Watson 1991: 66; Young 1992). Research on individuals, households, firms, and groups indicates that this motive is most powerful when the community is small and interconnected enough that individual reputation affects how an actor is treated in a range of interactions with several partners. The international system is not a small community if all the actors are taken into account, but the approximately two hundred national governments of the world can function like a small community if the fact of community is emphasized. Environmental regimes have an advantage in this regard because they can appeal to the underlying fact that "we all share one planet."

The value placed on good reputation, even in small communities, depends heavily on the prevailing social norms. The emphasis on national interest rather than on cosmopolitan concern in traditional world politics limits but has not eliminated the desire to maintain a good reputation. This desire is often weaker, however, in environmental affairs than in military and economic ones (Koskenniemi 1992). Governments that rule states with open political systems do pay considerable attention to their standing with major domestic constituencies. Intergovernmental organizations' efforts to appeal to these governments' concern for reputation will be more effective if international-level pressures can be coordinated with domestic-level ones. Intergovernmental organizations can contribute to this coordination by permitting nonstate actors access to meetings, by encouraging nongovernmental "parallel forums," or by allowing nongovernmental comment on government reports of activity.

Governments are likely to resist getting caught in a vise by keeping governmental and nongovernmental activity separate. Such resistance may occur when governments fear they may lose or are losing control of a negotiating process, as occurred in the climate change negotiations, or when they feel that nongovernmental actors are attempting to bring about a change in the regime that they do not endorse. The struggle between nonstate actors who seek an end to whaling and the few remaining whaling states that seek to maintain whaling as a legal activity (Stoett 1995: 132) provides the best example of the latter situation.

Intergovernmental organizations provide effective channels for the exercise of publicly or confidentially expressed peer pressure among governments. Intergovernmental forums are highly attractive to governments of weak states or to nonstate actors who lack good political access domestically, mainly because they permit the use of "outsider" strategies; that is, they alter a confrontation by attracting an audience and a set of potential allies (Edelman 1964; Cobb and Elder 1983). Such outsider strategies characterized the campaign against large-scale (longer than 2.5 kilometers) driftnets, which was taken to the UN General Assembly. At the same time, the corridors and private meeting spaces in or near the conference hall provide handy venues for starting or continuing the more private discussions favored by governments or nonstate actors who enjoy good access and considerable influence.

Although the mere existence of an intergovernmental organization provides opportunities for exerting peer pressure, the organization can be structured to make the peer pressure more effective. The most effective systems combine private and public channels: the effort to exert pressure begins quietly and privately, thus permitting the target government to save face, but then becomes more public if the target proves oblivious to the more quiet forms of persuasion. The managers of the London Dumping Convention used such a combined approach in addressing the issue of Soviet and Russian dumping of nuclear wastes at sea. The effort began in the relative quiet of expert panels but was moved to the public Meeting of Parties, at which the expert group came to broad consensus that the low level of Russian response represented foot dragging rather than transition problems (Handl 1995: 177).

Providing Material Rewards A few intergovernmental organizations, particularly the multilateral lending agencies, can provide material rewards for compliance. However, the process is seldom straightforward. The lending agencies face two obstacles in tying loans closely to compliance with environmental regimes. First, developing country governments have waged a long campaign against various forms of "conditionality"; they also strongly resist extending conditionality to environmental policy and take advantage of multiple sources to secure loans with fewer conditions whenever possible (Fairman and Ross 1996). Those countries able to raise money on the private capital markets can simply bypass the whole process. Second, the lending agencies are under internal pressure to make loans because doing so is the most important index of their activity and usefulness (Mosley et al. 1991; Kahler 1992). The situation is further complicated by the current norm of "shared but differentiated responsibility" for environmental improvement (see discussion in World Resources Institute 1994: chapter 14). The governments of developing countries can quite reasonably argue that the combination of the industrial states' greater historical responsibility for environmental degradation (or, the advantages they gained by misusing the environment to industrialize more cheaply) and their own need for resources means that provision of needed finance should be a prerequisite to, not an inducement for, good implementation of environmental agreements (an approach adopted in the climate change convention; see Werksman 1996: 91).

Despite these political factors, intergovernmental organizations can be used to review programs and proposals before rewards are actually given out. A long campaign of environmentalist and Western government pressure led the World Bank to incorporate more explicit environmental guidelines in its project specifications (Le Prestre 1989). When governments seek funding from the Global Environment Facility, they have to show that the activity to be financed will benefit the environment either by avoiding damage or by undoing earlier damage. A related type of reward system — dispensing individual rewards only on the provision that a certification of compliance has been given by intergovernmental organizations — has not been pursued. Most organizations lack the resources needed to run a compliance certification program. In addition, such programs would represent a considerable symbolic diminution of national sovereignty.

Inflicting Material Deprivations Intergovernmental organizations can inflict deprivations on member governments by excluding them from participation in meetings and other activities, by denying loans, or by suspending technical aid. In most cases, the degree of deprivation will be small. Even so, imposing deprivations can quickly become difficult. Denial of loans inspires the same negative effect as conditioning loans on actual or prospective good performance. Denial of technical aid or exclusion from participation is likely to be counterproductive because they block access to resources for capacity building or insulate officials from peer pressure.

Intergovernmental organizations do not have any authority to inflict deprivations on nonstate actors; in any event, they lack the monitoring and assessment capabilities needed for identifying nonstate noncompliers. Although it is difficult to determine whether the lack of resources effects this inability, or the lack of resources reflects governments' desire to maintain the inability, the net result is clear: governments deal with individuals, households, groups, and firms; and intergovernmental organizations deal with governments.

The principle of territoriality on which the current division of the world into separate states is based means governments and others expect unilateral enforcement action against any actor who operates within the land, air, and maritime jurisdiction of that state. Considerable controversy has arisen regarding government efforts to inflict deprivations on those whose actions produce effects felt inside a state but who are actually acting outside the state. In such cases, the same nonstate actor could be held accountable by two or more governments, quickly raising the question of which one's standards should prevail and when. International regimes are often created to reduce or eliminate those disputes. As disputes that arise in the intersection of trade and environmental protection show, many controversies center on the relative weight to be given to different social, economic, political, and environmental goals. Significant amounts of argument about efforts to exercise "long-arm" jurisdiction over actors outside the enforcing state's domain should be viewed by regime managers as a sign of differences in priorities that need to be resolved. Intergovernmental organizations can assist this process through general compliance reviews, country-specific discussions, or dispute-settlement procedures.

The activities of nonstate actors who operate in areas outside national jurisdiction, particularly the high seas, also inspire conflicts over unilateral enforcement efforts. The sharpest conflicts concern coastal state efforts to exert some control over fishing in high seas areas adjacent to their EEZs (Burke 1993; Meltzer 1994). Since the Rio conference identified straddling fish stocks as an issue that required more attention, governments have established some elements of a legal framework for improved cooperation in enforcing fishing rules on the high seas. The FAO Agreement to Promote Compliance includes provisions for flag state licensing of vessels to fish on the high seas. It stipulates that licenses should not be given to fishing vessels with a record of ignoring national or multilateral fisheries regulations and that governments should not permit transfer of fishing vessels onto their national registries if the transfer is merely an attempt to get around fisheries regulations. The UN Agreement on Straddling and Highly Migratory Fish Stocks outlines the elements of greater cooperation between flag and coastal states; it also provides legal reinforcement to management through international fisheries commissions.

Any unilateral measure, particularly the use of trade sanctions against a country as a whole, raises the thorny political question of whether environmental leaders should have the right to impose their views on other governments. At present, most governments oppose the use of unilateral trade sanctions for environmental purposes (Rio Declaration on the Environment 1992: Principle 12). Trade sanctions are, however, accepted more widely when applied pursuant to a multilateral treaty that clearly permits and defines their use. Intergovernmental organizations can materially assist the sanctioning process by developing procedures that will ensure greater consistency in the application of such measures (Koskenniemi 1992: 150). For example, an intergovernmental body (such as the UN Security Council) may need to give prior authorization for any unilateral inflictions, or the target government may be able to challenge other states' unilateral inflictions (through something like the General Agreement on Trade and Tariffs [GATT]).

Attaining Result Effectiveness

Even full compliance with regime prescriptions will fail to produce environmental improvement if they are poorly designed. The merits of their design can be determined only if regime participants are able to (1) monitor environmental conditions and compare the actual condition of the environment to the condition sought by the regime; (2) identify and cope with unintended environmental damage; and (3) assess whether even full implementation of the regime is producing the desired environmental improvement. All three tasks require development of feedback loops through which regime participants can review their situation and thus alter regime means or goals as required. The development of feedback loops, in turn, requires the development and maintenance of flexible mindsets in which the regime is regarded as an improvable mechanism—a revisable initial hypothesis—rather than a definitive solution. Both the common human tendency to fall into habit and the organizational impulses toward the development of vested interests that continue current programs work against the maintenance of such mindsets.

Intergovernmental Organizations and Feedback Loops

Environmental Monitoring   To assess the effect of recent and current activity on the environment broad-gauged environmental-monitoring systems need to be established and maintained. Unlike compliance monitoring, which focuses on actors, environmental monitoring requires coordinated observation over fairly wide geographic areas to assess the overall condition of the ecosystem or ecosystems that the regime is intended to protect.

The importance of environmental monitoring has been increasingly acknowledged and has inspired efforts to develop some fairly broad systems. These efforts began with the World Meteorological Organization's (WMO) World Weather Watch in the 1960s and UNEP's Global Environmental Monitoring System (GEMS) in the 1970s. Their ambition, however, has outrun their accomplishments (Rodenberg 1991), and particular regimes must often develop their own monitoring system rather than call on monitoring already underway. Particularly because economic, social, and ecological impacts must be assessed according to distinct policies, environmental monitoring requires a commitment of personnel, equipment, and other facilities beyond the resources of any single intergovernmental organization. They can contribute to effective environmental monitoring in four ways, however: by reminding other actors of the need for continuous monitoring; by encouraging more effective data gathering, aggregation, and analysis; by disseminating data and analysis to member governments and other actors; and by providing forums where the information that flows from various sources can be assessed and offered to decision makers.

Reminding others of the need for monitoring is easiest when the regime defines the desired forms of environmental monitoring and gives the intergovernmental body clear authority to discuss the results of monitoring efforts at regular intervals. Such rules ensure that environmental monitoring gets onto the agenda; it also provides opportunities for discussing possible changes in the environmental-monitoring scheme as better knowledge of the ecosystems involved or new monitoring techniques become available.

The effectiveness of condition-goal comparison depends heavily on how the monitoring obligations are defined. Until the late 1970s, monitoring was focused fairly closely on the direct effect of activity: how much oil was spilled, how much waste dumped, how many fish caught. Later agreements have reflected awareness of the need for broader environmental monitoring (Kimball 1996: particularly chapters 2 and 3). In the Long-Range Transboundary Air Pollution (LRTAP) and ozone layer regimes, monitoring began even before the regimes were established because it was needed to determine the dimensions of the problem and to indicate to the skeptical that international cooperation was essential (Levy 1993; Parson 1993). Over time, it continued and was adapted to the various forms of compliance monitoring added as emissions targets were defined. The Convention on the Conservation of Antarctic Marine Living Resources (CCAMLR) mandates the compiling of data on the sizes and changes of marine species populations and on factors that affect their distribution, abundance, and productivity (Article VII, paragraph 1a–c). The Madrid Protocol on Antarctic Environmental Protection requires that "regular and effective monitoring shall take place to allow the assessment of the impacts of ongoing activities, including the verification of predicted impacts" (Article 3, paragraph 2d).

A defined obligation to monitor encourages governments to include monitoring in their standard operating routines and to regard it as a "normal" government activity on par with collecting other national statistics. Intergovernmental organizations can foster better national monitoring efforts in several ways. First, they can develop standard reporting forms and sponsor the development and distribution of manuals that describe standard sampling methodologies and quality control techniques. These forms and manuals help countries with less scientific and technical capacity to complete monitoring tasks well enough to contribute usable information for global or regional assessments, thus improving the usefulness of the results for all governments. FAO has long offered such assistance in fisheries, and the UNEP regional seas secretariats have done so for their programs (Gerges 1994) though with uneven success (Kimball 1996: 77).

Unfortunately, information often flows from governments to international secretariats but does not flow back again (Kimball 1996: 56). Intergovernmental organizations need to provide channels of communication that permit governments to exchange data as well as receive aggregations and analyses. Such exchanges are accomplished either through an already established scientific advisory body, such as the International Council for the Exploration of the Sea (ICES) or the Joint Group of Experts on the Scientific Aspects of Marine Environmental Protection (GESAMP), or through a specially created body, such as the Intergovernmental Panel on Climate Change. As Kimball (1996: 97) notes, these bodies should not try to seek consensus when one does not exist, but they should try to convey to decision-making bodies a rounded picture of the areas of agreement and continuing disagreement among the relevant experts as well as assessments of different policy options.

Intergovernmental organizations can also promote methods of data dissemination and forms of data analysis that permit nonstate actors to participate in assessment of both environmental conditions and their implications for the regime. The LRTAP secretariat actively promoted the development and use of a standard mathematical model, runnable on laptop computers, for analyzing emissions and pollution impact data, which allowed university-based scientists and environmental groups themselves to assess conditions and suggest regime changes (Levy 1993: 87). In this way, scientific conclusions are thus exposed to peer review and to broader debate, which can help ensure that any advice is not unduly skewed by scientists' own biases or career interests (Stairs and Taylor 1992: 117–127; Boehmer-Christiansen 1994b).

Effective advice and debate depends on maintaining the quality of data and analysis. The quality of the data depends heavily on actors' incentives to report fully, accurately, and on time. Data are likely to be better if gathered by actors without any significant material stake in what the data say at any particular time and with a strong belief in the necessity of reporting the situation "as it really is." As in the area of compliance monitoring, however, reliability is improved if it can be cross-checked across several sources. Maintaining the quality of analysis requires competence in current analytical methods, as well as openness to new ideas. The IWC scientific committee was slow to incorporate population dynamics models into its work, and international fisheries commissions were slow to integrate economic and later ecosystem analyses of fisheries into their own analysis (Burke 1967: 153–154; Holt and Talbot 1978). More recently, a growing number of fisheries economists have concluded that standard catch-per-unit-of-effort data, which measure effort by vessel-days fishing, fail to convey the real situation in fisheries because they do not account for the increased catching efficiency of current fishing gear (Squires 1994). However, few fisheries regulators have yet sought to incorporate this insight into their analyses.

Assessing Unintended Consequences   The significance of unintended consequences, particularly negative ones, has only recently been acknowledged in the design of international environmental regimes. Recent Antarctic agreements express the concern quite strongly. The Convention on the Regulation of Antarctic Mineral Resources Activity (CRAMRA) specifically included detection of unforeseen consequences in the items to be covered by environmental monitoring; it also made provision for suspension or termination of exploration or exploitation if impacts beyond those foreseen in the initial environmental assessment of the project occurred (Article 51). The Madrid Protocol includes "early detection of the possible unforeseen effects of activities" as a goal of environmental monitoring (Article 3, paragraph 2e). The CCAMLR Commission has been sensitive to the problem of unforeseen effects and has sought to minimize such effects through the adoption of go-slow rules for new fisheries (Hofman 1993). On the other end of the spectrum, however, the history of fisheries management is replete with failures to deal with unintended consequences. The perverse effects of regulation by total allowable catch were not well understood; even when they became apparent, governments resisted giving fisheries commissions the authority to set national suballocations. The interrelations among different fishing activities were also poorly understood. To give two relatively recent examples, tuna stocks in the Pacific have been reduced because of failure to recognize and compensate for the combined effect of the purse-seine fishery that targeted relatively young tuna and the hook-and-line fishery that targeted more mature tuna (Campbell 1994). Canadian and U.S. success in pressuring Japan to limit their take of

Pacific salmon ended up intensifying Japanese fishing of stocks that originated in Russian rivers (Saguirian 1992: 4), and the closing of Namibian waters sent larger Spanish and Portuguese fleets to the Grand Banks (Fauteaux 1993).

The periodic reviews of performance under environmental regimes provided by recurrent Meetings of the Parties (those of the ozone layer and climate change regimes have attracted the most attention) create opportunities for identifying unintended consequences and for addressing whether they require modification of regime prescriptions. Intergovernmental organizations can contribute to the effectiveness of these reviews by ensuring that analyses of environmental-monitoring data point out areas of unintended effects and include time in the schedule of meetings for assessing both the extent of unintended results and their implications for regime management. When, as in the case of Antarctica, activity involves large projects, the international regime can encourage consideration of a wider range of potential consequences and later identification of unintended results by requiring a prior environmental impact assessment that will be reviewed by a multilateral body. The ozone layer regime shows that it is possible to institutionalize attention to unintended consequences even when a problem involves many sources of pollution rather than a few discrete activities. It defines both desired environmental end states and national commitments for emissions reduction. If the emissions reductions occur, but the goal is not met anyway, then participants' attention is drawn to figuring out why.

Goal Assessment   To determine whether even full compliance with the regime is producing the desired environmental situation, monitoring data must be gathered over a period of time, aggregated, and analyzed for trends and rates of change. As various private assessments (e.g., the World Resources Institute annual assessment) and national government assessments show, intergovernmental organizations are not the only entities capable of making such assessments. Intergovernmental organizations can, however, make the assessments more wide ranging and can ensure the inclusion of participants from all over the world in regime-stipulated reviews of activity. Such assessments have been a feature of the Montreal Protocol reviews (Parson 1993) and the Framework

Convention on Climate Change could be developed in this direction (Chayes and Chayes 1995: 247–248). However, the LRTAP experience shows that there is no guarantee this will happen (Chayes and Chayes 1995: 246–247).

Goal assessment also requires a continued awareness of new knowledge about how ecosystems function and are nested within one another. Although governments and the larger nongovernmental actors are the most prolific sources of information about the state of the environment, scientists and other intellectuals are the most prolific sources of the ideas and empirical research on which new knowledge is built. Fully effective assessment requires bringing together the data, the knowledge, and the authority to incorporate the knowledge into policy decisions. Although national government agencies and legislatures can do all this for individual countries, only intergovernmental organizations can do it at the international level. Nonstate entities can sponsor discussions, but only intergovernmental organizations can get governments formally engaged in the process of regime assessment and revision.

As the interrelation of environmental, economic, and social equity concerns has become more widely acknowledged, the process of policy review and regime modification has become more complex. Scientific and technical expert advice is only one of several streams of information needed by decision makers (Kimball 1996). Thus, the demands on intergovernmental organizations' talents as network managers and information disseminators will only become greater.

Sometimes an intergovernmental organization can do more than serve as a mechanism for assembling the elements. For example, it can step in to help when governments have reached an impasse that might be broken by adopting a new approach to the problem. The IWC helped erode resistance to the move away from the very crude "blue whale–unit" system of quota setting stipulated in the International Convention for the Regulation of Whaling by commissioning a "Committee of Four" widely respected cetologists familiar with the newer models of fisheries management to provide suggestions for improving management policy (Peterson 1992: 163). UNEP helped promote the development of scientific consensus regarding the extent and causes of ozone layer depletion by sponsoring a series of workshops for scientists and of meetings between scientists and national policymakers (Parson 1993: 65); governments took over this process in the climate change negotiations (through the work of the Intergovernmental Panel on Climate Change) to steer the process more closely (Ramakrishna and Young 1992).

The standing expert and other special committees of intergovernmental organizations are good ways to bring together experts from the full range of relevant academic disciplines, government representatives, and other affected actors for continuing discussion of the causal and value beliefs that underlie regime prescriptions. FAO-sponsored committees and workshops were prominent venues for criticizing prevailing single-species fisheries management models and for disseminating new multispecies and ecosystems models that were being proposed instead. More recently, they have provided opportunities for a coalition of environmentalists and anthropologists critical of current "industrial" fishing techniques and management to present their vision of fisheries: local groups would use low-technology fishing methods, manage their own local fishing grounds without outside intrusion, and supply food to local populations rather than to wealthy customers in other countries (see Fairlie, Hagler, and O'Riordan 1995 for an example). These standing committees have the advantage of meeting periodically and of being somewhat separated from the urgencies of day-to-day management decisions. At the same time, they may isolate themselves from management decisions in a way that makes their work seem less relevant.

The Conditions of Effective Intergovernmental Organization Activity

This chapter has defined some of the activities intergovernmental organizations can undertake and some of the conditions conducive or nonconducive to success. It is important to step back, however, and try to identify the conditions under which intergovernmental organizations will succeed in improving international environmental protection. Success depends on four sets of factors: (1) the broader context of the environmental protection effort, (2) the extent to which governments assign tasks to the intergovernmental organization, (3) the other features of the regime, and (4) how well the organization functions.

The Context and Organization Effectiveness

Even the most effective intergovernmental organization can be overwhelmed by changes in external conditions over which it has no control. In the final analysis, regime effectiveness depends on participants' ability to attain both compliance and result effectiveness. An international regime is thus no stronger than the material capability and intellectual resources of the coalition of participants that support it. Either requirement can be eroded by variables that intergovernmental organizations have little control over.

A coalition that supports a particular international environmental regime may collapse because it lacks or loses an agreed upon base of scientific knowledge that justifies regime rules. Both the IWC and other international fisheries commissions suffered setbacks in the 1960s and 1970s because the relevant experts were too divided among themselves to present governments with a consensual knowledge base on which to build regime rules (Peterson 1992: 168–171; Peterson 1993: 269–271). In contrast, UNEP's efforts to promote and then secure implementation of the ozone layer regime were greatly assisted by atmospheric scientists' strong consensus about relevant phenomena (Parson 1993: 35–44; Benedick 1991). Similarly, the mandate to practice ecosystems management has inspired the scientists who advise CCAMLR to develop a strong common knowledge base (Hofman 1993).

The importance of a consensual knowledge base for environmental regimes is demonstrated by some more recent experiences. The antiwhaling majority in the IWC has not been able to persuade or pressure Iceland, Japan, or Norway into giving up commercial whaling entirely. Rather, the conflict threatens to tear the IWC apart because it involves not only differences of opinion about the size and stability of whale stocks but also about the broader question of whether whales should be treated as a natural resource available for human use. The Norwegians in particular have responded to antiwhaling claims (e.g., Holt 1993) by arguing that nothing in the concept of sustainable development says that a strict preservationist approach, which makes whales off-limits for human taking, is more environmentally sound than careful resource management (Holt 1993). The entire process of moving from commitment in principle only to setting definite emissions targets on greenhouse gasses has been hobbled by lack of consensus on the environmental impact of current levels of atmospheric warming.

Issue linkages that occur during or after negotiations may ease or hinder both agreement and implementation. The identification of serious human health effects reinforced efforts to curb CFC and halon emissions because they strongly supported the calculations of interests that favored limitation. Overlaps between environmental and international trade issues, however, sometimes create problems that pull governments and other actors in conflicting directions (Esty 1993; Vogel 1995). International organization forums are open to both sorts of linkages, and the organization's staff will not be in a position to prevent governments from developing the linkages they prefer.

Political coalitions that support environmental regimes can also be reinforced or eroded because of changes in the government or in dominant social coalitions within major states. An intergovernmental organization has no control over such domestic politics; at most, it can serve as a forum for continued efforts to socialize new governments into the rules and rationales of the regime.

The ease or difficulty of implementing international environmental regimes also depends on whether significant activity precedes or follows the establishment of the regime. Regime managers whose regime is in place before much activity has developed enjoy a very advantageous situation. They can "go slow" and authorize or encourage only modest levels of activity until the environmental impact of that activity is more fully understood. CRAMRA would have adopted just such an approach, requiring a high threshold (i.e., unanimity in the relevant multilateral decision-making committees) before an area could be opened to resource exploration or exploitation (Article 41, paragraph 2). In the early 1990s, the CCAMLR Commission moved to impose limits on "new fisheries" (catching from hitherto unexploited stocks) rather than wait until catches approached or exceeded biologically sustainable levels (Hofman 1993: 535). Success of the campaign against large-scale driftnets also suggests that an activity can be limited early on, particularly when other users of the same resource can show that they would be harmed by the activity.

A decline in activity can also provide opportunities for imposing limits that would earlier have been resisted by actors interested in continuing the activity at the previous higher level. In the early 1990s, the

CCAMLR Commission was able to institute krill catch limits that were lower than the limits of the 1980s because actual catch had declined significantly when Bulgarian and Russian ships left the fishery (U.S. Marine Mammals Commission 1991: 130).

Intergovernmental organization efforts to promote compliance and result effectiveness also depend on their ability to recruit allies within governments and national societies. Such allies are more likely to be numerous and able to influence policy in countries that have open political systems (Chadwick 1995). Open systems permit greater public scrutiny and comment on government performance in implementing current commitments and on proposed changes in international environmental regimes. They are also more conducive to efforts to introduce new data or knowledge into discussions concerning compliance and results. When first introduced, new knowledge never has as much political support as the reigning orthodoxies. Open political systems provide a more favorable context for the introduction, dissemination, and evaluation of new knowledge by including a wider array of actors in the discussion and by being organized along principles that emphasize persuasiveness rather than brute force as the basis of choice among competing proposals.

Assignment of Tasks
The range of tasks assigned to intergovernmental organizations depends heavily on the form of cooperation that governments regard as necessary to meeting their goals. Establishing an international regime in the first place generally requires intergovernmental bargaining about the extent and terms of cooperation. Although international regimes can either develop spontaneously or be imposed by a particularly powerful state (Young 1983: 98–101), the current conditions of the international system and the sense of urgency felt in many environmental matters suggest that explicit negotiation will be the usual method of regime establishment. Implementing a regime, however, may or may not involve extensive interaction among governments. A regime might be designed for implementation through parallel national actions taken within the framework of regime rules; national actions subject to weak monitoring by an intergovernmental organization; continued joint decisions and

monitoring by an intergovernmental organization; or extensive joint decision making catalyzed as well as monitored by intergovernmental organizations (R. Bryant 1995: 8–11).

Some scholars contend that the form of implementation depends very much on the bargaining situation in which governments find themselves. Rational choice theorists have made the clearest arguments of this sort (e.g., Snidal 1985; Oye 1986; A. Stein 1990; Martin 1993), most frequently distinguishing between coordination and collaboration. According to this view, regimes that address coordination situations — ones in which all governments place high value on the same outcome — do not require joint decision making or monitoring because the governments will comply spontaneously, whereas regimes that address collaboration situations — ones in which different governments prefer different solutions or in which the rewards of "free riding" on others' efforts are significant — do require more monitoring because there are too many temptations to violate rules or slacken in efforts. These theorists speculate, then, that intergovernmental organizations would be irrelevant to coordination regimes, but that they would acquire more tasks in collaboration regimes as the temptations to violate rules or free ride increase.

Other considerations also influence the assignment of tasks, however. Because of the widespread belief that coordinated environmental monitoring is an essential element of regime implementation, the collation and dissemination of monitoring results is often assigned to an international secretariat even if the actual collection of data remains a national function. Weaker actors may also desire the continued participation of an intergovernmental organization to protect them against abuses of rules by stronger actors. The current practice of mandating periodic review of participant performance or of the condition of the environment also provides additional openings for intergovernmental organizations as the obvious forums for such meetings.

Regime Features and Organizational Effectiveness

Several features of international regimes can make it easier or more difficult for intergovernmental organizations to contribute to the goal of improved environmental protection. The initial rationales for a regime affect the ease with which particular new ideas can replace old ideas, thus making goal revision easier or more difficult. The decision rules can make it easier or more difficult to decide and influence how effectively states cooperate in implementation. Equally important, what happens if no decision is reached, can make it easier or more difficult to secure environmental protection when participants disagree about what to do next.

The ease of introducing new conceptions of goals or means into an international environmental regime depends heavily on the fit between the new ideas and the current rationale for the regime. The efforts of the antiwhaling coalition to shift the whaling regime to a nonexploitation rule have come up against the clear conservationist rationale advanced in the International Convention for the Regulation of Whaling. This rationale permits the Japanese and Norwegians to contend that antiwhaling proposals amount to a change in regime principles, which cannot be accomplished without unanimous consent to amend the convention. In contrast, within three years the Antarctic Treaty Consultative Parties were able to shift from a regime that would regulate mineral resource activity (CRAMRA) to one that would emphasize environmental protection first and ban resource activity for at least fifty years (the Madrid Protocol) because the wider Antarctic regime was built on principles designed to regulate human activity on and to protect the continent.

Decision-making rules also affect implementation. Unanimity (acceptance by all) and consensus (lack of strong objection by any significant number or group of participants) demand broad support before a decision can be made. The delays involved in building such a broad coalition and the compromises likely to be required often hobble result effectiveness. Attempts to move to less-demanding rules, however, run up against governments' continuing reluctance to accept binding majority decisions. This reluctance is particularly obvious in older environmental treaties in which provisions for decision by less than unanimity are almost always linked to "opt out" clauses that permit governments to remove their state and their nationals from application of the decision.

The disagreement about voting rules is so deeply entrenched because the large number of less powerful states want protection against tyranny by the few powerful states, whereas the small number of powerful states want protection against tyranny by the many less powerful states. Qualified majorities—whether constructed by weighting votes, by adopting chambered voting schemes in which votes are distributed among identifiable clusters of states that have similar interests and in which decisions need support from at least some members of all clusters (Zamora 1980), or by requiring parallel majorities of votes weighted by some criteria or of votes distributed on a one state–one vote basis—represent the most likely way out of the impasse.

The full implications of the decision-making rules depend on the basis of action. Advocates of the precautionary principle argue that the current basis of most regimes—that is, activity may proceed until harm is shown—unduly subordinates environmental considerations to other considerations; they want to shift the burden of proof so that activity may occur only when it can be shown to cause no significant harm. The impact of decision rules also depends on the "default" that will continue in the absence of decision. In most environmental regimes, no decision means that activity continues as before; no new limitations are adopted. The "default," then, is that activity continues as before and might even increase. In a few regimes, however, no decision means that current restrictions on activity remain in effect; the default is modest or means no activity. In the whaling regime, a three-fourths vote is necessary to lift the moratorium on commercial whaling, and in the Madrid Protocol, ending the resource activity ban will be permitted only after going through the amendment process. A low- or no-activity default is difficult to adopt if activity is already at a high level, unless the actors involved see some advantage for themselves in reducing activity or in shifting resources to other types of activity.

Internal Conditions of Organization Effectiveness

Being assigned a role is no guarantee, however, that an organization will carry it out effectively. Intergovernmental organizations, like any group of humans, can fail for lack of resources or lack of ability. Lack of resources is not an internal problem; most league-of-states type intergovernmental organizations have only those revenues allocated to them by member governments. Thus, an intergovernmental organization must devote real effort to securing resources adequate to carrying out its assigned roles. To some extent, however, funding is related to ability because an intergovernmental organization with a reputation for competence in supplying member governments with services they value has less trouble securing funds.

Maintaining the ability to carry out assigned roles or find new ones requires an intergovernmental organization to simultaneously maintain organizational independence from member governments; internal coherence based on a sense of organizational mission; competence in managing networks and information flows; and openness to the various intellectual, political, and material developments that indicate a need to revise organizational goals and routines. A considerable scholarly literature has explored the conditions under which these elements are or are not developed and maintained (e.g., Cox 1969; Cox and Jacobson 1973; Ness and Brechlin 1988; E. Haas 1990; Gallarotti 1991; Kardam 1993). The internal conditions most frequently mentioned include assembling a competent staff, infusing it with a sense of organizational mission, maintaining a solid working relationship with all the major coalitions of member states, and preventing organizational interest in the continued existence and maintenance of current routines and programs from ossifying. As several successive studies of the UN system have shown, assembling and motivating a competent staff is not easy; many intergovernmental organizations fail here because of the administrative style of their executive heads or various pressures from member governments (Jackson 1969; Meron 1977; Beigbeder 1988).

The existence of multiple intergovernmental organizations has advantages and disadvantages for different actors and in different contexts. On the one hand, proliferation of organizations dissipates the available resources of personnel, funds, and attention time. Yet, on the other hand, when different organizations are viewed as serving different constituencies, the constituencies have strong interests in keeping each organization alive and in assuring that it has a role in maintaining environmental cooperation. For example, the Multilateral Fund established under the Montreal Protocol and the Global Environment Facility are both comanaged by UNEP, UNDP, and the World Bank as a result of compromise between Western industrial states that want a World

Bank–managed fund and developing states that want a UNDP-managed one (Chayes and Chayes 1995: 199). Multiple agencies also serve governments' interests because they permit "forum shopping" either to affect problem definition and agenda setting by taking issues to one organization rather than another (e.g., Pistorius 1995) or to search for an organization willing to extend aid on terms preferred by the recipient (e.g., Connolly and List 1996). Thus, dreams of a fully "rational" set of intergovernmental organizations are unlikely to materialize.

Conclusion

Intergovernmental organizations have certain advantages over individual governments and transnational actors when it comes to serving as process managers charged with assuring the compliance and result effectiveness of international environmental regimes. Unlike individual governments, they represent the broader regional or global community affected by the activities being managed under the regime. Unlike transnational actors, they can bring together those who wield political power and public authority and can provide an institutional infrastructure within which private activity and the various forms of private governance can occur. They thus enjoy a far greater potential legitimacy as definers and promoters of international regimes than any other sort of actor.

  Their actual success as managers of the processes of implementing and revising international environmental regimes depends, however, on several factors, only some of which are within the organization's control. The basic shape of the regime is set, though the organization's forums and secretariat can influence the process of interpreting and developing the regime by sponsoring expert workshops and informal consultation sessions, by drafting possible revisions, and by disseminating relevant information. Similarly, the organization is unable to control, although it may be able to take advantage of, the contours of the bargaining situation that emerge from the constellation of governments' and other actors' beliefs and perceptions of interest. It is also unable to control (or even significantly influence) the features of domestic politics—that is, the openness of domestic political systems, the emergence of new governments, or the presence of prevailing social coalitions—that shape how a state participates in an environmental regime. The existence and depth of expert consensus on the scientific and technical questions relevant to any particular environmental regime is also beyond its control, although it can encourage efforts to build consensus by sponsoring workshops that bring together scientists and other experts.

However, the organization can control certain variables: the development and maintenance of an organizational ideology that gives its work direction and coherence; the competence with which the staff manages networks, collects information and analyses, and disseminates information and analyses to governments or other interested actors; and the opportunities it provides to various nonstate actors for involvement in the discussions of compliance and results. Even if they are taken together, these variables are not the major determinants of regime effectiveness. In some situations, however, they do make enough difference in compliance and result effectiveness to provide the margin that spells success or failure.

III

Issues

6

Managing International Rivers

Thomas Bernauer

Can transboundary freshwater resources be managed in a more sustainable way, and if so, how? Natural scientists, engineers, and international lawyers often seem to know the answer, as the significant body of literature on river management in these disciplines indicates. Their advice, however, obviously remains unheard or does not help to produce the desired results, for global freshwater resources are under growing stress as we approach the twenty-first century. The latter development suggests that effective management of transboundary freshwater is not merely a legal or technological problem, but rather primarily a political one — that is, a problem of designing and operating effective social institutions to govern the use of freshwater resources. This chapter develops a framework for thinking more systematically about the politics of managing international rivers, the conflicts that arise because of politics, and the strategies and instruments by which these conflicts are addressed with varying degrees of success.[1]

As noted in *Agenda 21* (1992: chapter 18) of the United Nations (UN) Conference on Environment and Development, freshwater is one of the most important natural resources. It is critical to agricultural development and food production (e.g., irrigated agriculture, fisheries) , energy supply (e.g., hydroelectric power production, cooling of nuclear power plants), transportation, industrial development, and public health. It also serves as a sink for the disposal of all sorts of industrial and household waste. Consequently, efficient use of freshwater resources is essential for sustainable socioeconomic development and human welfare in general.

Over the past few decades, rivers, lakes, and groundwater have become increasingly contaminated by chemical and biological waste.

Millions of people lack access to clean drinking water and sanitation, and they die from water-related diseases, including cholera, malaria, and typhoid. Water-development projects for irrigation, flood control, and hydropower production have eliminated many wetlands, destroyed precious ecosystems, displaced indigenous people, and reduced the fertility of farmland (Clarke 1991; Gleick 1993; World Bank 1995). Approximately eighty countries, inhabited by approximately 40 percent of the world's population, encounter serious water shortages (Falkenmark and Lindh 1993). Moreover, because freshwater is part of the global water cycle, freshwater problems are both causes and consequences of larger environmental problems, such as marine pollution, biodiversity, and even climate change.

To some extent, scarcity and uneven distribution of freshwater resources across time and space are caused by natural hydrological cycles.[2] In many instances however, these problems also result from unsustainable human consumption of freshwater. Political science theory and market failure theories developed by economists suggest that the principal reason for unsustainable use of natural resources is not primarily the technical and intellectual incapacity of human beings and their societies to recognize and cope with water scarcity problems. A more important reason is that certain incentive structures as well as political and institutional problems prevent riparian countries and their constituencies from collectively establishing and operating effective management systems for transboundary water courses.

At the most general (and also abstract) level, unsustainable use of freshwater resources can be traced back to problems of dealing with shared natural resources and to certain externalities in particular (see chapter 1 in this volume). Externalities are side effects — usually unintended but identifiable in terms of costs or, less often, benefits — that water-related activity by a household, firm, or other actors (e.g., states) produces for other actors or future generations and that are ignored in decisions made by the actors who cause them. Construction of a dam at the mouth of a river creates an obstacle to upstream actors' access to the sea, and it may reduce salmon catches upstream. Withdrawal of water for irrigation upstream can cause water shortages and salination problems for countries downstream. Or, by polluting a river today, the riparians impose costs on future generations. Such externalities lead to unsustainable or inefficient use of water resources because the consumers of the resource do not incur the full costs or benefits of consumption.

External effects and unsustainable use of scarce freshwater resources can generate serious economic problems and, as a consequence, political or social conflict over pollution, water distribution, navigation rights, flood control, and other issues (Bächler and Böge 1993; Homer-Dixon 1994; Libiszewski 1995). Vast irrigation projects in the former Soviet Union, for example, reduced the volume of the Aral Sea by 65 percent and tripled its salinity. Fisheries have been wiped out, health problems have increased, and the entire area is under threat of economic collapse. When Arab countries initiated a project to divert the headwaters of the Jordan, Israel conducted a series of military raids against these construction sites.

The resolution of problems resulting from the use of transboundary rivers often requires *international* policy coordination, not least because more than two hundred river or lake basins are shared by two or more countries.[3] These basins are populated by approximately 40 percent of the world's population and cover approximately 50 percent of the world's land area (World Resources Institute 1992: 171).[4] In addition, many countries located in international river basins have, because they are situated in arid areas, a low per capita water availability, which exacerbates human-induced freshwater shortages.[5]

We should not assume, a priori, that international water issues are more difficult to deal with than national or even local water issues. The many cases of domestic water pollution and other water scarcity problems suggest so. Yet, the international nature of freshwater problems and, consequently, the need for international cooperation often introduces additional difficulties. The most common solution to problems over shared natural resources at the domestic level is not available in the case of transboundary rivers: there is no central authority to solve these problems by imposing remedial policies, such as prohibitions, emission licenses, taxes on emissions, subsidies, or product and production process requirements. In most cases, no robust legal framework exists through which producers and victims of externalities might effectively settle their conflicts—for example, by engaging in legal action over liability for pollution.

Despite these difficulties, international and transnational cooperation frequently occurs. Transboundary rivers have been the subject of regulatory efforts for centuries. Early examples of such efforts include an agreement between Austria and Turkey, concluded in 1616, which regulated navigation rights on the Danube; the right of free navigation of international rivers established by the Congress of Vienna in 1815; an 1885 treaty governing the salmon fishery in the Rhine Basin; and a treaty regulating the transportation of corrosive and poisonous substances on the Rhine, signed in the year 1900 (Kiss 1985: 613–614; LeMarquand 1977: 8).

The UN Food and Agricultural Organization (FAO) has counted more than two thousand agreements that deal at least partly with transboundary water issues. Most of these agreements are bilateral, but the number of multilateral agreements is growing.[6] Three agreements even attempt to establish globally applicable rules for international watercourses (FAO 1978, updated). The latest example is the 1992 Helsinki Convention.[7] Several political programs have also been initiated, including the International Hydrological Decade in the 1960s, coordinated by UN Educational, Scientific and Cultural Organization (UNESCO), or the UN International Drinking Water Supply and Sanitation Decade in the 1980s. Moreover, the International Law Institute, the International Law Commission, the European Union (EU), and other bodies have been engaged in developing and interpreting international water law.

The outcomes of these cooperative ventures vary in many respects. In applying some of the broader social science questions about "governance without government" (such as those outlined in chapters 1 and 10 of this volume) to questions of managing international rivers, I focus largely on three types of phenomena: the existence or nonexistence of international river management institutions (IRMIs) and their geographical distribution; the features and functions of international river management; and the performance of institutions designed to manage international rivers, once they have been established.

Some conflicts over transboundary rivers are resolved quite speedily and effective institutions are established, whereas some serious conflicts persist (see Mandel 1992). More than forty of the major international rivers are currently subject to individual international regulation or management of one sort or another. A 1972 United Nations study (United Nations 1972) observed, however, that the distribution of international water management efforts was heavily skewed: 72 percent of all major international river basins are located in Africa, Asia, and Latin America, but less than 33 percent of the relevant agreements signed worldwide between 1948 and 1972 covered these rivers. As of 1995, it appears that international river management efforts are distributed somewhat more evenly across industrialized and developing countries, but considering that most international rivers are still located in developing countries, the relative distribution remains skewed.

The functions of IRMIs, and by implication their features, vary enormously. Some management efforts are directed at very narrowly framed issues, such as regulating salmon fisheries in the Rhine basin or curbing a salination problem created by irrigation drainage along the Colorado River. Other efforts are structured as broad attempts to foster socioeconomic development in an entire river catchment area—for example, in the Senegal and Paraná rivers. The instruments and strategies by which international rivers are managed also differ. They include, for example, joint research, jointly financed pollution reductions or dam projects, and liability frameworks.

Once they are established, IRMIs may differ considerably in terms of their performance over time and across cases. At one extreme, some IRMIs, such as those for the Niger and Kagera rivers in Africa, have largely remained paper tigers (Scudder 1989). At the other extreme, some institutions, such as those governing the Rhine and Indus rivers, are widely claimed to be successful.

Scientific knowledge on the questions raised here is seriously underdeveloped. Hydrologists, ecologists, and natural scientists in general have written extensively on international water courses—for example, the impact of climate change on the Rhine basin or the impact of increasing pollution on ecosystems. It seems, however, that the politics of managing international rivers, which is at least equally crucial to achieving sustainable use of these resources, has been largely neglected. The literature on the political and institutional aspects of river management consists largely of prescriptive studies that outline supposedly, but empirically untested, effective or efficient management schemes (e.g., United Nations 1972, 1988). These studies are purely descriptive or normative (most of the legal literature; e.g., Kiss 1985); or, where the approach is positive, they are based on single-case studies (e.g., Bernauer 1995; Mingst 1982), very few cases (LeMarquand 1977), or an unsystematic comparison (Vlachos, Webb, and Murphy 1986). Although case-specific, diagnostic approaches may produce valuable insights into problems and solutions in international river management, comparative empirical research, guided by coherent theory and systematic methodology, is also needed in order to arrive at more generalizable knowledge on the subject (see also chapters 1 and 10 in this volume).

This chapter constitutes but a first step in filling the research gap. It proposes a framework for thinking more rigorously about problems of governance in a key area of international environmental protection and resource management; it also illustrates the arguments by drawing on several cases of international river management. As a starting point, the second section conceptualizes international river management as an attempt to resolve problems of overuse of shared natural resources. It notes a number of constitutional and operational features by which most IRMIs are characterized and outlines some basic questions for research. The third section looks at how cooperation among riparian countries is achieved and which obstacles to cooperation have to be overcome. The fourth section discusses the question of whether and how variation in the features of IRMIs may relate to the performance of international river management. The concluding section summarizes the arguments and establishes the link between the subject of this chapter and more general social science questions concerning governance in international society.[8]

Basic Concepts and Questions for Research

Shared Natural Resources

Transboundary rivers are used for a variety of purposes, and the utility that individual riparian actors draw from consuming the resource may vary within and across different types of consumption and across time.

Table 6.1 shows that the riparian countries of the Rhine use the river for at least seven purposes. France, for example, does not draw its drinking water from the Rhine or depend on the river for its electric power production. Switzerland, on the other hand, derives a significant share of its electricity from hydropower plants along the Rhine. The Netherlands draws approximately 65 percent of its drinking water from the river.

Human consumption of scarce resources, such as water, often produces externalities—costs or, less often, benefits that one actor, by consuming the resource, imposes on other actors or future generations). Such externalities are particularly likely to occur in the case of shared natural resources (SNRs).[9] Such resources, which include most transboundary rivers, are characterized by the fact that various riparion actors' entitlements to quantities and qualities of water are ill defined or not defined at all. At the same time, no riparian can, at acceptable cost, be excluded from using the river. These two conditions imply that the choices and possibilities of riparian countries regarding the use of transboundary rivers are interdependent. Moreover, in many cases, they create incentives for individual actors to overuse the resource as long as they do not incur the full cost of consumption. Overuse may indicate growing pollution, diminishing water quality, and often both. Extreme

Table 6.1
Types of water consumption by Rhine riparian states

	Switzerland	France	Germany	Netherlands
Drinking water				x
Industrial processes	x	x	x	x
Energy production				x
Leisure	x	x	x	x
Waste water	x	x	x	x
Navigation	x	x	x	x
Irrigation				x

overuse leads to what is known as the "tragedy of the commons," which can mean, for example, the collapse of fisheries, the collapse of irrigated agriculture along transboundary rivers, or a shortage of drinking water (G. Hardin 1968).

Like rivers, externalities often flow in one direction: from upstream downward. Depending on the location of countries along a river and the type of consumption, use of the river in one country may positively or negatively affect the quantity and/or quality of the resource available to users in other countries. Table 6.2 lists the most important downstream effects of water consumption and indicates whether they are positive or negative.

Water consumption of the types indicated in Table 6.2 can have dramatic effects. Turkey interrupted the flow of the Euphrates for an entire month in 1990 as it began to fill the reservoir created by the Ataturk Dam, a key part of the Greater Anatolia Project. When the project itself is completed by the late 1990s, Syria and Iraq—the two downstream countries—could lose up to 40 and 90 percent, respectively, of their water from the Euphrates. In addition, water quality will suffer due to upstream irrigation runoff, which contains salts, fertilizer, and pesticide residues (McCaffrey 1993: 93).

Not all external effects flow from upstream downward. Construction of a dam at the mouth of a river, for example, may block the ascent of salmon, thus reducing or eliminating catches upstream. Similarly, excessive water withdrawal or dams in a downstream country may disrupt transportation routes of upstream countries to the sea.

Conflict and Cooperation

Externalities and the associated problems of overuse of freshwater are often major sources of conflict among riparian countries. It appears that such conflicts are more severe if (1) the quantity and quality of water available to the riparians is low, and no other sources are available at acceptable cost; (2) the entitlements of the riparians are ill defined, not defined, or contested; and (3) externalities and their impact are clearly discernible and direct.[10]

Conflicts emerge in many different ways. According to a long-term historical perspective, however, they often develop along the following

Table 6.2
Downstream effects of water consumption

Type of resource use	Downstream effect	Nature of externality
Hydropower production	Helps to regulate the river	Positive
	Creates additional peaks	Negative
Irrigation diversions	Remove water from the system	Negative
Flood storage	Provides downstream flood protection	Positive
Municipal and industrial diversions	Remove water from the system	Negative
Wastewater treatment	Adds pollution to the river	Negative
	Removes potential pollution	Positive
Navigation	Keeps water in the river	Positive
	Creates pollution, noise	Negative
Recreation storage	Keeps water out of the system	Negative
Ecological maintenance	Keeps low flow in the river	Positive
Groundwater development	Reduces groundwater availability	Negative
	Reduces stream flow	
Agriculture	Adds sediment and agricultural chemicals	Negative
Forestry	Adds sediment and chemicals	Negative
	Increases runoff	
Animal husbandry	Adds sediment and nutrients	Negative
Filling of wetlands	Reduces ecological carrying capacity	Negative
	Increases floods	
Urban development	Induces flooding	Negative
	Adds pollutants	
Fishing	Reduces fish stock	Negative
Recreation	Adds pollutants, depending on use	Negative
Dredging of gravel	Adds pollutants	Negative

Sources: Rogers 1992: 65; author.

lines. Downstream countries utilize the waters of a river before the upstream countries, mainly because their topography lends itself to irrigated agriculture on a larger scale. Examples of such downstream countries are the Netherlands, Egypt, and Iraq.

Some time later, upstream countries begin to develop more intensive forms of agriculture, and urban centers and industry emerge at a later stage. Increased water pollution and the negative effects of dam projects or upstream flood control measures are the typical results of such development, which bring upstream countries into conflict with downstream countries. The latter claim to have acquired the right to a certain quantity or quality of the water. They usually employ the widely respected customary norm of international law that riparian countries shall not harm each other. They also argue that upstream countries have hitherto acquiesced to a specific level of water consumption downstream and that downstream countries have relied on this acquiescence. Mexico and the Netherlands made such claims with regard to the chloride concentrations in the Colorado River and the Rhine, respectively.

In justifying their increased consumption of water, upstream countries then tend to resort to two arguments. Hard-liners often evoke the so-called Harmon doctrine, a legal doctrine that emphasizes the unlimited sovereignty of each riparian country over its natural resources. Countries with a more cooperative attitude will stress the principle of equitable utilization. They will argue that, up to the present, they did not need to increase consumption or did not possess the technology or financing for water development projects. They will also claim, however, that strict application of the principle not to harm downstream riparians would now unduly jeopardize their socioeconomic development. Despite being latecomers, upstream countries will thus demand an equitable share of the resource (see also McCaffrey 1993: 99).

In international cooperation, which is required to resolve such disputes, the riparians will normally pursue the following objectives: (1) organize entitlements to political authority among riparian countries with a view to defining property rights to the resource (ill- or undefined or unenforced property rights are to a large degree responsible for external effects and thus conflict); (2) redistribute existing rights or entitlements; and/or (3) reduce the entitlements or property rights of riparians in order to achieve a sustainable level of water consumption.[11] In practical terms, as Gleick (1993: 9) notes, the principal goal of managing freshwater resources more efficiently as populations grow should be to "demand reduction through rationing, improved distribution of available supplies, increased efficiency of water use, restructuring of societal activities, such as cultivating low–water use crops, and avoiding water pollution as human activities per unit of water intensify."

In some, albeit rarer, cases, cooperation does not result from the need to solve an existing conflict. Rather, it evolves around the possibility of jointly exploiting hitherto un- or underexploited freshwater resources. Cooperation may, for example, allow riparian countries to capitalize on economies of scale and prevent in advance any potential conflicts that may result from the external effects of individual river development projects.[12] When, how, and how effectively riparian states achieve these objectives remains to be explained. Research on local SNRs or common pool resources (e.g., Libecap 1993) clearly shows that changing property rights or entitlements to political authority often involves long and conflict-prone processes of policy coordination. We still don't know, however, whether this insight and the results of other research on local SNRs can be applied at the international level.

In a considerable number of cases, riparian countries have been able to establish formal or informal governance systems that organize political authority to allocate freshwater resources directly. Allocation may be determined in terms of quantities of water that each party can withdraw for irrigation, pollution thresholds, burden-sharing formulas for joint dam projects, and so on. Beyond the most general function of allocating freshwater, IRMIs perform many different tasks, which means that their features also vary.

The most basic proposition in this chapter is that variation in IRMI features has an impact on whether transboundary rivers can be successfully managed. Explication of two IRMI features — constitutional design and operational elements — serves as a starting point for further discussion of this proposition.

International versus National Rivers   In some cases, hitherto international rivers (that is, SNRs) are by agreement transformed into a set of national rivers; that is, international rivers are nationalized so that each riparian country can autonomously manage its part of the resource. The most prominent example of autonomous management is the Indus River. In 1960, particular tributaries of the Indus and their associated irrigation systems, which had been built under colonial rule, were divided up between India and Pakistan. India received the eastern rivers of the Indus basin, Pakistan the western rivers. In some rare cases, the reverse occurs: hitherto national waterways are transformed into international ones. Through the treaty of Versailles, the North Sea–Baltic Canal was transformed from a formerly German waterway into an international one. At the end of the World War II Roosevelt proposed to internationalize the main waterways of continental Europe, but this proposal did not result in any substantive political action.

Single versus Multi-Issue IRMIs   As noted, some IRMIs deal with a single river pollution problem (e.g., the salination problem of the Colorado River or the Rhine), whereas others are constructed as catch-all efforts at socioeconomic development of a river basin (e.g., the Senegal and Mekong Rivers institutions).

Liability Framework   Liability rules offer one method of dealing with externality problems. Probably the most developed framework for taking transboundary legal action against polluters exists for the area along the Rhine. A ruling by the European Court of Justice has established the right of any victim to take legal action against any polluter in either the polluter or the victim country of the European Union (Romy 1990). In most river basins, however, it seems nearly impossible to engage, with any reasonable prospect of success, in a lawsuit against the actor who produces an externality in another country.

Extent of Transnational Activity   Some efforts to manage international rivers are exclusively intergovernmental, which is the case with most IRMIs in developing countries. Often, these IRMIs also involve international agencies (usually the World Bank, the United Nations

Development Program [UNDP], and the United Nations Environment Program [UNEP]. In other cases, we can observe considerable nongovernmental activity. In the Rhine case, a basin-wide association of waterworks (the International Association of Waterworks in the Rhine Basin [IAWR]) seems to have been rather effective in lobbying governments on water quality issues. Moreover, other subnational actors (e.g., the city of Rotterdam; chemical firms upstream in France, Germany, and Switzerland; groups of farmers in the Netherlands; environmental nongovernmental organizations [NGOs] have been involved in transboundary civil law contracts and lawsuits over pollution issues involving the Rhine.

Sources of Financing   Dealing with externality problems or developing international rivers is often very costly. These costs can be met in three ways. First, in the rare case, internationally agreed upon measures are jointly financed by riparian countries. The riparians of the Rhine, for example, have jointly paid for chloride reductions at a potash mine in France (Bernauer 1996). Second, in the most common case, actions to be taken under international agreements are financed by each government individually. Reductions of Rhine pollution caused by heavy metals and pesticides have been financed this way. Third, river development programs in particular are often financed to a considerable degree by sources external to the river basin. The Senegal and Mekong are typical examples.

Questions for Research
As shown, international river management can vary along several dimensions. First, in relation to the distribution of international rivers across the globe, there are more IRMIs in industrialized countries than in developing countries. Second, IRMIs vary in terms of their functions and, by implication, their features. Third, once established, IRMIs appear to vary in terms of their performance.

All this variation raises questions about the factors that influence the possibilities of establishing IRMIs and about the conditions that shape the performance of these institutions. Are IRMIs inherently more difficult to set up in developing countries than in industrialized countries,

and if so, why? Are narrowly framed (single-issue) IRMIs more successful than broadly framed ones? Do IRMIs with large transnational
participation perform better? Should IRMI designers attempt to nationalize international rivers, as happened in the Indus River case and in
ocean fisheries, in which exclusive economic zones were established? Or
should they strive to internationalize resources—that is, transform them
into the common heritage of mankind—and manage them jointly, as
happened with Antarctica and celestial bodies? Which mode of IRMI
financing is more propitious to their performance? Are transboundary
liability frameworks effective means of reducing externality problems?

The third and fourth sections of this chapter provide some preliminary
answers to these questions. The third section explores how international
cooperation is achieved and which strategies and instruments are used
to achieve such cooperation. It thus explains the existence and the
features of IRMIs. In the fourth section, the features of IRMI become
part of the effort to explain the performance of these institutions.

When and How Is Cooperation Achieved?

Managing international rivers is circumscribed by the interests of the
riparian countries and by several other structural variables. These
variables, however, are not constant over time, nor do they fully
determine the possibilities and features of international river management. They serve merely as starting points for a political process in
which the negotiating parties try to harmonize their interests and to
achieve cooperation. This harmonization of interests can be achieved
through a variety of instruments and strategies.

Structural Explanations

As noted in the previous section, international river management issues
can be characterized as conflicts that arise over shared natural resources
(SNRs). SNRs tend to be overused because one or more riparians'
consumption of water resources affects the quantity and/or quality of the
resource available to other riparians; plus, no riparian can, at least in
principle, be excluded from consuming the resource. Overuse occurs
because users can, in this situation, externalize some or even all costs of

their consumption—that is, pass them on to other actors or future generations. Depending on the types of resource consumption, overuse varies in intensity, which in turn influences the possibility of cooperation.

Benign SNR Problems   Transboundary navigation issues tend to pose rather benign SNR problems. As long as the benefits of a functioning navigation system are significant, rivalry effects (externalities) appear only gradually, and both the effects and the benefits are distributed quite uniformly among the riparians, as is often the case with international rivers. Oftentimes, it is to each riparian's benefit to establish a system of free navigation on a transboundary river. Upstream countries need to transport goods and people downstream, and downstream countries wish to trade with upstream actors and to facilitate their people's upstream travel. Contingent on the navigability of a river and the availability of alternative routes of transportation as well as their costs, the joint gains of free navigation of transboundary rivers can thus be very high. The costs of establishing free navigation and of regulating river traffic, on the other hand, tend to be rather low, and the rivalry problem among riparian actors tends to emerge only gradually. Navigation may generate externalities for all (e.g., congestion of shipping lanes) or for only some actors (e.g., pollution from ships affecting riparians downstream from discharge points). These problems are more difficult to deal with than simple navigation issues. If governance structures for the simple issues have been firmly in place for some time, however, they may facilitate cooperation over gradually evolving externality problems associated with increasing navigation.

These propositions are quite compatible with what we can observe in reality. Navigation is usually among the first issues covered by IRMIs. Austria and Turkey, for example, regulated navigation rights on the Danube in 1616. A similar agreement for the Rhine was reached between France and Germany in 1697. The Congress of Vienna, held in 1815, established the right of free navigation of international rivers (LeMarquand 1977: 8). Cooperation among riparians of transboundary rivers located in developing countries, such as the Senegal, also appears to support the proposition.

The Central Commission for the Navigation of the Rhine, founded in 1815, was in fact the first international organization in history (Kiss 1985: 620). Compared to other international organizations, the Rhine navigation commission has surprisingly important powers: it can issue mandatory regulations concerning navigation issues, and violations of the rules are punished by tribunals designated as Rhine Navigation Tribunals. This governance structure was instrumental in dealing with more extensive problems as they gradually appeared. In 1900, for example, it introduced regulations governing the transportation of corrosive and poisonous substances on the river.

Malign SNR Problems   In less benign circumstances, SNR problems can develop into "tragedies of the commons." River pollution or problems over large-scale water withdrawals may exhibit the characteristics of such tragedies. Each country along the river has an incentive to appropriate water (e.g., in terms of its capacity for waste assimilation) as long as the marginal private benefit of appropriating the resource is larger than the marginal private cost. The private cost is smaller and the net private benefit larger, the more an actor can externalize the costs of its resource consumption by passing them on to other actors or to a larger group to which it belongs, and the less externalities are imported from other users of the resource. This proposition and the often asymmetrical distribution of external effects explain the empirical observation that pollution and water distribution issues tend to be more difficult to deal with than navigation problems. In contrast, little evidence supports the hypothesis sometimes put forward that water distribution problems are more difficult to solve than water pollution problems.

Heterogeneity of Preferences and the Number of Riparians   Both the degree to which riparian countries can externalize the costs of their resource consumption and the extent to which each of them is affected by the externalities of other riparians vary. The greater the variation, the more heterogeneous the preferences of riparian countries are likely to be regarding the possible measures needed to deal with externality problems. Such heterogeneity does not necessarily prevent cooperation (as the third section of the chapter shows), but it is bound to make cooperation more difficult.

Among the most difficult situations to deal with is the well-known upstream-downstream problem in which an upstream country can largely externalize the costs of its resource consumption and by doing so can negatively affect a downstream country. Similar cooperation problems occur in the case of positive upstream-downstream effects. An upstream country may wish to regulate a river by building dams. This measure will benefit the country taking the action, but it may also reduce floods downstream, thus creating a positive externality. Obviously, the upstream country will have an incentive to seek the participation of downstream countries in this project. Downstream countries, on the other hand, will have an incentive to ride free on the efforts of the upstream country unless the latter can signal in a credible manner that it will not go ahead with the project unless the downstream country's participation is assured. Once a joint dam project is agreed upon, the participants must overcome additional obstacles. The most fundamental difficulty is that many different projects for the use of a resource are possible, each one entailing a different distribution of costs and benefits. In the case of the Columbia River, for example, these distributional conflicts complicated the establishment of a joint network of hydropower and flood control projects (Le Marquand 1977: 53–77, 79–93).

This variation proposition can be combined with the standard hypothesis of collective action theory that cooperation problems grow with the number of parties involved (e.g., Sandler 1992). We can thus argue that SNR problems are most difficult to solve—and IRMIs most difficult to establish—when many riparians and heterogeneous preferences are involved, as is the case in most upstream-downstream scenarios. The most propitious situation for collaboration exists when the group is small and preferences are homogeneous. If these conditions do not exist, then the chances of cooperation are probably moderate. These relationships are summarized in Table 6.3.

In the case of most transboundary rivers, the number of riparian countries per river basin is quite small, usually two to four. But there are important exceptions, including the Danube (12), Niger (10), Nile

Table 6.3
Heterogeneity of preferences, group size, and cooperation

	Homogeneous preferences	Heterogeneous preferences
Large group	Cooperation possible	Cooperation unlikely
Small group	Cooperation likely	Cooperation possible

(9), Zaire (9), Rhine (8), Zambezi (8), Amazon (7), Mekong (6), Volta (6), Ganges-Brahmaputra (5), and LaPlata (5) river basins (United Nations 1978). In virtually all of these cases, the external effects of resource use are asymmetrically distributed, resulting in heterogeneous preferences, and they have created protracted political conflict among the riparian countries. We can observe extensive international cooperation in very few of these cases (notably the Rhine). In most cases, cooperation exists among only an insufficient subset of riparians (e.g., the Nile), is largely restricted to joint research (e.g., the Mekong), is more declaratory than real (e.g., the Niger, the Zaire, the Volta), or has begun only recently (e.g., the Danube). In comparison, several international rivers with only two riparian countries seem to be managed more successfully (e.g., the Columbia, the Colorado, the Indus).

Economic Development and Integration   If there is indeed a correlation between the number of riparians and the heterogeneity of preferences, on the one hand, and the extent of cooperation (the existence of substantive IRMIs may serve as an indicator), on the other hand,[13] we should remain sceptical as to whether small groups and homogeneous preferences are sufficient or even necessary conditions for successful river management. The international relations literature suggests that several other structural variables are likely to play an equally relevant role. The most important among these variables are probably the level of economic development of concerned riparian countries and the degree of social, political, and economic integration among them.

Riparian countries with a higher level of economic development usually have a greater administrative, technological, and financial capacity for engaging in pollution reductions and other measures needed to deal with externality problems. As witnessed in many areas of environmental cooperation and resource management, countries with a low capacity will be more reluctant to commit themselves internationally (Bedarff et al. 1995). The fact that IRMIs tend to appear later in developing countries (one exception is the Mekong Commission) makes this proposition plausible.[14] Because environmental protection is allegedly a "normal" good (i.e., the demand for it grows with income), richer countries tend to be more sensitive to ecological and intergenerational aspects of managing transboundary rivers. This greater sensitivity facilitates environmental protection efforts. A case study of the Rhine shows that growing environmental awareness had a critical impact on the evolution of pollution reduction efforts (Bernauer and Moser 1996).

A high degree of social, economic, and political integration between countries increases the possibility of cooperation in various ways. First, preexisting cooperative frameworks reduce the transaction costs of negotiating agreements. Second, integration creates more opportunities for issue linkages and for other types of intertemporal and cross-issue trade. The next section shows that such trades are often essential for overcoming adverse structural conditions, such as upstream-downstream problems, and for achieving cooperation. Third, incentives to cheat on agreements, and thus on monitoring costs, decline with growing integration because the riparians will meet again in many other contexts — in other words, in *iterated interactions*. Iterated interactions also reduce concerns about relative gains in negotiations, which in turn alleviates the problem of distributional bargaining over the costs and benefits of cooperation. Fourth, because of growing integration, collateral issues such as recognition of borders or governments are less likely to interfere with river management efforts. Despite at least a moderate will to cooperate on water issues, the riparian countries of the Jordan have until recently been forced into informal talks and tacit forms of river management, particularly because the Arab countries refused to cooperate publicly with Israel. Fifth, the degree of integration can also have a significant impact on the possible forms of cooperation, which in turn influence the performance of river management (discussed in the fourth section of the chapter).

One of the very rare empirical studies on international rivers that is based on a larger number of cases (Durth 1995) clearly shows that integration is a key variable in explaining the likelihood of cooperation. The cross-sectional analysis of 127 agreements made before 1993 on transboundary waters in North America and Europe—as well as case studies of the Rhine, the Elbe, and the Euphrates—demonstrates that in more integrated contexts (e.g., EU, European Free Trade Association [EFTA], European Economic Space) cooperation on transboundary waters is more frequent and occurs earlier. Although no empirical analysis has yet been done on this point, this finding does suggest that the impact of water scarcity,[15] heterogeneity of preferences, and the number of actors[16] on the likelihood of cooperation is heavily mediated by the degree of integration. Neither a low degree of water scarcity, nor homogeneity of preferences, nor a small number of riparians constitutes a necessary or sufficient condition by itself for cooperation.

Process-Oriented Explanations

Even if the constellation of riparian countries preferences and other structural conditions are propitious to cooperation, the establishment and operation of IRMIs is by no means automatic. As we know from the theoretical literature on collective action (Sandler 1992; Morrow 1994), informational and distribution problems, as well as monitoring and enforcement difficulties, may still stand in the way of effective cooperation. Conversely, adverse structural conditions, such as those found in many upstream-downstream situations, do not necessarily prevent cooperation,[17] but they do necessitate the use of particular strategies designed to overcome such problems such as coercion, compensation, issue linkage, and changes in the group of participants and in bargaining forums.

Consequently, the likelihood of cooperation cannot be explained by structure alone. It must also be explained through answers to particular questions. When is a certain type of strategy used during the *processes* of establishing and operating governance systems for transboundary rivers? Or, what problems arise during the processes? It is impossible in this chapter to discuss comprehensively the conditions that determine when bargaining processes get under way or when and how they lead to the establishment of IRMIs. Instead, I can focus only on when and how one type of adverse structural condition—upstream-downstream problems—tends to be resolved. In such situations, riparian countries are likely to resort to coercion, compensation, issue linkage, or efforts to change the set of parties or bargaining forums in order to arrive at cooperative outcomes.

Coercion The most straightforward but rarest strategy to resolve upstream-downstream deadlocks is for downstream countries to threaten the use of force if upstream countries do not internalize their external effects. In 1967, Israel conducted military raids on Arab waterworks at the headwaters of the Jordan when it concluded that these projects could cut by half the water supply to Israel's National Water Carrier. Egypt has threatened to go to war against upstream riparians of the Nile should they ever divert major quantities of Nile water. Treaties between Sudan and Egypt in 1929 and 1959 allocated all Nile waters to these two countries, and Egypt receives approximately twelve times more water than Sudan. At the time when these treaties were concluded, most of the other upstream countries were still colonies. As their economies grow, however, they are likely to demand more water, which is likely to bring them into conflict with Sudan and Egypt. Whether these two countries will then be able to offset their disadvantageous strategic location downstream through coercion remains to be seen. Coercion has two important drawbacks, however. First, it is useful only to the extent that the downstream country has more power resources and the will to employ them. Because it lacks both the power and the will, the Netherlands has been unable to resort to coercion to obtain pollution reductions upstream in France and Germany. Second, coercion can result in "collateral damage"—that is, adverse effects on other areas of relations between the riparian countries. Israeli attacks against upstream countries of the Jordan, for instance, would probably derail the entire Middle East peace process.

Compensation Actors who suffer from external effects can compensate producers of these effects for their reduction. Even though this solution contravenes the "polluter pays" principle, it can be an economically efficient solution under some circumstances according to the economic theory of property rights (Coase 1960). In the case of chloride pollution of the Rhine, France engaged in reductions only when it was compensated by the other riparian countries (Bernauer 1996).

External financing is a special case of compensation in which non-riparian countries finance certain activities of riparian countries in exchange for benefits usually not directly related to the freshwater resources in question.[18] Most river development projects in developing countries and economies in transition are financed on this basis. At least in some cases, external financing seems to have had a positive influence on the likelihood of cooperation.

The relative success of the Indus case is partly explained by the fact that the World Bank was able to enlist the financial support of (mainly) Western countries for various projects to separate existing irrigation systems and to build new works. This approach also increased the amount of water available to India and Pakistan. External assistance probably more than compensated for the inefficiencies inherent in splitting up the previously unified irrigation system and in separately using individual tributaries to the Indus. It can also exert a moderating impact on riparian countries. The World Bank, on whose funding many river development projects depend, provides money only if the other riparians give their consent to a project. This rule is quite rational because international conflicts over a water development project may well hamper its economic viability. In the Jordan case, for example, a joint dam project by Jordan and Syria is currently stalled because in the absence of Israeli consent the World Bank refuses funding. This project would supply Syria with electricity and Jordan with water, but it would decrease the water supply to Israel. For similar reasons, the Greater Anatolia Project did not receive World Bank funding, although it was nonetheless undertaken. The five riparian governments of the River Plate basin are currently engaged in a project that would establish a waterway from the Upper Paraguay River through the Paraná River to the Uruguay River. They are trying to solve the associated problems with the help of UNDP and the Inter-American Development Bank (Cano 1992: 305).

Issue Linkage   The victim of an externality may seek to link the issue to another issue in which it has more bargaining leverage. The Netherlands could have threatened to close its part of the Rhine to ships registered in upstream countries if the latter countries did not reduce pollution. Or, it could have imposed a special tax on upstream ships to raise money for cleaning up the Rotterdam Harbor basin, where the pollutants emitted by upstream countries settle. The Netherlands did not do so, however, mostly because the costs of carrying out the threat would obviously have been high, which would by itself have rendered the threat itself incredible. What the Netherlands did, was to escalate the pollution issue by linking it to broader political relations between the riparian countries: it recalled its ambassador to France in the mid-1980s, thereby signaling credibly that, unless France made an effort to reduce its chloride emissions, overall relations between the two countries could turn increasingly sour.

In other cases, less direct linkages are at work in transforming otherwise adverse structural configurations. For example, the United States became willing in 1971 to desalt parts of Colorado River water (irrigation water drainage) that flows from the United States into Mexico. Given the upstream-downstream context, the United States had no direct incentive to invest in such an effort. What drove the United States toward cooperation was the attempt to avoid deteriorating relations with Mexico and to avert the image of a strong industrialized country damaging a poorer neighboring country (LeMarquand 1977: 25–51).

In the case of the Columbia River, a combination of the strategies was used to induce cooperation. The planned Libby Dam on the Kootenay River in Montana would have flooded some Canadian territory. The United States offered to compensate Canada for the land loss and dislocations but was unwilling to give Canada a share in the hydroelectric power benefits of the project, which Canada also demanded. Canada, unable to prevent the dam as such, threatened to construct a dam further upstream to divert the Kootenay River into the Columbia if the United States went ahead with its plans. It also suggested that it might divert waters of the Columbia into the Fraser River, which would have damaged U.S. hydroelectric power investments downstream. Threatening to impose considerable costs on the United States in the case of no agreement, Canada succeeded in obtaining a comprehensive river development scheme in which it receives one half of the additional hydropower created by the projects on the Canadian side and compensation for flood control benefits (McCaffrey 1993: 96; Le Marquand 1977: 13).

The above examples notwithstanding, it appears that explicit compensation or issue linkage is used quite rarely, particularly among industrialized countries, because countries with close relations often seem to prefer issue-isolation strategies over issue linkage. The reason for this preference may be that these countries expect to interact frequently in all sorts of areas in the future. Thus, giving in on one issue will establish some credit that can be used in future negotiations on other issues. In such a situation, issue isolation is only superficial; issues are linked sequentially and rather loosely. Issue linkage seems to become more direct if relations between countries are tense, perhaps because of continued frustration over the lack of progress on a pollution issue (the Rhine chloride case is an example). An additional reason for the low preference for issue linkage is that it poses a variety of difficulties. It increases the complexity of negotiations because negotiators have to attribute values to individual issues that are traded and, moreover, to compare these values (Sebenius 1984). In addition, negotiations may stall as governments carry more and more issues into the ring.

Why is financial compensation used so infrequently, particularly among industrialized countries? As in the case of explicit issue linkage, compensation might be more necessary in less integrated settings. Moreover, it is a key to solving capacity problems, which exist particularly in developing countries. Lack of capacity to implement transboundary river management policies may induce riparian countries to refuse river management agreements in the first place or to accept them but insufficiently implement these obligations (Bedarff et al. 1995). In integrated settings at high levels of economic development, more indirect linkages can serve to offset upstream-downstream asymmetries, and capacity problems are not as serious. In addition, bargaining over compensation arrangements is often complicated by information, monitoring, enforcement, and fairness issues (Morrow 1994; Albin 1993; Bedarff et al. 1995). Indeed, one of the only cases of direct compensation in Western countries occurred in the context of Rhine chloride pollution—a case likely to remain an exception.

These arguments suggest that upstream-downstream problems in developed countries and in integrated settings can often be resolved without explicit coercion, compensation, or issue linkage, a view that supports the previously defined structural arguments. This view also highlights the possibility that increasing integration—not necessarily vertical integration but primarily the growth of transboundary social interaction or the emergence of civil society—may facilitate the establishment and functioning of governance systems (see also chapters 1, 2, 3, and 10 in this volume). Solving upstream-downstream problems in developing countries and less integrated settings will, however, be more difficult. Coercion, direct issue linkage, or compensation might often be necessary to overcome upstream-downstream deadlocks. In most cases, coercion will not produce stable cooperation, as indicated by the Nile case, nor may issue linkage increase the possibilities of cooperation, particularly if capacity problems exist, the issues to be linked are complex, or linkage raises fairness and legitimacy problems. In addition, financial resources for compensation on a sufficient scale are usually not available in the developing world. These somewhat pessimistic propositions suggest that external funding must play a key role in transboundary river management in developing countries or economies in transition.

Changing Negotiating Forums and Bargaining Parties   In some cases, if victims of externalities are unable to obtain reductions from producers of these effects, they may carry the issue into bargaining forums more favorable to their cause. Normally they will choose forums where they can solicit the support of other countries or international agencies. Bangladesh, for example, was affected by an Indian dam project at Farakka. This dam reduced the water flow of the Ganges (needed for irrigation in the dry months), increased siltation and as a consequence flooding, and led to growing saltwater intrusion from the Bay of Bengal. Between 1968 and 1976, Bangladesh carried the issue into the UN General Assembly. In 1977, following a UN General Assembly statement, the two countries concluded an agreement that solved the problem of sharing the Ganges waters at least to some extent.

The change of the bargaining forum had clearly pushed India into a more moderate bargaining position.

In summary, the theoretical arguments and empirical examples in this section suggest that the likelihood of and the stability of cooperation, particularly if upstream-downstream river management problems are involved, are influenced by the following variables: the number of riparians; the homogeneity of their preferences; the level of development; the degree of integration among riparian countries; and the difficulties of bringing coercion, issue linkage, compensation, and other strategies to bear. These factors appear to explain why cooperation has generally been more frequent and has occurred earlier in Western countries. They also show why external financing plays a key role in determining the likelihood and stability of transboundary river management in developing countries and economies in transition.

Features of River Management and Performance

This section defines success in river management not merely in terms of whether countries are able to establish some form of cooperation but also in terms of whether some features of transboundary river management are likely to render these efforts more successful than others. This step moves the features of river management institutions from phenomena to be explained to explanatory factors. The performance of IRMIs, in some specific meaning of the term, becomes the outcome to be explained.

The performance of international river management is a multidimensional concept (Wettestad 1995; Young and von Moltke 1994; Bernauer 1995). Because this chapter does not aim at offering a rigorous comparative analysis, but rather at outlining an analytical framework for doing so, I can afford to operate on the basis of very crude assessments of performance. The following arguments rely on a notion of performance based on goal attainment as the evaluative yardstick — that is, the extent to which the goals that motivated the establishment of an IRMI are achieved.

No larger-scale comparative work analyzing the effects of institutional features on the performance of international environmental management efforts has so far been carried out (Young 1994a; Wettestad 1995). Some modest comparative studies are under way, but they continue to face daunting research design problems, including identifying and measuring indicators of effectiveness or some other type of outcome, identifying relevant institutional or organizational features, and controlling noninstitutional variables (Young and von Moltke 1994; Bernauer 1995). These problems have led some analysts to question the usefulness of such variation-finding analysis and to suggest more emphasis on tendency-finding analysis—in other words, more diagnostic and case-specific modes of research—which by nature produces few generalizable results (see chapter 10 in this volume). The literature on international river management is deficient in both types of research. Because tendency-finding analysis is in many ways more straightforward and both theoretically and methodologically less challenging than variation analysis, I focus here on the latter without denying the usefulness of the former.

Elinor Ostrom and her colleagues (1990) have carried out perhaps the most systematic analysis of the effects of particular features of institutions. They have found that long-enduring institutions for shared natural resources at the local level tend to be associated with the following: clearly defined boundaries; congruence between appropriation and provision rules and local conditions; collective-choice arrangements; monitoring; graduated sanctions; conflict-resolution mechanisms; minimal recognition of rights to organize; and nested enterprises (Ostrom 1990: 90). Some of these results remain contested and/or cannot be easily transposed to the international level (Taylor 1992). In the international relations literature, the following institutional features are often referred to as potential explanations of the effectiveness of institutions: type of rules (e.g., legally binding obligations versus recommendations, best available technology versus hard targets); scope of issues covered; number and composition of membership; openness to NGO involvement; nature of secretariats; decision-making rules; and verification and compliance mechanisms (Wettestad 1995; Bernauer 1995).

Which IRMI features account for variation in the performance of river management? As Wettestad notes (1995: 24), it might be worthwhile to "identify a limited set of 'specific' regime features as points of departure—acknowledging that such an identification to some extent must be arbitrary." To keep the task to manageable proportions, I discuss only six features of IRMIs. Although these features constitute a fraction of those features that might potentially affect the performance of river management, they are frequently mentioned in the literature on international river management. Moreover, we have at least some theoretical handle on them to the extent that they are related in particular ways to four key functions that IRMIs perform: they provide information, affect the incentives of riparians, provide procedures that may serve in overcoming constraints and conflicts, and affect the capacity and/or authority of riparians to tackle resource-use problems (Underdal 1990; Wettestad 1995: 24).[19] The six features are: the nature of property rights as constituted by an institution; the scope of IRMIs; the legal framework supporting river management efforts; financial transfers and other market instruments; monitoring arrangements; and the openness of river management to policy innovation.

Property Rights

As I previously noted, IRMIs can constitute rivers as international SNRs, or they can nationalize (privatize) rivers. The economics literature usually argues that the latter solution is associated with a better performance of resource management, a proposition based on two assumptions. First, countries and their population will be more careful not to overuse their own resource if the costs of overuse are more difficult to externalize. Because externalities occur when property rights are ill defined, they are likely to decrease when property rights are clearly defined and enforced. Second, if an international SNR is transformed into a national SNR and unsustainable use of the resource continues, it will be easier for individual governments to impose remedial policies than for international institutions to establish some sort of control over the international SNR.

Following this logic, many countries have tried to tackle fisheries problems by extending their jurisdiction—in other words, by appropriating areas of the sea that were hitherto an international SNR (Scott 1980). This action has in some cases succeeded. In other cases, it has imposed external effects on other countries as fishing fleets simply began to catch more fish outside the appropriated area. Or, it has failed because the hitherto international SNR was simply converted into a national SNR, and the government was unable to prevent the same "tragedy of the commons" from occurring at a lower level.

The Indus River basin is one of the rare cases in which a hitherto shared river system was divided up between the riparian countries. The tributaries and irrigation systems of the Indus were assigned to Pakistan and India in such a way that the resource consumption of one country would not affect the consumption of the other country. This solution has been widely regarded as economically inefficient and would probably not have materialized without the important financial support of international agencies. Also, it remains unclear whether this solution has in fact led to a more sustainable use of the now national freshwater resources. Nevertheless, the division of the river system has removed a major source of conflict between India and Pakistan and, at least from this perspective, may be regarded as successful.

Resolving river management problems by dividing up a shared river system has, however, not been emulated by the riparians of other transboundary rivers, mainly because the geography of these rivers has not allowed for such a solution. For example, if an upstream polluter is passing pollution costs to downstream countries (i.e, externalizing the costs), nationalizing the river as such does not necessarily internalize these costs and restore the correct price signals. Nationalization might also interfere with navigation, so most transboundary rivers have been explicitly constituted as international watercourses—that is, as SNRs (Frey 1993). Efforts to solve externality problems have therefore focused on defining property rights in terms of resource consumption (e.g., water withdrawals, pollution thresholds, etc.) rather than in terms of exclusive jurisdiction or control over the resource. Future research might concentrate on whether particular forms of property rights or mechanisms for assigning them (e.g., end of the pipe rules, environmental effect–oriented prescriptions, best available technology approaches, market versus non-market approaches) can account for variation in the performance in river management.

Scope of IRMIs

Riparians of transboundary rivers usually encounter more than one river management problem. Accordingly, the issues addressed by IRMIs can be manifold—including flood control, river traffic, irrigation, drainage, dredging, water quality and pollution, nature conservation, aesthetic management, flood plain management, and so on (Wessel 1993: 15). In their efforts to jointly manage the Senegal River, for example, the riparian countries of the area are facing problems of flood control as a result of two dam projects; they are having difficulty managing the construction and operation of these dams, as well as the associated hydropower facilities and irrigation schemes; and they must also deal with navigation issues (Horowitz et al., 1991).

Various river management issues can be dealt with by only one institution, or they may require the services of more than one institution. The riparians of the Senegal have dealt with all of the aforementioned issues in the framework of the Organization pour la Mise en Valeur due Fleuve Senegal (OMVS). Navigation and pollution control issues concerning the Rhine are dealt with by two separate institutions: the International Commission for the Navigation of the Rhine and the International Commission for the Protection of the Rhine against Pollution.

Deciding which issues are packed together or when and how to deal with them is rarely the result of rational and purposeful policys. It may depend on the substantive relationships among these issues; the timing of their appearance on the political agenda; the tactical considerations of negotiators; the institutional context, including the "repertoire" of preexisting organizations; and many other factors. Hence, it seems nearly impossible to define the scope of IRMIs in a general way. In most cases, however, IRMIs seem to evolve from more simple forms of water allocation management or navigation regulation into more complex schemes for pollution control and ecosystems management—as happened with the Rhine, for example.

The literature on international river management frequently distinguishes between integrated- and single-issue management by suggesting that the two methods have different levels of environmental effectiveness. Many experts tend to regard integrated-issue river management as the more promising approach, but whether it really performs better than single-issue management depends on a variety of conditions. Integrated management perhaps makes more sense from a ecological viewpoint, and it may also provide more opportunities for issue linkages, which may improve the possibilities of cooperation. On the other hand, integrated management significantly complicates negotiations and poses a greater challenge to the capacity of the actors involved. Consequently, we should remain skeptical about whether the scope of IRMIs in this respect has a decisive influence on the performance of river management.

Legal Framework

It is often argued that, besides nationalizing or privatizing international SNRs, effective environmental management will be enhanced by liability rules because they internalize externalities (e.g., pollution damage). Ideally, the possibility of successful liability claims will raise the polluter's expected costs to the point where it will be worthwhile to curb pollution or compensate victims even in the absence of legal action.

Several legal doctrines exist in international water law. The Harmon doctrine advocates absolute sovereignty of each riparian country over its part of a river. Another doctrine establishes absolute rights of riparian countries to the water, entitling the downstream country to an unaltered environment. Yet another doctrine stresses the community aspect of river basins by advocating the joint development and mutual respect of riparian countries. The most widely supported doctrine today is the doctrine of limited territorial sovereignty or equitable utilization. It allows for the use of water resources to the extent that such use does not harm other actors. As expressed in the documents of the 1972 Stockholm Conference and the Organization for Economic Cooperation and Development (OECD), it stresses the liability principle and the polluter pays principle, both of which imply the internalization of external effects. These principles have been supported by the International Law Commission, the International Law Association, and the Institut de Droit International (McCaffrey 1993: 98; Cano 1992).

In most areas of the world, however, the polluter pays principle does not carry much weight; moreover, victims of pollution are rarely in a position to obtain emission reductions from a polluter by threatening transboundary legal action. In contrast to the relatively well-developed (at least de jure) international liability rules regarding nuclear power production and maritime or landborne transport, the liability rules concerning transboundary freshwater are weak (Doeker and Gehring

1992). The only exception can be found in the European Union, where the European Court of Justice has ruled that any victim of pollution can take legal action against polluters either in victim or polluter countries.

The effect of the EU's legal framework is difficult to determine because it may influence outcomes either directly or through processes of anticipation. Despite several lawsuits in the Rhine chloride case (Romy 1990), in only one instance was small-scale compensation paid to the victims. In other cases, such as the toxic spill of 1986, the threat of legal action may have induced the Swiss chemical firm Sandoz to reach relatively generous out-of-court settlements rather quickly. In negotiations with firms upstream in Germany, France, and Switzerland, the city of Rotterdam has used the threat of legal action as one among several strategies to exert pressure on those upstream actors.

Whether threats or anticipation of legal action influence polluters enough to internalize external effects, and to what extent, would have to be determined through the analysis of decision-making processes, an analysis that cannot be undertaken in this chapter. However, there are reasons to be skeptical about the effectiveness of these methods. The Rhine case clearly shows that when threats of legal action have to be carried out, the situation is rarely as simple as it may seem. First, it is often difficult to find the smoking guns — that is, whether a particular actor has in fact emitted a specific substance at a given point in time and in what quantities. Second, even if such proof is possible, there may be (many) other actors emitting the same or a similar pollutant at the same time, thus making it difficult to determine which actor is responsible for the excess pollution that caused the damage. Third, the extent of damage may be difficult to express in monetary terms. For example, if crop damage is the issue, analysts will have to show what the crop and its value would have been if pollution had been lower, in the process controlling for exogenous variables, such as weather and market prices. Fourth, it is often unclear how clean the water should be that the victim is entitled to receive, particularly if the doctrine of equitable utilization is applied. As previously noted, this problem of ill-defined property rights is in fact the cause of externalities. Finally, in virtually all transboundary and national liability laws, only human beings possess entitlements to the resource. If plants and animals suffer damage, liability rules do not apply as long as no direct damage to human beings is involved.

In domestic politics, these difficulties were recognized some time ago, and proposals to solve environmental and resource-use problems solely through liability rules quickly gave way to more comprehensive approaches to environmental policy making. In brief, we should expect that although liability rules may contribute to a better performance of transboundary river management, they are not sufficient for internalizing external effects and solving conflicts over SNRs. This proposition is clearly in need of testing, however.

Financial Transfers and Other Market Instruments

As in most other cases of international resource and environmental cooperation, market instruments have so far played only a marginal role in managing international rivers. They have been restricted to liability rules and financial transfers (examples include the Rhine, Colorado, Indus, and most river development projects in developing countries). Other market instruments, such as taxes or tradable emission or water allocation permits, have not been employed. The Rhine is probably the most interesting case in this regard. As noted, efforts to manage this river have probably benefited from a rather well-developed liability framework. Several pollution stand-still or reduction agreements concluded by the Rhine riparians have defined pollution thresholds for individual countries and for branches of industry. The agreements on chloride pollution have even envisaged a possible redistribution of property rights, but these provisions never developed into a tradable pollution permit scheme. The Rhine case also involve joint international financing of pollution reductions (Bernauer 1996).

Financial transfers can facilitate international cooperation in the first place by influencing the recipients' preferences and capacities, but their effect is limited by problems in negotiating and implementing them. This proposition is substantiated by empirical research, and applies to transfers among riparians and to transfers from external sources to riparian countries (Bedarff et al. 1995; Keohane and Levy 1996).

There are good reasons to argue that financial transfers also have an impact on the performance of IRMIs, once they are established. Building financial transfer arrangements into IRMIs influences performance in two respects. First, they can help to solve capacity problems that might otherwise hamper the implementation of agreements. Second, they can, at least theoretically, enhance the cost efficiency of river management by financing pollution reductions or other management activities. Both propositions need to be tested, however. The only evidence we have, so far, is that financial transfers are instrumental in starting international river management, particularly in developing countries.

Monitoring

Most studies on SNR management argue that monitoring is a key task of institutions (Mitchell 1994a). In accordance with collective action theory, we should assume that the extent and performance of river management increase with the possibility of monitoring the behavior of riparian actors and their compliance with transboundary agreements.

Monitoring functions can be performed by international river agencies, by riparian countries, or even by private actors. The principal reasons for involving international agencies in monitoring activities are threefold. First, the international approach allows for standardized measurement techniques. Second, it is more legitimate and fair, particularly in the eyes of those whose behavior is being monitored. International agencies monitor everybody with the same techniques, whereas other types of agencies—NGOs, for example—tend to focus more on actors whom they regard as culprits. Third, funding agencies favor international monitoring within the framework of an IRMI, usually for reasons of legitimacy and accountability, and most notably in cases where rirarian countries are relatively poor and external funding is required for any significant monitoring activity. The constraints on international monitoring are that it requires explicit agreement by the riparian countries and that it often results in monitoring commitments convenient to the riparian countries, thus having very little impact on them. Individual governments or private agents tend not to have these constraints. It would seem, therefore, that the ideal case will involve both international and decentralized forms of monitoring.

International and decentralized monitoring are facilitated by two additional factors. First, when transboundary rivers are legally constituted as international SNRs, actors willing to monitor the behavior of riparians can, at least theoretically, do so much more easily than they can monitor the behavior of CFC producers, for example. Who withdraws how much water and which major point sources are responsible for how much pollution by which substance will then be easier to establish if the finances, technology, and know-how are available. In other cases, however, free movement on a river and the possibility of monitoring may be impaired by tense relationships between riparian countries. Second, both types of monitoring are likely to be more extensive in integrated settings, which increases the extent and performance of river management efforts.

A cursory review of transboundary river management efforts suggests that the above propositions are plausible. In cases where the extent of monitoring is small — that is, limited to international monitoring, or even absent — river management efforts tend to be more limited in terms of their scope, intensity, and probably performance. Examples of how limited monitoring affects management efforts include the Danube River before 1989 and the Mekong River until recently. In the case of managing the Rhine, widely regarded as more successful than the Danube or the Mekong cases, both international and decentralized monitoring is pervasive. For instance, the city of Rotterdam, Greenpeace, and the IAWR have conducted their own investigations of Rhine water quality at many different points along the river. At the international level, the Rhine Commission operates an ambitious monitoring program.

Openness to Policy Innovation

The final institutional feature to be discussed here pertains to the openness of transboundary river management to policy innovation. This feature extends our perspective from problem solving — in the extreme case, clear-cut and final solutions — to process management, which involves more incremental and piecemeal approaches to solving more complex and long-term problems (see chapter 10 in this volume). IRMIs tend to develop slowly over longer periods of time, which in principle enables riparians to experiment with various policy options. To allow for such experiments and learning processes, however, negotiating bodies and decision-making procedures have to be flexible and open to new ideas.

To date, the record for openness and flexibility is not very encouraging. Most IRMIs are based on conventional command-and-control measures, such as agreements that allocate percentages of a river's water to the various riparians or provide for the reduction of certain pollutants by agreed quantities or percentages. Decision makers have often focused on a narrow range of policy options and the most innovative steps in river management have frequently taken place outside the purview of IRMIs.

In combating chloride pollution of the Rhine, for example, the riparian countries settled, prematurely I would argue, on a policy option that took an extremely long time to put into practice and that eventually proved quite ineffective: the jointly financed reductions at a state-owned potash mine in France. Perhaps more innovative and effective options for curbing chloride pollution, such as a joint trust fund or bids by polluters and suppliers of reduction technology for reduction projects, were never even considered.

In other areas of Rhine pollution, the most innovative policies were usually initiated outside the International Rhine Commission. The city of Rotterdam, Dutch farmers, and Dutch waterworks, for example, engaged in lawsuits against upstream polluters and directly negotiated contracts on pollution reductions with upstream polluters. Only comparatively late, after many years of stalemate, the Rhine Commission abandoned its traditional approach of negotiating framework agreements with broad reduction targets and subsequently developed implementation protocols. Adopted in 1987, the Rhine Action Program provides for a more flexible approach based on a gentlemen's agreement that also involves general reduction targets. In contrast to earlier efforts, however, it addresses a broader range of pollution and ecosystems issues, directly engages specific industries, and is based on the principle of "best available technology." Many observers believe that this approach has worked better than the previous ones.

Arguably one of the more successful examples of transboundary river management, the Rhine case highlights several propositions that might be pursued in further research. It suggests that binding agreements and hard targets do not necessarily lead to a better performance of river management than softer and more flexible approaches, such as action plans. Also, because river management often involves a host of different resource problems and possible solutions, it is often useful to pursue multiple options that actively involve the principal stakeholders. Finally, the number of options and solutions that can be pursued by riparians at the transboundary level tends to increase with the degree of integration. Horizontal forms of integration, such as empowering nongovernmental actors, in particular appear to offer new and innovative avenues for addressing more complex problems of river management.

Conclusion

Neither the 1972 Stockholm conference nor the Brandt and the Brundtland Commissions, which are regarded as milestones in the international environmental debate, paid much attention to freshwater resources. Other environmental problems, such as desertification, deforestation, ozone depletion, global warming, or biodiversity clearly had higher places on the agenda.

By the mid-1990s the neglect of freshwater resource issues was significantly reversed due to two developments: (1) freshwater resources are becoming scarcer, and political conflict over these resources has increased steadily; and (2) scientists and policymakers have become more aware that many of the world's major environmental and resource problems—such as climate change, deforestation, food production, marine pollution, or energy supply—are interrelated and that these problems all have an impact on and, at the same time, are influenced by freshwater problems. Gleick (1993: 10) notes that "as we now look to the 21st century, several challenges face us. Foremost among them is how to satisfy the food, drinking water, sanitation, and health needs of ten or twelve or fifteen billion people, when we have failed to do so in a world of five billion."

Given its strong relationship to other environmental problems and to social conflict, freshwater scarcity will be one of the most serious environmental problems of the twenty-first century. It is hardly surprising, therefore, that water issues have moved into the "high" politics domain, where ambassadors are recalled in protest, heads of government get involved to deal with water crises, and even threats or use of military force occur. The demand for effective governance systems in this domain has clearly risen.

This chapter has discussed some of the causes of unsustainable use of transboundary rivers, the associated conflicts among riparians, and the factors that may influence the possibility of managing these rivers. It proceeds from the assumption that by itself, the analysis of organizational structures of international river commissions and international treaties, which dominates the literature on international rivers, will not sufficiently explain the emergence and performance of river management efforts. Such analysis requires a comprehensive look at the structures, actors, and processes whereby governance can be regarded as a social function that operates in a largely nonhierarchical setting. The "new institutionalism" in political science and economics, on which this chapter draws, provides a sound basis for this comprehensive look and also directs our attention to new and potentially more innovative approaches to governance. Larger-scale comparative research on international river management, however, remains to be undertaken (see note 8). The theoretical arguments, empirical illustrations, and propositions put forward in this chapter can give some guidance to such a research program.

The chapter suggests that the difficulties of transboundary river management increase with the heterogeneity of preferences among riparian actors (an extreme case being upstream-downstream asymmetries) and with the number of actors involved. These problems are, however, strongly mitigated by the degree of economic, social, and political integration among the riparians and by their level of development. Development and integration are, therefore, the best long-term recipes for success in transboundary river management.

IRMIs designed to nationalize hitherto international rivers can, in some rare circumstances, contribute to a more effective management of transboundary rivers, but this approach is often not feasible because the nature of the resource makes it impossible to internalize external effects.

The scope of IRMIs is not directly related to their performance. It seems, that although IRMIs designed to manage transboundary rivers in an integrated manner are probably more difficult to establish and operate, they may contribute to better performance of river management.

As the experience of environmental protection at the domestic level shows, sustainable management of transboundary rivers cannot be achieved solely through liability rules that operate across national boundaries. Nonetheless, such rules can enhance transboundary river management efforts.

Financial transfers can facilitate the establishment of IRMIs and the implementation of agreed upon measures when strong asymmetries of preferences and capacities are involved. The costs of designing and implementing financial transfers may be high, however. Market instruments other than financial transfers and liability rules have not been used so far.

Monitoring is indispensable for successful river management. To increase flexibility and coverage of monitoring, a broadly based monitoring activity by governmental and nongovernmental actors is desirable.

Openness of transboundary river management to policy innovation is crucial to performance. Decision makers should be careful not to close bargaining processes prematurely. Policy options should be kept open for debate as long as possible, and policy experiments should have a firm place in river management. Particularly in the case of more complex problems that involve attempts to deal with international rivers as ecosystems, process management instead of once-and-for-all solutions appears to be more appropriate. The framework convention and protocol approach does not necessarily perform better with difficult tasks than informal action programs. Neither do supranational solutions necessarily produce better results. Perhaps the greatest advantage of integrated settings and "civil society," which denotes the nongovernmental element of integration, is that they facilitate the pursuit of multiple options or solutions by a greater number of stakeholders.

How, then, can effective river management be fostered in less integrated settings, particularly in developing countries and in situations where upstream-downstream asymmetries are strong. First, international river commissions can reduce the costs of negotiating and implementing river management schemes. They may serve to curb the monopoly of governments on information about rivers and their management; they may also open the door for the involvement of nongovernmental stakeholders. Second, the creation of political symbols and prestige effects (e.g., turning a river into a national heritage or making the Rhine inhabitable for salmon) may increase the benefits to governments that might otherwise be less interested in transboundary river management. Third, capacity problems and problems of heterogeneous preferences can be addressed through external financing of river management efforts.

On a more general note related to global governance, this chapter raises questions about the extent to which systematic comparative research on river management is possible and sensible, and the extent to which the study of one issue area can produce findings relevant to governance in other issue areas. International rivers may be a more suitable topic for comparative analysis than, for example, such disparate issues as ozone depletion, fishery problems, and tropical deforestation. The cases discussed here also show, however, that transboundary rivers and efforts to manage them differ in many respects, which implies that comparisons are complicated because few variables can be held constant. Moreover, in order to be generalizable across different transboundary rivers or even beyond the issue area, propositions have to be highly abstract. The more abstract they are, however, the less valuable they are likely to be to decision makers who seek practical knowledge on how to manage transboundary rivers more effectively or sustainably.[20] The difficulties involved in such a trade-off between generalizability and policy relevance cannot be definitively solved, but they can to some extent be mitigated if research on the management of international rivers uses a combination of variation-finding and tendency-finding analysis (see chapter 10 in this volume). It seems, in any event, that some of the lessons of international river management may apply to other issue areas of international environmental politics.

Finally, this chapter suggests that the new institutionalism need not be conservative in the sense of focusing on and implicitly legitimizing the state system. On the contrary, the above discussion indicates that river management can strongly benefit from broader transformative processes in the international system. In particular, increasing social, economic, and political integration—which is not supranational in the traditional sense of governance, but is based on subsidiarity, decentralized action, and elements of what is often termed international society (see chapter 3 in this volume)—is likely to increase the performance of river management because it increases flexibility and leaves more room for the involvement of nongovernmental stakeholders. Conversely, transboundary river management may, at least to a small degree, also influence processes of transformation by opening up the possibilities for nongovernmental relations across national boundaries. Consequently, further research on transboundary rivers is likely not only to yield usable knowledge on how to manage freshwater resources more sustainably, but also to produce some insights on the evolving nature of the international system and on questions of governance.

7

Ecosystem Governance: Lessons from the Great Lakes

Marcia Valiante, Paul Muldoon, and Lee Botts

The Great Lakes basin is a significant international ecosystem. Shared between Canada and the United States, it contains approximately 20 percent of the Earth's fresh surface water and is home to some 35 million people as well as to intense industrial and agricultural development.[1] Significant environmental stress is also characteristic of the region, including eutrophication; contamination of all media from toxic substances; shoreline erosion with fluctuating water levels; interbasin and intrabasin diversion of waters; introduction of exotic species, such as zebra mussels; loss of native fish species; and loss of wetlands and biodiversity. New environmental stresses, such as climate change, continue to be identified.

Many of these stresses, particularly pollution-related stresses, have been apparent and have created conflicts in the bilateral relationship between Canada and the United States for the better part of this century. Despite the continued presence of significant pollution, however, the experience of Canada and the United States in governing the Great Lakes ecosystem is often cited as a model for international governance of a shared natural resource.[2]

A thorough analysis of all the elements of the governance regime in the Great Lakes is beyond the scope of this chapter. The recently completed report of a major research study about the Great Lakes Water Quality Agreement (Botts and Muldoon, 1996) provides a more complete analysis. It describes in detail the history of the regime and both identifies and discusses seven key characteristics of the regime that contribute to its effectiveness: promotion of community; binationalism; equality and parity in structure and obligations; adoption of common objectives; joint fact finding and research; flexibility to adapt to changing circumstances; and accountability and openness in information exchange (Botts and Muldoon 1996: chapter 4). Instead of discussing each of these characteristics separately, this chapter combines the themes of the larger study by focusing on three crucial elements that have allowed this regime to endure and make progress in improving environmental quality:

1. Binationalism in mechanisms for fact finding on contentious issues;

2. Substantive objectives of the regime that provide progressive direction and flexibility; and, most importantly;

3. Development of an influential binational "community" that is external to the formal regime and that enhances the legitimacy and accountability of the formal regime

This chapter suggests that, in combination, these essential elements have allowed this regime to flourish and make progress in cleaning up the Great Lakes.

The chapter begins with a description of the formation and operation of the formal regime as it has evolved to its present form. Next, it discusses the extent to which the regime has been effective and considers the reasons why it has been effective. Finally, it draws some conclusions as to the transferability of the Great Lakes experience to other internationally shared ecosystems or resources.

Formation and Operation of the Great Lakes Governance Regime: Legal and Institutional Framework

The Great Lakes environmental governance system is a complex but fairly well-integrated network of legal agreements, institutions, and organizations that started to develop in the last century. The legal foundations of the present environmental protection regime are the Boundary Waters Treaty of 1909 and the Great Lakes Water Quality Agreements (GLWQAs) of 1972 and 1978, as amended by a protocol in 1987.

The Boundary Waters Treaty

The Boundary Waters Treaty concluded between the United States and Great Britain (for Canada) in 1909 built upon earlier efforts to regulate rights of navigation and use of shared waters. The treaty sought to regularize the methods for dealing with the inevitable conflicts over uses of such waters.

The principles set out in the treaty include free navigation (Boundary Waters Treaty 1909: Article I), jurisdiction over use on each side of the border, and equal rights for injury caused by such use (Boundary Waters Treaty, 1909: Article II). Article IV states that boundary waters "shall not be polluted on either side to the injury of health or property on the other."

The treaty established the International Joint Commission (IJC) as the primary organization to carry out its purposes. The commission has three members from each country, appointed by the president of the United States and the Canadian Cabinet. All costs for operating the IJC are shared equally.

The commission was given four functions to realize its principal purpose of settling questions between the two countries involving rights, interests, or obligations "along the common frontier." First, the IJC has a quasi-judicial power of decision on applications to use, obstruct, or divert waters forming or flowing across the boundary when the flow or level of those waters would be altered. The treaty sets out guiding principles and an "order of precedence" of uses for the IJC to apply in deciding on these applications (Boundary Waters Treaty 1909: Articles III, IV, and VIII).

Second, the IJC has a "reference" or advisory function when the two governments apply to it regarding any "questions or matters of difference arising between them involving the rights, obligations, or interests of either in relation to the other or to the inhabitants of the other, along the common frontier" (Boundary Waters Treaty 1909: Article IX). Following an investigation, the commission submits a joint report to both governments that offers its conclusions and recommendations for action.

Third, the treaty gives the IJC the powers of a tribunal to decide any "questions or matters of difference" between the parties (Boundary Waters Treaty 1909: Article X). A decision made under this power is binding on the two governments. This authority has never been used, however, perhaps because ratification would be required by the U.S. Senate and such ratification would be very difficult to obtain.

Fourth, the commission is given a number of administrative functions with respect to the measurement and apportionment of two transboundary rivers, the St. Mary's and the Milk (Boundary Waters Treaty 1909: Article IV) and to the operation of control structures that allow limited regulation of levels in Lake Superior, Lake Erie, and Lake Ontario.

The first two functions have made up the bulk of the commission's work. About three-quarters of its cases before World War II were applications under the quasi-judicial power, mainly for purposes of navigation and of hydroelectric generation. Major developments in the basin include the St. Lawrence Seaway and damming of the Columbia River.

Use of the reference power to address major environmental issues has dominated the workload of the IJC in the second half of this century,[3] including major studies on air and water quality and on fluctuating water levels in the Great Lakes.[4] The 1964 reference on water quality in Lakes Erie and Ontario was the most important reference for development of the Great Lakes; it led directly to negotiation of the first Great Lakes Water Quality Agreement, signed in 1972.

By 1972, the IJC had an established method of operation and was well respected on both sides of the border. Its approach on a reference was to establish a study board with equal numbers of technical experts from each country (usually government agency personnel) to investigate the details of the issues and recommend options for action. The study board's conclusions and recommendations would then usually be adopted or sometimes modified by the commission in its recommendations to the two governments. The joint fact-finding approach was eventually incorporated into the day-to-day operations of the Great Lakes regime and became one of its most important elements.

The commission itself reaches its final decisions by consensus. Throughout its history, it has rarely been divided along national lines

(Carroll 1983: 49–50), thus operating as a truly "binational" institution. Although it has no power to implement its recommendations, its advice has been followed by the governments in most cases.

The Great Lakes Water Quality Agreements[5]

The first GLWQA was made in 1972 following IJC recommendations in the report on the 1964 reference concerning pollution in Lakes Ontario and Erie. The report concluded that extensive pollution of boundary waters was coming from both sides of the border to the detriment of health and the environment in the region. The two national governments decided to address the problem through an international agreement because of the strong binational scientific consensus, the unanimous recommendation by the IJC for a new agreement, and the strong expressions of public support for coordinated action. The agreement created a standing reference to the IJC under the Boundary Waters Treaty to study the Great Lakes' water quality, and it set out the principles, policies, and objectives needed to guide the two governments in their actions to clean up the Great Lakes. In effect, the agreement "breathed life into Article IV" of the Boundary Waters Treaty, which states that neither country should cause harm to the other by polluting boundary waters (Bourne 1974: 488).

The 1972 agreement largely addressed the issue of eutrophication, which had been highlighted in the report on the 1964 reference (GLWQA 1972: Article VII). The primary objective of the 1972 agreement was the reduction of the loadings of phosphorus, identified as the limiting nutrient that triggered excessive algal growth and ultimately the eutrophication that had caused Lake Erie to be declared "dead." Addressing only the improved treatment of municipal and industrial waste as the key to reducing phosphorus loadings, the agreement set an effluent limit on phosphorus for all sources — in both countries — discharging more than a million gallons a day.

The other important feature of the 1972 agreement was organizational: it placed the binational IJC in a central position with respect to research, data gathering, and oversight of agreement implementation. New binational bodies were created to assist the IJC in carrying out these functions, including the Great Lakes Water Quality Board, the

Science Advisory Board (known as the Research Advisory Board until 1978), and a Great Lakes Regional Office, which was established in Windsor, Ontario. The current regime is built upon this organizational foundation, although a second revised agreement in 1978 provides the central substantive directives.

Under the 1978 agreement, the governments committed themselves to an "ecosystem approach"—that is, to an approach that views the entire Great Lakes basin as an integrated ecosystem, thus requiring cooperative efforts not just on water quality, but also on sediments, air pollution, and land-based activities. The agreement's overall goal is "to restore and maintain the chemical, physical, and biological integrity of the waters of the Great Lakes Basin Ecosystem" (GLWQA 1978: Article II). To achieve this purpose, a number of policies are to be followed: the "discharge of toxic substances in toxic amounts [is] prohibited," and "the discharge of any or all persistent toxic substances [will] be virtually eliminated" (GLWQA 1978: Article II). The agreement then enunciates a number of general objectives and specific water quality objectives, and in a series of annexes, it details actions for a number of programs.

The IJC was given several roles and responsibilities, to help it implement the agreement's objectives:

1. To collate, analyze, and disseminate data pertaining to the quality of Great Lakes water and to the general and specific objectives under the agreement and all adopted measures

2. To verify independently any data or information given to it by the parties

3. To tender advice and make recommendations to the parties on all matters relating to Great Lakes water quality—including objectives, legislation, standards, programs, and other measures, covered by the annexes and regarding research needs

4. To provide assistance in the coordination of the joint activities under the agreement

5. To assess the effectiveness of programs and other measures established under the agreement and to review and report biennially on progress toward achieving the goals of the agreement

6. To investigate matters referred to it by the parties.[6]

The 1987 protocol amending the 1978 agreement effected a number of changes. First, it made the regime more comprehensive by adding a number of issue areas for which the parties were to initiate specific programs, including contaminated groundwater, sediments, and airborne toxic substances (GLWQA Protocol 1987: Annexes 16, 14, and 15). Second, it adopted new, common means for addressing more localized issues: the Remedial Action Plans for local "areas of concern" and the Lakewide Management Plans for each of the lakes (GLWQA Protocol 1987: Annex 2). In the Remedial Action Plans, if agreement objectives are not being achieved in a contaminated area (such as a bay or harbor), the problems are to be identified, options for remedial actions studied, and then efforts to implement those remedial measures made. The Lakewide Management Plans operate in a similar way on a lake-by-lake basis.

Third, the protocol initiated direct activities between the parties that realigned their relationships with the IJC under the agreement. Most importantly, the parties were required to undertake "jointly" a number of tasks that the IJC had previously done.[7] This requirement led to the establishment of a Binational Executive Committee consisting of representatives of federal agencies from each country. This committee has sponsored two activities to date: a biennial State of the Lakes Ecosystem Conference and the development of a draft binational toxics strategy (Environment Canada and U.S. Environmental Protection Agency 1996). To accomodate all these changes, the function of the advisory structures within the commission was changed.

In summary, the formal organizational elements of the regime include the IJC—a long-standing, binational, generalist organization that has been adapted to take on a particular role in the Great Lakes. Through its subordinate structures, its role involves data gathering and analysis, national program assessment, policy formulation, and provision of information to the public.

Implementation of the agreement is the responsibility of the two national governments. State and provincial governments are not parties to the formal agreements, but they do participate in the regime in many capacities from data gathering to program implementation. The roles of all these actors were fairly constant until recently when the 1987 protocol implemented certain changes.

Effectiveness of the Great Lakes Governance Regime

The regime that evolved in the Great Lakes around these formal arrangements is a dynamic one with continual activity conducted by the primary organizations and by committed and active informal constituencies. The complex factors that allowed the regime as a whole to develop and contribute to progress in restoring environmental quality to the ecosystem make it difficult to isolate singular causes and effects.[8] Nevertheless, Botts and Muldoon (1996: chapter 4) concluded that the Great Lakes regime has been "effective" according to the criteria proposed for evaluation of international regimes[9] and the criteria they developed in their study. They reached this conclusion despite the fact that the problem of toxic substances in the ecosystem has yet to be completely "solved."

The regime is rightly considered effective for several reasons. First, it has made progress toward its stated goals. The goals of the 1972 agreement — that is, the reduction of phosphorus loadings and slowing of eutrophication — have been achieved. The vast majority of large municipal sewage treatment systems in both countries have achieved the effluent limit; moreover, the total target loadings set for each lake and the target levels of concentration set for the open waters have by and large been maintained for at least ten years.

Although the goals of the 1978 agreement — in particular, the virtual elimination of persistent toxic substances from the ecosystem — have not be fully realized, progress has been made. This incomplete success to date is not due to any lack of effort. The regime created by the agreement has spawned important research initiatives that have increased scientific understanding of not only the effects of exposure to toxics but also the complexity and intractability of the problems. In addition, programs developed to carry out the formal requirements of the agreement have led to dramatic reductions in the loading of many toxic substances into the ecosystem.

Second, the regime has been effective because it is largely responsible for dramatic changes in behavior over the last twenty-five years. Governments have committed significant resources to studying the ecosystem and to carrying out clean-up programs, and industries have responded by changing their polluting practices. The agreement has been a catalyst for greater commitments of resources for research and program development; it has also prompted innovative federal, provincial, and state policies and regulatory programs that are specifically tailored to this region but that have led the way for more general toxics management in both countries. Other participants in the regime, particularly environmental and citizens organizations, have also invested energy, resources, and innovative ideas in achieving the goals of the regime.

Third, the regime has been effective in the sense that the parties have adopted the agreement's objectives into their domestic policies, programs, and laws. Although they are not parties to the agreement, states and provinces have also adopted laws and programs consistent with agreement objectives.

Fourth, the regime has contributed to stability in U.S.-Canadian interactions over potentially divisive environmental issues. Despite serious disagreements at times, the two countries (as well as some states and provinces) have continued to participate in the structures of the regime. These structures—namely, both the IJC and newer bilateral arrangements—have provided a depoliticized forum for discussing and resolving these differences.

Three characteristics of this regime have been essential to its effectiveness: common fact finding; progressive and flexible substantive objectives i.e., (the ecosystem approach and the virtual elimination of persistent toxics); and a process that has allowed for broad participation and has fostered the development of a strong Great Lakes community. In combination, these characteristics have led to a balance of power between Canada and the United States that has allowed progress to be made. Whether the balance can be maintained with the changes now underway and whether other changes may be necessary to meet existing and future challenges are questions considered in the larger study made by Botts and Muldoon (1996).

Common Fact Finding

As noted, the Boundary Waters Treaty resulted from the desire to facilitate dispute settlement and to avoid prolonged conflicts along the international border. The GLWQA maintains this objective and gives the IJC the additional role of evaluating the progress of the parties in achieving agreement goals. The routine reporting of progress by the commission is designed to make the parties more accountable for their actions or inaction. It also provides an important source of information to the general public and establishes a forum for "binational" negotiation, discussion, and problem solving.

The IJC has no power to enforce the agreement, implement programs, or order any actions. However, its power to collect, verify, analyze, and disseminate information on all aspects of both the ecosystem and government actions has provided a sound, independent information base that leaves governments exposed and empowers the environmental sector to press for greater efforts. Its ability not only to identify problems but also to make recommendations (which are most often derived from and supported by its advisory boards, some of whose members are government agency staff) has given the IJC an important policy development function, even if its recommendations are not fully adopted by the parties. This function has been a crucial component of progress in Great Lakes governance.

Whether the commission is working to avoid or settle disputes or to enhance governmental accountability and policy development, the key mechanism that makes it effective in these roles has been the provision of a binational forum for data collection and technical analysis. Both the Boundary Waters Treaty and the GLWQA presume that common fact finding by the parties within the framework of the binational commission will depoliticize many sensitive or controversial bilateral issues. In most instances, the parties need to agree on the definition of a problem and on its possible solutions before implementation of specific solutions can begin. Many commentators have regarded the key role of the commission as a "conflict dampening, technically oriented, fact-finding, advisory bilateral body."[10]

The common fact-finding approach[11] is manifest in the GLWQA, which requires the commission to report every two years to the governments on progress toward achieving agreement objectives. Until the 1990s, the commission based its progress assessment on reports from its advisory bodies: the Water Quality Board, the Science Advisory Board, and the Council of Great Lakes Research Managers. Each of these bodies is composed of equal numbers of Canadians and Americans.

In common fact finding, experts from each country—acting in their personal and professional capacities and not as representatives of their home agencies—attempt to define the problem and fashion solutions while insulated from narrow political and other interests that often pervade international negotiations. Historically, these bodies have prided themselves on the fact that their members—drawn largely from federal, state, and provincial agencies—have achieved their objectives. There is ample testimony that the result of this approach in the Water Quality Board (WQB) was the development of an esprit de corps among government officials, which has often allowed them to advance positions that reflect their expertise rather than their agency allegiance (Carroll 1983: 61; Willoughby 1979: 55–56; Cohen 1975: 257; Ross 1974: 240). In the twenty-five year history of the agreement, there developed a strong core of agency experts who took back to their home agencies their allegiances to the Great Lakes. This approach likely influenced national agendas and allowed specific agencies to pursue a Great Lakes program that differed from national programs. Often in the past, advisory boards were comprised of key managers of environmental programs of the responsible agencies. If the binational process convinced them of a course of action, they were particularly well placed to further that course of action in their own jurisdiction. In this way, the international forum served as a lever to initiate change in domestic arenas.

The expectation that WQB members could actually serve independently of agency affiliations was suspect and heavily criticized virtually from the inception of the agreement. The criticism came from scholars, independent researchers, environmental advocacy groups, and the IJC itself. Others, including members, however, have loyally voiced their belief in the integrity and success of the board. In fact, it may have been the intense scrutiny of the suspected conflict between agency affiliation and board membership that helped the board work successfully. In any case, the WQB clearly helped forge the technical consensus on which IJC recommendations and the two parties' remedial programs were based for twenty years.

Since the early 1990s, a number of changes have been made to the common fact-finding approach, in part due to criticisms of it,[12] whose consequences remain to be seen. One of the more controversial, albeit subtle, changes pertains to how and from whom the IJC receives information, technical data, and advice. In addition, the 1987 protocol altered the coordination process by requiring the agencies who represent the parties to meet twice a year to coordinate their workplans, to evaluate any progress made, and to report this evaluation to the IJC (GLWQA Protocol 1987; Article X, Section 3). The intent of the alteration was to increase government accountability and to allow the commission to make more of an arm's length assessment of the parties' programs.

Up to the early 1990s, the Water Quality Board, as the principal IJC advisor, undertook two tasks. First, it provided a comprehensive "state-of-the-lakes" report that collected data and analyzed progress made in improving the quality of the Great Lakes. These often lengthy reports, which sometimes included several appendices, provided the binational technical consensus as to what was going right or wrong in the Great Lakes. Second, the WQB reviewed the parties' legislative and policy initiatives directed at achieving the goals of the agreement. In completing both tasks, the members of the board evaluated the findings through negotiation so that the outcome usually did appear to be independent.

Now, the WQB no longer provides technical data in the form of state-of-the-lakes reports or programmatic assessments to the commission. Instead, Environment Canada and the U.S. Environmental Protection Agency (EPA) sponsor a State of the Great Lakes Ecosystem Conference (SOLEC) that alternates every year with the IJC's own biennial meetings, which are open to the public. SOLEC is intended to gather and analyze information necessary for the parties to submit a joint report to the IJC on the state of the lakes.

SOLEC was created and workplans were coordinated through the Binational Executive Committee because the lead government agencies felt that the IJC boards and committees required too many resources, especially personnel, and that there was inadequate recognition of the contribution of the parties. Also, environmentalists supported the new arrangement as a means of increasing accountability for government actions or inaction by requiring them to report directly to the IJC rather than indirectly through the WQB.

Concerns have been raised about the consequences of these new arrangements. Technical experts and program managers no longer have the opportunity to step out of their parochial roles in working jointly to reach consensus. Instead, they always act as agency representatives, which potentially undermines their ability to reach consensus and likely influences the nature of that consensus.

Another concern about the new arrangement is whether the IJC and the public are receiving enough information and whether sufficient data are being collected and analyzed to allow independent scrutiny of the effectiveness of programs. Now that the WQB is limited to providing policy advice, no independent process is in place to determine what programs need to be undertaken by the parties.

Still another concern is whether the IJC retains the capacity to evaluate the information that comes from the parties. Without assistance from its own advisory boards, the IJC is hampered in its ability to verify independently and to analyze whatever data are submitted. The commission attempted to deal with this issue in part by establishing a Task Force on Ecosystem Indicators charged with developing a methodology to supplement information and results derived from SOLEC (IJC Task Force 1996).

Finally, it is of concern whether Canada will still be able to influence the Great Lakes agenda because, with the altered role of the WQB, it has lost an important binational forum where it participated equally with the United States.[13] In the WQB, Canada previously had the ear of U.S. decision makers. Now, in a subtle but important change, the two governments meet outside of the binational forum. But despite these recent changes, common fact finding remains crucial to the continued effectiveness of the Great Lakes regime.

Substantive Objectives

Progress under the Great Lakes regime is also due to the adoption of particular substantive objectives that were expansive enough to allow evolution of the regime as information revealed changing concerns. The GLWQA sets out a number of general environmental goals as well as specific numerical objectives for individual pollutant levels. The principles reflected in the general goals have allowed the regime the flexibility to evolve over time while providing the public and the developing Great Lakes community with powerful concepts around which to organize and advocate. The agreement allows for flexibility because it only specifies *what* the goals and objectives are; it does not specify *how* each jurisdiction should achieve those goals. The two most important objectives are discussed in the next two sections.

The Ecosystem Approach   One of the most important contributions of the GLWQA is the adoption of an ecosystem approach in 1978.[14] This approach is not specifically laid out in the GLWQA but is necessarily implied in the definition of the boundaries of the regime as the "Great Lakes Basin Ecosystem."[15] The adoption of the ecosystem approach has had three general impacts on the regime.

First, by this definition, the scope of the regime expanded from the waters of the Great Lakes to the entire drainage basin, which is more than twice the size of the lakes themselves, and to all interconnecting biophysical and social components therein. Expansion of the scope of the regime to include the entire range of human activities on land—from agriculture to urban development—and in the air or underground, has made the regime more comprehensive. The title "GLWQA" is thus misleading because the agreement now goes far beyond water quality alone.

Second, the ecosystem concept not only imports a multimedia perspective that requires consideration of the interactions of water, air, and land in the physical environment, but also embraces issues of human health, economy, culture, and ecology.[16]

The third and perhaps most important effect of adopting an ecosystem approach to Great Lakes governance was to define a new zone or entity for governance. With the agreement, the Great Lakes basin took on greater significance as an identifiable region for both governments and nongovernmental actors alike (Manno 1993: 31). Certainly, the basin has long been recognized as a focus for numerous institutions, not affiliated with GLWQA institutions, including more than twenty binational governance arrangements, pertaining to Great Lakes issues.[17] However, formal adoption of the ecosystem approach coincided with greater awareness of the links between environmental and economic well being and of the limits of political boundaries; it also catalyzed enormous interest and momentum for protection of the basin as a whole. Recognition of the Great Lakes as an ecosystem provided an important foundation for the development of numerous new governmental and nongovernmental organizations, of coordinated and innovative scientific investigation, and, for lack of a better term, of an ecosystem ethic that began to pervade the legal and political culture of the regime and its participants.

The importance of the ecosystem principle should not be overstated, however. It has not turned the basin into a new state where political boundaries no longer matter. It has not led to an immediate cleanup of sites or stopped industry from polluting. Nevertheless, the ecosystem concept has provided the framework whereby the ecologically defined region is recognized as having common environmental, economic, political, and social concerns and strengths. As the concept has expanded, it has in effect become the prism through which present and future actions are viewed and evaluated.

Under the ecosystem approach, coordinating work that pertains to water quality with work that pertains to other stresses on the Great Lakes has been difficult under the agreement. Contrary to its recognition of the need for an ecosystem approach to address water quality, the agreement does not address certain related issues such as fisheries management, the introduction of exotic species, and the loss of habitat and biodiversity. Both public interest groups and the IJC have argued, though, that the agreement need not be renegotiated. The IJC commented that "the Agreement's purpose, objectives, and programs remain a firm foundation for the work that is needed to restore and maintain the Great Lakes Ecosystem. The Agreement provides a legitimate framework for economic and social futures that are sustainable and supportive of human life and prosperity" (IJC 1992: 45–46). Despite this view, regime participants continue to make efforts to fashion common principles that apply to a fuller range of issues affecting the Great Lakes ecosystem—for example, the Ecosystem Charter developed by the Great Lakes Commission (Great Lakes Commission 1994).

Recognizing the Great Lakes basin as an ecosystem has also led, at least in part, to the recognition that more specific laws and programs may be needed in the region. For example, in the United States the federal Clean Water Act was amended by the Great Lakes Critical Programs Act of 1990 to require the U.S. EPA to carry out programs considered necessary for achieving GLWQA objectives. The Great Lakes Water Quality Initiative is an attempt to fashion common guidance for the eight Great Lakes state governments in setting water quality standards.[18]

The Goal of Virtual Elimination   One of the most important but controversial objectives of the GLWQA is found in Article II—namely that "the discharge of any or all persistent toxic substances be virtually eliminated." This goal was adopted when understanding of the effects of persistent toxic chemicals was still in its formative stages and the notion of their virtual elimination from the environment had few precedents.

In Annex 12 to the 1978 GLWQA, the parties agreed that the goal of "virtual elimination of persistent toxic substances" was to be accomplished by control of releases based on a "philosophy" of "zero discharge." Although this goal was derived from U.S. domestic legislation, its meaning for the binational context was vague. As a result, in order to address the significant problems caused by toxic contaminants in the Great Lakes, the regime has had to define more specifically what it meant by "zero discharge" and address the inherent limitations of the existing regulatory approach in achieving it. Led by the work of environmental groups, the development of a strategy for virtual elimination has become a major issue on the binational agenda.[19] In addition, to serving as a benchmark for measuring progress under the GLWQA, the concept of zero discharge has become a focal point in nongovernmental efforts to organize and motivate Great Lakes citizens to participate in and influence the direction of the regime.[20]

An understanding of what is meant by "virtual elimination" is derived not only from the agreement but also from the commentary and interpretation of the IJC. In its biennial reports, the IJC has provided direction and policy innovation in providing advice and recommendations to the parties. The recommendations that breathe meaning into the objective of virtual elimination include the need for a reverse onus, the furtherance of a weight of evidence approach, the development of a "sunsetting" regime, and—the most controversial recommendation— the call to eliminate chlorine as a feedstock.

The *reverse onus* concept was developed by the commission as a preventive principle that would assist in implementing the goal of zero discharge. As stated by the commission, "when approval is sought for the manufacture, use or discharge of any substance which will or may enter the environment, the applicant must prove, as a general rule, that the substance is not harmful to the environment or human health." (IJC 1990: 21) The *Eighth Biennial Report* reiterated the call for a reverse onus approach (IJC 1996: 17). Although the idea of a "weight of evidence" approach was discussed in earlier reports, the *Sixth* and *Seventh IJC Biennial Reports* elaborated on the approach (IJC 1992: 22; IJC 1994: 10) by responding to the challenge of how to make legislative and policy decisions in the face of scientific uncertainty.[21]

Moreover, in its *Sixth Biennial Report*, the IJC recommended the adoption of a *sunsetting* approach to the most harmful toxic substances. Sunsetting is a systematic process designed to restrict, phase out, or even ban designated substances from manufacture, use, transport, and re- lease.[22] The process involves the development of criteria (e.g., persist- ence of a chemical in the environment) that, if met, would engage the framework for chemical phase-out. Although sunsetting is not necessar- ily a new process, the IJC did adapt it to the circumstances of the Great Lakes basin and recommended to the parties that it be applied to the entire ecosystem.

In the *Sixth Biennial Report*, the IJC extended the sunsetting concept beyond individual substances to classes or families of substances and to industrial feedstocks. In doing so, the IJC made one of its most controversial recommendations: the use of chlorine and chlorine-con- taining compounds be phased out over time.[23] This particular recom- mendation had a number of important consequences[29] First, industry was galvanized into fighting against the recommendation, which ensured that its voice was heard by the IJC. Second, considerable scientific debate was fuelled, which in turn raised the overall issue of how to make public policy decisions in the face of scientific uncertainty.[25] Third, those opposing the recommendation argued that the process the commission had followed in developing the recommendation was inappropriate and that there was an insufficient justification for the recommendation.

The IJC has deflected such criticism and vigorously defended its procedures and recommendations. In fact, it has reiterated its support for the recommendation in the subsequent two biennial reports with unabated enthusiasm.[26] Public interest groups continue to support the IJC for its bold, comprehensive approach to the problem and to advocate the acceptance and implementation of the recommendation (Great Lakes United 1995) The chlorine recommendation remains an important issue not only in the work of the IJC and in the Great Lakes area, but also around the world, as the use of chlorine continues to be debated in Europe, North America, and elsewhere.

There is little doubt that the goal of zero discharge has driven policy development and, perhaps less so, legislative change at all levels of government in Canada, although these developments have not completely fulfilled IJC recommendation. For example, in 1992 the federal government initiated multistakeholder discussions on the concept. Industry then initiated a voluntary program aimed at reducing or eliminating targeted chemicals.[27] In 1994, the federal and Ontario governments concluded a new Canada-Ontario Agreement that contained a strategy for implementation of the GLWQA in Canada. The strategy identifies specific substances whose use is to be phased out (Canada-Ontario 1994). In addition, although heavily criticized by environmental groups, the federal government initiated a Chlorine Substances Action Plan (Environment Canada 1995) in an attempt to respond to the IJC's recommendation in its *Sixth Biennial Report* to "develop timetables to sunset the use of chlorine and chlorine-containing compounds as industrial feedstocks and that the means of reducing or eliminating other uses be examined" (IJC 1992: 30). In June 1995 the federal government released its Toxic Substances Management Plan (Canada 1995a), which establishes the criteria for identifying substances that are toxic, bioaccumulative, and persistent and therefore candidates for virtual elimination.[28]

More recently, a parliamentary committee called for a new program to phase out use of persistent toxic contaminants within a set timeframe, a program that is supported by a range of measures in the Canadian

Environmental Protection Act (House of Commons 1995). However, the government response to the *Sixth Biennial Report* (Canada 1995a) has called for a less ambitious series of amendments to the legislation.[29] Nevertheless, the response does accept the need to virtually eliminate substances of concern and to incorporate the key components of the *Toxic Substances Management Plan.*

Ontario's primary legislative program pertaining to water quality — the Municipal-Industrial Strategy for Abatement (MISA) — adopted as its goal the "virtual elimination" of toxic substances. (Ontario Ministry of the Environment 1986). Moreover, the province has used the agreement as a rationale to develop a list of substances to phase out (Ontario Ministry of Environment and Energy 1993) and to introduce new pulp and paper regulations that also require virtual elimination of toxic substances.

In the United States, federal and state programs have been developed that attempt to implement the goal of virtual elimination, including the Great Lakes Critical Programs Act of 1990 and the Great Lakes Water Quality Initiative. The act formalized a cooperative process between U.S. EPA and the Great Lakes states to reform water quality standards and to implement these standards so that they are made consistent among all the states and move toward virtual elimination of persistent toxics. Adopted in 1993, the initiative defined the criteria each state was to use in developing new water quality standards. Other programs or projects of the U.S. EPA include a virtual elimination pilot project, a mass balance study of toxic contaminants in Lake Michigan, and demonstration projects on treatment technologies for contaminated sediments.

Despite the attention to the issue, the goal of virtual elimination of persistent toxic substances has not been reached. Although the levels of some toxic contaminants declined in the 1970s, the levels of other toxics rose slightly in the 1980s, probably because of the growth of long-range atmospheric sources (National Research Council and Royal Society of Canada 1985). Few substances in either the United States or Canada have actually been banned. Moreover, although total pollution releases have declined significantly, the quantities present in and still being discharged in the ecosystem are substantial. When Environment Canada combined data from its new emissions inventory with an existing U.S. emissions inventory, the result showed that more than 173,000 metric tonnes of emissions were still being released to the Great Lakes environment (Environment Canada 1995a).

Governments continue to publish fish consumption guidelines that outline what quantities of fish are safe to eat. As noted in a 1990 study, the "edible portions of fish tissue in the larger specimens of some Lake Ontario sportfish—most frequently salmon and trout—exceed Canadian and/or U.S. standards for PCBs, mirex, chlordane, dioxin, 2,3,7,8-TCDD and mercury. They also exceed more stringent U.S. Environmental Protection Agency guidelines for hexachlorobenzene, DDT and metabolites and dieldrin" (Colborn et al. 1990: 98).

These examples remind us that achieving virtual elimination will be difficult, costly, and time consuming because it requires more than simply phasing out a few substances. Instead, it calls for a larger, more involved transition by society to cleaner production technologies and sustainable materials, a move that could take more than one generation of technology change and that involves rethinking of industrial policy. Although some substances and classes of substances can be dealt with quickly and efficiently, eliminating the use of others will require the development of alternative methods and a fundamental change in industrial processes.[30]

Another reason why virtual elimination will be difficult is that scientific understanding of effects of toxic chemicals has expanded since the 1970s. Although the concern about cancer risks remains, additional evidence has been found that some substances can affect reproduction and development of both wildlife and humans.[31] Scientists still do not understand exactly how the hormonal effects occur or which substances act as so-called "hormone copycats," however.

Elements of the toxics problem are intractable in the short term. The fact that a considerable proportion of Great Lakes contamination comes from sources outside the drainage basin speaks to the need for continental and global conventions for problems that cannot be dealt with regionally. In the past the IJC has recognized the need to address sources of contaminants outside the Great Lakes region but has recently heightened activity in this regard. For instance, there are proposals for the United Nations Environment Program to commence formal negotiations for an international agreement on persistent organic pollutants (POPs). Discussions are already underway to expand the Economic Commission for Europe's (ECE) Convention on the Long-Range Transport of Air Pollution to include POPs. Further, the Commission on Environmental Cooperation (an institution created by a side agreement to the North American Free Trade Agreement) is in the process of furthering Resolution 95/5, which is intended to develop workplans in each member country to reduce four specific pollutants—DDT, PCBs, chlordane, and mercury. The control of these substances is of obvious importance to the water quality of the Great Lakes.[32] Finally, the problem of reservoirs of pollutants located in contaminated sediments, soils, and stored chemicals speaks to the need to develop safe remediation and disposal options that, at the present time, are still being researched and developed.[33]

Despite the fact that the goal of virtual elimination is yet to be fully realized, it has been enormously important. It has influenced national, provincial, and state law and policy and has altered corporate behavior. It can also be reinterpreted as new data, problems, and solutions emerge, thus allowing flexibility in the operation of the regime.

Informal Governance Structures: A Great Lakes Community

Reference to formal governance structures reveals only part of the story of governance in the Great Lakes regime. It is also necessary to discuss how the vitality and relevance of the regime depend on nongovernmental participation and on a broad community that includes government personnel, scientists and technical experts, and environmental activists. This chapter and the larger study from which the research is derived argue that the formal regime and the community have developed a synergy that is the most important factor contributing to the regime's effectiveness in improving Great Lakes water quality. That is, a strong and diverse nongovernmental community developed as a result of the formal structures, and the formal structures have been energized and legitimized because of the continuing active involvement of that community.

After the GLWQA was adopted, the Great Lakes became a focus of interest and action for a diverse range of associations, organizations, and individuals, which together constitute the Great Lakes community. By community, we mean a network of interests or constituents who share a common interest in Great Lakes issues and who devote their time, resources, and energy toward these issues because they believe it is important to do so. Some constituents focus on local or regional issues, others on basin-wide issues — thus paralleling the agreement, which creates different levels of public involvement: basin wide (through the boards and the biennial meeting); regional (through the Lakewide Management Plans; and local (through the Remedial Action Plans). Some constituents participate occasionally, others on a full-time basis. In this section, we consider a number of the more important components of the community — except governmental agencies, even though they are part of the community.

One of the oldest and most influential components of the Great Lakes community is the scientific sector. Since the 1950s and 1960s, U.S. and Canadian scientists with an interest in the Great Lakes have worked together to advance knowledge about the basin and its ecological decline (National Research Council and Royal Society of Canada 1985: 113–114). Since the late 1950s, scientists have shared and publicized their research in an annual conference. In 1968, the International Association for Great Lakes Research (IAGLR) was formed to coordinate this conference, to assist scientific investigation, and to publicize these investigations in a journal. Through the 1964 reference to the IJC, the joint work of both academic and government scientists formed the basis for government action in establishing and refining the Great Lakes Water Quality Agreement, and their influence has expanded since the agreement was adopted in 1972.

Scientists from both countries have had a strong presence within formal agreement structures and a high level of influence on the direction of the regime. The working boards of the IJC and the regional office relied on and promoted strong links with Great Lakes scientists. Some scientists have been members of the advisory boards, but advancement of the regime has also depended on continuing research and on workshops in which the research community, including nonscientists, took an active role. This work was instrumental in the adoption of the ecosystem approach in the 1978 agreement. Moreover, in 1985 an independent review of the agreement by the U.S. National Academy of Sciences and the Royal Society of Canada strongly influenced the parties in the formal review that led to the adoption of the 1987 protocol.

Environmental and citizens' organizations are a second important component of the Great Lakes community (Manno 1993; Becker 1993). Hundreds of such organizations have at least some interest in the Great Lakes and most of these are small, locally based groups with few resources. Despite varied interests, more than two hundred of them have joined together to form a binational coalition known as Great Lakes United (GLU). Formed in 1983, GLU became an active and influential participant in Great Lakes governance to the extent that it was allowed to participate in the formal negotiations for the 1987 protocol amending the agreement. Because they are part of this influential coalition, smaller environmental and citizens organizations have gained a broader perspective, basin-wide contacts, and the ability to participate in many agreement processes.

The environmental sector of the community is also characterized by the presence of large, long-established national environmental organizations such as the Sierra Club and the National Wildlife Federation in the United States and such as Pollution Probe and the Canadian Environmental Law Association in Canada. Although these organizations work on many issues in many regions, they have included Great Lakes issues as a focus of their work, especially since the mid-1980s. The community also includes strong regional organizations such as the Lake Michigan Federation and the Societé pour le Vaincre de Pollution in Quebec. Recreational users associations, such as Michigan United Conservation Council and the Ontario Federation of Anglers and Hunters, also play an important role, both on their own and as part of the GLU.

Environmental organizations participate in the regime by monitoring and publicizing the parties' progress in implementing the agreement's principles and requirements—processes very similar to the IJC's formal review. They actively participate in the IJC and in Agreement activities and events; they work to influence domestic policy agendas in ways favorable to achievement of regime principles; and they organize and educate citizens about the agreement's ecosystem approach to management and its goal of zero discharge. Generally led by trained, knowledgeable individuals who work closely with scientists and other experts, environmental nongovernmental organizations (NGOs) have had a significant influence on the progressive direction of the regime. For example, their views about the need for more aggressive action on toxic contaminants are reflected in the IJC's recommendations to the parties for the phaseout of chlorine.

A third major group participating in Great Lakes governance is industry. Before 1990, commercial and industrial interests participated only occasionally in binational processes as individual firms or industry associations tried to influence the direction of the regime on specific issues, such as phosphate detergent bans.[34] Industry on both sides of the border did not take an active role in policy development but generally concerned themselves with national regulatory initiatives (Allardice et al. 1994).

In 1990, industries with a stake in Great Lakes issues joined together in a binational coalition known as the Council of Great Lakes Industries (CGLI), at least partly in response to the success of the environmental sector in influencing the regime. Since then, the CGLI has actively tried to influence the direction of policy at the binational level, not just by lobbying of legislatures and agencies but also by participating in agreement institutions and forums.

Other sectors of the Great Lakes community include organized labor, First Nations, municipal politicians, and educators.[35] Members of local and regional community groups also participate through Remedial Action Plans and Lakewide Management Plans.

Before the signing of the first Great Lakes Water Quality Agreement in 1972, there was little organized nongovernmental participation in IJC processes. Public outcry over the state of the environment, particularly the condition of Lake Erie, was instrumental in causing the two national governments to act, first in referring the issues to the International Joint Commission and second in negotiating the agreement. NGO participation, however, remained ad hoc and, except for the scientific sector, not well organized (Sinclair 1974; Weller 1990: chapter 6).

With the creation of the agreement institutions, the level of organization and the nature of participation changed. The GLWQA gave the IJC responsibility for informing the public, but it left it up to the commission to determine how to do so. Prior to this, the IJC had operated under quite formal rules of procedure, had kept a low profile with the public, and had opened its work to scrutiny only at structured public hearings. Early in the operations of the Great Lakes Regional Office, however, the commission and its advisors became convinced of the need to change to a more open process as a way of building public support for the agreement and for the IJC itself. Several initiatives were undertaken to make the IJC's actions under the agreement more visible. For example, an information officer was hired, a newsletter began publication, and a new policy supporting wide release of reports and open meetings was adopted to open up those actions to greater public participation (Sinclair 1974; Becker 1993: 244; Swinehart 1988: 137–147).

One of the most significant experiments in expanded participation was undertaken in connection with the Pollution from Land-Use Reference Group (PLUARG) (Becker 1993; Swinehart 1988; Grima and Mason 1983). The study board members were all from government agencies, but seventeen multistakeholder consultation panels were convened to discuss basin issues. Public hearings were held; fact sheets, issue papers, and reports were widely distributed. The intention was to get broad public input into the reference group's draft report and to generate knowledge and support for the agreement and the IJC. Although the PLUARG recommendations were never formally adopted by the two governments, this experiment had a lasting influence on the direction of governance regarding water quality, and it created a pool of individuals from many sectors who had an expanded knowledge of and enthusiasm for protecting the Great Lakes and who continued to be actively involved in Great Lakes issues.

In the aftermath of PLUARG, the IJC has increasingly opened its processes to broad participation and has supplied the public with more information.[36] Thus, the development of a strong Great Lakes community is due in part to the deliberate efforts of the IJC. Moreover, although growing interest in Great Lakes issues cannot be separated from the growing public interest in environmental issues throughout

North America in general, the development of groups with a strong regional focus was fostered because of the number and serious nature of Great Lakes issues. In fact, many continental-wide environmental issues were first identified in the Great Lakes region. The issue of toxics in Love Canal adjacent to the Niagara River galvanized the environmental movement in general, but it was an especially important focal point for binational cooperation and for organizing in the Great Lakes region. Other regional threats, in particular the diversion of water out of the basin, also led to successful binational organizing.

The provision of funding by regionally based private charitable foundations to NGOs and multistakeholder forums was also important to development of the community. The support of the Joyce, Mott, Gund, and Donner Foundations as well as others, has been essential in bringing many organizational efforts and crucial projects to fruition.

Strong links between the different elements of the community, particularly between scientists and the NGOs, helped the development of sophisticated participants and enhanced their credibility. Finally, the NGOs used the principles of the regime, especially the ecosystem concept and zero discharge goal, that had been adopted by the parties, to focus attention on whether agreement obligations were being met.

The binational processes of the IJC—including the advisory boards, workshops, and the annual (later biennial) meetings—provided a forum for different community sectors to participate and helped legitimize their participation. In addition to participating in IJC processes, environmental organizations initiated other activities, such as monitoring and publicizing progress under the agreement, holding public hearings to review the agreement, and holding an annual lobbying week in Washington, D.C., on Great Lakes issues to seek conversion of the principles of the agreement into government policies.[37] The overall result has been significant political influence on the IJC, on leading agencies of the parties, and on legislative processes in both countries. Accountability of the parties has also been enhanced accordingly.

The IJC's employment of these combined strategies enhanced the synergy between the regime and the community: the regime helped the community to develop and evolve, and the community has helped form, maintain, and legitimize the regime.

Some changes in IJC process and in the Great Lakes community have made the future uncertain, however. The changes in the IJC process mean fewer opportunities to participate in a binational forum. In addition, the changes in the relationship between the parties and the IJC have not led to equivalent approaches to public involvement. Some community sectors have been hit hard by budget cuts: government-funded scientific research (both within government and in universities) has been reduced, and environmental groups have lost both government and public funding. Governments have been slow to pledge funds for the implementation of the Remedial Action Plans and Lakewide Management Plans, both important vehicles for local organizing and participation. Finally, Great Lakes issues, particularly the toxics issue, are being addressed through many other governmental and quasi-governmental activities, thus diverting the energies of the groups involved.

Relevance beyond the Great Lakes

The Great Lakes experience in managing the environmental degradation of a shared ecosystem is clearly linked to its particular political and social context. However, a number of characteristics that have made it an effective system might have relevance in other contexts.

In terms of the formal relationship of the national governments within the system, one important characteristic has been the equality of the parties—that is, each country has equal representation in all binational institutions. Dating from the creation of the IJC, this equality has been of greatest importance to Canada, which has a smaller population and economy and has never held much political influence with any U.S. government.

Through formal agreement processes, Canada regularly commands the attention of U.S. officials, thus exercising an influence beyond what it would otherwise have. The equality of the relationship at this level has had a positive effect on the continued commitment of both governments to cleaning up the Great Lakes.

Another important characteristic of the formal structure of Great Lakes governance is the use of an independent, binational organization, the IJC, for crucial elements of the system. In particular, the IJC's tasks—gathering, evaluating, and verifying data, reviewing and reporting on national programs to implement the agreement, controlling the spread of information to the public, and providing an open forum for debate and resolution of conflicts—have had an enormous influence on the direction and effectiveness of the system. This particular organization had the advantage of a long history, a small staff, and a mode of operating that allowed it to start off with a high level of respect and little sense of threat to existing agencies.

Although not planned for in the formal structure, a large and diverse binational community focused on the Great Lakes developed both spontaneously and partly in response to the concerted efforts of the IJC, foundations, existing groups, and individuals.

The binational scientific community played a leading role in the development of a consensus on the scientific basis for action, which convinced the governments of the need for cooperative action and which formed the basis for the principles of the regime. Interaction with scientists and with government agency personnel made NGO leaders more knowledgeable, thus rendering the whole community more credible.

The larger binational community has been a necessary element in making the system effective. Its great influence is the result of building political support for the principles of the agreement and its institutions and of orchestrating, well-prepared and well-organized participation in binational forums. Such influence also results from self-initiated activities that influence both the issues on the binational agenda and the direction of policies and from lobbying efforts at the national level that determine policies and actions leading to implementation.

Lastly, the adoption of expansive principles rather than specific numerical objectives as goals of the regime was essential in allowing the regime the flexibility to respond to the increasing complexity of the challenges facing the ecosystem. These goals provided the impetus for more integrated research and allowed the system to shift focus as priorities changed. They also provided a framework for building public support and for measuring the success of implemented actions.

It is the combination of these characteristics, not any one of them alone, that has allowed this system to function and make progress. The complex, supportive relationships among all of them have given the regime its particular strength and vitality so that it dynamically continues to evolve. Most important, while its flexibility, willingness, and ability to adapt to changing circumstances have kept students of the regime interested in its operation, the regime itself has made progress in regional environmental protection.

A note of caution must be sounded, however. What has made for success in the recent past may not be what makes for success in the future, for two reasons: (1) the regime is now faced with very difficult, intractable issues around which it will be difficult to build consensus for action; and (2) the parties and the IJC itself have made recent changes in the operation of the regime whose consequences are unclear. These changes have diluted the influence of the IJC, but it is not yet known whether they will contribute to a less effective regime, and it will likely be many years before this can be determined.

Nevertheless, the Great Lakes experience to date can and should inform those involved in regime formation and operation. Many of the attributes described under the Great Lakes agreement are found in other regimes, at least to some degree. Whether these attributes will be the controlling factors in the continued effectiveness of those regimes involves a wide variety of complex factors.

Perhaps the most important and difficult attribute to duplicate is the constituencies' desire and ability to achieve the sense of community that is so important for the Great Lakes regime. The ability depends both on the constituencies' sense of their own importance in dealing with the issues at hand and on the extent to which individuals within those constituencies are willing to assume a leadership role.

One of the understated factors in the evolution of the Great Lakes is the role that various individuals — including scientists, IJC commissioners, staff and members of advisory boards, government officials, and citizen activists — played at crucial times throughout the history of the regime, especially in the development of the sense of community. There is no reason why, given the appropriate circumstances, this factor could not be duplicated in the context of other regimes.

8

The Environmental Legacy of Bretton Woods: The World Bank

David Reed

The thesis of this chapter is that the environmental performance of the World Bank has changed considerably during its fifty years of operation, evolving from a legacy of general environmental neglect and irresponsible behavior to a record now characterized by standard setting for the international development community.[1] Further, this chapter argues that the Bretton Woods institutions (BWIs), although poorly prepared, may be better positioned than any other multilateral arrangements to respond to new environmental demands on the international community created by the rapidly changing world economy.

In seeking to capture the general historical contours and important transitions of the World Bank's environmental performance, this chapter does not pretend to be either an inclusive or exhaustive statement. At best, it summarizes the overall policy trends of the bank as it has tried to respond to changing external pressures, such as the public demand for improved environmental performance and the new role of the private sector in driving the development enterprise on a global level. The chapter focuses on the World Bank, with only passing reference to the International Monetary Fund (IMF), an emphasis that reflects the fundamentally different mandates of these sister organizations as well as their respective corporate capacities to address the rapidly evolving environmental agenda.

The Environmental Legacy

Operational Premises

Since the formation of the World Bank, its basic function has been the intermediation of private savings to governments of developing and transition countries on advantageous financial terms to facilitate the development process (International Bank for Reconstruction and Development 1989). This initial function was expanded in 1960 with the creation of the International Development Association (IDA) (International Development Association 1960), which broadened the bank's scope of operations to include provision of public financial resources to governments of the poorest developing nations on highly concessional terms. This grafting of two functions created a yet unresolved tension as to the fundamental character of the bank: was it to function as a lending institution or a development agency? Although these functions are not necessarily mutually exclusive, they have created policy and implementation conflicts throughout the past three decades of operation.

In addition to this underlying institutional tension, the bank has been constrained to lend either to governments that seek financial and technical support for implementing specific development projects and for undertaking economic policy reforms or to other economic agents that act with full financial guarantee from the member government (International Bank for Reconstruction and Development 1989). Primary responsibility for lending to the private sector has been delegated to the International Finance Corporation (International Finance Corporation 1986), and providing loan guarantees for private sector operations has been delegated to the Multilateral Investment Guarantee Agency (Multilateral Investment Guarantee Corporation 1990), both of which are in the World Bank group. This restriction of lending directly to or under the aegis of governments coincided with the development strategies pursued by a large majority of developing countries during the first fifty years of the bank's activities. In that period, the preeminent role of the state as the driving force of economic and social development arose from several different yet complementary imperatives. In many countries, the lack of dynamic entrepreneurial classes indigenous to the country led national policy makers to invest the government with many of the country's principal economic functions. Some countries relied on the state to guarantee the "economic sovereignty" previously controlled by the colonial powers from which many had recently gained independence. Other countries opted for centrally planned economies in which the state dictated economic priorities and controlled the mechanisms of economic activity. Regardless of the specific reason, many governments remained at the crossroads of the development process as they attempted to establish strategies, set priorities, and implement a wide range of development activities.

Given the objectives established by its Articles of Agreement, the World Bank promoted a development strategy that sought to use government intervention as a vehicle for creating economic conditions under which private sector expansion and accumulation could occur. Its lending operations have given priority, in varying mixtures, to developing economic infrastructure, particularly energy and transportation, and to addressing the "basic needs" of rural and urban poor. That strategy viewed the state as the agent for creating economic conditions under which both the national and international private sectors could generate ever growing employment opportunities. Ultimately; expansion of the private sector would facilitate the transition from traditional to modern or industrial societies, as well as from informal to formal economic structures and relations.

Before the early 1980s, environmental issues found no consistent place in the World Bank's development strategy or lending activities. Natural resources were viewed essentially as "factor constraints"—that is, as limitations in natural resource endowment, which set boundaries on the productive potential of a country or project. For example, a country's having only so much water would constrain the amount of land to be irrigated and thereby limit the potential economic contribution of the agricultural sector to gross domestic product (GDP). The bank considered environmental issues only when natural resources imposed problems for successful project implementation—problems such as siltation of dams, waterlogging and salinization of irrigation projects, or soil erosion resulting from forestry sector projects. It viewed natural resources as free, public goods of inexhaustible character that did not need to be considered in economic calculations. Natural capital existed only to the degree that it could be converted into marketable goods, and nonmarketed environmental goods and services occupied little or no place whatsoever in the development equation promoted by the bank. Consistent with neoclassical economics, visible environmental damages resulting from project implementation were relegated to the realm of negative externalities that were considered an unavoidable part of the development process.

Public Outcry

In the early 1980s, the negative environmental impacts of this grossly deficient development approach generated public condemnation from many quarters of civil society. The World Bank's failures were widespread and covered the entire gamut of environmental desecrations: major deforestation projects, environmentally destructive resettlement programs, infrastructure programs that encouraged internal migrations accompanied by environmental despoliation, pesticide-intensive agricultural projects, energy projects that failed to examine least-cost and demand-side alternatives. Moreover, it failed to calculate the impact those programs would have on human health, on the economic performance of different sectors, and on the provision of life-guaranteeing goods and services. In short, the bank's portfolio was replete with textbook examples of failure to integrate environmental issues into the mitigation, not to mention the core logic, of development activities[2] (Bank Information Center 1989).

The appointment of an environmental advisor in 1970, followed by the creation of the Office of Environmental Affairs in 1973 under the bank's president Robert McNamara, had no demonstrable impact on the environmental performance of the bank prior to the early 1980s. At that juncture, U.S.-based nongovernmental organizations (NGOs) coalesced to form the Multilateral Development Bank (MDB) Campaign that targeted the environmental performance of the World Bank. The MDB Campaign logically focused on the World Bank not only because of its global reach and leadership functions in the development community, but also because it was more vulnerable than the governments of developing countries to public pressure exercised through the U.S. government's appropriation process.

The MDB Campaign has undergone several important changes in the past decade. First, during its initial stage in the mid-1980s, the MDB Campaign focused on bank projects already completed or under implementation. The physical environmental damage caused by the projects was easily documented and an estimate of associated environmental costs was readily calculated. The choice of specific targets was also relatively easy given the multitude of bank-funded projects that had been implemented with neither environmental assessments nor mitigation components. Second, as the MDB Campaign's sophistication increased in the late 1980s, the NGOs in the campaign began to target bank projects not yet formally approved by its executive board, often using information obtained through the U.S. Freedom of Information Act. This step in their public lobbying efforts required that these NGOs acquire more intimate familiarity with the bank's operational procedures, institutional arrangements, and the specific sectoral regulations with which all bank projects had to comply. Third, at approximately the same time, the MDB Campaign also came to recognize its own northern biases and limited accountabilities; its response was to slowly increase partnership building and resource transfers to strengthen NGO partners in developing countries.

Fourth, the MDB Campaign's ability to forge a multifaceted, largely professional relationship with the U.S. government proved central to its effectiveness in promoting enduring reforms in the World Bank and in other MDBs. Using Congress as its springboard, the MDB Campaign shaped the agenda of the U.S. government concerning development banks by establishing reporting requirements, by requiring public information sharing standards, and by forcing the executive branch of the government to create a number of staff positions to meet the legislated environmental performance requirements. Those environmental standards were translated into government policy by the Treasury Department, the Department of State, the United States Agency for International Development, and other agencies, and their impact was often felt far beyond the activities of the World Bank and other MDBs. As the bank's largest shareholder, the United States has enjoyed significant influence in shaping the bank's policy agenda, investment priorities, and institutional arrangements since its formation. During the mid-

1980s and early 1990s, U.S. executive directors promoted policy, managerial, and institutional reforms that became the basis for the World Bank's subsequent environmental reform program. These reforms often created serious conflicts with the executive directors (EDs) from other countries, however. At times, the tension reached the point where bank management and other EDs were no longer willing to share documents with the U.S. office for fear they would find their way to the nongovernmental organization (NGO) community.

Contrary to the public impression conveyed by the NGO campaign, the design and implementation of any World Bank–funded project was and still is the responsibility of the agencies of recipient governments. Counterpart funds are required to strengthen government "ownership" of projects, and most projects in which the bank invests are cofinanced by other multilateral lenders or bilateral development agencies. Although the government capacity to develop and implement the wide range of development activities varies significantly from country to country, governments must approve projects and accept responsibility for implementing those activities.

The Bank Responds

At first, the World Bank's response to public charges of environmental desecration and to various lobbying activities was defensive, arrogant, and, in both the short and long term, counterproductive. Its subsequent distortion of events and specious refutation of documented damage, coupled with its denial of responsibility, deepened the antagonism between public critics and the bank staff and management. Even honest, well-documented research efforts from United Nations (UN) development agencies, such as the UNICEF study on structural adjustment, garnered little more than contempt and refutation from the bank (Cornia 1987). Because of its inability to respond constructively and creatively to public oversight and criticism, the bank failed to engender a public debate about the trade-offs involved in undertaking development activities. It also failed to explain the shared responsibilities of stakeholders in the development enterprise and dodged an honest examination of the distribution of costs and benefits of various development strategies.

Having failed to understand the enduring character of the NGO efforts, which were in reality but one expression of a far wider growth of organizations within civil society, the bank missed early and easy opportunities to embark on an internal reform program. The unrelenting pressure from the international NGO community ultimately forced governments of industrialized member countries to demand policy and operational changes from bank management. For the better part of a decade beginning in 1985, the bank slowly and reluctantly embarked on a reform process that significantly changed its environmental performance by reversing its own project portfolio and by establishing performance standards to be respected by the international community. Those changes began taking institutional hold with the creation of the Environment Department and Regional Environment Divisions in 1987 and have expanded to include the following salient reforms.

Institutional Changes

1. In January 1983, the bank created a Vice Presidency for Environmentally Sustainable Development, which brought together the bank's Environment, Agricultural and Natural Resources, and Transport, Water, and Urban Development Departments. Also, a New Social Policy and Resettlement Division was created within the Environment Department (World Bank 1993).

2. Environmental technical units were formed within regional operations. Whereas environmental policy is formulated in the Environment Department, environmental experts have been placed in the technical units and country departments of each region to ensure that environmental issues are integrated into project development and implementation.

3. In 1994, the World Bank assumed the chair and financial responsibility for the Consultative Group for International Agricultural Research (CGIAR), which had experienced financial problems and institutional decline in recent years. From the bank's perspective, sustaining the work of the agricultural research institutes is critical in increasing food production and in helping countries sustainably manage their natural resources.

Procedural Changes

1. In addition to expanding the number of projects subject to project-level environmental assessments (EAs), the bank now requires that sectoral and regional EAs be applied in appropriate projects. A 1993–1994 internal review of the environmental assessment process led to the identification of on-going problems in the application of EAs and to a subsequent strengthening of the EA process.

2. The recently revised information policy now calls for public release of project information documents (PIDs): summary documents that inform the public of project development prior to formal approval. Staff appraisal reports (SAPs) are to be released to the public following formal board approval. In addition, the bank is establishing public information centers to house bank materials where it has resident missions.

3. In 1995, the bank established a formal review process by which the public can submit complaints to a three-person independent review panel. The panel will review allegations that the bank has failed to comply with its own internal policies and procedures in developing and implementing projects.

4. The bank has established no fewer than twenty operational directives that address environmental issues. These issues range from those that concern specific resources, such as forests, water, natural habitats, and wetlands to those that concern impacts on indigenous peoples and policy-based lending (World Bank 1994).

Policy Reforms

1. The World Bank has also revised the composition of its lending portfolio. Cumulative funding for environmental projects has increased to approximately $9 billion from 1986 to 1994 for 118 projects. The greatest borrowers are middle-income countries that emphasize pollution control. The environmental portfolio of lower-income countries includes a higher percentage of rural-based projects (World Bank 1994). (The figures provided by the bank must be used cautiously, however.)

2. The bank has also created new policies regarding the environment. Over recent years, it has undertaken reviews and subsequent reforms in

its approach to uses of forests, water, and energy.[3] A similar review involving 192 bank-financed projects for involuntary resettlement led to strengthened bank requirements and supervision to ensure compliance with bank standards.

3. Finally, the bank developed its National Environmental Action Plans (NEAPs). In efforts to comply with agreements in IDA-9 replenishment, NEAPs have been developed in some forty-seven IDA countries and sixteen IBRD countries (World Bank 1995). The quality and utility of those action plans varies significantly, however.

A Tentative Assessment

These reforms are more ambitious and inclusive than institutional changes implemented by any other multilateral development bank. They have enabled the World Bank to set the pace and standards by which other international organizations are held accountable by governments and the broader public. Moreover, through its leadership, the bank has been able to leverage additional resources for environmental purposes from other multilateral and bilateral donor agencies. Despite the scope and pace of this institutional change, it also has a number of important limitations:

• The main shortcoming remains the disjuncture between the formal requirements of the bank's improved policies and procedures and actual respect for those standards in the design and implementation of projects. This disjuncture exists for two reasons. First, bank staff have been reluctant to follow required procedures methodically because of distorted internal incentives, lack of responsibility for failure of projects to meet objectives, and the cumbersome, time-consuming nature of those requirements. Second, although counterpart agencies in developing countries often accede to the strict, formal requirements established by the bank, they lack the ability and the will to respond adequately or to respect the standards in practice.

• In maintaining a privileged dialogue with governments, bank staff often exclude important segments of civil society, even direct stakeholders and intended beneficiaries, from all stages of project design and implementation. As a consequence, projects often reflect the vested interests of privileged sectors of developing societies who have greater access to government decision making and resources. Although operational directives now require that stakeholders be consulted in the project cycle, consultation still remains perfunctory and marginal in many projects.

• Environmental issues have not been fully integrated into the core logic of the World Bank's development strategy. The dependence of the productive process on environmental goods and services, the internalization of environmental costs in calculation of costs and benefits, and the distribution of environmental costs and benefits across various sectors (and generations) of developing societies are not yet integral aspects of the bank's development planning, national development strategies, or calculations of net results of the development enterprise.

• In undertaking structural reforms in scores of developing countries throughout the past decade and a half, the bank has failed to differentiate the impacts of adjustment on extractive economies, agricultural economies, and diversified manufacturing economies. Its structural adjustment programs have been driven by the logic of "getting the prices right" without recognizing the social and environmental impacts of the restructuring process and without considering integration into the global market system. In this context, the bank has not understood how restructuring economies also restructures social classes and institutions, which in turn fundamentally alters the rate and composition of natural resource use in developing societies, often with significant negative consequences (Reed 1996).

Although the World Bank has remained the main target of environmental critics for the better part of a decade, the evolution of its responses in that ten-year period has now established it as a trendsetter among other multilateral institutions regarding environmental standards of behavior. Furthermore, the bank has often obliged borrowing governments to respond to standards that are higher than those set by the countries' own legal and regulatory requirements. The following areas represent some of the ways in which the bank has raised the level of international environmental performance:

• The World Bank has established sector- and industry-specific policies that are frequently formally required by or informally respected by borrowers. It requires that projects in which it participates provide guarantees for the protection of indigenous peoples and that the resettlement of people be carried out only if the displacees' prior income levels are restored. Furthermore, through technical and financial operations it has encouraged governments to develop national environmental action plans as the basis for lending operations to all economic sectors.

• As a result of more than a decade of contentious public squabble, in 1995 the World Bank implemented a new information policy that makes available the basic information about approved projects and projects under appraisal, it has also established public information centers in countries where it has missions.

• Since 1990, the World Bank has considerably expanded the number of resource-based projects, as well as the number of other project loans that have natural resource components, in its lending portfolio. The bank claims that its total investments in these sectors now total upward of $9 billion for 118 projects. Although these figures should be taken with a good dose of caution, they do reflect an important shift in the bank's lending priorities.

• World Bank management and staff were instrumental in establishing the Global Environment Facility (GEF) in 1990. Although originally beholden to the three implementing agencies — World Bank, United Nations Development Program (UNDP), United Nations Environment Program (UNEP) — the GEF has shown considerable independence and leadership since completion of its restructuring process in 1994.

The World Bank's attempt to integrate these standards and policies into its own operations continues to elicit criticism from civil society. However, a significant shift has taken place: although the bank has already operationalized many of the reforms, it has nevertheless sought support from civil society — including NGOs from both the North and the South — to implement new operational policies through consultative processes, technical inputs, and professional contracts. Positive responses to those overtures have come mainly from community-based groups and NGOs in developing countries, but not often from the more ideological northern groups that lack the technical or operational capacity to translate their criticisms into alternative development practices.

Among other changes in international relations, the UN Conference on Environment and Development (1992), the formation of the Global Environment Facility, and the signing of international environmental protocols are, in many ways, reflections of how governments are reacting to the pressures of civil society in both the North and the South to address the deepening environmental crisis. An important outcome of these pressures on the World Bank has been to reinforce its internal commitment to integrate environmental issues into its lending activities and policies. Perhaps the most direct external impact of the changing international climate has been the bank's favorable response to the growing number of requests from developing countries to fund environmental projects.

In contrast, the IMF has remained relatively insulated from criticisms regarding the environmental impacts of its stabilization programs. This differentiation is in large part attributable to the different mandates of the sister institutions: the IMF gives exclusive attention to short-term currency stabilization and balance of payments corrections, whereas and the World Bank assumes responsibility for longer-term development processes. This difference does not imply, however, that IMF actions have had no impact on the environment because such impact has been documented by recent research (Reed 1996). Despite the managing director's efforts to broaden its environment activities, the IMF Board of Directors has steadfastly refused to expand the authorization given to its staff to become directly involved in environmental issues. Consequently, staff are limited to learning from the work of other agencies and institutions and must rely to a large degree on World Bank data, analysis, and policy prescriptions.

Evolving Demands: New Opportunities and New Forces of Change

During the past decade, the demand for change in the World Bank's environmental performance has come from the civil society that has borne the brunt of the bank's deficient development policies. Often unable to influence the policies of developing country governments themselves, NGOs have targeted the World Bank as representing the source of environmental failures in the development process. Today, however, a new set of forces pose equally fundamental challenges to the role and functions of the World Bank and, at the same time offer the bank new opportunities to expand its role in global environmental affairs.

The evolving international conditions to which the bank must respond reflect the greater role of the private sector in setting the direction and priorities of economic growth in the developing world. Growth in world trade captures, in part, the integration of the world economy. World trade now amounts to approximately $4 trillion a year. Although three-fourths of that volume is among Organization for Economic Cooperation and Development (OECD) countries, trade expansion in developing counties has nearly kept pace with that in industrialized societies. An unprecedented increase in private capital flows, the second major characteristic of the past decade, eclipses the merchandise flows on a daily basis by two orders of magnitude. Moreover, foreign direct investment and portfolio investment reached $66 billion and $14 billion in 1993 (Stedman 1995).

In addition to its responses to changes in international trade regimes, the World Bank has played a central role in restructuring the world economy through the policy-based lending operations it initiated in 1980. Through structural adjustment loans the bank has accelerated the integration of developing countries into the emerging development model that is premised on (1) outward-oriented growth, (2) liberalized trade regimes, (3) diminution of the economic role of the state, (4) increased private sector growth, and (5) deregulation of labor markets. Structural adjustment programs do not differ in any fundamental way from the emerging development paradigm; they, along with liberalized trade regimes, have been the programmatic vehicle for accelerating the integration of developing country economies into the global market system.

In many ways, we are in a transitional period in the restructuring of the world economy. Formerly a major economic actor in many developing countries, the state is now being decisively supplanted by the private sector. The new export-led development model holds many opportunities for diversified manufacturing economies in the developing world that can attract international capital and advanced production technologies, although it offers lower wage opportunities relative to those offered by industrial societies. In contrast, the new international division of labor offers significantly fewer opportunities for extractive and agricultural economies because the export value of manufactures continues to increase more than that of primary commodities (Borensztein 1994).

In this transitional period, the importance of multilateral funders as providers of development finance to many governments, particularly those of middle-income countries, is diminishing. The role of the state as an economic agent in middle-income countries has decreased as governments have undertaken sweeping privatization programs. In the current ideology of liberalized markets and privatization, the other functions of the state — including administration and management of a country's environmental patrimony — have diminished dramatically in most countries. The role of the state in low-income countries is also undergoing major changes. Although governments have divested themselves of many state-owned enterprises, they have also limited their roles as providers of social services, environmental managers, and guarantors of conditions of social equity (Reed 1996). Not surprisingly, still on the margins of the emerging global economy, low-income countries have increased their reliance on the donor community (and on multilateral banks, in particular) to meet their pressing financial needs.

These changes in the world economy have profound implications for the prospects of promoting socially defined, socially agreed upon development objectives. The international *rapport des forces* has shifted clearly in favor of the private sector, which is able to move with greater speed and freedom to all corners of the globe. The opportunities for private capital to generate profit in the international marketplace now determine the development strategies and options of both countries and social groups. Relative to the growing strength of the private sector, the functions and influence of the state has been weakened significantly, particularly in developing countries. Not only has the state's economic influence been diminished, but its ability to regulate the social costs of private enterprise, to promote social equity through redistributive programs, and to shape the direction of national development has also been drastically reduced (Reed 1996). As a consequence of this shift in relative control over the development process, civil society has been placed in a defensive position. Many social groups' access to services and wages has been weakened; reliance on their governments to protect them from the negative impacts of private enterprise has reduced; and the expectation that their needs and long-term interests will be integrated into the national development strategy has been undermined.

New Opportunities for the World Bank

The changing conditions in the world economy and the corresponding changes in the role of the state are creating new demands and new opportunities for the World Bank. Sharper differentiation will emerge in the bank's relations with low-income and middle-income developing countries. Provision of concessional finance for infrastructure development, human capital development (above all, health and education), and even specific projects will remain the backbone of the bank's activities in low-income countries. Middle-income countries, in contrast, will be able to rely more on national savings and private sector flows to finance many investments in those same development areas. In both low- and middle-income countries, the demand for the development of public sector goods and services, with particular emphasis on the environment, offers an opportunity for potential World Bank involvement. This trend has already begun and can be expected to intensify as the social and environmental costs of the expanding private sector continue to rise in coming years.

Many developing countries have not willingly come to recognize the importance of the environmental agenda in the development process. Their resistance stems from many sources. First, they resent the objective constraints that the previous and present environmental performance (that is, the irresponsibility) of industrialized societies imposes on their own development options. Second, they often view the international environmental agenda as a method for industrialized countries to extend their own development and lending criteria to a developing world that has severely limited resources to respond to those demands. Third, they are often faced with crisis conditions that require urgent responses to address the survival needs of millions of people. In that context, environmental issues are often given low priority. Fourth, representatives of developing countries on the World Bank's Executive Board often act as a bloc to resist efforts from their industrialized counterparts to strengthen environmental measures in the bank's and the IMF's operations. National sovereignty issues weave themselves through all of those objections. Despite their resistance, the urgency of addressing environmental issues is rising in the ranks of the priorities of developing countries because of the increasingly apparent link between basic issues of survival and the protection of water, soil productivity, fisheries, and forests. With growing populations and growing demand for diminishing resources, we can expect demands for external support from the World Bank to increase.

The private sector will continue to expand its involvement in many areas that were once the reserve of the World Bank. Its growing influence will invariably increase pressure on World Bank shareholders to decide whether the bank will be, first and foremost, a merchant bank or a development agency. If it relinquishes its function in intermediating development resources, its ability to leverage policy reforms in developing countries will decrease. The current and successive rounds of negotiations on IDA replenishment may decide the issue without the World Bank's Executive Board having to act decisively on the matter. If it relinquishes its role as a development agency, its ability to address the growing threat of poverty will be significantly diminished, and its underlying mission in the eyes of the public will be brought into question.

Regardless of which policy choice bank shareholders make, the demand to address environmental externalities — namely, increased consumption of resources and increased pressure on environmental sink functions — will continue to rise. The World Bank can provide the following specific functions to national governments through its future operations:

1. Develop meaningful national environmental action plans
2. Integrate those plans into national economic growth strategies

3. Rebuild national regulatory and enforcement capacity

4. Integrate environmental performance and oversight units into government ministries with responsibility for specific economic sectors

5. Improve data collection capabilities on a national level

6. Develop market-based environmental incentive structures to meet the specific needs of individual countries

7. Strengthen participation of civil society in management of natural resources

8. Develop national environmental education programs to strengthen public awareness and participation

On an international level, the World Bank should increase its capacity to collect environmental data, to monitor trends in environmental performance and issues, to share information with the broader public, and to help develop strategies for addressing environmental problems. No other international institution is better positioned or in command of such an extensive range of resources than the World Bank to address these evolving environmental issues.

A Final Comment

In closing, I must make one further point. The foregoing analysis is based on the assumptions, categories, and criteria of neoclassical economics. The neoclassical economic framework deals with environmental goods and services in terms of relative scarcities that can be reflected to a certain degree in the price mechanism and pursuit of microeconomic equilibria. In this context, I have argued that the World Bank's environmental performance has undergone important change over the past decade. It has moved from a negative record characterized by neglect and widespread environmental damage to a more positive legacy of providing leadership to the international development community in correcting short-term environmental failures of growth economics. Moreover, my analysis has suggested that important changes in the world economy and in the functions of the state in the development enterprise pose many new challenges and opportunities for the bank. Whether this preeminent development institution will rise to those new challenges by clarifying its mandate and by addressing the needs of civil society — rather than by facilitating private sector expansion — is not at all certain.

However, in addressing environmental issues from the vantage point of relative, not absolute, scarcity, the World Bank has not accepted the premise that humankind has inherited limited environmental stocks, which imposes irreducible constraints on the economic system. As a consequence, it perpetuates a basic myth that economic growth need not be constrained by external frontiers because the substitutibility of human-made for natural capital, coupled with technological innovation, will allow the human community to overcome the "alleged" environmental constraints. Perpetuation of this myth is a failure of immeasurable proportions, though. It allows the human community to cling to unrealistic expectations regarding achievable standards of living for the great majority of humanity and to believe that global inequalities and poverty can be addressed by more growth in both the North and the South. Moreover, this perspective allows the present generation to expand the current economic system without any recognition of the fact that depleting or overtaxing environmental goods and services today will reduce the options of future generations as they try to address their own survival needs.

In highlighting this failure, I do not assume that the World Bank alone can alter the basic nature of the growth enterprise, despite the central role that it has played in promoting and guiding capitalist expansion around the world in the past five decades. The ecological restructuring of the growth economy will require a concerted, protracted effort by many institutions and societies that today remain quite hostile to such a proposal. If, however, the bank were to question the growth predicate of its development strategies, it could provide urgently needed intellectual leadership to the world community by

1. Helping interpret the indications of when countries approach environmental thresholds

2. Exploring transitional approaches for shifting economies toward sustainable development strategies

3. Strengthening the political foundations of sustainable development by supporting international environmental regimes and mechanisms for redistributing global wealth and opportunity

Breaking with the assumptions of unlimited growth represents the most difficult challenge yet laid before the World Bank and perhaps the human community in general. The World Bank's ability to face this issue in the immediate future may well determine whether it will again become the target of a civil society tired of bearing the social costs of private sector growth. During the past fifteen years of protest, the bank has often served as a proxy for governments of developing countries when they failed to address their nations' environmental problems. As the social costs of private sector expansion accumulate, and as these costs consequently remain the motivation of civil society's protests in the future, the World Bank may find itself serving as the proxy for private capital and private enterprise rather than the governments of developing countries. This quite plausible scenario may finally oblige it to clarify its basic character: will it be a development institution committed to addressing the broader needs of civil society, or will it be a lending institution that seeks to expand the private sector and the growth enterprise? The answer the bank offers will also determine its role in addressing the basic challenges of survival of the human community as we move into the twenty-first century.

9

Institutional Interactions: The Structure of Regimes for Trade and the Environment

Konrad von Moltke

Environment and Trade[1]

In 1991, the trade and environment agenda burst upon the international scene, catching the trade community unawares and the environmental community unprepared.[2] It is surprising that it took so long for this issue to emerge. The potential for overlaps between international environmental regimes and trade regimes are many.

International Nature

At the most mundane level, environment and trade policies interact because they both have an essential international component. This fact is so obvious that it hardly requires elaboration. The overlap between trade policy and domestic policy issues, such as social welfare or even human rights, is much less obvious and thus much more controversial. Although it is possible to argue from a position of national sovereignty that trade policy and domestic policies should not be commingled, no comparable argument can be made against the interaction between environmental matters and trade policy.

Structural Economic Change

The economic goals of trade liberalization and environmental policy are the same. This statement may seem outrageous, but it does reveal that both policy interventions ultimately aim to promote structural economic change. Although it offers an acceptable description of trade policy, however, it focuses only on the economic component of environmental policy. The entire argument on trade liberalization and comparative advantage is that some countries should do less of what they do poorly and more of what they do better—in other words, restructure their economy to benefit from their comparative advantage rather than seek to do everything, as postulated by theories of autarky. Similarly, the aim of environmental policy is that countries should do less of what harms the environment and more of what harms it the least—in other words, restructure their economy to create more welfare at less environmental cost. Yet the implied criteria of efficiency are different in trade and environmental policies. Trade policy is limited to criteria of efficiency that are internal to the economic system (e.g., productivity, economies of scale, cost reduction), whereas environmental policy aims to achieve results that are, at least in part, external to the economic system (e.g., conservation, environmental quality, emission reduction).

Pollution Havens

There has been a persistent fear that trade liberalization would promote measures to capture the economic benefits of unpolluted environments or to trade long-term environmental harm for short-term financial gain. Such a fear would seem, at least theoretically, a direct outgrowth of the theory of comparative advantage—that is, a "pollutable" environment or a "pollution haven" would be considered little more than an economic good waiting to be culled. The result would be a "race to the bottom" as countries came under competitive pressure to lower environmental standards. In practice, the search for pollution havens and for companies that relocate to escape environmental restrictions has come up empty. In most cases, other factors predominate in location decisions, particularly such classic factors as market access, availability of (skilled) labor, and availability of raw materials. In some instances, more careful consideration of the evidence has shown that the environment is used to cover up other problems, such as managerial failure. The remaining considerations are too few to constitute a reasonable basis for assuming that pollution havens exist. Moreover, no correlation can be shown between vigorous environmental protection measures and economic decline; if anything, the opposite appears to be the case. In focusing on manufacturing and new investments, the debate about pollution havens may in fact have been looking at the wrong things. The steady move to developing countries of commodity extraction and commodity manufactures may have been promoted by less stringent environmental controls—in addition to low wages and poor protection of worker rights.

Commodities Trade
The global trade regime was constructed to meet the needs of trade and industry. The concerns of commodity producers, however, were largely left out of the regime. Commodity production entails inescapable environmental impacts because commodities are by definition primary economic goods extracted directly from the environment. The existence of international markets and trade has been crucial to the continuing process of reducing the price of natural resource inputs to market economies. Markets focus exclusively on the characteristics of the commodities, generally defined as narrowly as possible to facilitate trade; they do not recognize whether production occurred in an environmentally sound (i.e., sustainable) manner or not. They thus effectively exclude themselves from the "polluter pays" principle, leaving the primary producer to carry the entire environmental burden of extraction and shielding subsequent consumers from the costs. The polluter pays principle is frequently understood to mean that environmental protection comes at the cost of manufacturing profits. More accurately, however, it is a principle of cost attribution that assumes costs will be passed on to the ultimate polluter, the consumer, thereby creating appropriate incentives not to pollute. Where this price mechanism is interrupted, as in the commodity trade, the polluter pays principle does not apply.

Changed International Agenda
It is by now a truism to point out that the end of the Cold War changed the nature of international relations. The international agenda is no longer dominated by the perceived needs of security and ideology. Rather, it is increasingly defined by the needs of an emerging international civil society supported by both economic policy and environmental management.

Presumably, the complex relationship and conflict between environment and trade did not emerge before the nineties because neither trade nor international environmental regimes had matured sufficiently to make the relationship apparent and the conflict inescapable. In a real sense, the emergence of the trade/environment linkage is a result of the remarkable successes achieved by both trade negotiators and those who created international environmental regimes.

The conflicts between trade and environmental policy have so far been revealed episodically. Some events (for example, the negotiation of the North American Free Trade Agreement or a trade panel report) focus attention on a particular issue, forcing consideration of certain elements of the relationship. Such episodic attention follows the classic structure of international policy, which is largely a system of crisis management. The congruences between trade and environmental policy that have occurred in such episodes indicate that this approach has been at least partially successful in allaying the immediate crisis. Nevertheless, the possibility exists that structural differences in trade and environmental regimes may render the long-term management of the relationship between them particularly onerous and may create major challenges for the structure of the international system itself.

The notion of structural characteristics assumes that a set of regimes—in this instance, those concerned with trade and with environmental management—is likely to exhibit certain regularities not only in terms of their legal doctrines but also in terms of their operation and the manner in which they relate to other regimes. In essence, these regimes share certain common institutional characteristics that distinguish them from other regimes, define their coherence as a group, and significantly impact their effectiveness.

The Structure of the Trade Regime

Like all other international economic regimes created in the postwar years—the Bretton Woods institutions, the United Nations Economic Commissions, the Organization for European Economic Cooperation (OEEC) (subsequently the Organization for Economic Cooperation and Development (OECD), and the three European communities—the trade regime was first and foremost a response to World War II. It reflected the widespread view that the post–World War I order had failed to stand the test of the economic crisis of the late 1920s. The authors of the new order were determined not to repeat the mistakes of Versailles and the early 1920s. As we look back, we can see that they were remarkably successful. The limits of their mandate were defined by the willingness of the Congress of the victorious United States to support multilateral action rather than to exercise its sovereign power unilaterally. These limits were reached in the case of the trade regime (at least, the negotiators were convinced that they had been reached). In an act of self-fulfilling prophecy, they extracted the central obligations of the draft charter establishing the International Trade Organization (ITO) and implemented them as the General Agreement on Tariffs and Trade (GATT) through something known as the Provisional Protocol of Application. This remarkable legal and diplomatic sleight of hand created an international trade regime that was institutionally hobbled from the outset. Because the GATT existed, the U.S. Senate had no reason to ratify the Havana Charter establishing the ITO, which consequently failed to enter into force.

For decades, this amputation of the trade agenda and GATT's lack of institutional capacity were not perceived as obstacles to achieving the basic goals of trade liberalization. The GATT left the so-called "contracting parties" firmly in charge. The initial rounds of negotiation under the GATT focused on tariff reduction, a politically difficult but administratively straightforward enterprise that had little need of international implementing machinery. Related interests that had been lost when the ITO was dropped — mainly labor and the commodities trade — were not perceived as critical to the success of this venture.

Beginning with the Tokyo Round, the GATT regime turned to more complex issues that required subsequent implementing interpretation and continuing international vigilance to ensure that the principal goals were achieved. Dispute resolution became increasingly important in this round, and the parties' inability to modify the agreement led to fragmentation of the trade regime as new agreements were created separate from the GATT itself. Moreover, many countries counted on increased institutional strength of the GATT to curb the ability of the more powerful members (in particular the United States) to act unilaterally. These issues, as much as the need to make agriculture and trade-related intellectual property rights (TRIPs) part of the trade regime, were the central concerns of the Uruguay Round of trade negotiations, which led to the creation of the World Trade Organization (WTO). Again a subterfuge was used to slip the WTO past a U.S. Senate that would presumably have been unable to muster a two-thirds majority to ratify a formal treaty. A "fast-track procedure" was employed not only to get the agreement on trade liberalization and its domestic implementing legislation sanctioned but also to bring into existence a new international organization. It remains to be seen whether this lack of due process will again exact a price as the new WTO is implemented. Whether the WTO rests on a broad public consensus in key member states — one that is sufficient to tide it over during periods of crisis — remains untested for the moment.

The success of the trade regime rests on the conceptual clarity of its underlying premises and the ability of the regime to carry out these premises in an effective manner. The trade regime is constructed around a limited number of central principles that give institutional form to its fundamental premises. The two most important principles are *most-favored nation treatment* (MFN) and *national treatment*, which insulate trade from many vagaries of national policy making. In other words, they constitute trade a matter of international economic negotiation alone. Equally important, these two principles define the structure of trade regimes and accommodate it to an international society that is based on sovereign states. Threats to these principles are widely regarded as threats to the trade regime itself. The most serious conflicts between trade and environment are liable to arise when international environmental regimes threaten to impinge on MFN and national treatment.

Both MFN treatment and national treatment focus on what are termed "like" goods. The use of such an indeterminate term as "like" goods reflects the reality that the full range of legitimate variation between traded goods cannot be anticipated and, consequently, that the determination of what goods are "like" remains a matter of subsequent interpretation. The most vehement trade disputes involving environmental issues have generally revolved around attempts to introduce environmentally based distinctions between what are usually designated as like goods: "dolphin-safe" tuna, fur from animals not caught in leghold traps, beef produced without the use of artificial hormones, reformulated gasoline produced with less pollution, and "undersize" lobster, for example. The central conflict between trade and environmental policy arises because trade policy abhors such distinctions, which always entail the risk of protectionist capture, whereas environmental policy cannot manage without them.

The trade regime is hierarchical in structure, so all regional trade regimes are—theoretically at least—structured like the GATT and WTO with the nation as the basic unit. The regime has never displayed any difficulty in dealing with the concept of nation states and sovereignty as an organizing principle of international relations. Even though trade is carried on mainly by private interests that have also been the primary beneficiaries of the process of trade liberalization, these interests have not had any formal representation within the GATT/WTO structure, which usually has turned trade disputes between private enterprises into disputes between states. This aspect of the trade regime puts it at odds with recent insights concerning the new institutionalism of international regimes, which utilize international institutions to design complex responses to situations that require a balance between conflicting interests.

The basic process of implementing trade agreements is "multi-unilateral": each country implements the appropriate policies and is responsible for primary adjudication. The international regime helps ensure transparency of each country's implementation and provides a forum for resolving disputes that cannot be handled either unilaterally or bilaterally. This approach limits the need for active involvement of an international organization in the management of trade.

The trade regime is designed to manage economic competition and is essentially neutral concerning outcomes. It does depend quite heavily, however, on the general perception that economic competition increases welfare in a manner beneficial to both importing and exporting countries.

This brief outline of the trade regime identifies some of the salient characteristics of the trade regime: its conceptual clarity, hierarchical organization, and structural congruence with international society based on sovereign nation states. Many of the undeniable successes of the trade regime may be attributable to the manner in which it has been able to innovate without challenging traditional approaches to the management of international relations.

The International Environmental Agenda

While the Uruguay Round was building the GATT regime, a long series of environmental negotiations were also being conducted.[3]

1. After the stalemate of the Vienna Convention in 1985, the discovery of the hole in the ozone above Antarctica changed the dynamics of negotiations on the stratospheric ozone layer, leading to the Montreal Protocol in 1987, which was subsequently amended in London and Copenhagen.

2. After fractious negotiations, the Basel Convention was adopted in 1989. African states unhappy with the outcome of the Basel negotiations created the Bamako Convention soon thereafter. After the Basel Convention was ratified and entered into force, the Second Meeting of the Parties moved to adjust the convention to emphasize more strongly the principle that hazardous wastes should not be traded internationally.

3. After remarkably short but difficult negotiations, the Framework Convention on Climate Change was concluded and opened for signature in Rio de Janeiro in June 1992. The first Conference of Parties took place in Berlin in March 1995.

4. To the surprise of many observers, the United Nations Environment Program succeeded in concluding negotiations for the Convention on Biological Diversity, which also was opened for signature in Rio de Janeiro in June 1992 and attracted many signatures. The convention has since entered into force, and the First Conference of Parties occurred in 1994.

5. Following the collapse of efforts to establish a minerals regime for Antarctica, agreement was quickly reached on the Madrid Protocol to the Antarctic Treaty, which declared the region a protected area.

6. The Global Environment Facility was established as a cooperative venture of the World Bank, the United Nations Environment Program

(UNEP), and the United Nations Development Program (UNDP) (Sjöberg 1994).

This extraordinary sequence of global environmental negotiations represents the capstone of a twenty-year effort to construct regimes able to respond to the pressing need for international environmental management. If they are taken to their logical conclusion and implemented properly, these six agreements will have greater impact—both environmental and economic—on the world of the twenty-first century than the Uruguay Round.

The dramatic environmental negotiations of the 1980s did not occur in a vacuum, however. In fact, they supplemented an already impressive number of multilateral environmental agreements (for various lists of multilateral environmental agreements, see Burhenne n.d.; Brown Weiss et al. 1992). Although these sources include a large number of core agreements, they differ in their definition of what other agreements need to be included. The number of agreements covered ranges from 25 to more than 200. The result is a fairly confusing number of new international regimes, which, taken together, constitute the essential core of current international environmental management.

International environmental management represents a dramatic challenge to traditional international relations because it has engendered many innovative approaches to the construction and operation of international regimes, which are an integral part of the changing nature of international relations themselves (Young 1994a).

Each one of the many international environmental regimes established during the past twenty years was negotiated separately and was rarely linked to other international regimes. All of them do, however, exhibit common structures and dynamics. Moreover, they increasingly overlap other international regimes, especially those concerned with economic policy, human rights, and security affairs. Such an overlap can create new opportunities for environmental management, but it can also give rise to conflicts.

Clearly, international environmental management represents something broader than the six recent global agreements, indeed broader than the many multilateral environmental agreements. It represents an extraordinary effort of regime formation that encompasses hundreds of multilateral agreements; thousands of bilateral agreements between national governments; even more agreements between regional and local authorities that happen to share a boundary; and untold private international forms of cooperation as well as newer joint public/private regimes such as debt-for-nature swaps and the environmental trust funds that have frequently flowed from them. Although most of these regimes respond to an immediate and limited need—otherwise they would not have been created in an era of great public skepticism about the expansion of international regimes—they by now constitute an overall system or structure that responds to the overarching demands of the environment.

Perhaps nothing characterizes the difference between environmental regimes and most other international regimes more clearly than the extraordinary position occupied by the United States in these environmental negotiations. These negotiations took place during a period when the United States was emerging as the only uncontested superpower, equally powerful in both its economy and its military. Conventional theory of international relations suggests that the United States should have been able to dictate the terms of the agreements if it so chose. At the very least, the negotiations could not proceed or any agreements be reached without U.S. support. Despite talk of U.S. leadership on environmental management, however, the United States was in reality an obstacle in most international environmental negotiations. Moreover, several negotiations resulted in agreements that were contrary to expressed U.S. priorities. The only period of uncontested U.S. leadership occurred during the process of negotiating the Montreal Protocol. The following list offers examples of negotiations in which the United States was either a leader or, more often, an obstacle:

1. The United States championed "prior informed consent" as the principle for the transport of hazardous waste. It also succeeded in blocking broader international agreement on this issue until a common OECD position was worked out, an approach reminiscent of trade negotiations. The U.S. failure to ratify the Basel Convention, however, left the initiative in the Conference of Parties to others, specifically to the developing countries with Chinese leadership.

2. The United States was visibly an unwilling participant in the climate negotiations, and although the final agreement carries the stamp of its reluctance, the first Conference of Parties again demonstrated that the United States was confronted by an invidious choice between accepting unwelcome developments or appearing obstructionist (Mintzer and Leonard 1994).

3. U.S. opposition to the Convention on Biodiversity contributed in a backhanded manner to the convention's success at the Rio Conference, as virtually every country other than the United States signed the agreement, leaving the United States painfully and visibly isolated.

4. The United States was the principal champion of the Antarctic minerals regime, which fell when France and Australia announced their opposition, presumably pressured by nongovernmental environmental interests.

5. The Global Environment Facility (GEF) was launched at European initiative, and the United States had to scramble to stay involved. It ultimately pledged its support only after the other major countries had allowed it to pretend to participate by counting some of its bilateral aid.

Clearly, international environmental policy responds to different dynamics than those to which security or economic policies respond. The creation and implementation of those environmental regimes with at best grudging support from the U.S. government can only be explained if one recognizes that other U.S. interests groups—notably scientists, nongovernmental environmental organizations, and (often forgotten) the media—were playing a very different role than their government. All environmental policy developments of the past decade cannot be understood without reference to the emergence of international civil society as an independent force in international relations, capable of driving developments even against the will of the most powerful government provided that government subscribes to basic tenets of democratic rule.

Seen from this perspective, the international arena constitutes another level of governance—albeit subject to special rules—instead of just a privileged forum for intergovernmental action. In this context, the role of governments changes from that of primary actors to the more traditional one of process managers and arbiters who provide a vital but well-defined social function. The emergence of international civil society is a complex phenomenon driven by a number of interlocking developments in science, technology, the economy, and the environment (Wapner 1996).

The conflict between trade and environmental policy creates a number of challenges to international governance. First, trade and environmental policy have responded differently to the emergence of international civil society. Trade regimes have accommodated themselves to changes in governance options, but they have not utilized these options creatively. In contrast, environmental regimes depend significantly on the emergence of new structures of international governance that integrate governments and civil society at the international level. Second, international society has not traditionally confronted the issue of policy conflicts that arise from overlapping policy concerns. It has little experience in resolving such conflicts in a manner that is acceptable to all concerned.

Several of the environmental agreements have direct implications for the trade regime, either because they directly affect trade (e.g., the Basel Convention), or because they use trade measures as part of their implementation strategy (e.g., the Montreal Protocol), or because they affect the potential supply of commodities (e.g., the Madrid Protocol), or because they are so comprehensive that it is difficult to conceive of long-term development of the regime without trade impacts (e.g., the Framework Convention on Climate Change; von Moltke 1992). However, the obvious relationship between multilateral environmental agreements and the trade regime did not attract the attention it deserved. For example, during the Uruguay Round and specifically at the time of the Brussels meeting, which sought unsuccessfully to conclude the round in December 1990, attempts to introduce the environmental dimension into the negotiations were widely resisted. It is worth recalling that by December 1990 most of the major environmental negotiations were well under way, and the United Nations Conference on Environment and Development (UNCED) was but eighteen months distant. Only in the final days of the Uruguay Round in December 1993, after the main deals had been struck and while details were being finalized for the signing in Marrakech, was it possible to introduce some basic environmental provisions into parts of the round and into the structure of the World Trade Organization: modest provisions in the accords themselves, a weak reference to sustainable development in the document establishing the WTO, and the creation of a Committee on Trade and Environment within the WTO.

In fact, the linkages between trade and environment came into sharp focus for the first time through the negotiation of a regional trade agreement, the North American Free Trade Agreement (NAFTA). A number of factors may have favored this development. Because political support for NAFTA was razor thin in the United States, negotiators were forced to take into consideration all factors that might help or hinder approval of the final package, including some environmental factors that the negotiators themselves might have otherwise disregarded. Despite growing evidence of the need for them, only a very few significant bilateral institutions and no trilateral environmental institutions existed on the North American continent, which rendered tenuous any government assertions that environmental concerns were adequately taken care of. Finally, any regional agreement usually involves matters of greater detail than a broadly multilateral one. As the practical implications of day-to-day management of NAFTA emerged, it became increasingly obvious that these details would have a significant impact on the manner in which the authorities in the region went about protecting the environment and that protection of the environment would have an impact on day-to-day management.

The outcome of the NAFTA negotiations confirmed many of the lessons learned in the preceding twenty years by the European Community (von Moltke 1996). However, because of the unique character of the EC (now the European Union), the applicability of these lessons to the North American context was far from clear. As a result, NAFTA became the first "traditional" trade agreement to attempt to integrate some environmental considerations into the text of the agreement itself. It also demonstrated clearly if trade agreements lack or include only weak international environmental management, they will have a difficult time avoiding the shoals of environmental concern (von Moltke 1996). This particular lesson was powerfully reinforced by the vehement reaction of those concerned primarily with environmental management to a (then GATT) panel report on a dispute between Mexico and the United States concerning the use of trade measures to protect dolphins from incidental mortality in tuna fisheries, in particular in the eastern tropical Pacific. Again, the implication was that unmanaged environmental problems threaten to become trade problems.

Seen from this perspective, the negotiators of the Uruguay Round should have welcomed the parallel development of global environmental agreements. It can reasonably be argued that without these agreements the WTO would soon have been confronted with a range of global environmental problems that it was manifestly not equipped to handle, mainly because the problems had both environmental and trade implications. Conceivably, they might have been able to handle the problems if the nature and structure of international environmental management was more obvious and if its implications for the trade regime were clearer. In reality, however, the structure of international environmental management is still far from clear. Although the related international legal regime has been analyzed quite comprehensively (Brown Weiss et al. 1992; Sands 1995), little attention has been devoted to the structural characteristics of individual regimes or to the manner in which they interrelate (Young 1996; von Moltke 1996). For historical reasons, the international order has few effective mechanisms with which to analyze the manner in which regimes interrelate — whether they are congruent, as environmental regimes appear to be, or conflicting, as environment and trade regimes appear to be.

To the extent that such structural characteristics exist, in general, when we compare the structure of environmental regimes to the structure of trade regimes, we can see that the emerging structure of environmental regimes is manifestly incommensurate with the structure of the trade regimes. This incongruity ultimately renders the management of conflict between these policy areas extremely difficult.

The Structure of International Environmental Management

Several reasonable definitions exist for what does and what does not belong to "environmental policy." For example, some include nature protection, some nuclear safety, and some accident prevention measures.

What unites all definitions, however, is the effort to use human laws to affect trends in the natural environment, which responds to the laws of nature. This discontinuity of action, akin to shooting around corners, is one of the dominant features of environmental management. Large areas of uncertainty exist because we lack an adequate understanding of natural phenomena. Discontinuity and uncertainty also effectively defeat any attempt to control environmental conditions through isolated measures so that we end up having to construct complex, interacting systems of law, policy, and action through international environmental regimes, which themselves become characterized by discontinuity, uncertainty, and complexity.

The international environmental management structure that has evolved over the past twenty years has not been designed according to central principles. It has no conscious architecture that defines the position and role of each of its many constituent parts. There is not even a single agency or forum that can articulate the common interests of all the participants. Nevertheless, it represents a coherent endeavor and can be expected to reflect a recognizable pattern defined by the common purposes and the general principles underlying environmental management. In this regard, international environmental management may represent a harbinger of more complex and more comprehensive international relations within an interactive structure that will involve numerous public and private actors in a large number of international regimes.

Some may argue that the UNCED forum encompassed the full range of current international environmental management. UNCED was an emanation of the United Nations system and reflected many of its strengths and weaknesses (Childers and Urquhart 1994). Many parts of the international environmental management structure described in this chapter were not represented at UNCED. Despite the fact that UNCED offered some representation of the international environmental agenda, the overall agenda proved too unwieldy to handle at one conference alone. Thus, one of the lessons from UNCED is that a single comprehensive structure for international environmental management is currently not possible. (For a fuller discussion of UNCED and its successes or failures, see Spector et al. 1994.)

It is premature to conclude, however, that finding a forum able to represent the full range of international environmental issues will remain permanently impossible. Proposals to create a multilateral environmental organization are based on an incomplete understanding of the issues and an excessive focus on a limited number of global environmental issues that cannot be separated in practice from the broader environmental agenda. Presumably, a global environmental organization would need formal links to environmental regimes at all levels, essentially a kind of standing conference of regimes.

It would be a mistake to conclude that a way around all these difficulties cannot be found. International environmental management has been an innovative endeavor that has repeatedly confounded conventional wisdom by its ability to make progress against the odds. In the meantime, however, we must recognize that dealing with environmental issues is an extremely frustrating experience for those engaged in building other, more clearly articulated regimes—such as the trade regimes. The environmental agenda must appear inchoate to them, with a disconcerting tendency to reveal new issues unexpectedly. There are several reasons for this tendency.

First, the environmental agenda is still relatively new. We are still uncertain about whether some issues—for example, pesticide residues in food or the use of bovine growth hormone—are truly environmental issues or simply matters of consumer policy. Second, the agenda is based on uncontrollable developments in the natural environment and frequently driven by unanticipated occurrences—such as the Bhopal accident, the Waldsterben phenomenon in Germany, the Chernobyl accident, the Exxon Valdez spill, or the discovery of the hole in the ozone layer over Antarctica—which can change priorities suddenly and dramatically. Finally, even scientific knowledge is uncertain regarding many environmental issues. Moreover the environmental agenda continues to evolve as scientific knowledge evolves. New discoveries (such as the phenomenon of pesticide resistance) and sometimes even new hypotheses (such as the role of acidification in forest dieback, the concept of biodiversity, or the idea that endocrine disrupters exist) can abruptly change the agenda.

The existence of these difficulties indicates a real need to tackle the practical problem that international environmental activities must be structured in some reasonable fashion to permit an assessment of their relationship to other priority areas of international concern and to trade policy in particular. Although the environmental agenda seems to remain inchoate, specific decisions nevertheless need to be made, which in turn implies a need to set priorities and to identify the relevant actors who must participate in the critical phases of decision making. A number of approaches can be taken in fulfilling these needs.

The most common approach from an environmental perspective is to list all substantive environmental issues — for example, water quality management, wildlife protection, the threat of global climate change, and so on. The problem with this approach is that it does not always lead to clear institutional roles.

The most practical approach from the perspective of other policy concerns is to identify levels of action or organizations that can serve as surrogates for substantive environmental concerns — for example, "multilateral environmental agreements," the United Nations Environment Program or the Commission on Sustainable Development. In this approach, the issue of representativeness would be set aside.

In some instances, individual countries have become champions for certain environmental issues; they are willing to pursue the issues through a wide range of institutions and to provide both leadership and coordination. No single country can be progressive on all environmental issues, but certain countries are often further along than others in managing some issues.

A different approach seeks to identify the structural characteristics that define the emerging system — in other words, to identify certain general principles that are broadly applicable to all environmental regimes. To be meaningful, such principles must meet tests of both necessity and sufficiency; that is, they must be necessary to achieving the goals of international environmental management and sufficient in the sense that they include all essential aspects of that management. These principles are related to the traditional principles of environmental policy (e.g., the polluter pays principle, the principle of prevention, and the precautionary principle), although these traditional principles were originally designed to guide specific policies rather than to explain the structure of environmental management itself.

The Winnipeg Principles on Trade and Sustainable Development (International Institute for Sustainable Development 1994), for example, were created to inform important areas of policy relating to the environment, particuarly those areas linked to trade policy and to the issue of sustainability. A number of these principles stand out as clearly identifiable parts of the emerging structure of international environmental management: specifically the principles of environmental integrity, science and precaution, openness and subsidiarity.

Environmental Integrity

It seems like a tautology to observe that the goal of environmental management is the preservation of environmental integrity. Nevertheless, we have to acknowledge that the quest for environmental integrity lies at the heart of the difficulties encountered in developing a systematic understanding of international environmental management.

Many areas of policy regularly confuse the means and the ends of goal achievement. Once a decision has been made to adopt certain measures to achieve certain policy goals, it is easier to focus on the effective implementation of these measures rather than on the question of whether the goals are actually being met. The problem is particularly acute in environmental management because the only variables subject to policy control are the means; the ends are subject to the laws of nature. The driving forces behind environmental management are, however, the quality of the environment and people's perceptions of the quality of the environment. All countries have at some time felt frustrated when, although they have faithfully executed stringent environmental policies, they discover that the result is unacceptable environmental quality.

Those actors who are primarily concerned with other areas of policy find it particularly difficult to accept the principle of environmental integrity because it acts like an Archimidean lever. Environmental processes are governed by the laws of nature and thus are not accessible to the normal bargaining of the policy process. Some actors whose primary concern is environmental management have recognized that they can turn environmental integrity into an absolute mandate. In the course of practical implementation, however, all principles are subject to a process of assessment and bargaining.

Cooperation

International environmental policy is a cooperative venture. At the heart of most international environmental regimes are "soft" structures of cooperation and accountability. The number of environmental regimes created over the past twenty years, a period of superpower tensions, is remarkable. We now have to confront the problems associated with using this large and complex structure to achieve the desired goal of maintaining environmental integrity. Neither military coercion nor economic leverage can ensure this goal; ultimately, it depends on willing cooperation, which in turn requires a high degree of accountability to ensure that burdens are fairly shared.

Science and Precaution

Science makes the environment speak. Without science, trees have no legal standing, ecosystems degrade unrecognized, and species are lost without our knowing. Scientists are deeply implicated in the process of environmental policy formation. However, although science is the only means we have of making environmental phenomena manifest, it is actually quite unsuited to the task of policy formation. The best science can do is to provide hypotheses that have stood up well under repeated scrutiny. The policy process, in contrast, focuses on a specific decision at a given time and does not worry greatly about the likelihood of different decisions being required at other times.

From the outset, environmental policy has struggled with the issue of "scientific uncertainty." Risk assessment and the precautionary principle are two approaches to this issue. In particular, the precautionary principle recognizes that science will not provide clear policy prescriptions and that criteria are needed to systematically address the resultant uncertainties in the policy process. Implementing the precautionary principle involves finding appropriate legal and economic bounds for action and taking the need to act as a given despite the continuing reality of scientific uncertainty.

Openness

The experience of most countries is that government action on the environment is frequently driven by public perceptions of environmental hazards. Environmental protection is indeed a matter of public concern rather than of particular interests. Thus, although science makes the environment speak, public pressure and organized environmental groups articulate the environmental interest in a manner that is politically effective in societies that view government as a balanced set of conflicting organized interests. This set of circumstances has created a constant demand for expanded opportunities for public participation and access to environmental information. In some instances, requiring public access to information and public participation can cause delays in administrative procedures. In general experience, however, the advantages of public participation in environmental management—including occasional acceleration of decision making—outweigh its disadvantages. The support for public participation in environmental management is founded on a potent combination of basic democratic principles and increased effectiveness of policy. Such participation is not bound by national frontiers, but broad democratic rights are not effectively protected at the international level. Countries, even democratic ones, differ widely in their attitudes toward public participation and freedom of information. Nevertheless, international environmental regimes are characterized by unprecedented levels of participation by nongovernmental actors—including scientists, business representatives, environmental organizations, and the media.

Subsidiarity

The principle of subsidiarity is central to environmental management. It recognizes that action must occur at different levels of jurisdiction, depending on the nature of the issues. It assigns priority to the lowest level of action consistent with effectiveness. For environmental policy, it recognizes the impossibility of capturing problems in precise political boundaries or of imposing extraordinary requirements for cooperation between jurisdictions at all levels. Moreover, although most environmental phenomena are local in origin, they have wide-ranging, sometimes even global effects. They can be managed only through cooperation between the level at which they originate and the level at which they produce effects.

Subsidiarity pervades environmental action. Most countries have struggled to balance the need for coordinated national action with the need to take specific steps at the local or regional level. In most instances, national legislation creates a framework for action, frequently with detailed standards, but implementation occurs at subnational levels, which retain significant discretion in setting priorities and determining strategies for the attainment of standards.

The need to apply the principle of subsidiarity is reinforced by the fact that environmental threats and environmental conditions differ from one region to another. Consequently, different measures may be needed to achieve comparable levels of environmental quality. For example, economic activities in areas with high concentrations of population benefit in many ways from direct access to finance, labor, and markets. Regions with direct access end up with higher concentrations of economic activity. The concentration of both population and economic activities, however, places a heavier burden on environmental resources so that environmental policy will need to be more stringent in such a region to attain environmental quality. Even with strict policy, the environmental quality of the region will remain lower than it is in areas with sparse population and few economic activities.

Establishing rules to govern these variations is one of the challenges of environmental policy, requiring a delicate balance between local autonomy and national requirements and between economic goals and environmental imperatives at all levels. The result is a complex, dynamic decision-making structure best described in terms of subsidiarity: the underlying rule must be to keep decisions as open as possible for the lowest level of centralization. Extending environmental policy to the international level — in response to inescapable demands for environmental quality that arise from threats to the environment — extends the application of the principle of subsidiarity to the international level.

In addition to these five basic principles for environmental management, the Winnipeg Principles include *efficiency* and *equity*. The efficiency principle forges an essential link between environmental management and economic policy, and the equity principle links management and social policy. Together, they circumscribe the agenda of sustainability that has frequently supplanted the more narrowly defined original environmental agenda.

These seven principles define an increasingly complex international structure of regimes for environmental management. To some extent, they represent a challenge to traditional approaches to international relations. Meeting the requirements of these principles, or at least recognizing their validity, has been the source of numerous innovations in the design and operation of international regimes.

The Structure of International Regimes: A Critical Task of International Governance

What was once a sparse landscape of international regimes has become increasingly verdant. The number of both intergovernmental and nongovernmental international regimes has expanded rapidly. Some hybrid public/private regimes such as the International Standards Organization have evolved. Overall, the most dramatic developments have taken place in the private sector, where rapidly expanding international business activity, further integration of scientific research, consolidation of media, and a burgeoning of nongovernmental environmental and policy research institutions have occurred. The environmental segment of the regime landscape has been largely self-organizing and has created a structure of international environmental management that reflects common principles even though it has no organizational coherence. The economic segment has also been self-organizing and includes such institutions as commodity markets and global commodity chains (Gereffi and Korzeniewicz 1994).

Little attention has been given to the problem of relationships between international regimes, whether they be governmental or nongovernmental. The United Nations, long the primary focus of attention as the main global international organization, does not represent an appropriate framework for the economic and social dimensions of the international system: its failures in this regard are due less to the inadequacy of the organization than to its incompatibility with the issues. Reform of the United Nations has long ceased to be the critical issue for international social and economic policy (including environmental management) because many crucial developments within regimes—some of them private in nature—have no relationship to the UN. Indeed, strengthening non–United Nations regimes and rendering them more effective and coherent are more important to the future of international governance than any conceivable adaptation or reform of the United Nations.

The lack of a coherent organizational structure for all relevant international regimes has created a situation in which competition between organizations is rampant; even organizations that form part of the United Nations compete with each other. The reason for this competition is relatively straightforward: each intergovernmental regime has been established as if it existed alone, with its own individual institutional structure and governing bodies. Even within the United Nations system, the secretary general does not exercise formal authority over the many constituent parts; he or she does not even have the right to nominate the administrative heads of the so-called specialized agencies. Consequently, coordination between parts occurs primarily when the incentives are right—that is, when financial resources or some other perceived source of influence is at stake.

In theory, intergovernmental regimes are the creation of sovereign states and remain under their control. In practice, such control has not extended to the sphere of coordination, mostly because it is difficult for countries to pursue the same policies in all of the regimes to which they belong. Large countries are overloaded with the number and complexity of the issues. Smaller countries frequently lack the personnel and resources needed for effective participation, much less for coordination efforts. Equally important, the emergence of international civil society has effectively removed full control of intergovernmental regimes from governments.

Two types of relationships stand out in the landscape of international environmental management: (1) relationships between international environmental regimes, and (2) relationships between environmental and other international regimes that deal with environmental impacts and economic policy. In the first type of relationship, regimes can be assumed to have convergent interests. Even when they pursue quite different aspects of environmental policy they will reflect similar underlying principles. In the second type of relationship, avoding potential conflicts and limitating their impacts are the focus of attention.

Relations among Environmental Regimes

An ongoing study of transboundary relations in North America indicates that several hundred agreements exist at the state/province and regional levels and that a much larger number of continuing relationships between nongovernmental organizations need to be taken into account. International environmental regimes are probably even more numerous in Europe. Rapid regime growth has not yet taken place in most other regions of the globe, but it is reasonable to assume that it will sooner or later occur. For example, we do not generally appreciate how extensive the phenomenon of international river basins is. There are thirteen river basins that involve five or more nations. Fifty countries have 75 percent or more of their territory in international river basins. Worldwide there are 215 international river basins that cover 47 percent of the global land area (Gleick 1993: 436–439). The current total of governmental agreements concerning international river basins runs to roughly twenty thousand, with an at least equal number of relevant nongovernmental arrangements.

Relations between these regimes are defined geographically and by subject matter. Regimes that operate in a given region can be presumed to interact as necessary, but the same cannot be said of all regimes that operate between two countries or of all regimes concerned with a particular issue. In all instances, however, the dynamic of subsidiarity applies to the relationships between the regime and the institutions that implement the specific provisions of the regime.

Structures to ensure the integration of these regimes are extremely rare. UNEP sponsored the Regional Seas Program, which encompasses most (but not all) the regimes that address matters of marine pollution at a regional (rather than global) level. UNEP also provides secretariat functions for several global environmental regimes and is actively involved in others. It often coordinates regime activities as far as appears reasonable. The Global Environment Facility is involved in the financial arrangements for several global environmental regimes consequently representing a potential vector of coordination. Recently, the Swedish government took the initiative in creating an Intergovernmental Forum on Chemicals to provide a means of ensuring better coordination and information flow between those concerned with chemicals policy. Efforts to draw together regimes designed to improve forest management and the trade in forest products have thus far not met with success, but two new initiatives have been launched. The recently established North American Commission for Environmental Cooperation is puzzling over its relations with existing international environmental regimes in North America. In addition, the so-called post-Dobris process in Europe has created a forum for both ministers of the environment and some international institutions in an attempt to promote more effective environmental management in the changing political landscape of Central and Eastern Europe. Certainly, the UN Commission on Sustainable Development may conceivably contribute to greater coordination in the field of environmental management. Although all of these examples serve to illustrate the nature of the problems in coordinating regimes, none of them presents a solution.

Relations between International Environmental and Economic Regimes
Environmental policy is a form of economic policy in that, when successful, it can create structural reform of the economic system. Relations between environmental and economic regimes are thus close and frequently difficult. The major problem in achieving better coordination between economic and environmental regimes is their structural incommensurability: although environmental regimes have clear economic impacts, their structure is not defined by these economic impacts.

The central reality of relations between economic and environmental regimes is that their goals overlap without being congruent. In many areas they act in mutually reinforcing ways so that coordination, although desirable, is not essential. If the outcomes of actions by environmental regimes are economically desirable, no conflict occurs between the two types of regimes. Coordination may improve the outcomes in significant ways, but it is not an inescapable necessity. In other areas, the steps that one type of regime takes to achieve its goal may have more or less detrimental impacts on the other type of regime.

In other words, alternative strategies are available to achieve certain goals that may be either more or less desirable from the perspective of the other type of regime. In these instances, coordination is essential to ensure that the approach most acceptable to the other type of regime is used. Finally, in some instances, the goals of environmental and economic regimes are in conflict — perhaps for structural reasons, perhaps because of temporary circumstances, or perhaps because of differing perceptions and assessments of outcomes.

As the foregoing analysis suggests, the structurally defining principles of the respective regimes are critical. In the case of the trade regimes, the critical principles are economic efficiency and its cognate comparative advantage. These principles are institutionalized in trade regimes through the most-favored nation principle and the national treatment principle. In the case of environmental regimes, the critical principles are environmental integrity, subsidiarity, international cooperation, science and precaution, and openness. Unlike the principles of the trade regime, these principles have not yet been given clear institutional form.

Focusing on the structural characteristics of regimes also opens up new avenues of analysis of nongovernmental international regimes. Such analysis may help us to identify criteria we can use to assess the appropriateness of such regimes for the tasks at hand, to locate areas in which they require strengthening, or to pinpoint times when they need to form strategic alliances. Without such criteria it may prove difficult to develop any systematic understanding of the nature, appropriateness, and effectiveness of these regimes.

10

Global Governance: Toward a Theory of Decentralized World Order

Oran R. Young

The demand for governance in world affairs has never been greater. Broadly speaking, this development is a product of rising interdependencies among the members of international society and what we have come to think of as global civil society. It is increasingly difficult for states and various nonstate actors to isolate themselves from events taking place in other parts of the world, however much they may wish to do so. Even for individuals who live on the opposite side of the planet, the political repercussions of the disintegration of the former Soviet Union and the bloody civil war in the former Yugoslavia are inescapable. The economic consequences of financial crises in Mexico or Russia reverberate throughout the global monetary system. Likewise, greenhouse gases emitted anywhere in the world affect the global climate system. These examples are merely illustrative of a broad spectrum of problems that make it impossible for individual actors to isolate themselves from the impact of outside events.

The end of the Cold War triggered a moment of euphoria when it seemed that the emergence of a new world order was at hand and that the promise of the United Nations as an intergovernmental mechanism for solving problems of international governance would finally be realized. This moment soon ended, however, with euphoria giving way to mounting skepticism about the capacity of the United Nations to cope with an array of pressing problems. The failure of UN peacekeeping missions in Bosnia, Rwanda, and Somalia has raised profound questions about the ability of the organization to deal effectively with current threats to international peace and security. The pronounced tendency of the group of seven most-developed countries (G-7), the Organization for Economic Cooperation and Development (OECD), the European Union (EU), and the North American Free Trade Agreement (NAFTA) to circumvent the United Nations in dealing with consequential economic issues has marginalized the world organization in the arena of the global economy (Lyons 1995). In the realm of environmental affairs, the obvious inadequacy of initiatives such as the Commission on Sustainable Development, established as a legacy of the 1992 United Nations Conference on Environment and Development, highlights the limited capacity of the UN to solve problems involving the relationship between humans and the environment.

What is to be done to close the dramatic gap between the demand for governance and the capacity to supply governance in international society? Some observers react to this question with growing frustration and a deepening sense of pessimism regarding our ability to cope with the world's troubles. Anticipating a coming anarchy, they offer no clear recipe for coming to grips with the crisis of governance they foresee.[1] Others respond by emphasizing efforts to reform the United Nations as a preferred mechanism for supplying global governance. Those who espouse this approach have devoted much time and energy to drawing up blueprints for restructuring the organization to increase its capacity to deal with a wide range of governance problems. The latest in a long line of such prescriptive programs is articulated in the report of the Commission on Global Governance, *Our Global Neighborhood*, published in January 1995.[2]

A third response points out the distinction between governance and government. Those who offer this response direct attention to a variety of innovative social practices that have come into existence in recent years to solve discrete or distinct problems: the creation of regimes or sets of roles, rules, and relationships that focus on specific issues but do not require elaborate organizations to administer them (Levy, Young, and Zürn 1995). Whereas the second option looks to the United Nations system and calls for a comprehensive, legally binding, and state-centered approach to international governance, the third response looks to piecemeal or issue-specific arrangements that may or may not be legally binding, that may or may not assign some role to the United Nations and its specialized agencies, and that may often accord important roles to nonstate actors. Creative efforts of this sort are particularly notable in—but by no means confined to—the realm of environmental issues (Young 1994a).

Without passing judgment on other responses, the Dartmouth Conference on International Governance in the Twenty-first Century set for itself the task of critically assessing this third response's potential ability to face the challenge of governance in world affairs as we prepare to enter the next millennium. There is no denying the appeal of this approach, with its pragmatic focus on well-defined problems, its promise of crafting regimes that do not require expensive bureaucratic organizations, and its sense of optimism about the prospects for solving problems without radically transforming the character of international society. The attractiveness of this approach should not prevent us critically assessing it however. On the contrary, it highlights the importance of taking a hard look at the real potential of issue-specific regimes. Proceeding in this spirit, the participants in the Dartmouth Conference posed and sought to answer the following questions:

• What exactly are regimes and how do they differ from organizations such as the United Nations that have occupied our attention in earlier efforts to meet the demand for governance in international society?

• Are we witnessing the emergence of a global civil society alongside international society, and what are the implications of this development for governance in world affairs?

• Are some sorts of problems better suited than other sorts to treatment through the formation of international or transnational regimes?

• Under what conditions are issue-specific regimes likely to prove successful or effective in solving the problems that motivate their creation?

• What broader (often unintended) consequences for international society or for global civil society are likely to flow from the formation and operation of a growing collection of regimes?

Regimes as Sources of Governance

The blossoming of interest in international regimes as mechanisms for solving problems of governance has defined a number of new concepts and has redefined a number of old concepts. In addition to regimes, we now find ourselves talking about social institutions, social practices, governance systems, mechanisms of social control, and organizations. This poses two problems (Young 1994a). As Olav Schram Stokke reminds us in his chapter in this volume, few analysts can agree on the definition and use of some key terms, a fact that complicates efforts to compare and contrast arguments about fundamental questions regarding the formation and effectiveness of regimes. Additional difficulties arise when we attempt to operationalize these concepts for purposes of empirical analysis. As a result, it is often difficult to subject the diverse views of theoreticians to empirical testing in order to single out those propositions that stand up well to testing and to discard those that do not.

Even more fundamental is the split between those who adopt a *contractarian* perspective and those who think in *constitutive* terms in seeking to identify and understand international regimes. Contractarians assume the prior existence of actors with a clear sense of their own identities and of the interests flowing from these identities. Such actors will be motivated to create institutional arrangements when they discover that proceeding individualistically leads to joint losses or to an inability to reap joint gains. According to this account, then, regimes are devices created by self-interested actors to solve or at least to ameliorate collective-action problems (e.g., security dilemmas, trade wars, tragedies of the commons) and thus to increase social welfare (R. Hardin 1982). The constitutive perspective, on the other hand, assumes that institutions play a major role in defining the interests of participants and even in shaping their identities. Membership in the European Union, for example, requires states to adjust their domestic systems to conform to the requirements of the union. According to this account, institutions have formative effects on their members rather than the other way around (Wendt 1987, 1992).

In one sense, there is no need to choose between these analytic perspectives. They offer different starting points that produce distinct lines of inquiry, each of which should be encouraged to broaden and deepen our knowledge of governance in international society. What is more, it is perfectly possible to adopt the view that actors and institutions are mutually constitutive: participation in social institutions can affect how members frame their interests and understand their identities, even though their distinct identities were established prior to participation (Wendt 1994). Yet clashes between advocates of these distinct perspectives, who often disagree about matters of epistemology as well as about conceptual or analytic issues (Kratochwil and Ruggie 1986), have served to heighten the problem facing those analysts who want to devise a practical means of identifying the universe of international regimes. Such clashes prevent these analysts from getting on with the task of assessing the potential of this approach to meet the rising demand for governance in international society.

How should we proceed in the face of these conceptual complications? The answer that emerged from the discussion at the Dartmouth Conference is a highly pragmatic one. Despite the conceptual problems, most observers have little trouble recognizing international regimes in operation, and there is a high level of agreement among them when it comes to identifying specific regimes. With regard to environmental concerns, for example, regimes govern an array of functional problems (e.g., the dumping of wastes at sea, intentional discharges of oil, international trade in endangered species of fauna and flora, transboundary fluxes of airborne pollutants, international shipments of hazardous wastes, ozone depletion, the loss of biological diversity, climate change, and so on), as well as a variety of geographically delimited areas (e.g., the Great Lakes, the Rhine River, the Svalbard Archipelago, Antarctica, and various regional seas). Some regimes reflect functional and geographical concerns at the same time, as in the case of the regime designed to protect the North Sea from the disposal of chemical wastes at sea and from land-based runoffs. Some observers, of course, disagree about whether a particular regime exists, especially when a regime is embryonic or in its earliest stages of development (e.g., the arrangements spelled out in the 1992 Framework Convention on Climate Change). What is most noteworthy for analytic purposes, however, is that such disagreements typically involve marginal cases. In general, there is a high degree of consensus regarding the identification of most members of the set of international regimes.

What do the members of this set of international regimes have in common that can help to pinpoint the defining attributes of regimes in general? Regimes are sets of rules, decision-making procedures, and programs that define social practices, assign roles to the participants in these practices, and govern their interactions. Regimes can and certainly do vary along a number of dimensions. Most obviously, they differ greatly in their functional scope, geographical domain, and membership. Consider the differences between the Great Lakes water quality regime, which has two members and focuses on water quality in a limited area, and the climate regime, which is global in scope and is likely to draw in almost all members of international society as it develops. Regimes also vary considerably in their decision-making procedures, compliance mechanisms, revenue sources, and dispute-resolution processes. They may have significantly different degrees of formalization: some rest on legally binding conventions or treaties, and others are founded on soft law agreements (e.g., ministerial declarations, executive agreements, or even more informal understandings).

Beyond this, a number of more analytic distinctions have emerged in the literature on international regimes (Levy, Young, and Zürn 1995). Although complex mixes of characteristics are common, individual regimes may be (1) largely regulative in the sense that they emphasize the formulation of rules or behavioral prescriptions; (2) predominantly procedural in the sense that they focus on procedures for arriving at collective choices; (3) essentially programmatic in the sense that they lead to joint or collaborative projects; or (4) fundamentally generative in the sense that they highlight new ways of thinking about problems. Regimes also vary in strength, which is measured in terms of the specificity, density, range, and depth of their operative provisions. Many regimes (e.g., the Antarctic Treaty System, the European transboundary air pollution regime) become stronger as they develop over time. Additionally, as Konrad von Moltke's discussion of institutional structures makes clear (see Chapter 9 in this volume), individual regimes are often nested within overarching institutional arrangements or integrated into larger structures pertaining to broader issue areas (e.g., the regime for high seas fishing is subject to the encompassing law of the sea; or the regimes that deal with specific commodities such as sugar, coffee, or tin are parts of the overarching regime that deals with international trade in goods and services).

Like other social institutions, international regimes come in many sizes and shapes, yet they share a number of features that place them in the same universe of cases and set them apart from entities that are emphasized in other approaches to governance in international society. (e.g., the various components of the United Nations system). Regimes such as the ones designed to protect stratospheric ozone and to regulate trade in endangered species of fauna and flora indicate that, international regimes are almost invariably responses to specific problems; they do not seek to provide comprehensive systems of public order for geographically or socially defined areas. Although states loom large in such arrangements, a variety of nonstate actors (including the intergovernmental organizations [IGOs] discussed in chapters 5 and 8) have become important players in these institutional arrangements. Taken together, regimes form a horizontal rather than a vertical or hierarchical system of public order. The result is a complex pattern of decentralized order. One of the strengths of this arrangement is the capacity of individual regimes to survive serious failures that occur in other components of the system. A weakness, however, is an underdeveloped capacity to sort out overlaps and intersections among issue-specific arrangements. Individual regimes are created for different purposes by different actors who often make little or no effort to coordinate their efforts or to identify the links between regimes.

Relatively speaking, regimes are lightly administered. If we draw a distinction between regimes as institutions and organizations as material entities possessing offices, budgets, personnel, and legal personalities, it is possible to say that the regime approach to governance highlights the idea of "governance without government" and holds out the prospect of fulfilling the function of governance while minimizing the establishment of new bureaucracies or administrative entities (Rosenau and Czempiel 1992). Of course, as Helmut Breitmeier makes clear (see chapter 4 in this volume), IGOs frequently play significant roles in the processes of regime formation. Much of the work of implementing the provisions of international regimes is left to individual members that are typically highly organized, whether they are states or various types of nonstate actors. Moreover, regimes vary in the extent to which their day-to-day operation requires the presence of organizational capacity at the international or transnational level. For instance, the 1959 Antarctic Treaty, the core element of the Antarctic Treaty System, is operated without any standing administrative apparatus; however, the organizational arrangements initially envisioned in connection with deep seabed mining—the International Seabed Authority and the Enterprise—would have brought into existence an unprecedentedly elaborate set of organizations. No doubt, this is one reason why the original deep seabed mining provisions set forth in part XI of the 1982 Law of the Sea Convention have fallen by the wayside, even though the convention itself finally entered into force in 1994, almost twelve years after being opened for signature in 1982.

Regimes frequently acquire increased organizational capacity as they evolve through time. As Peterson observes (chapter 5 in this volume), IGOs often assume increasingly important roles in implementing or operating regimes as the social practices they launch become more and more complex. To take the case of Antarctica again, the addition of new elements dealing with living resources and environmental protection has added to the Antarctic Treaty System an increasingly complex administrative apparatus. Even so, the secretariats and associated organizations that have grown up to perform various functions for environmental regimes are more likely to have only five to twenty staff members in contrast to the hundreds employed by the various entities included in the United Nations System, such as UNDP, WHO, FAO, UNESCO, or the World Bank (Institute on International Environmental Governance 1995).

Regimes and Societies

International regimes do not operate in a social vacuum. Just as students of domestic systems draw a distinction between the state and civil society, those concerned with international affairs have long recognized that the states system itself can be looked upon as a society of states. Reasonably well-defined principles spell out the criteria for membership in international society, and explicit rules govern interactions among its members (e.g., the rule prescribing nonintervention in the domestic affairs of individual members).[3] Although there is no state as such in international society, we can still pose questions about the relationship between regimes as elements of a decentralized system of public order and the society of states in which they operate. These questions parallel the questions that students of domestic systems ask about the relationship between state and society.

Both the constitutive principles of the states system and the more specific rules that have emerged to put them into practice are violated from time to time, and the constitutive underpinnings of international society evolve steadily over time. Recently, for example, there has been much discussion of de facto shifts in the idea of sovereignty as a constitutive principle of international society (Lyons and Mastanduno 1995). Nonetheless, there can be no doubt that in their focus on international society, many (perhaps most) students of international regimes have assumed that the members of regimes are states and have proceeded to analyze the effectiveness of regimes within an analytic framework tied to the states system (Krasner 1983).

This state-centric perspective, however, runs the risk of introducing a conservative bias into regime analysis and fails to confront many interesting developments currently underway in world affairs. A number of the participants in the Dartmouth Conference argued forcefully that there is no reason to believe that states are on their way out as centers of power and authority. Led by Paul Wapner and Konrad von Moltke, they also suggested, however, that a second social system is growing up around the society of states and that this second system is coming to form a part of the social environment within which regimes operate. Described by Wapner and others as *global civil society*, this system is made up of a variety of nonstate actors—including interest groups, professional associations, and corporations—that operate above the level of the individual but below or apart from the level of the state (Wapner 1995a, 1996; Lipschutz 1996).

As a number of conference participants noted, the concept of global civil society is currently fraught with ambiguities. Does global civil society qualify as a society in the sense that it has identifiable constitutive principles covering such matters as membership and interactions among its members? Is global civil society a single phenomenon to be considered on a par with international society? Does it make sense, for instance, to include the world economy or the worldwide system of modes of production as part of global civil society, or are we better off reserving the idea of civil society for essentially noneconomic and nonpolitical actors and interactions (Thompson 1983)? Does global civil society have a life of its own, or is it more appropriately treated as a set of developments that modify the character of international society?[4] At the end of the day, can we define the concept of global civil society with sufficient precision so that we can distinguish it from international society and make confident judgments concerning its strength and the degree to which its strength is increasing or decreasing?

These are formidable questions. Even so, the discussion at the Dartmouth Conference made it clear that the concept of global civil society is a rich one, with a great deal to offer to students of international or transnational governance. As von Moltke and Wapner pointed out at the conference, one danger of regime analysis is that it can become excessively state centric; that is, it assumes that membership in international regimes is (or should be?) limited to states. There is no doubt that we are experiencing the emergence of a variety of recognized and significant roles for nonstate actors in the development and operation of international regimes (Princen and Finger 1994). Some of these actors (e.g., multinational corporations) have proven remarkably adept at finding ways to achieve their goals within institutional frameworks established by international regimes. Beyond these frameworks (if we are to take Wapner's ideas seriously) lies the realm of organized relations between nonstate actors and global civil society. Just as international regimes have proliferated to deal with a variety of problems arising in international society, transnational regimes have been created as mechanisms for solving problems arising in global civil society. Consider, for example, the global insurance regime that has evolved in conjunction with the dramatic growth in world trade during the postwar era, or the global communications regime that has emerged among users of the World Wide Web. Moreover, it is fair to say that membership in global civil society has constitutive significance for many nonstate actors (e.g., the Worldwide Fund for Nature or Greenpeace) in the same way that membership in international society has constitutive implications for states (Wapner 1995a). Under these circumstances, it makes no more sense to try to grasp the identity of many nonstate actors without understanding their involvement in global civil society than it does to define the identity of states without paying attention to their connection to international society.

One discussion at the Dartmouth Conference focused on Wapner's suggestion that global civil society should be regarded as a mechanism for the performance of governance in its own right. Interesting as this suggestion may seem, it runs the risk of confusing the issue rather than clarifying it. Regimes are sets of roles, rules, and relationships created to deal with issue-specific problems, whether these problems are associated primarily with the society of states or with global civil society. In order to make progress in the analysis of the relationships among these various systems, we need a clear distinction between regimes, on the one hand, and both international society and global civil society on the other.[5] The point of drawing such a distinction (which parallels the distinction between state and society with regard to domestic systems) is not to argue that regimes and society are unrelated to each other. On the contrary, the distinction opens up a new research agenda that focuses precisely on the links between regimes and societies. Are regimes easier to create and operate successfully in some societal settings than in others? Can we draw useful distinctions between international regimes whose members are states and transnational regimes whose members are various types of nonstate actors? Are some types of regimes better suited to operate in conjunction with international society or with global civil society? What about the prospects for regimes whose membership comprises a mix of states and nonstate actors? How should we think about the argument advanced by Marcia Valiante, Paul Muldoon, and Lee Botts (see chapter 7 in this volume) that the presence of a broader community treated as an element of society is necessary for regimes to operate effectively? These and other similar questions indicate important issues that come into focus once we make a clear distinction between regimes and society; they cannot be posed, let alone answered, in the absence of such a distinction.

To sum up this discussion, we can distinguish initially between two pure types of regimes relevant to world affairs. International regimes, the central concern of most contributors to the new institutionalism in international relations, are institutional arrangements whose members are states and whose operations center on issues arising in international society. Arms control regimes, such as the arrangements governing nonproliferation of nuclear weapons, exemplify this category of institutions. Transnational regimes, in contrast, are institutional arrangements whose members are nonstate actors and whose operations are pertinent to issues that arise in global civil society. The rapidly emerging social practice governing relations among users of the World Wide Web is a case in point. Although these pure types of regimes are interesting for analytic purposes, real-world regimes are often (perhaps typically) mixed types: nonstate actors often play significant roles in international regimes, and states often have important roles to play in transnational regimes, What is more, societal influences can and often do cut across the pure types of regimes. The forces at work in global civil society can exert considerable pressure on the operation of international regimes, and international society can exert pressure on the operation of transnational regimes. It follows that we must pay greater attention to arrangements in which states and nonstate actors interact with one another in complex ways, rather than cling to the familiar assumptions of a state-centric world. To facilitate discussion, we might agree to use the term *global governance* to refer to the combined categories of international, transnational, and mixed regimes.

The Effectiveness of Regimes

It would be a mistake to expect too much of individual regimes as devices for meeting the growing demand for governance in world affairs. Although the number of such arrangements has increased rapidly in recent decades, especially in the realm of environmental affairs, regimes do not arise to deal with every problem that makes its way onto the global political agenda. In fact, the effort to explain why regimes form to deal with some problems but not with others is a major preoccupation of students of global governance. Thus, the striking contrast between international efforts to regulate various forms of air pollution and efforts to conserve forests with global environmental significance is a phenomenon that calls for sustained analysis. Even when regimes do come into being, the absence of any hierarchical structure capable of welding these issue-specific arrangements into an integrated world order means that gaps between and overlaps among discrete regimes are common. Some institutional linkages are beneficial in the sense that separate regimes serve to reinforce each other, thereby contributing to the fulfillment of their respective goals. But as von Moltke observes, mutual interference is also inevitable from time to time (Young 1996). Under the circumstances, therefore, we have no basis for expecting regimes to offer a simple and comprehensive solution to the problem of governance in world affairs.

It is natural, however, to raise questions, as Thomas Bernauer does in discussing regimes for river basins (see chapter 6 in this volume), about the effectiveness of specific regimes or their success in solving the problems that motivate their creators to establish them. As the discussion at the Dartmouth Conference made clear, a number of criteria are widely used to assess the performance of regimes over and above considerations relating to the substantive features of particular problems. An *economic criterion* stresses efficiency and asks whether the same results could have been achieved at a lower cost or, alternatively, better results achieved at the same cost. A *political criterion* directs attention to equity and raises questions about the fairness both of the results of institutional arrangements and of their procedures or processes. Although equity is notoriously difficult to define and operationalize, it cannot be set aside as a major concern or criterion. Assessments of environmental regimes also use an *ecological criterion* that emphasizes the degree to which the results flowing from institutional arrangements are sustainable in the sense they do not disrupt key biotic or abiotic systems. A well-known example of this concern is the vigorous debate in recent years about an analytic construct known as the "tragedy of the commons"; this debate centers on issues that relate to the consequences of alternative structures of property rights (McCay and Acheson 1987).

A particularly interesting feature of the discussion of the performance of regimes at the Dartmouth Conference was the introduction of the idea of process management as an alternative (or supplement) to problem solving in the assessment of social institutions. Articulated with particular clarity by Angela Cropper of the United Nations Development Program, this idea suggests we need to recognize that some problems are extremely difficult or even impossible to solve within any reasonable time frame. Many cases of ethnic conflict immediately come to mind to illustrate this phenomenon. Environmental examples, such as the problems associated with the treatment of toxic wastes or anthropogenic interferences in the global carbon cycle, are easy to identify as well. In such cases, regimes may be more effective in managing or containing problems than in solving them. The idea of process management also helps us to grasp the role that regimes can play in deepening or even transforming our understanding of the problems that led to their creation. In cases such as climate change, where the physical and biological systems involved are poorly understood, this form of process management can become a central feature of the performance of institutional arrangements. Without doubt, the development of the concept of process management was one of the more striking ideas to emerge from the conference, and it certainly deserves greater attention in future analyses of institutional effectiveness.

Even so, this concept is by no means free from controversy. The debate over process management resembles the well-known debate among students of conflict: one group focuses on conflict resolution and sees management as a process that is likely to reduce pressures on the parties to resolve their differences; the other group emphasizes conflict management and sees resolution as an ideal whose pursuit may prove detrimental to the effort to manage or contain conflicts. As this comparison suggests, success in the development of regimes that emphasize process management may sometimes reduce the pressure to solve problems, but the single-minded pursuit of regimes capable of solving problems can turn out to be a counsel of perfection that leads to outright failure. There is no simple way to resolve this debate; the arguments on both sides have merit, at least under some circumstances. The idea of process management is nevertheless a welcome addition to the growing stream of work that hitherto has looked at institutional effectiveness primarily in terms of problem solving.

Whatever way we choose to approach the effectiveness of international and transnational regimes, virtually everyone agrees that they vary dramatically in terms of their performance and that many individual regimes undergo substantial changes over time with regard to effectiveness. The prevailing view (reinforced by Valiante, Muldoon, and Botts) is that the regime created to deal with Great Lakes water quality has been relatively successful. But, as Bernauer reminds us in chapter 6, many other arrangements that deal with lakes or river basins have performed poorly.[6] Similarly, the regime governing problems of pollution in the North Sea has grown stronger with the passage of time, whereas many international fisheries regimes have proven increasingly ineffectual. There is general agreement, moreover, that the regime dealing with intentional discharges of oil at sea became markedly more effective following a switch during the 1970s from a system of discharge standards to a system based on equipment standards (Mitchell 1994b). The regime for whales and whaling became increasingly effective during the 1970s and early 1980s, before undergoing a transformation of constitutive principles from conservationism to preservationism. Such a transformation raises questions about whether it is meaningful to compare the regime's current effectiveness with its earlier performance. Overall, the effectiveness of international and transnational regimes varies greatly, which leads us to search for factors that serve as determinants of success or failure. We must also determine whether assessment should focus only on problem solving or open up to considerations of efficiency and equity or of process management in contrast to problem solving.

This conclusion suggests the need for a large and profoundly important research program focusing on governance in world affairs. Not only is it important for analytic purposes to focus attention on the determinants of institutional effectiveness, but it is also essential to make progress in this area if the study of regimes is to yield results of interest to practitioners. It is hardly surprising, then, that in recent years students of regimes have devoted more and more attention to various aspects of effectiveness (Levy, Young, and Zürn 1995). Any definitive judgment regarding the results of these studies would undoubtedly be premature; this is a case in which it is surely accurate to say that more research is needed. Still, asking for a midterm report regarding efforts to understand the forces that explain the variance in the performance of international and transnational regimes would not be an unreasonable request.

As the discussion at the Dartmouth Conference made clear, the report we can offer at this time is by no means clear-cut. Recent work — represented most clearly in this volume by the contributions of Bernauer and Valiante, Muldoon, and Botts (see chapters 6 and 7) — has produced a long and rapidly growing list of factors that appear to have some bearing on the effectiveness of regimes, at least in specific cases. Robust generalizations about the relative importance of these factors and well-grounded propositions that state necessary or sufficient conditions for regimes to succeed as problem solvers or as process managers still need to be developed, however. Some analysts emphasize the nature of the problem to be solved and draw a distinction between benign and malign (or easy and difficult) problems (Rittberger and Zürn 1991; Andresen and Wettestad 1995). Others differentiate between distinct social forces (e.g., material conditions, interests, and ideas); they seek to sort out the relative importance of factors such as population growth, technology, conflicts of interests, and values as determinants of performance (Cox 1986). Another approach features the distinction between endogenous and exogenous factors. Those analysts who look to endogenous factors focus on the role of various institutional attributes — such as the nature of decision rules, revenue sources, and compliance mechanisms (Mitchell 1994b). Those analysts who focus on exogenous factors, in contrast, tend to see regimes as relatively fragile structures influenced by societal forces that range from material conditions, such as technology, to intangible conditions, such as the emergence of consensual knowledge. Yet another perspective emphasizes the extent to which individual regimes are embedded in larger institutional structures (Ruggie 1983, 1991). How deeply the regimes are embedded is partly a matter of international or transnational linkages that can affect performance and partly a matter of whether regimes complement or clash with the social institutions that operate at the domestic and local levels. A particularly interesting thought expressed at the Dartmouth Conference suggests that effectiveness will often be a function of the compatibility of top-down arrangements reflected in the content of international regimes themselves and bottom-up arrangements reflected in features of the societal setting (e.g., the presence of a well-defined community). The issue of the links between regimes and society thus will be particularly pertinent in cases such as climate change because the problem to be solved involves behavior that reaches all the way down to the actions of individual users of motor vehicles or home appliances.

The most striking feature of this type of analysis is the proliferation of factors that appear to have some bearing on the effectiveness of regimes. The factors identified in the preceding paragraph by no means exhaust the list of determinants of effectiveness uncovered by case studies. These studies lend support to a wide range of claims about the importance of one factor or another in determining effectiveness, at least in specific cases. What does the discovery of this list of determinants mean, however, and how should we respond to it in our ongoing efforts to understand the effectiveness of regimes? For one thing, the list raises searching questions about the efficacy of classic procedures of *variation-finding analysis* in regime analysis. It is difficult, perhaps impossible, not only to identify necessary or sufficient conditions for the success of regimes, but also to explain proportions of the variance in effectiveness — treated as the dependent variable — in terms of specific independent variables. To some degree, these problems stem from the difficulty of conducting empirical research that uses large enough samples of comparable cases to make the results meaningful (King, Keohane, and Verba 1994). But there is a deeper issue here as well. The array of factors somehow involved is so large and so prone to surfacing in different combinations that the familiar techniques of variation-finding analysis may yield only inconclusive and disappointing results in attempts to identify exactly which features determine regime effectiveness.

Without doubt, we need to continue the search for robust generalizations about regime effectiveness; we may be able to simplify the analysis dramatically once we identify the right variables and organize them into a powerful model of effectiveness. Nonetheless, the discussion at the Dartmouth Conference suggests that we need to direct more attention to the techniques of *tendency-finding analysis* and to probe the uses of what is often called genetic explanation in seeking to improve our understanding of the determinants of regime effectiveness.[7] As David Dessler (1992) puts it, variation-finding analysis seeks to answer the question, "Under what conditions will regimes prove effective?" Tendency-finding analysis, on the other hand, directs attention to the question, "How is it possible for regimes to solve or manage specific problems?"

Tendency-finding analysis does not yield generalizations about regular relationships between dependent and independent variables. Rather, it leads to the identification of combinations of forces that, taken together, can be said to cause outcomes in individual cases. The particular combinations of forces in specific cases may be unusual or even unique. As a result, the testing of genetic explanations does not feature efforts to compare hypothesized regularities with empirical evidence obtained from collections of comparable cases. Rather, those who engage in tendency-finding analysis tend to study individual cases in depth in order to construct persuasive narrative accounts of the forces affecting the performance of regimes and to assess the merits of rival hypotheses. Their objective is to develop detailed accounts of the dynamics of individual cases rather than to assemble data sets of the sort required to test the hypotheses that come from variation-finding analysis.

What are the implications of this argument for the application of regime analysis to matters of public policy and, more specifically, to the design of individual regimes so that they have the best possible chance of proving effective? The answer is that regime analysis should be looked upon, at least in part, as a diagnostic tool rather than as a source of straightforward generalizations to be applied to well-defined and sizable sets of cases with little need for interpretation. The analyst here is much like the physician rather than the physiologist: the physician focuses on individual cases and runs through a relatively long checklist of potentially relevant factors in search of the particular combination that accounts for the condition of each patient, who is treated as a unique individual. It would thus be inappropriate for regime practitioners to expect regime analysts to formulate simple and generic rules to guide the process of institutional design (e.g., try to maximize transparency regarding compliance with regime rules, or strive to include extensive implementation review mechanisms as a prominent feature of regime design). Rather, regime analysts should be treated as diagnosticians who can use the results of tendency-finding analysis to provide an in-depth understanding of the forces at work in a specific case and to recommend institutional arrangements to enhance effectiveness.

Broader Consequences of Regimes

Whether or not regimes succeed in solving or managing particular social problems, their presence may have broader consequences for the social settings in which they operate. Some regimes produce spillover effects by influencing the relationship of members in functional areas beyond their nominal scope.[8] As Valiante, Muldoon, and Botts observe (see chapter 7), regimes, especially those widely regarded as successful, can also generate demonstration effects by creating precedents that influence the thinking of both their own members and the members of other regimes as they confront new problems. The role that issue-specific regimes play as vehicles for the introduction of institutional innovations is even more significant in the long run because such innovations propagate throughout international society or global civil society in ways that have profound consequences over time. Students of regimes have devoted relatively little attention so far to the analysis of these broader consequences (Levy, Young, and Zürn 1995). It is clear, however, that we must invest more time and energy in such analysis if research on governance in world affairs is to flourish in the future.

The discussion at the Dartmouth Conference emphasized the importance of avoiding inflated expectations about the capacity of regimes to deal with the world's troubles. Some participants suggested that a preoccupation with problems amenable to treatment through regimes may actually divert attention from larger or more pervasive concerns in international society and in global civil society. These concerns include the resurgence of ethnic violence that is leading to the breakdown or failure of multinational states; the steady growth of human population to a level that raises questions about the Earth's carrying capacity; the surging tides of both documented and undocumented migrants and refugees that threaten to produce open conflict in a number of areas; and the spread of technologies that are leading human communities to expend the Earth's natural capital at an unprecedented rate. These problems are systemic not in the sense that they focus on global systems (e.g., the global climate system) but rather in the sense that they involve large-scale processes occurring all over the world. Problems of this sort may be appropriate targets for the articulation of general international norms or broad principles of international law. It is difficult, however, to see how they can be solved through the creation of issue-specific regimes designed to deal with more circumscribed problems.

We should also bear in mind that international or transnational regimes have a limited capacity to alter the behavior within societies that frequently underlies the problems to be solved. (e.g., the combustion of fossil fuels or the destruction of old-growth forests). Their capacity is limited partly because securing compliance with international or transnational rules is difficult.[9] and partly because regimes are top-down arrangements whose ability to solve problems will be determined in considerable measure by the extent to which they complement bottom-up arrangements centered on the same issues. These limitations are particularly apparent in cases where the behavior in question is not so much a matter of actions on the part of regime members themselves but rather a matter of actions on the part of numerous actors (including individuals) who are operating below the level of regime members. The accounts of management arrangements for transboundary lakes and rivers presented by Bernauer (chapter 6) and by Valiante, Muldoon, and Botts (chapter 7) are particularly illuminating in this regard.

Consider climate change and in particular the combustion of fossil fuels as a prominent case in point (Rowlands 1995). The emission of carbon dioxide from the burning of fossil fuels is a consequence of the actions of individuals using automobiles for work and pleasure, corporations using fossil fuels to drive their production lines, municipalities using oil-fired power plants to generate electricity, and so forth. This complex combination of behaviors does not mean that the 1992 Framework Convention on Climate Change (FCCC) is irrelevant or that it will prove ineffective — far from it. Acknowledging the importance of individual behavior, however, reminds us that the FCCC can achieve results only if it is coupled with effective efforts to influence behavior deep within the economic and social systems of the member states. What is more, the behavior in question will be affected by values and local institutional arrangements that the FCCC, whose official members are states, cannot alter in any direct sense. Under the circumstances, we clearly need to think more systematically about institutional linkages and the interplay of institutions operating at different social scales (Young 1994b).

In more practical terms, it is also worth noting that both the creation and the operation of regimes are costly enterprises. Direct costs, intangible as well as tangible, include the expenditure of time and energy to negotiate the terms of international agreements, the allocation of resources to pay for the operation of secretariats, or the restrictions that participation places on the freedom of individual members to do as they please. Regimes also entail opportunity costs because the expenditure of resources on any given regime ordinarily reduces the resources that remain to be invested elsewhere. Such opportunity costs are particularly severe for less affluent societies, which is why many criticisms of the climate regime are articulated by representatives of developing countries who are preoccupied with a range of other pressing concerns (e.g., food production and disease control). Beyond these two types of costs, the creation and operation of regimes can sometimes produce perverse results by generating a false sense that certain problems have been taken care of and thus do not require additional attention. New problems may also be introduced in the process of solving old ones. For example, a number of responsible observers have expressed concern about various chemicals being substituted for chlorofluorocarbons (CFCs) and about some sources of energy that may be substituted for fossil fuels. Although we can argue that there is nothing unique in the expression of such concerns to international or transnational institutions — that such concerns arise at all levels of social organization — we should also temper enthusiasm for regimes with a healthy respect for the costs incurred in forming and operating them.

That said, let us now focus explicitly on the question of the broader consequences of regimes. Broadly speaking, there are two approaches to this question. Some observers regard social institutions as conservative forces, regardless of the social setting in which they operate. Institutional arrangements are thus mechanisms of social control created by the dominant members of society to secure or advance their own interests.[10] A liberal twist on this argument treats institutions as public goods that enhance the welfare of all members, even as they yield results that are particularly beneficial for the most powerful members. Familiar in studies pitched at all levels of social organization, this line of thinking has focused on international and transnational trade regimes, which are sometimes regarded as a means of institutionalizing neocolonialism, and on environmental regimes, which are sometimes viewed as a means of imposing the newly emerging environmental values of affluent countries on the rest of the world (Kindleberger 1973). Needless to say, such arguments are difficult to resolve. In essence, the debate turns on three issues: (1) the capacity of leading actors to impose institutional arrangements on others in the first place; (2) the incidence of the benefits and costs of institutions once the arrangements become operational; and (3) the extent to which regimes acquire a life of their own over time, which makes it difficult for leading actors to manipulate them. Each of these issues raises profound concerns that students of international and transnational regimes will need to address in analyzing the broader consequences of institutional arrangements.

The second approach to the question of broader consequences centers on the view that regimes are agents of social change in international society, and probably in global civil society as well. Individuals and groups who seek to reform international society have had little success in their direct efforts to redefine its constitutive principles. Given the decentralized or nonhierarchical nature of international society, they may not even be able to see the general rules governing membership or relations among the members of this society, much less go about changing those rules. International law, for instance, is essentially a set of rules that spell out the requirements for membership in a society of states and guide the interactions of states with one another. Yet today we face growing problems that are difficult to solve in the context of a states system and that have given rise to powerful pressures to alter the character of international society as we have known it. How is this alteration to be made? The answer lies, in considerable measure, in efforts to introduce innovative institutional arrangements at the level of specific problems and then to take steps to encourage their diffusion through international society as a whole. Nowhere is this type of regime-based innovation more in evidence than in environmental regimes formed during the last several decades. They accord significant roles to nonstate actors, introduce decision-making procedures designed to avoid the paralysis associated with consensus rules, and initiate processes intended to facilitate institutional growth and development.

Two distinct forms of this piecemeal approach to societal reform are worthy of particular notice. The first focuses on the role of nonstate actors in the creation and operation of international regimes (Wapner 1995b). The striking growth in the number of roles that environmental nongovernmental organizations (NGOs) play in international regimes exemplifies this point. Representatives of these organizations are now routinely included as members of national delegations in forming and managing regimes. Meetings once closed (e.g., the Antarctic Treaty Consultative Meetings) are now open to NGO representatives who participate actively as observers. NGOs also provide the brain trust for the participation of many smaller states in international regime s (e.g., the role of leading environmental groups as providers of intellectual capital for the Alliance of Small Island States in negotiations pertaining to the climate change regime).

Furthermore, institutional initiatives that once would have gone through without controversy are now derailed and redirected in considerable part as a result of the efforts of environmental groups. Although Australia and then France became outspoken opponents of the 1988 Antarctic minerals convention, for example, a number of NGOs brought significant pressure to bear on governments to abandon this laboriously negotiated arrangement and to replace it with the Environment Protocol of 1991, which bans the exploitation of minerals in Antarctica during the foreseeable future. Environmental NGOs stalled the adoption and implementation of the Revised Management Procedures in the whaling regime and therefore barred any resumption of commercial or artisanal whaling sanctioned by the International Whaling Commission. Does the active participation of nonstate actors signal the end of states as the most important members of international society or the coming dominance of global civil society? Certainly not. Does it mean that international society is undergoing significant change regarding the role of other types of players as a consequence of the creation and operation of an array of issue-specific regimes? It is difficult to avoid an affirmative answer to this question.

Consider also the constitutive principles governing the interactions among members of international society (Onuf 1989). It is difficult to imagine a successful effort to redefine rules derived from the principle of sovereignty, for example, if the task is approached at the generic or systemic level. There is a widespread feeling, however, that these rules are now evolving in ways that will have profound consequences. How is this possible? Again, the engine of change is fired by a growing number of innovations introduced in connection with the creation and operation of issue-specific regimes. The idea that states are responsible for the external effects not only of their own actions but also of the actions of various actors operating within their jurisdictions has been strengthened immeasurably by the development of regimes dealing with marine pollution, transboundary air pollution, nuclear accidents, ozone depletion, and so forth. Given the traditional insistence on the right of states to use their natural resources and environmental systems as they see fit, the trend toward imposing restrictions on state sovereignty is a remarkable one. A similar observation can be made regarding the emergence of an obligation to share benefits derived from the use of global commons—for example, the deep seabed, the electromagnetic spectrum, and celestial bodies. In effect, the traditional view of sovereignty as a basis for the assertion of rights on the part of the members of international society is being joined by a complementary view that sovereignty also entails duties or obligations. The long-term consequences of this conjunction, which has emerged largely in connection with the evolution of an array of issue-specific regimes, are likely to be profound.

A second form of the piecemeal approach to broader consequences can be seen in the growth of global civil society. As suggested early in this chapter, global civil society is in one sense a separate social system growing up around international society and giving rise to regimes of its own. Even so, its emergence has far-reaching implications for the dynamics of international society because it provides a social base for nonstate actors that helps them to participate effectively in the creation and operation of international regimes, which in turn influence the character of international society. The emergence of a global civil society is partly a simple matter of material resources. The introduction of the fax machine and the dramatic growth of the World Wide Web, largely as a function of global civil society rather than international society, has allowed nonstate actors to forge effective global alliances that are not subject to national governmental control and that are, as James Rosenau

(1990) puts it, sovereignty free. The emergence of global civil society is also partly a matter of providing more intangible forms of support. Because they have strong roots in global civil society, many nonstate actors can afford to operate in a freewheeling fashion and to ignore the efforts of states to rein in their activities. In the minds of some observers, this has raised questions about the extent to which nonstate actors are accountable for their own behavior. Whatever the merits of arguments claiming the emergence of a "democracy deficit" in global civil society, it is apparent that nonstate actors now have remarkable freedom to operate as they see fit in their dealings with international regimes. The fact that this has had and will have broader consequences for international society is undeniable.

Drawing Inferences from the Environmental Experience

Finally, what can we say about the wider applicability of insights drawn primarily from the study of environmental or resource regimes? Interestingly, the discussion at the Dartmouth Conference did not stress the distinction between environmental issues and other issues. Although the papers presented at the conference intentionally focused on environmental regimes, either in their own right or in association with economic regimes, the discussion was wide ranging. What can we infer from this about the applicability of ideas and insights drawn from the environmental experience to other issue areas and to the phenomenon of global governance itself?

Participants in the Dartmouth Conference expressed a variety of views about applicability, ranging from the familiar idea that each case is unique to the equally familiar notion that outcomes flowing from environmental as well as other types of regimes are by and large a function of some master variable, such as power in the structural or material sense. Several points worthy of note did, however, emerge little by little as the discussion of applicability progressed. To begin with, an examination of specific environmental regimes serves to reinforce a number of observations that have arisen from the study of regimes in general. Most regimes are driven by the need to deal with more or less acute problems, even though they may perform significantly different mixes of regulative, procedural, programmatic, and generative functions. The extent to which members or a regime share a sense of community or a common culture makes a difference not only to the process of regime formation but also to the success of the regime. State capacity is also an important determinant of the performance of international regimes, but the capacity of states in this connection does not correlate well with simple measures of development or modernization. Although it is important to draw a distinction between regimes and organizations, organizations do play important roles in both the creation and the operation of regimes (see chapters 4 and 5 in this volume).

Drawing on experience with environmental regimes, the conference discussion of applicability also identified a number of less familiar concerns that certainly warrant systematic examination in the future. Regime analysis to date has been too state centric. Not only are we faced with the growth of transnational regimes whose principal members are not states at all, but we also need to pay more systematic attention to the participation of nonstate actors in international regimes. No matter how complex regimes become, in the final analysis they generally rest on a dominant vision or discourse (Litfin 1994). These generative visions may center on any of a variety of ideas (e.g., achieving maximum sustainable yield from renewable resources; eliminating consumptive uses of living resources; adopting a holistic view of large ecosystems; focusing on the planet as a single system; directing attention to global environmental changes), and they typically have normative as well as analytical and empirical content.

Although it makes sense for certain purposes to study individual regimes in depth, we must also examine the complex linkages between individual regimes and other institutional arrangements. As von Moltke argues convincingly in a discussion of economic and environmental regimes, in order to sort out all these complex relationships it will prove helpful to think in terms of institutional structures encompassing a number of regimes that deal with a broad range of issues (e.g., trade, pollution). The performance of international and transnational regimes will be affected, moreover, by their compatibility with the societal settings in which they operate. Thus, success is typically a matter of making the right connections between top-down arrangements and bottom-up arrangements operative in the same issue area. Regimes change continuously, but these changes are often nonlinear in character. It will not do, therefore, to assume that we can model regime dynamics in terms of analytic constructs built, explicitly or implicitly, on linear processes.

To what extent are all of these concerns peculiar to environmental arrangements? No doubt, important differences exist both among regimes and among the problems they address. Coordination problems in which there is no incentive to cheat once an agreement is struck are clearly different from collaboration problems in which individual members can gain from cheating so that issues of compliance and the design of compliance mechanisms are of central importance (Martin 1992). Regimes themselves differ markedly in how they mix regulative, procedural, programmatic, and generative provisions. Whereas compliance is a central concern in regulative arrangements, decision-making mechanisms constitute the primary concern in procedural arrangements; programmatic arrangements would focus on the step-by-step development of common projects or substantive activities. The extent to which individual regimes are embedded in larger institutional structures is another important variable. As von Moltke reminds us (see chapter 9), there is a major difference between commodity regimes embedded in the overarching arrangements governing trade and much more self-contained regimes that deal with the conservation of individual species (e.g., whales, seals, polar bears). We must also consider the degree to which regimes anticipate pressures for change and incorporate orderly procedures for adjusting or adapting their provisions to changes in the nature of the demand for governance.

The question remains, however, whether the differences between regimes correlate with the division of problems and institutional responses into functional categories (e.g., economic, environmental, human rights, and security problems and regimes). Although this question cannot be answered in the course of a single conference session, the discussion at the Dartmouth Conference yielded the strong impression that many regime features cut across or transcend distinctions among social functions. To the extent that this is true, an examination of environmental cases may yield broader or more generic insights regarding the supply of global governance.

Notes

Chapter 2

1. For a recent, compact summary of the various types of liberal theories of international relations, emphasizing neoliberal institutionalism, see Baldwin (1993a). A particularly clear statement that generating policy advice is a major purpose of regime theory is given in Haas, Keohane and Levy (1993:18).

2. Concepts and propositions in the interdependence tradition, especially their contrast to structural realism, are reviewed by Keohane and Nye (1977); a comparison with integration theory is offered in Nau (1979).

3. For an interesting example of such linkages, demonstrating the role of the transnational insurance industry in enforcing international regulation of maritime transport, see Mitchell (1994a).

4. See Stokke and Vidas (1996b).

5. On interactions between military activities and environmental protection, see Holst (1989) or Westing (1990); for a discussion applied to the Arctic situation, see Stokke (1991).

6. For a comparative analysis of a number of recent regionalization processes across the old East-West divide in Europe, see Veggeland (1994).

7. For a comparison, Young (1991b); see also Keohane (1993: 29).

8. For a study of the significance of regime adaptation to the effectiveness and legitimacy of the Antarctic Treaty System, see Stokke and Vidas (1996b).

9. Using terminology compatible with both approaches, Young (1982: 282) distinguishes imposed and negotiated orders from what he terms spontaneous orders, which do not result from planned, coherent design but rather—like markets or language systems—from the actions or practices of many. On the notion of political engineering, see Underdal (1991).

10. For a review of a number of ongoing projects on regime consequences, see Young and von Molkte (1994); and Bernauer (1995). A presentation of preliminary results of some of these projects is given in Haas, Keohane, and Levy (1993), Andresen and Wettestad (1995), and Jacobson and Brown Weiss (1995).

11. For a corresponding, influential definition of performance at the domestic level, see Lipset (1983: 65); clear discussions of the various components of the regime effectiveness concept are offered by Underdal (1992) and Young (1994a).

12. See also Levy, Osherenko, and Young (1991); this research design was developed by a transnational research team that included the author of the this chapter.

13. This is not necessarily borne out by *changes* in behavior. The purpose of the voluntary moratorium on mining in the Antarctic in the period of negotiations for CRAMRA was precisely to keep actors from changing their behavior and from initiating mining activities. In discussions of the impact of regimes, therefore, behavioral *adaptation* is the preferred notion because it includes cases when the impact of the regime has been to impede undesired changes in behavior.

14. See, for instance, Weale (1992); see also Article 32 of the 1969 Vienna Convention on the Law of Treaties, *United Nations Treaty Series* 1155: pp. 331 ff.

15. For two very different accounts of this transition, see Rochester (1986) and Kratochwil and Ruggie (1986).

16. For two very suggestive and also very different early outlines of the regime agenda, compare Ruggie (1975) and Young (1980). It may be useful to note that the transition from integration theory to interdependence, which occurred in the late 1960s and early 1970s, coincided with setbacks in the European regionalization process.

17. See, for instance, Strange (1982); the classical text on modern political realism is Waltz (1979).

18. For an interesting overview of new institutionalism that emphasizes this distinction in somewhat different terms, see Thelen and Steinmo (1992); see also Yarbrough and Yarbrough (1990).

19. See Peter Katzenstein's contribution to Kohli et al. (1995), especially page 12.

20. Those alternative strategies correspond to the distinction between benign and malign hegemony; see Snidal (1985b).

21. A broad account of the Barents region process is given in Stokke and Tunander (1994); Stokke (1990) analyzes the potential for institutionalized collaboration in this region at the time when the shift in the Soviet attitude to westward cooperation was fairly recent.

22. On the use of behavioral mechanisms in causal analysis of international regimes, see Young and Levy (1996): here, a number of general mechanisms are elaborated, including impacts on the incentive structure. The various mechanisms imply different causal pathways between an international regime and the solution of the problem addressed. See also Haas, Keohane, and Levy (1993).

23. See in general Oye (1986). In Young and Levy (1996), those two versions of the utility modification mechanism are singled out as separate mechanisms. There is little doubt, however, that both refer to processes in which the regime has affected the incentives of actors.

24. For a central discussion of this, see George (1979).

25. For an analysis of this dispute, which is nested in the global United Nations process on the negotiation and implementation of a global treaty on straddling stocks and highly migratory species, see Stokke (1995a).

26. See also Malnes (1995).

27. For a discussion of legitimacy that is sensitive to both the international law and the international relations literature, see Franck (1990); Stokke and Vidas (1996b) relate the concept to international regimes and regime effectiveness.

28. Franck (1990: 49, 209); for a more compact discussion, see Franck (1992: 51).

29. For an account of the significance of programmatic activities to regime formation and effectiveness in the Barents region, see Stokke (1994).

30. The journal *International Organization*, 46(3) (1992), published a number of articles from a symposium on multilateralism; see also Ruggie (1993a).

31. For an early exploration of the relationship between the authority of regimes and their embeddedness in shared conceptions of interest, see Ruggie (1975: 580).

32. See the discussion below.

33. Andresen (1989: 109) portrays how wider membership and growing outside attention to the IWC were important in modifying the priorities of that organization from the prevention of over-exploitation of whales to the prevention of all whaling. For a discussion of how the management of whaling has been related to the beliefs and the causal understandings of experts, see Peterson (1992).

34. According to the conventional realist view, the foreign policy of a state is so controlled by its position in the international system that we do not lose much insight by ignoring differences at the domestic level. For a discussion of this assumption, see Goldmann (1988: 5–7).

35. For an early attempt to forge such a link to assess the relative bargaining strength of actors and the likelihood of agreement, see Putnam (1988); in this context, see also Evans, Jacobson, and Putnam (1993), especially Evans (1993).

36. For a similar distinction, see Ikenberry, Lake, and Mastanduno (1988); interesting efforts to condense various approaches that link international relations and various features of domestic politics are offered by Moravcsik (1993) and by Zürn (1993), who focuses in particular on international regimes.

37. The more critical perspective on the latter function terms it cooptation: societal opposition is pacified by the state system and tied to a given policy by their participation in its formulation.

38. A large-scale transnational project, "Implementation and Effectiveness of International Environmental Commitments," organized by the International Institute of Applied Systems Analysis, tries to forge such a link. See Andresen, Skaerseth, and Weltestad (1995).

39. The journal International Organization, 46(1) (1992) is a special issue edited by Peter Haas on the usefulness of the epistemic community concept in clarifying relations between knowledge, power and the international policy coordination; see also Haas (1989). For an early linkage of epistemic communities, which are somewhat differently conceptualized, to international regimes, see Ruggie (1975).

40. See also Behnke (1995) and Wendt (1995). In their conclusion to the special *International Organization* issue on epistemic communities, Adler and Haas (1992) explicitly portray their approach as contributing to an empirical research program of the type Keohane (1988) has insisted on.

Chapter 3

1. This broader understanding of civil governance extends back to the Aristotelian notion of *koinonia politike*, the forebear of *societas civilas* (Cohen and Arato 1992: 85) and helps account for later understandings associated with Locke, Kant, Rousseau, and others that conflate the state and civil society. (See Kumar 1993: 376).

2. According to John Keane, Hegel's role in distinguishing the state from civil society is exaggerated. Between 1750 and 1850, scores of political thinkers wrestled with the distinction through reflection on the limits of state action (see Keane 1988: 63).

3. It should be noted that, although Hegel characterizes civil society as taking place outside the *household* and below the state, I locate it above the *individual* and below the state. I do so because I am persuaded by arguments that claim that the household is a part of civil society. See Pateman (1988) and Singerman (1996).

4. The relationship between the state and civil society in Hegel is admittedly abstract. As I understand it, the state makes apparent what already exists in civil society by disciplining the particularist dynamics of civil society to more universalist, public aims. Put differently, as a moment of social organization, civil society sits at an intermediate stage between the family and the state. The state's job, as it were, is to enable universal interest—in contrast to private interest—to prevail. In Hegelian terminology, it allows for the realization of ethical life in contrast to the abstract morality available in civil society. See Knox (1967).

5. This acknowledgement was part of a broader development of rationalized law that eventually circumscribed such freedom and codified such rights. See Serif Mardin, "Civil Society and Islam," in Hall (1989: 279–280).

6. The idea that the economy is separate from other social spheres leads some to conceptualize it outside the domain of civil society (Cohen and Arato 1992; Parsons 1971). Following the Hegelian tradition, I include the economy within civil society.

7. To be sure, the result of the coordinated mode of economic life is not a homogeneous private domain but a stratified one wherein separate classes possess only circumscribed interests and partial social affiliations. Nonetheless, a coherent domain is, in fact, created where people can pursue private aims. See Lewis (1992: 37–38).

8. For a list of such sentiments as articulated by the Scottish moralists, see Perez-Diaz (1995: 82).

9. Fukuyama argues that international society is becoming liberal in the sense that liberalism has finally triumphed over other ideologies (Fukuyama 1989). My point is not that the system is liberal in character but that it has elements that serve the same purposes as those that gave rise to liberal understandings of civil society.

10. For a discussion of problems associated with the term *nongovernmental organization*, see Gordenker and Weiss (1995), Korten (1990: 95), and Rosenau (1990).

11. See, for example, Lipschutz (1992). Although they do not use the term *global civil society*, Princen and Finger (1994), and Boli and Thomas (1995) suggest that NGO activity is undertaken primarily by politically progressive organizations.

12. James Rosenau persuasively argues that the term NGO places too much attention on states and thus perpetuates the state centrism of international relations scholarship. He suggests using the term "sovereignty-free" actors. I prefer the term NGO simply because of its common currency, although I realize that there are certain costs involved with employing it. See Rosenau (1990).

13. See note 6.

14. On the differences between "voluntary," "nonprofit," and "independent," see Fisher (1993: 8–9).

15. Implicit in this formulation is the idea that what is of concern to the public is necessarily political. For background on this idea of the public and on the conjunction between it and politics, see Dewey (1954: 15–16).

16. END's efforts, along with those of other peace groups, may have contributed to the eventual breakup of the Soviet Union and superpower accommodation (see, for example, Deudney and Ikenberry (1992).

Chapter 4

1. I am grateful for comments on an earlier draft of this paper from Mlada Bukovansky, Angela Cropper, Oran R. Young and the participants in the

Dartmouth Conference on International Governance in the Twenty-first Century, 14–16 September 1995.

2. At the United Nations Conference on Environment and Development (UNCED) in Rio de Janeiro 1992, nation states again stated in *Agenda 21* that all agencies of the United Nations system should play a key role in implementing international environmental policies. See chapter 38 of *Agenda 21* (1992: 456).

3. The number of international nongovernmental organizations increased even more significantly to 5,121 in 1995. See *Yearbook of International Organizations* (1995–1996: 1670–1671).

4. Different interests can prevail among international organizations, and some of their efforts can be conflicting rather than reinforcing, though they need not represent "important sources of disorder" (Gallarotti 1991: 219).

5. A more detailed discussion about the overlaps between international environmental regimes and trade regimes can be found in Chapter 9 by Konrad von Moltke in this volume.

6. For a more comprehensive study on these regime formation processes, see Breitmeier (1996).

7. For an overview about the different approaches about regime formation, see Efinger et al. (1990); Rittberger and Mayer (1993); Osherenko and Young (1993a); Young and Osherenko (1993); Young (1994a); and Wolf (1991).

8. Parts or single book chapters of volumes about the rise of international environmental politics focus on the role of international organizations. See for instance Caldwell (1990), Birnie (1993), Brenton (1994), Sands (1995), Thacher (1992), Thomas (1992). For a more recent volume on international organizations in the field of the environment, see Bartlett, Kurian, and Malik (1995).

9. See Osherenko and Young (1993a: 17, 20) and Rittberger and Mayer (1993). A more detailed consideration of international organizations can be found in Young (1994a: 163–183).

10. On epistemic communities, see Peter M. Haas (1990, 1992a).

11. One of the few efforts to integrate the policy cycle into the analysis of international relations was made by Soroos (1986). For a discussion about the sequence of different stages of regime formation, see also Chapter 1 in this volume by Oran Young.

12. For a study about environmental agenda building at the international level, see Breitmeier (1992).

13. For an elaborate discussion about such types of regulating factors, see Cobb and Elder (1972).

14. On the role of international organizations in regime management, see Chapter 5 by M. J. Peterson in this volume.

15. On the structure of international organizations, see Rittberger (1994: 92–93) and Jacobson (1984: 86–89).

16. For their early role as facilitators of technical interstate collaboration in the field of telecommunication, see Codding and Rutkowski (1982). On categor-

ization of IOs' roles, see Jacobson (1984: 83), Archer (1993: 161–177), and Weiss, Forsythe, and Coate (1994: 228–241).

17. See E. B. Haas (1990: 20–23). For an early study on the influence of the work of scientists and technical experts on international organizations, see Haas, Williams, and Babai (1977).

18. On relationships between states and nonstate actors, consult Haufler (1993).

19. See Molina and Rowland (1974). On the early years of the issue of ozone depletion, see Breitmeier (1992); Dotto and Schiff (1980); Gehring (1994); Lobos (1987); Miller and Mintzer (1986); Morrisette (1989); Parson (1993); and Roan (1989).

20. Ground-based measurement techniques were, for instance, the Dobson Spectrophotometer, the Standard Dobson Umkehr, Balloon and Rocket Ozonesondes, the Brewer Spectrophotometer, lidar measurements, and microwave radiometry. Satellite measurements were carried out on board the U.S. NIMBUS-7 spacecraft with the Solar Backscatter Ultraviolett Spectrometer and the Total Ozone Mapping Spectrometer (WMO 1989: 164–174).

21. See Final Statement of the First World Climate Conference in WMO (1979: 714).

22. See WMO/UNEP (1988c).

23. See United Nations GA/Res 43/53, 12 December 1988.

24. Such criticism was raised by Lanchberry and Victor (1995).

25. On the attitude of the European Community see Jachtenfuchs (1990). On the political process until 1987 see Benedick (1991), Breitmeier (1996), Gehring (1994).

26. On the climate negotiations that occurred up to Rio 1992 and the follow-up that took place up to the first Conference of the Parties in Berlin 1995, see Bodansky (1993, 1995). On the achievements under the climate convention, see also Victor and Salt (1994).

27. The address by Mostafa K. Tolba, 29 October 1990, appears in Jäger and Ferguson (1991: 3).

28. For a discussion about the role of science during the climate negotiations, see Boehmer-Christiansen (1994b).

29. See *Nature* 382 (1996: 287).

30. On the role of knowledge during the ozone negotiations and during the stages after initial regime formation, see Litfin (1994).

31. On counterfactuals see Biersteker (1993).

32. For a review of the state of the art of regime analysis, see Levy, Young, and Zürn (1995).

Chapter 6

1. I would like to thank the participants of the Dartmouth Conference and, particularly, Genady Golubev, Frank Magillian, Oran Young, and the anony-

mous reviewers at the MIT Press for their very helpful comments on an earlier version of this chapter.

2. The uneven distribution of water resources is indicated, for example, by the fact that the annual per capita water availability (10^3 m^3 per year) in 1990 in Oceania was 76, in South America 35, in North and Central America 16, in Africa 6.5, in Europe 4.7, and in Asia 3.4 (Gleick 1993: table A.10).

3. By the same token, 75 percent of the territory in many countries lies in international river basins—including 23 countries in Africa, 0 in North and Central America, 6 in South America, 8 in Asia, and 13 in Europe (United Nations 1978; Gleick 1993: 437).

4. According to United Nations statistics (United Nations 1978; Gleick 1993: 436), 57 international river basins lie in Africa, 34 in North and Central America, 36 in South America, 40 in Asia, and 48 in Europe. As the number of states in the international system increases, the number of international rivers will also grow.

5. Consider, for example, the following figures. The first number in the parentheses indicates the area of the country that lies in an international river basin; the second number indicates the per capita water availability in 10^3 m^3 per year: Ethiopia (80/2.39), Gambia (91/4.48), Ghana (75/3.65), Sudan (81/ 1.31), Togo (77/3.66) Peru (78/1.93), Afghanistan (91/2.76), Iraq (83/2.00), Belgium (96/0.85), Bulgaria (79/1.97), Czechoslovakia (100/1.79), Hungary (100/0.56), Poland (95/1.31), Romania (98/1.59). Source: Gleick (1993: 439).

6. Cano (1992), for example, discusses twenty-four multilateral agreements and instruments relating to transboundary freshwater.

7. Convention Relating to the Development of Hydraulic Power Affecting More than One State (1923); Convention and Statute on the Regime of Navigable Waterways of International Concern (1921); UN Convention on the Protection and Use of Transboundary Watercourses and International Lakes (1992).

8. A current research project at the Swiss Federal Institute of Technology (ETH), which began in August 1996 and is led by the author of this chapter, will examine ten cases of international river management and will lead to propositions based on larger-scale and more systematic empirical research.

9. The relationship between externalities and shared natural resources (SNRs) can be relatively complicated because, in the case of SNRs, externalities can be multidirectional and need not be symmetrically distributed. One actor's resource consumption (e.g., in terms of waste discharge) may uniformly affect the entire group, in which case the externality is the difference between total damage and self-imposed damage. In other cases, damage resulting from waste discharges by one actor may be imposed either entirely and uniformly or asymmetrically on other actors. Similar arguments may be made about externalizing costs to future generations, which is an alternative to the usual treatment of intergenerational issues in terms of discount rates.

10. Libiszewski (1995) makes a similar argument.

11. In this context, defining property rights does not necessarily imply the transformation of a transboundary SNR into a national and nonshared resource. Property rights can also be defined in terms of the right to consume the resource in certain quantities and/or in certain ways.

12. For reasons of simplicity, I assume in this chapter that most IRMIs are designed to deal with externality problems or to capture gains by jointly exploiting freshwater resources. In some cases, however, which I largely ignore, IRMIs may be set up and operated merely to improve neighborly relations, to create a forum for the discussion of more general development issues, to mobilize funding by international agencies, or to create a catalyst for cooperation in other areas. IRMIs may also serve to reinforce territorial claims or to legitimize new boundaries (many river agreements have indeed been signed after major domestic or international crises or wars; see United Nations 1963).

13. Systematic empirical research on this proposition remains to be done.

14. A detailed empirical analysis of this proposition would have to control for the degree of water scarcity. In some cases, IRMIs may have appeared earlier in industrialized countries simply because pollution problems occurred earlier.

15. I assume here that water scarcity as such does not affect the likelihood of cooperation (even though it may affect the demand for cooperation) because water in North America and Europe is not less scarce than it is in other parts of the world, but the extent of cooperation in North America and Europe is greater. See Gleick (1993: table A.10).

16. In North America all international river issues are bilateral, whereas 75 percent of the territory in Europe is located in international river basins (United Nations 1978; Gleick 1993: 437). The fact that cooperation on transboundary water issues is more frequent in Europe contradicts the proposition concerning the number of actors. However, some doubt about the validity of this finding must remain because it is unclear whether Durth (1995) has accounted for the simple fact that there are more boundaries in Europe, which per se tends to increase the number of agreements. Another weak point in Durth's analysis is that his sample includes only one case involving developing countries (the Euphrates).

17. This view is, of course, simplified. The geography of rivers often results in more complex patterns of externalities than those discussed here. At one point, riparian countries may border a river sequentially. At other points of the same river, the border between two countries may run along the middle of the river. Another factor that complicates the picture is that different countries attach different values to different types of resource use. As noted above, the riparians of the Rhine draw different types of utility from the resource and may weigh each type differently. For example, chloride emissions by France have not posed much of a problem for Germany, but they have significantly affected the Netherlands due to the characteristics of its freshwater supply system. Differences in valuation of a resource may also give SNR situations that have a physically uniform distribution of externalities the characteristics of an upstream-down-

stream problem. The ozone layer problem affects everyone, but for a variety of reasons developing countries are not as concerned about the issue as many industrialized countries.

18. On the reasons why countries provide foreign aid, see B. Frey (1985: 86–102).

19. These functions resemble the three functions that Haas, Keohane, and Levy (1993) attribute to international environmental institutions. They argue that institutions affect concern, capacity, and the contractual environment. Levy, Osherenko, and Young (1991) refer to six causal pathways. The central research question in this context is, Which institutional features influence the performance of the mentioned functions?

20. Also for this reason, I have focused on transboundary rivers and have excluded other, equally important, freshwater issues, such as transboundary lakes and groundwater.

Chapter 7

1. A number of sources outline the environmental history and features of the Great Lakes, including: Tom Kuchenberg, *Reflections in a Tarnished Mirror: The Use and Abuse of the Great Lakes* (Sturgeon Bay, Wis.: Golden Glow, 1978); *The Great Lakes: An Environmental Atlas and Resource Book* (Ottawa and Washington, D.C.; Environment Canada and U.S. Environmental Protection Agency, 1988). Theodora Colborn et al., *Great Lakes: Great Legacy?* (Washington, D.C.: Conservation Foundation and Institute for Research on Public Policy, 1990); Phil Weller, *Fresh Water Seas: Saving the Great Lakes* (Toronto: Between the Lines, 1990).

2. There is a rich literature on the importance of the Great Lakes to the development of international environmental protection. Some historical perspectives on this matter include Richard B. Bilder, "Controlling Great Lakes Polution: A Study in the U.S.-Canada Environmental Cooperation," *Michigan Law Review* 70 (1972): 469–556; Maxwell Cohen, "The Regime of Boundary Waters: The Canadian-U.S. Experience," *Recueil des Cours* 146 (1975): 219–291; Canada, Standing Senate Committee on Foreign Affairs. *Canada-U.S. Relations, vol. 1: The Institutional Framework for the Relationship* (Ottawa: Queen's Printer, 1975).

3. This change in workload is due largely to the fact that, by the early 1960s, after the development of the St. Lawrence Seaway and the Columbia River basin, all major transboundary and boundary waters had been developed.

4. There have been references in 1912, 1946, 1948, 1964 and 1975 on air and water pollution in the basin in addition to two references mandated by the 1972 Great Lakes Water Quality Agreement: Pollution of the Upper Great Lakes and Pollution of the Great Lakes from Land-Use Activities. There have also been references on levels in 1964 and 1986 and on diversions and consumptive uses.

5. This chapter discusses three agreements. The first, the "Agreement Between the United States of America and Canada on Great Lakes Water Quality," signed at Ottawa, 15 April 1972, was superseded by the "Agreement between Canada and the United States of America on Great Lakes Water Quality," signed at Ottawa, 15 November 1978. The 1978 Agreement was amended in important ways by the "Protocol," signed 18 November 1987. These agreements are collectively referred to hereafter as GLWQA.

6. GLWQA, 1978, Article VII sets out the "Powers, Responsibilities and Functions of the International Joint Commission."

7. For example, Article X now requires the parties to meet twice a year, along with state and provincial governments, to coordinate their work plans and to evaluate progress made. Prior to this, evaluation of progress was done exclusively through the IJC.

8. The study examined the Great Lakes regime in light of the following criteria: (1) results of the agreement for the Great Lakes (including the reduction of phosphorous and other pollutants); (2) the Great Lakes as a model for ecosystem management; (3) contributions to science; (4) Great Lakes and the U.S-Canada relationship; and (5) growth and evolution of the Great Lakes community.

9. In his book *International Governance: Protecting the Environment in a Stateless Society* (1994a: Chapter 6), Professor Oran Young developed the following criteria, which were employed in this study: (1) effectiveness as problem solving, (which asks whether the regime solves the "problems that motivate the parties to create them in the first place"; (2) effectiveness as goal attainment, which is the "measure of the extent to which a regime's (stated or unstated) goals are attained over time"; (3) behavioral effectiveness, which asks whether its operation affects behavior of the parties themselves or of others under their jurisdiction, such as nongovernmental organizations, industry, or members of the general public; (4) process effectiveness, measured by "the extent to which the provisions of the international regime are implemented in the domestic legal and political systems of the member states as well as the extent to which those subject to a regime's prescription actually comply with the requirements"; (5) constitutive effectiveness, whose "formation gives rise to a social practice involving expenditure of time, energy, and resources on the part of its members", and (6) evaluative effectiveness, which asks whether the regime produces results that are "efficient, equitable, sustainable or robust".

10. See Don Munton, "Paradoxes and Prospects" in R. Spencer, J. Kirton, and K. R. Nossal (eds.), *The International Joint Commission Seventy Years On* (Toronto: Centre for International Studies, 1981), p. 88. However, it should be mentioned that Professor Munton himself questions common fact finding as a panacea for dispute resolution. He notes that:

The fact-finding approach to settlement makes the assumption that the technical and political issues in a given dispute are identical, or at least the former largely account for the latter. Once again, that seems rarely the case. Often the lack of technical facts is not the difficulty at all. Indeed, political disputes frequently arise precisely because "the facts" become well known.

11. It is recognized that the fact-finding approach to dispute settlement has its limits. For a further discussion of this approach with respect to the GLWQA, see: David LeMarquand, "The International Joint Commission and Changing Canada-United States Boundary Relations" *National Resources Journal* 33(1) (1993): 59–91, particularly pp. 77–79.

12. It should be noted that the reforms put in place did not emanate from those who criticized the working of the board in the past. The most prevalent suggestion had been to appoint nongovernmental experts to the board, but this change was not made.

13. Former Canadian chairman of the IJC, Dr. Maxwell Cohen explained it in this way:

. . . here was an asymmetrical relationship between a small Canada, still almost semi-colonial, and a great power, which together in 1909 were able to devise a system to create symmetry in the relationship of the two countries . . . through the theory of equality on the Commission and equality on the boards in the field . . .

See "Testimony before the Senate Standing Committee on Foreign Affairs," 18 February 1975, quoted in Canadian Parliament, Senate Standing Committee on Foreign Affairs, *Canada–United States Relations, vol. 1: Institutional Framework for the Relationship* (Ottawa: Queen's Printer, 1975), 41.

14. For a history of the approach generally, see Stephen Bocking, "Visions of Nature and Society: A History of the Ecosystem Concept," *Alternatives* 20(3) (1993): 12–18. For the document prepared in anticipation of the renegotiation of the agreement to possibly include the concept, see Great Lakes Science Advisory Board, *The Ecosystem Approach: Scope and Implications of an Ecosystem Approach to Transboundary Problems in the Great Lakes Basin* (Special report to the International Joint Commission, presented July 1978, Windsor, Ontario). For a more recent discussion of the concept applied to the Great Lakes, see George Francis, "Great Lakes Governance and the Ecosystem Approach: Where Next?" *Alternatives* 13(3) (1986): 61–70; R. L. Thomas, J. R. Valentyne, K. Ogilvie, and J. D. Kingham, "The Ecosystems Approach: A Strategy for the Management of Renewable Resources in the Great Lakes Basin," in L. K. Caldwell (ed.), *Perspectives on Ecosystem Management for the Great Lakes: A Reader* (Albany: State University of New York Press, 1988), pp. 31–58, Lynton Keith Caldwell, "Disharmony in the Great Lakes Basin: Institutional Jurisdictions Frustrate the Ecosystem Approach," *Alternatives* 20(3) (1994): 26–31.

15. The Great Lakes basin ecosystem is defined as "the interacting components of air, land, water, and living organisms, including humans, within the drainage basin of the St. Lawrence River" (GLWQA 1978, as amended: Article I[g]).

16. For an expanded view of this notion, see Royal Commission on the Future of the Toronto Waterfront, *Regeneration: Toronto's Waterfront and the Sustain-*

able City: Final Report (Toronto: Minister of Supply and Services, 1992), pp. 19–61.

17. At least twenty binational governance arrangements outside of the Great Lakes Agreement cover areas such as fisheries, air pollution, and water pollution. These arrangements are listed and described in Henry A. Regier, "Progress with Remediation, Rehabilitation and the Ecosystem Approach," *Alternatives* 13(3) (1986): 47–54.

18. The Great Lakes Water Quality Initiative is found in *Federal Register*, vol. 58, no. 72, 16 April 1993, and is discussed in relation to the GLWQA in the Great Lakes Science Advisory Board, *Report to the International Joint Commission* (1993).

19. See, for example, the work of the Virtual Elimination Task Force of the IJC, *A Strategy for Virtual Elimination of Persistent Toxic Substances*, vols. 1 and 2 (Windsor, Ont.: IJC, 1993). For commentary on this goal, see National Wildlife Federation and the Canadian Institute for Environmental Law and Policy, *Prescription for Healthy Great Lakes*: Report of the Program for Zero Discharge (February 1991); and P. Muldoon and M. Valiante, *Toxic Water Pollution in Canada: Regulatory Principles for Reduction and Elimination* (Calgary: Canadian Institute of Resources Law, 1989).

20. For example, Great Lakes United, a coalition of 150 groups, undertook a series of public hearings around the Great Lakes and solicited support for the concept. See Great Lakes United, *Unfulfilled Promises* (1986), and P. Mjuldoon and J. Jackson, "Keeping Zero in the Goal of Zero Discharge," *Alternatives* 20(4) (1994): 14-20.

21. As defined by the IJC (1994), this approach would take into account the findings of scientific studies:

If, taken together, the amount and consistency of evidence across a wide range of circumstances and/or toxic substances are judged sufficient to indicate the reality or a strong probability of a linkage between certain substances or class of substances and injury, a conclusion of a causal relationship can be made.... Once this point is reached, and taking a precuationary approach, there can be no defensible alternative to recommending that the input of those substances to the Great Lakes be stopped. (p. 10)

22. The history of the concept is discussed in depth in National Wildlife Federation and Canadian Institute for Environmental Law and Policy, *A Prescription for Healthy Great Lakes: Report of the Program for Zero Discharge* (February 1991).

23. The report recommended that the parties "develop timetables to sunset the use of chlorine and chlorine-containing compounds as industrial feedstocks and that the means of reducing or eliminating other uses be examined." (IJC 1992: 30).

24. The issue of chlorine and the role of the IJC is complex. For some additional background and commentary, see Alana M. Fuierer, "The Anti-Chlorine Cam-

paign in the Great Lakes: Should Chlorinated Compounds Be Guilty Until Proven Innocent?" *Buffalo Law Review* 43 (1995): 181–229 and Gordon Durnil, *The Making of a Conservative Environmentalist* (Bloomington: Indiana University Press, 1995).

25. The contrasting views of the chlorine issue can be discerned from two appendices to the Report on Virtual Elimination Task Force. See G.N. Werezak, "A Report on Chlorine to the Virtual Elimination Task Force"; D. K. Phenecie, "Virtual Elimination in the Pulp and Paper Industry"; and T. Muir, T. Eder, P. Muldoon, and S. Lerner, "Case Study: Application of a Virtual Elimination Strategy to an Industrial Feedstock Chemical-Chlorine," in *Three Background Reports to the Virtual Elimination Task Force on the Subject of Chlorine and Organochlorines* (Windsor, Ontario: IJC, 1993). See also John R. Ehrenfeld, "Science, Scientists and Chlorine: Or It's a Wicked World Out There," (paper presented at *The Future Uses of Chlorine: Symposium on the Role of the University*, Massachusetts Institute of Technology, Cambridge, Mass., 14–15 November 1994).

26. The Science Advisory Board called for the phaseout of persistent toxic substances and, in particular, of halogenated organics. See Great Lakes Science Advisory Board, *1989 Report*, 71; Great Lakes Science Advisory Board, *1991 Report to the International Joint Commission*, 41. For an in-depth review of the decision-making processes following the 1991 biennial meeting, which included interviews with the IJC commissioners, see Craig Waddell, "Saving the Great Lakes: Public Participation in Environmental Policy," in Carl G. Herndl and Stuart C. Brown (eds.), *Green Culture: Environmental Rhetoric in Contemporary America* (Madison: The University of Wisconsin Press, 1995), 153.

27. The program is called "Accelerated Reduction/Elimination of Toxic Substances" (ARET).

28. This policy, although supported in its general direction, has been criticized on a number of fronts. See Canadian Institute for Environmental Law and Policy and the Canadian Environmental Law Association, *A Response to the Proposed Toxic Substances Management Policy for Canada*, a report submitted to Environment Canada (November 1994).

29. The response has been subject to extensive comment. See CELA and CIELAP, *It's Still about Our Health! A Submission on the Document, CEPA Review: The Government Response to Environmental Protection Legislation Designed for the Future, a Renewed CEPA — a Proposal* (March 1996). New legislation was expected late fall of 1996.

30. Also, there has been a trend to think about "transition planning," a process in which all stakeholders meet to ensure that workers and communities are not inequitably affected by the move to cleaner technologies. For a proposal, see Clean Protection Task Force, Great Lakes United, *Planning for the Sunset: A Case Study for Eliminating Dioxins by Phasing Out PVC Plastics* (May 1995).

31. For a summary of these concerns, see Great Lakes Science Advisory Board, Chapter 2, Section 4 in *1993–95 Priorities and Progress under the Great Lakes*

Water Quality Agreement (1995). Also see Mark Nichols, "The Sperm Scare: Pollution and Chemicals May Be Threatening Human Fertility," *Maclean's*, 1 April 1996: 50–55; and T. Colborn, Dianne Dumanoski, and Johnm Peterson Myers, *Our Stolen Future* (New York: Dutton, 1996).

32. There is evidence that the amount of some of these substances declined or levelled off in the Great Lakes during the 1970s and 1980s but have slightly increased in recent years. See Environment Canada and U.S. EPA, *State of the Great Lakes*, a report (1995), 19.

33. For a recent progress report, see United States Environmental Protection Agency and the New York State Department of Environmental Conservation, *Reduction of Toxic Loading to the Niagara River from Hazardous Waste Sites in the United States* (February, 1996).

34. Industry became most involved when activities at the binational level directly threatened their interests. For example, the detergent industry associations in Canada and the United States vigorously participated in the public hearings and debates on the reports that led to the negotiation of the 1972 GLWQA.

35. Organized labor and Aboriginal communities are becoming increasingly visible and important participants. They participate on their own and also through membership in Great Lakes United. Municipal politicians meet annually on matters of common interest through a coalition known as the Great Lakes Mayors' Association. Educators participate on the IJC's Educators Advisory Council and through a series of summer institutes around the basin.

36. For example, the reference on Great Lakes Water Levels has a diverse study group that includes representatives of environmental, recreational user, and rate payers groups. (See Becker 1993 and note 30 above) Since 1989, IJC biennial meetings have included thousands of basin citizens, and IJC boards and task forces now include membership from the broader Great Lakes community.

37. For example, leading up to the 1985 review of the 1978 GLWQA, Great Lakes United convened a series of public hearings around the basin and prepared a report on progress under the agreement that was influential in getting GLU status in the negotiations (see Manno 1993 and note 26 above). In addition, the NGO community has organized regional networks of citizens and local groups, including the Lake Erie Alliance. The larger environmental groups have been very influential in pushing the principles of the agreement into programs such as the Great Lakes Initiative in the United States, the Canada-Ontario Agreement and the Municipal-Industrial Strategy for Abatement in Ontario.

Chapter 8

1. I would like to thank Oran Young, Konrad von Moltke, Kevin Lyonette, Alex Wood, Andrew Steer, Colin Reese, Robert Goodland, and Sheila Mulvihill for their comments and advice during various stages of writing this paper.

2. One of the earliest publications in the extensive literature produced by NGOs criticizing the World Bank is *Funding Ecological and Social Destruction: The World Bank and the International Monetary Fund.* It was published by the Bank Information Center on behalf of an NGO coalition in 1989. Literally thousands of articles, books, and mimeo publications have subsequently documented the environmental and social impacts of Bank-financed projects.

3. A review of the forest policy was precipitated by an internatonal lobbying campaign led by the World Wildlife Fund (WWF) on the impact of a forest sector loan to Cote d'Ivoire in 1991. A one-year lending moratorium led to a far more inclusive and sensitive forest policy.

Chapter 9

1. This paper is based on work supported by the International Institute for Sustainable Development, Winnipeg. See von Moltke (1996).

2. There was a debate about trade and environment in the seventies, but it did not have implications for policy. The earliest papers in the trade and environment debate of the nineties were written in August 1990 for the U.S. National Advisory Council on Environmental Policy and Technology Subcommittee on Trade and Environment.

3. Texts of international conventions are now widely available on the World Wide Web. Two useful sites are http://www.unep.ch, which also provides access to secretariat documents, and http://www.tufts.edu/departments/fletcher/multi-laterals.html

Chapter 10

1. The phrase "coming anarchy" is from Kaplan (1994). For a thoughtful discussion of the "new pessimism," see Maynes (1995).

2. A succinct summary of the commission's recommendations can be found in Carlsson (1995).

3. The elaboration of this idea is the defining feature of the British school of thought on international affairs (Bull 1977; Young 1995a).

4. For an account suggesting that global civil society is presently a source of criticism of international society rather than an alternative source of world order, see Falk (1995).

5. Whereas regimes are issue-specific arrangements focused on supplying governance, societies are socially defined groups of actors that interact with one another across a broad range of issues and that share general rules regarding membership in the group and prescriptions pertaining to interactions among their members. For relevant background, consult Cohen and Arato (1992).

6. Some close observers think that the Great Lakes water quality regime is facing growing threats to its effectiveness at the present time (Environmental Law Institute 1995)?

7. For a general account of genetic explanations, which are common in biology and geology as well as in the social sciences, see Nagel (1961).

8. Readers will recognize this idea as a familiar element in the logic of neofunctionalist integration theory (E. Haas 1964).

9. For an account that explains why it is a mistake to overemphasize the distinction between domestic societies and international society in these terms, see Chayes and Chayes (1995).

10. Interestingly, both realists and Marxists espouse arguments of this kind. For a prominent realist exposition, see Gilpin (1987).

References

Adler, Emanuel, and Peter M. Haas. 1992. "Conclusion: Epistemic Communities, World Order, and the Creation of a Reflective Research Program." *International Organization* 46 (1):367–390.

Agenda 21. 1992. UN Document A/CONF.151/4.

Aggarwal, Vinod K. 1983. "The Unraveling of the Multi-Fiber Arrangement, 1981: An Examination of International Regime Change." *International Organization* 37 (4):617–645.

Albin, Cecilia. 1993. "The Role of Fairness in Negotiation." *Negotiation Journal* 9 (3):223–244.

Allardice, David R., Richard H. Mattoon, and William A. Testa. 1994. "Industry Approaches to Environmental Policy in the Great Lakes Region." *University of Toledo Law Review* 25:357.

Andrassy, Juraj. 1970. *International Law and the Resources of the Sea.* New York: Columbia University Press.

Andresen, Steinar. 1989. "Science and Politics in the International Management of Whales." *Marine Policy* 13:99–117.

Andresen, Steinar, and Jorgen Wettestad. 1995. "International Problem-Solving Effectiveness: The Oslo Project So Far." *International Environmental Affairs* 7:127–149.

Andresen, Steinar, Jon Birger Skjaerseth, and Jorgen Wettestad. 1995. *Regime, the State, and Society: Analyzing the Implementation of International Environmental Commitments.* Working Paper WP-95-43. Laxenburg: International Institute for Applied Systems Analysis.

Ann-Zondorak, Valerie. 1991. "A New Face in Corporate Responsibility: The Valdez Principles." *Boston College Environmental Affairs Law Review* 18.

Antarctic Treaty. 1959. 402 *United Nations Treaty Series.*

Archer, Clive. 1993. *International Organizations.* 2nd edition. New York: Routledge.

Axelrod, Robert. 1984. *The Evolution of Cooperation.* New York: Basic Books.

Bächler, Günther, and Volker Böge, eds. 1993. *Umweltzerstörung: Krieg oder Kooperation?* (Environmental Destruction: War or Cooperation). Münster, Germany: Agenda Verlag.

Baldwin, David A. 1993a. "Neoliberalism, Neorealism, and World Politics." In *Neorealism and Neoliberalism: The Contemporary Debate,* edited by D. A. Baldwin. New York: Columbia University Press, pp. 3–25.

Baldwin, David, ed. 1993b. *Neorealism and Neoliberalism: The Contemporary Debate.* New York: Columbia University Press.

Bank Information Center. 1989. *Funding Ecological and Social Destruction: The World Bank and the International Monetary Fund.* Washington, D.C.: World Bank.

Bartlett, Robert V, Priya A. Kurian, and Madhu Malik. 1995: *International Organizations and Environmental Policy.* Westport, Conn.: Greenwood Press.

Becker, Mimi Larsen. 1993. "The International Joint Commission and Public Participation: Past Experiences, Present Challenges, Future Tasks." *Natural Resources Journal* 33:235.

Bedarff, Hildegard, Thomas Bernauer, Cord Jakobeit, and Martin List. 1995. "Umwelthilfe als Tausch: Transferzahlungen in der internationalen Umweltpolitik" ("Environmental Aid as an Exchange: Financial Transfers in International Environmental Politics"). 1995. *Zeitschrift für Internationale Beziehungen* 2 (2):317–346.

Behnke, Andreas, "Ten Years After: The State of the Art of Regime Theory." 1995. *Cooperation and Conflict* 30 (2): 179–197.

Beigbeder, Yves. 1988. *Threats to the International Civil Service.* London: Pinter Publishers.

Bellah, Robert N., 1991. "Breaking the Tyranny of the Market." *Tikkun* 6 (4):30–32.

Benedick, Richard Elliott. 1991. *Ozone Diplomacy: New Directions in Safeguarding the Planet.* Cambridge, Mass.: Harvard University Press.

Bernauer, Thomas. 1995. "The Effect of International Environmental Institutions: How We Might Learn More." *International Organization* 49 (2):351–377.

Bernauer, Thomas. 1996. Protecting the River Rhine against Chloride Pollution." In *Institutions for Environmental Aid,* edited by Robert O. Keohane and Marc A. Levy. Cambridge, Mass.: MIT Press, pp. 201–232.

Bernauer, Thomas, and Peter Moser. 1996. "Reducing Pollution of the River Rhine: The Influence of International Cooperation." *Journal of Environment and Development.* 5:389–415.

Biersteker, Thomas J. 1993. "Constructing Historical Counterfactuals to Assess the Consequences of International Regimes: The Global Debt Regime and the Course of the Debt Crisis of the 1980s." In *Regime Theory and International Relations,* edited by Volker Rittberger and Peter Mayer. Oxford: Clarendon, pp. 315–338.

Birnie, Patricia. 1993: "The UN and the Environment." In *United Nations, Divided World: The UN's Roles in International Relations,* 2nd edition, edited by Adam Roberts and Benedict Kingsbury. Oxford: Clarendon Press, pp. 327–383.

Blaney, David L., and Mustapha Kamal Pasha. 1993. "Civil Society and Democracy in the Third World: Ambiguities and Historical Possibilities." *Studies in Comparative International Development* 28 (1).

Bodansky, Daniel. 1993. "The United Nations Framework Convention on Climate Change: A Commentary." *The Yale Journal of International Law* 18 (2):453–558.

Bodansky, Daniel. 1995: "The Emerging Climate Change Regime." *Annual Review of Energy and the Environment* 20: 425–461.

Boehmer-Christiansen, Sonja. 1994a: "A Scientific Agenda for Climate Policy?" *Nature* 372:400–402.

Boehmer-Christiansen, Sonja. 1994b. "Global Climate Protection Policy: The Limits of Scientific Advice." *Global Environmental Change* 4:185–200.

Boli, John, and George Thomas. 1995. "The World Polity in Formation: A Century of International Non-Governmental Organization." Unpublished manuscript, Atlanta, Ga. 1995.

Borenzstein, Eduardo, Mohsin S. Khan, Carmen M. Reinhart, and Peter Wickham. 1994. *The Behavior of Non-oil Commodity Prices.* Washington, D.C.: International Monetary Fund.

Botts, Lee, and Paul Muldoon. 1996. *The Great Lakes Water Quality Agreement: Its Past Successes and Uncertain Future.* Hanover: Institute on International Environmental Governance.

Boundary Waters Treaty. 1909. "Treaty between the United States and Great Britain Relating to Boundary Waters and Questions Arising between the United States and Canada." Reprinted in Edith Brown Weiss, Daniel Barston McGraw, and Paul C. Szesz, *International Environmental Law.* Transnational Publishers, 1992, pp. 413–419.

Bourne, C. B. 1974. "Canada and the Law of International Drainage Basins." in *Canadian Perspectives on International Law and Organization,* edited by Morris MacDonald and Douglas Johnston. Toronto: University of Toronto Press, pp. 458 et. seq.

Breitmeier, Helmut. 1992. *Ozonschicht und Klima auf der globalen Agenda.* Tübinger Arbeitspapiere zur internationalen Politik und Friedensforschung. No. 17. Tübingen.

Breitmeier, Helmut. 1996. *Wie entstehen globale Umweltregime? Der Konfliktaustrag zum Schutz der Ozonschicht und des globalen Klimas.* Leske-Budrich: Opladen.

Brenton, Tony. 1994. *The Greening of Machiavelli: The Evolution of International Environmental Politics.* London: Earthscan.

Bromley, Daniel W., ed. 1992. *Making the Commons Work: Theory, Practice, and Policy*. San Francisco: ICS Press.

Brown, Seyom, Nina W. Cornell, Larry L. Fabian, and Edith Brown Weiss. 1977. *Regimes for the Oceans, Outer Space, and Weather*. Washington, D.C.: Brookings Institution.

Brown Weiss, Edith, Daniel Barston Magraw, and Paul C. Szasz, eds. 1992. *International Environmental Law: Basic Instruments and References*. New York: Transaction Publishers.

Brubaker, Sterling, ed. 1984. *Rethinking the Federal Lands*. Washington, D.C.: Resources for the Future.

Brunnée, Jutta. 1988. *Acid Rain and the Ozone Layer Depletion: International Law and Regulation*. Dobbs Ferry, New York: Transnational Publishers.

Bryant, Christopher G. A. 1995. "Civic Nation, Civil Society, Civil Religion." In *Civil Society: Theory, History, Comparison*, edited by John A. Hall. Cambridge: Polity Press, pp. 136–157.

Bryant, Ralph C. 1995. "Alternative Forms of Cooperation." In *International Coordination of National Stabilization Policies*. Washington, D.C.: Brookings Institution, chapter 2, pp. 6–34.

Bull, Hedley. 1977. *The Anarchical Society: A Study of Order in World Politics*. New York: Columbia University Press.

Burhenne, Wolfgang. N.d. *International Environmental Law: Multilateral Treaties*. The Hague: Kluwer.

Burke, William T. 1967. "Aspects of Internal Decision-Making Processes in Intergovernmental Fisheries Commissions." *Washington Law Review* 43:115–162.

Burke, William T. 1994. *The New International Law of Fisheries: UNCLOS 1982 and Beyond*. Oxford: Clarendon.

Caldwell, Lynton Keith. 1990. *International Environmental Policy: Emergence and Dimensions*. 2nd edition. Durham, N.C.: Duke University Press.

Calhoun, Craig. 1992. "Introduction: Habermas and the Public Sphere." In *Habermas and the Public Sphere*, edited by Craig Calhoun. Cambridge, Mass: MIT Press.

Campbell, Harry F. 1994. "Investing in Yellowfin Tuna," *Marine Policy* 18:19–26.

Canada. 1995a. *Toxic Substance Management Plan*, June.

Canada. 1995b. *CEPA Review, the Government Response: Environmental Protection Legislation Designed for the Future—A Renewed CEPA, Proposal*, December.

Canada-Ontario. 1994. "The Canada-Ontario Agreement Respecting the Great Lakes Basin Ecosystem.".

Cano, Guillermo J. 1992. "Transboundary Freshwaters." In *The Effectiveness of International Environmental Agreements*, edited by Peter Sand. Cambridge: Grotius Publications, pp. 302–308.

Carlsson, Ingvar. 1995. "The UN at 50: A Time to Reform." *Foreign Policy* 100:3–18.

Caron, David D. 1995. "The International Whaling Commission and the North Atlantic Marine Mammal Commission: The Institutional Risks of Coercion in Consensual Structures." *American Journal of International Law* 89:154–173.

Carroll, J. E. 1983. *Environmental Diplomacy: An Examination and a Prospective of Canadian-U.S. Transboundary Environmental Relations*. Ann Arbor: University of Michigan Press.

CCAMLR. See Convention on the Conservation of Antarctic Marine Living Resources.

Chadwick, Bruce P. 1995. "Fisheries, Sovereignties, and Red Herrings." *Journal of International Affairs* 48:558–584.

Charnovitz, Steve. 1995. "Improving Environmental and Trade Governance." *International Environmental Affairs* 7:59–91.

Chayes, Abram, and Antonia Handler Chayes. 1991. "Compliance without Enforcement: State Behavior under Regulatory Treaties." *Negotiation Journal* 7:311–330.

Chayes, Abram, and Antonia Handler Chayes. 1993. "On Compliance." *International Organization* 47:175–205.

Chayes, Abram, and Antonia Handler Chayes. 1995. *The New Sovereignty: Compliance with International Regulatory Agreements*. Cambridge, Mass.: Harvard University Press.

Childers, Erskine, and Brian Urquhart. 1994. *Renewing the United Nations System*. Development Dialog Number 1. Uppsala, Sweden: Dag Hammarsjöld Foundation.

Chossudovsky, Evgeny, 1988. *East-West Diplomacy for the Environment in the United Nations: The High-Level Meeting within the Framework of the ECE on the Protection of the Environment*. New York: United Nations Institute for Training and Research.

Choucri, Nazli, ed. 1993. *Global Accord: Environmental Challenges and International Responses*. Cambridge, Mass.: MIT Press.

Clark, Margaret. 1994. "The Antarctic Environmental Protocol: NGOs in the Protection of Antarctica." In *Environmental NGOs in World Politics: Linking the Local and the Global,* edited by Thomas Princen and Matthias Finger. London: Routledge, pp. 160–185.

Clarke, Robin. 1991. *Water: The International Crisis*. London: Earthscan Publications.

Claude, Inis L. Jr. 1962. *Power and International Relations*. New York: Random House.

CLOS. See Convention on the Law of the Sea.

Coase, Ronald H. 1960. "The Problem of Social Cost." *Journal of Law and Economics* 3:1–44.

Cobb, Roger W., and Charles D. Elder. 1983. *Participation in American Politics: The Dynamics of Agenda-Building*, 2nd edition. Baltimore, Md.: Johns Hopkins University Press.

Codding, George A., and Anthony M. Ruttowski. 1982: *The International Telecommunication Union in a Changing World*. Dedham, Mass.: Artech House.

Cohen, Jack, and Ian Stewart. 1995. "Taxing the Rat Farms: Pollution in Context." *Marine Pollution Bulletin* 30:236–238.

Cohen, Jean L., and Andrew Arato. 1992. *Civil Society and Political Theory*. Cambridge, Mass.: MIT Press.

Cohen, Maxwell. 1975. "The Regime of Boundary Waters: The Canadian-U.S. Experience," Hague Academy Lectures, *Recueil des Cours* 146 (1975), 219–291.

Colborn, T., A. Dandson, S. N. Green, R. A. Hodge, C. J. Jackson, and R. A. Liroff. 1990. *Great Lakes, Great Legacy?* The Conservation Foundation and Institute for Research in Public Policy.

Commission on Global Governance. 1995. *Our Global Neighborhood: The Report of the Commission on Global Governance*. New York: Oxford University Press.

Conca, Ken. 1995. "Greening the United Nations: Environmental Organisations and the UN System." *Third World Quarterly* 16 (3):103–119.

Connolly, Barbara, and Martin List. 1996. "Nuclear Safety in Eastern Europe and the Former Soviet Union." In *Institutions for Environmental Aid: Promises and Pitfalls,* edited by Robert O. Keohane and Marc Levy. Cambridge: MIT Press, pp. 233–279.

"Convention on the Conservation of Antarctic Marine Living Resources" (CCAMLR). 1980. 33 *United States Treaties* (UST) at 3476.

"Convention of International Liability for Damage Caused by Space Objects." 1972. *United Nations Treaty Series* (UNTS), 961 at 187.

Cornia, Giovanni Andrea, Richard Jolly, and Frances Stewart, eds. 1987. *Adjustment with a Human Face: Protecting the Vulnerable and Promotoing Growth*. Vols. 1 and 2. Oxford: Clarendon Press.

Cox, Robert W. 1969. "The Executive Head: An Essay on Leadership in International Organizations." *International Organization* 23:205–230.

Cox, Robert W. 1986. "Social Forces, States and World Orders: Beyond International Relations Theory." In *Neorealism and Its Critics*, edited by Robert O. Keohane. New York: Columbia University Press, pp. 204–254.

Cox, Robert W., and Harold K. Jacobson, eds. 1973. *The Anatomy of Influence: Decision-Making in International Organizations*. New Haven: Yale University Press.

Cristol, Carl Q. 1982. *The Modern International Law of Outer Space.* New York: Pergamon Press.

Deihl, Colin. "Antarctica: An International Laboratory." *Boston College Environmental Affairs Law Review* 18 (3):423–456.

De la court, Thijs. 1990. *Beyond Bruntland: Green Development in the 1990s.* New York: Horizon Books.

Dessler, David. 1992. "The Architecture of Causal Analysis." Unpublished paper.

Deudney, Daniel, and G. John Ikenberry. 1992. "Who Won the Cold War?" *Foreign Policy* 87:123–138.

Dewey, John. 1954. *The Public and its Problems.* Chicago: Swallow Press.

Doeker, Günther, and Thomas Gehring. 1992. "Liability for Environmental Damage. In *The Effectiveness of International Environmental Agreements,* edited by Peter Sand. Cambridge: Grotius Publications, pp. 392–409.

Dotto, Lydia, and Harold Schiff. 1980. *The Ozone War.* New York: Doubleday.

Downs, George W., and David M. Rocke. 1990. *Tacit Bargaining: Arms Races and Arms Control.* Ann Arbor: University of Michigan Press.

Downs, George W., David M. Rocke, and Peter N. Barsoom. 1996. "Is the Good News about Compliance Good News about Cooperation?" *International Organization* 50:379–406.

Dunne, Timothy 1995. "International Society: Theoretical Promises Fulfilled?" *Cooperation and Conflict* 20:125–154.

Durth, Rainer. 1995. *Internationale Oberlauf-Unterlauf-Probleme und Regionale Integration: Zur politischen Ökonomie von Umweltproblemen an grenzüberschreitenden Flüssen (*International Upstream-Downstream Problems and Regional Integration: The Political Economy of Environmental Problems concerning Transboundary Rivers). Hamburg: Graduiertenkolleg für Integrationsforschung.

Easton, David. 1965. *A Systems Analysis of Political Life.* New York, London, Sydney: Wiley.

Edelman, Murray. 1964. *The Symbolic Uses of Politics.* Urbana: University of Illinois Press.

Efinger, Manfred, Volker Rittberger, Klaus Dieter Wolf, and Michael Zürn. 1990. "Internationale Regime und internationale Politik." In *Theorien der Internationalen Beziehungen. Bestandsaufnahme und Forschungsperspektiven,* edited by Volker Rittberger. Westdeutscher Verlag: Opladen, pp. 263–285.

Ellickson, Robert. 1991. *Order without Law: How Neighbors Settle Disputes.* Cambridge, Mass.: Harvard University Press.

Environment Canada. 1995a. *Chlorinated Substances Action Plan Progress Report,* October.

Environment Canada. 1995b. *Industrial Releases within the Great Lakes Basin: An Evaluation of NPRI and TRI Data,* November.

Environment Canada and U.S. Environmental Protection Agency (EPA). 1996. *Canada–United States Strategy for the Virtual Elimination of Persistent Toxic Substances in the Great Lakes Basin.* Draft for Consultation, August.

Environmental Law Institute. 1995. *An Evaluation of the Effectiveness of the International Joint Commission.* Washington, D.C.: Environmental Law Institute.

Esty, Daniel C. 1993. *Greening the GATT.* Washington, D.C.: Institute for International Economics.

Evans, Peter B. 1993. "Building an Integrative Approach to International and Domestic Politics: Reflections and Projections." In *Double-Edged Diplomacy: International Bargaining and Domestic Politics,* edited by P. B. Evans, H. K. Jacobson, and R. D. Putnam. Berkeley: University of California Press, pp. 397–430.

Evans, Peter B., Harold K. Jacobson and Robert D. Putnam eds. 1993. *Double-Edged Diplomacy: International Bargaining and Domestic Politics.* Berkeley: University of California Press.

Fairlie, Simon, Mike Hagler, and Brian O'Riordan. 1995. "The Politics of Overfishing." *The Ecologist* 25:47–73.

Fairman, David, and Michael Ross. 1996. "Old Fads, New Lessons: Learning from Economic Development Assistance." In *Institutions for Environmental Aid: Pitfalls and Promises,* edited by Robert O. Keohane and Marc Levy. Cambridge, Mass.: MIT Press, pp. 29–51.

Falk, Richard. 1992. *Explorations at the Edge of Time: Prospects for World Order.* Philadelphia: Temple University Press.

Falk, Richard A. 1995. "The World Order between Inter-State Law and the Law of Humanity." In *Cosmopolitan Democracy: an Agenda for a New World Order,* edited by Danielle Archibugi and David Held. Cambridge, Mass.: Polity Press, pp. 163–179.

Falkenmark, Malin, and Gunnar Lindh. 1993. "Water and Economic Development." In *Water in Crisis: A Guide to the World's Fresh Water Resources,* edited by Peter Gleick. New York: Oxford University Press. pp. 80–91.

FAO. See Food and Agricultural Organization.

Fearon, James. 1991. "Counterfactuals and Hypothesis Testing in Political Science." *World Politics* 43:169–185.

Fisher, Julie. 1993. *The Road from Rio: Sustainable Development and the Nongovernmental Movement in the Third World.* Westport, Conn.: Praeger.

Food and Agricultural Organization (FAO). 1978. Systematic Index of International Water Resources Treaties, Declarations, Acts and Cases by Basin. Rome: FAO. Legislative Study No. 15.

Food and Agricultural Organization (FAO). 1993. "Agreement to Promote Compliance with International Conservation and Management Measures by Fishing Vessels on the High Seas." *International Legal Materials* 33:971–976.

Forsythe, David. 1989. *Human Rights and World Politics*, 2nd edition. Lincoln: University of Nebraska Press.

"Framework Convention on Climate Change." 1992. *International Legal Materials* 31:849–873.

Franck, Thomas M. 1992. "The Emerging Right to Democratic Governance." *American Journal of International Law* 86 (1):46–91.

Franck, Thomas M. 1990. *The Power of Legitimacy among Nations*. New York: Oxford University Press.

Frey, Bruno S. 1985. *International Political Economics*. London: Basil Blackwell.

Frey, Frederick W. 1993. "The Political Context of Conflict and Cooperation over International River Basins." *Water International* 18:54–68.

Fukuyama, Francis. 1989. "The End of History?" *National Interest* 16:3–18.

Gallarotti, Giulio M. 1991. "The Limits of International Organisation: Systematic Failure in the Management of International Relations." *International Organization* 45 (2):183–220.

Galtung, Johan. 1989. "The Peace Movement: An Exercise in Micro-Macro Linkages." *International Social Science Journal* 40 (117):377–382.

Gehring, Thomas. 1994. *Dynamic International Regimes: Institutions for International Environmental Governance*. Frankfurt: Peter Lang.

George, Alexander L. 1979. "Case Studies and Theory Development: The Method of Structured, Focused Comparison." In *Diplomacy: New Approaches in History*, edited by P. C. Lauren. New York: The Free Press, pp. 43–68.

George, Alexander L., and Timothy J. McKeown. 1985. "Case Studies and Theories of Organizational Decision Making." *Advances in Information Processing in Organizations* 2:21–58.

Gereffi, Gary, and Miguel Korzeniewicz, eds. 1994. *Commodity Chains and Global Capitalism*. Westport, Conn.: Praeger.

Gerges, Makram. 1994 "Marine Pollution Control Monitoring, Assessment, and Control: UNEP's Approach and Strategy." *Marine Pollution Bulletin* 28 (4):199–210.

Gilpin, Robert. 1987. *The Political Economy of International Relations*. Princeton: Princeton University Press.

Gleick, Peter, ed. 1993. *Water in Crisis: A Guide to the World's Fresh Water Resources*. New York: Oxford University Press.

Glenn, William P., Jr. 1995. "Maritime Commerce: Reducing Environmental Losses." *Natural Resources and Environment* 9 (4):40–43 and 69.

GLWQA. See Great Lakes Water Quality Agreement.

Goldman, Robert. 1993. "International Humanitarian Law: Americas Watch's Experience in Monitoring Internal Armed Conflict." *The American University Journal of International Law and Policy*.

Goldmann, Kjell. 1988. "The Concept of 'Realism' as a Source of Confusion." *Cooperation and Conflict* 23:1–14.

Goldstein, Judith, and Robert O. Keohane, eds. 1993. "Ideas and Foreign Policy: An Analytical Framework." In *Ideas and Foreign Policy: Beliefs, Institutions, and Political Change*. Ithaca, N.Y.: Cornell University Press, pp. 3–30.

Goldstein, Judith, and Robert O. Keohane, eds. 1993. *Ideas and Foreign Policy: Beliefs, Institutions, and Political Change*. Ithaca, N.Y.: Cornell University Press.

Gordenker, Leon, and Thomas G Weiss. 1995. "Pluralising Global Governance: Analytical Approaches and Dimensions." *Third World Quarterly* 16.

Government of Canada. See Canada.

Gramsci, Antonio. 1985. *Selections from the Prison Notebooks of Antonio Gramsci*, edited and translated by Quintin Hoare and Geoffrey Nowell Smith. New York: International Publishers.

Great Lakes Commission. 1994. *Ecosystem Charter for Great Lakes–St. Lawrence Basin.*

Great Lakes United. 1995. *Our Lakes, Our Health, Our Future*, chapter 3. A Presentation to the International Joint Commission, 22–25 September.

Great Lakes Water Quality Agreement (GLWQA). 1972. "Agreement between the United States of America and Canada on Great Lakes Water Quality," signed at Ottawa, 15 April 1972. Superseded by "Agreement between Canada and the United States of America on Great Lakes Water Quality," signed at Ottawa, 15 November 1978, as amended by Protocol, signed 1987. 33 *United States Treaties* (UST) at 1383.

Grima, A. P., and R. J. Mason. 1983. "Apples and Oranges: Toward a Critique of Public Participation in Great Lakes Decisions." *Water Resources Journal* 8:22–50.

Haas, Ernst B. 1964. *Beyond the Nation-State: Functionalism and International Organization*. Stanford: Stanford University Press.

Haas, Ernst B. 1976. "Turbulent Fields and the Theory of Regional Integration." *International Organization* 30 (2):173–212.

Haas, Ernst B. 1990. *When Knowledge is Power: Three Models of Change in International Organizations*. Berkeley: University of California Press.

Haas, Ernst B., Mary Pat Williams, and Don Babai. 1977. *Scientists and World Order: The Uses of Technical Knowledge in International Organziations*. Berkeley: University of California Press.

Haas, Peter M. 1989. "Do Regimes Matter? Epistemic Communities and Mediterranean Pollution Control." *International Organization* 43:377–403.

Haas, Peter M. 1990. *Saving the Mediterranean: The Politics of International Environmental Cooperation*, New York: Columbia University Press.

Haas, Peter M., ed. 1992a. *Knowledge, Power, and International Policy Coordination. International Organization* (special issue) 46(1):1–390.

Haas, Peter M. 1992b. "Introduction: Epistemic Communities and International Policy Coordination." *International Organization* (special issue) 46:1–35.

Haas, Peter M., Robert O. Keohane, and Marc A. Levy, eds. 1993. *Institutions for the Earth: Sources of Effective International Environmental Protection.* Cambridge, Mass.: MIT Press.

Haggard, Stephan, and Beth A. Simmons. 1987. "Theories of International Regimes." *International Organization* 41:491–517.

Haglund, Paul. 1991. "Environmental Policy." In *The State of the European Community*, edited by Leon Hurwicz and Christian Lequesne. Boulder, Col.: Lynne Reinner, pp. 259–272.

Hall, Peter A., ed. 1989. *The Political Power of Economic Ideas: Keynsianism across Nations.* Princeton: Princeton University Press.

Handl, Günter, ed. 1995. *Yearbook of International Environmental Law.* Vol. 4. Oxford: Oxford University Press.

Hardin, Garrett. 1968. "The Tragedy of the Commons." *Science* 162:1343–1348.

Hardin, Russell. 1982. *Collective Action.* Baltimore: Johns Hopkins University Press.

Haufler, Virginia. 1993. "Crossing the Boundary between Public and Private: International Regimes and Non-State Actors." In *Regime Theory and International Relations*, edited by Volker Rittberger and Peter Mayer. Oxford: Clarendon Press, pp. 94–111.

Herr, Richard A. 1995. "Antarctica Offshore's Order: The Cacophony and Harmony of Overlapping Regimes." In *Antarctica Offshore: A Cacophony of Regimes?*, edited by R. A. Herr. Hobart, Tasmania: Antarctic CRC Monograph Number 1, pp. 1–10.

Hofman, Robert J. 1993. "Convention for the Conservation of Antarctic Marine Living Resources." *Marine Policy* 17:534–536.

Holst, Johan Jorgen. 1989. "Security and the Environment: A Preliminary Exploration." *Bulletin of Peace Proposals* 20:123–128.

Holst, Johan Jorgen. 1993. "Foreign Minister's Statement to Parliament." English translation printed in *Our Planet* (UNEP) 5 (5):11 and 13.

Holt, Sidney. 1993. "What is Sustainable Development: The Test Case over Whaling." *Our Planet* (UNEP) 5 (5):10 and 12.

Holt, Sidney, and Lee M. Talbot. 1978. "New Principles for the Conservation of Wild Living Resources." *The Journal of Wildlife Management* 43 (2):(supplement).

Homer-Dixon, Thomas F. 1994. "Environmental Scarcities and Violent Conflict: Evidence from Cases." *International Security* 19:5–40.

Horowitz, Michael M., Muneera Salem-Murdock, Curt Grimm, Oumer Kane, Andre Lericollais, John Magistro, Madiodio Niasse, Christophe Nuttal, Thayer Scuder, and Monica Sella. 1991. *The Senegal River Basin Monitoring Activity,*

Phase I: Final Report. Binghamton, New York: Institute for Development Anthropology.

House of Commons, Standing Committee on Environment and Sustainable Development. 1995. *It's About Our Health! Toward Pollution Prevention/ CEPA Revisited,* June. Ottawa:

Hurrell, Andrew. 1992. "Brazil and the International Politics of Amazonian Deforestation." In *The International Politics of the Environment,* edited by Andrew Hurrell and Benedict Kingsbury. Oxford: Clarendon Press, pp. 398– 429.

ICSU. See International Council of Scientific Unions.

IJC. See International Joint Commission.

Ikenberry, G. John, David A. Lake, and Michael Mastanduno. 1988. "Introduction: Approaches to Explaining American Foreign Economic Policy." *International Organization* 42 (1):1–14.

Institute on International Environmental Governance. 1995. "International Secretariats." Background paper prepared for a workshop on international secretariats. Pocantico, New York.

"International Convention for the Regulation of Whaling." 1946. 161 *United Nations Treaty Series* (UNTS) at 72.

International Council of Scientific Unions (ICSU), United Nations Environmental Program (UNEP), and the World Meteorlogical Organization (WMO). 1986. *Report of the International Conference on the Assessment of the Role of Carbon Dioxide and of other Greenhouse Gases in Climate Variations and Associated Impacts.* Villach, Austria, 9–15 October 1985. WMO, Number 661, Geneva.

International Institute for Sustainable Development (IISD). 1994. *Trade and Sustainable Development Principles.* Winnipeg: IISD.

International Joint Commision (IJC). 1990. *Fifth Biennial Report to the Governments of the United States and Canada.*

International Joint Commission (IJC). 1992. *Sixth Biennial Report to the Governments of the United States and Canada.*

International Joint Commision (IJC). 1994. *Seventh Biennial Report to the Governments of the United States and Canada.*

International Joint Commission (IJC). 1996. *Eighth Biennial Report to the Governments of the United States and Canada.*

International Joint Commission (IJC). Task Force. 1996. *Ecosystem Indicators.*

Jachtenfuchs, Markus. 1990. "The European Community and the Protection of the Ozone Layer." *Journal of Common Market Studies* 28 (3):261–277.

Jackson, Sir Robert. 1969. *A Study of the Capacity of the United Nations Development System,* 2 vols. UN Document DP/5.

Jacobson, Harold K. 1984. *Networks of Interdependence: International Organizations and the Global Political System,* 2nd edition, New York: McGraw Hill.

Jacobson, Harold K., and Edith Brown Weiss. 1995. "Strengthening Compliance with International Environmental Accords: Preliminary Observations from a Collaborative Project." *Global Governance* 1 (2):119–148.

Jäger, Jill, and H. L. Ferguson. 1991. *Climate Change: Science, Impacts, and Policy: Proceedings of the Second World Climate Conference*. Cambridge, U.K.: Cambridge University Press.

Jodha, N. S. 1993. "Property Rights and Development." Paper available from the Beijer International Institute of Ecological Economics. Stockholm, Sweden.

Jonsson, Christer. 1993. "International Organization and Cooperation: An Interorganizational Perspective." *International Social Science Journal* 138:463–489.

Joseph, Paul. 1993. *Peace Politics*. Philadelphia: Temple University Press.

Kahler, Miles. 1992. "External Influence, Conditionality, and the Politics of Adjustment." *The Politics of Economic Adjustment*, edited by Stephan Haggard and Robert R. Kaufman. Princeton: Princeton University Press, pp. 89–133.

Kaplan, Robert D. 1994. "The Coming Anarchy." *The Atlantic Monthly* 273:44–76.

Kardam, Nuket. 1993. "Development Approaches and the Role of Policy Advocacy: The Case of the World Bank." *World Development* 21:1773–1786.

Keane, John. "Despotism and Democracy: The Origins and Development of the Distinction between Civil Society and the State, 1750–1850." In *Civil Society and the State*, edited by John Keane. London: Verso, pp. 35–72.

Keeley, James F. 1990. "Toward a Foucauldian Analysis of Regimes." *International Organization* 44 (1):83–106.

Kennedy, Paul. 1993. *Preparing for the 21st Century*. New York: Random House.

Keohane, Robert O. 1984. *After Hegemony: Cooperation and Discord in the World Political Economy*. Princeton: Princeton University Press.

Keohane, Robert O. 1988. "International Cooperation: Two Approaches." *International Studies Quarterly* 32 (4):379–396.

Keohane, Robert O. 1989: *International Institutions and State Power: Essays in International Relations*. Boulder, Col.: Westview Press.

Keohane, Robert O. 1993. "The Analysis of International Regimes: Toward A European-American Research Programme." *Regime Theory and International Relations*, edited by Volker Rittberger and Peter Mayer. Oxford: Clarendon Press, pp. 23–48.

Keohane, Robert O., and Marc A. Levy, eds. 1996. *Institutions for Environmental Aid*. Cambridge, Mass.: MIT Press.

Keohane, Robert O., and Lisa L. Martin. 1995. "The Promise of Institutionalist Theory." *International Security* 20 (1):39–51.

Keohane, Robert O., and Joseph S. Nye, Jr. 1977. *Power and Interdependence: World Politics in Transition*. Boston: Little, Brown.

Keohane, Robert O., and Joseph S. Nye Jr. 1987. "Power and Interdependence Revisited." *International Organization* 41 (4):724–753.

Keohane, Robert O., and Elinor Ostrom, eds. 1995. *Local Commons and Global Interdependence: Heterogeneity and Cooperation in Two Domains.* London: Sage Publications.

Kimball, Lee A. 1996. Treaty Implementation: Scientific and Technical Advice Enters a New Stage. *Studies in Transnational Legal Policy.* No. 28. Washington, D.C.: American Society of International Law.

Kindleberger, Charles P. 1973. *The World in Depression 1929–1939.* Berkeley: University of California Press.

King, Gary, Robert O. Keohane, and Sidney Verba. 1994. *Designing Social Inquiry: Scientific Inference in Qualitative Research.* Princeton: Princeton University Press.

Kingdon, John. 1995. *Agendas, Alternatives, and Public Policy,* 2nd edition. New York: Harper Collins.

Kiss, Alexandre. 1985. "The Protection of the Rhine Against Pollution." *Natural Resources Journal* 25 (3):612–637.

Knox, T. M., trans. 1967. *Hegel's Philosophy of the Right.* London: Oxford University Press.

Kohler-Koch, Beate. 1989."Zur Empirie und Theorie internationaler Regime." In *Regime in den internationalen Beziehungen,* edited by Beate Kohler-Koch. Baden-Baden, Germany: Nomos, pp. 17–85.

Kohli, Atul, Peter Evans, Peter J. Katzenstein, Adam Przeworski, Susanne Hoeber Rudolph, James C. Scott, and Theda Skocpol. 1995. "The Role of Theory in Comparative Politics: A Symposium." *World Politics* 48 (1):1–49.

Korten, David. 1990. *Getting to the 21st Century: Voluntary Action and the Global Agenda.* Hartford, Conn.: Kumarian Press.

Koskenniemi, Martii. 1992. "Breach of Treaty or Non-Compliance? Reflections on the Enforcement of the Montreal Protocol." *Yearbook of International Environmental Law* 3:123–162.

Krasner, Stephen D. 1982. "Structural Causes and Regime Consequences: Regimes as Intervening Variables." *International Organization* 36 (2):185–206.

Krasner, Stephen D., ed. 1983. *International Regimes.* Ithaca, N.Y.: Cornell University Press.

Kratochwil, Friedrich. 1984. "The Force of Prescriptions." *International Organization* 38 (4):685–708.

Kratochwil, Friedrich. 1993. "Contract and Regimes: Do Issue Specificity and Variations of Formality Matter?" In *Regime Theory and International Relations,* edited by Volker Rittberger and Peter Mayer. Oxford: Clarendon Press, pp. 73–93.

Kratochil, Friedrich, and John G. Ruggie. 1986. "International Organization: A

State of the Art on an Art of the State." *International Organization* 40 (4):753–175.

Kumar, Krishan. 1993. "Civil Society: An Inquiry into the Usefulness of an Historical Term." *British Journal of Sociology* 44 (3):375–395.

Lagoni, Rainer. 1984. "Convention on the Conservation of Antarctic Marine Living Resources: A Model for the Use of a Common Good?" In *Antarctic Challenge: Conflicting Interests, Cooperation, Environmental Protection, Economic Development*, edited by R. Wolfrum. Berlin: Duncker & Humblot, pp. 93–108.

Lambright, Henry W., and Rosemary O'Leary. 1991. "Governing Global Climate Change: Can We Learn from the Past in Designing the Future?" *Policy Studies Journal* 19 (2): 50–60.

Lanchberry, John, and David Victor. 1995. "The Role of Science in the Global Climate Negotiations." In *Green Globe Yearbook of International Co-operation and Development 1995*, edited by Helge Ole Bergeson and Georg Parman. Oxford: Oxford University Press, pp. 29–40.

Larkin, P. A. 1977. "An Epitaph for the Concept of Maximum Sustainable Yield." *Transactions of the American Fisheries Society* 106:1–11.

LeMarquand, David G. 1977. *International Rivers: The Politics of Cooperation.* Vancouver: University of British Columbia, Westwater Research Centre.

Le Prestre, Philippe. 1989. *The World Bank and the Environmental Challenge.* Selinsgrove, Penn.: Susquehanna University Press.

Levy, Marc A. 1993. "European Acid Rain: The Power of Toteboard Diplomacy." In *Institutions for the Earth: Sources of Effective International Environmental Protection*, edited by Peter M. Haas, Robert O. Keohane, and Marc A. Levy. Cambridge, Mass.: MIT Press, pp. 75–132.

Levy, Marc A., Gail Osherenko, and Oran R. Young. 1991. *The Effectiveness of International Regimes: A Design for Large-Scale Comparative Research.* Hanover, N. H.: Dartmouth College, Institute on International Environmental Governance.

Levy, Marc A., Oran R. Young, and Michael Zürn. 1995. "The Study of International Regimes." *European Journal of International Relations* 1:267–330.

Lewis, Peter. 1992. "Political Transition and the Dilemma of Civil Society in Africa." *Journal of International Affairs* 46 (1): 31–54.

Libecap, Gary D. 1993. *Contracting for Property Rights.* Cambridge: Cambridge University Press.

Liberatore, Angela. 1991. "Problems of Transnational Policymaking: Environmental Policy in the European Community." *European Journal of Political Research* 19:281–305.

Libiszewski, Stephan. 1995. *Internationale Konflikte um die Nutzung fliessender Gewässer* (International Conflicts over the Use of Transboundary Waters).

Zürich: Eidgenössische Technische Hochschule (ETH), Forschungsstelle für Sicherheitspolitik und Konfliktanalyse.

Lipschutz, Ronnie. 1992. "Restructuring World Politics: The Emergence of Global Civil Society." *Millennium* 21:389–420

Lipschutz, Ronnie. 1996. *Global Civil Society and Global Environmental Governance.* Albany: State University of New York Press.

Lipset, Seymour Martin. 1983. *Political Man: The Social Basis of Politics* (expanded edition). London: Heinemann. First edition published by Doubleday: New York, 1959.

List, Martin, and Volker Rittberger. 1992. "Regime Theory and International Environmental Management." In *The International Politics of the Environment: Actors, Interests, and Institutions,* edited by Andrew Hurrell and Benedict Kingsbury. Oxford: Clarendon Press, pp. 85–109.

Litfin, Karen T. 1994. *Ozone Discourses: Science and Politics in Global Environmental Cooperation.* New York: Columbia University Press.

Lobos, Melissa S. 1987. "Thinning Air, Better Beware: Chlorofluorocarbons and the Ozone Layer." In *Dickinson Journal of International Law* 6 (1):87–117.

Lyons, Gene M. 1995. "International Organizations and National Interests." *International Social Science Journal* xlvii:261–276.

Lyons, Gene M., and Michael Mastanduno, eds. 1995. *Beyond Westphalia: State Sovereignty and International Intervention.* Baltimore: Johns Hopkins University Press.

Malnes, Raino, " 'Leader' and 'Entrepreneur' in International Negotiations: A Conceptual Analysis." *European Journal of International Relations* 1 (1):87–112.

Mandel, Robert. 1992. "Sources of International River Basin Disputes." *Conflict Quarterly* 12 (4):25–56.

Manno, Jack. 1993. "Advocacy and Diplomacy in the Great Lakes: A Case History of Non-Governmental Participation in Negotiating the Great Lakes Water Quality Agreement." *Buffalo Environmental Law Journal* 1:16 et. seq.

Mardin, Serif. 1995. "Civil Society and Islam." In *Civil Society: Theory, History, Comparison,* edited by John A. Hall. Cambridge: Polity Press.

Marin, Bernd, and Renate Mayntz, eds. 1991. *Policy Networks: Empirical Evidence and theoretical Considerations.* Frankfurt am Main: Campus Verlag.

Martin, Lisa L. 1992. "Interests, Power, and Multilateralism." *International Organization* 46:765–792.

Martin, Lisa L. 1993. "The Rational State Choice of Multilateralism." In *Multilateralism Matters: The Theory and Praxis of an Institutional Form,* edited by John G. Ruggie. New York: Columbia University Press, pp. 91–121.

Maynes, Charles William. 1995. "The New Pessimism." *Foreign Policy* 100:33–49.

McCaffrey, Stephen C. 1993. "Water, Politics, and International Law." In *Water in Crisis: A Guide to the World's Fresh Water Resources*, edited by Peter H. Gleick. New York: Oxford University Press, pp. 92–104.

McCay, Bonnie, and James Acheson, eds. 1987. *The Question of the Commons: The Culture and Ecology of Communal Resources*. Tucson: University of Arizona Press.

McCormick, John. 1995. "Environmental Policy and the European Union." In *International Organizations and Environmental Policy*, edited by Robert V. Bartlett, Priya Kurian, and Madhu Malik. Westport, Conn.: Greenwood Press, pp. 37–50.

McCubbins, Mathew, and Thomas Schwartz. 1984. "Congressional Oversight Overlooked: Police Patrols versus Fire Alarms." *American Political Science Review* 78:165–79.

McKean, Margaret A. 1992. "Success on the Commons: A Comparative Examination of Institutions for Common Property Resource Management." *Journal of Theoretical Politics* 4:247–281.

Meltzer, Evelyne. 1994. "Global Overview of Straddling and Highly Migratory Fish Stocks." *Ocean Development and International Law* 25:255–344.

"Memorandum of Understanding on Port State Control in Implementing Agreements on Maritime Safety and Protection of the Marine Environment." 1982. *21 International Legal Materials* at 1 et. seq.

Meron, Theodore. 1977. *The United Nations Secretariat: The Rules and the Practice*. Lexington, Mass.: Lexington Books.

Mfodwo, S. K. B., B. M. Tsamenyi, and S. K. N. Blay. 1989. "The Exculsive Economic Zone: State Practice in the African Atlantic Region." *Ocean Development and International Law* 20:445–99.

Miller, Alan S., and Irving M. Mintzer. 1986. *The Sky is the Limit: Strategies for Protecting the Ozone Layer*. Washington, D.C.: World Resources Institute.

Mingst, Karen A. 1982. "The Functionalist and Regime Perspectives: The Case of Rhine River Cooperation." *Journal of Common Market Studies* 10 (2):161–173.

Mintzer, Irving, and J. Amber Leonard, eds. 1994. *Negotiating Climate Change: The Inside Story of the Rio Convention*. Cambridge, U.K.: Cambridge University Press.

Mitchell, Ronald B. 1994a. *International Oil Pollution at Sea: Environmental Policy and Treaty Compliance*. Cambridge, Mass.: MIT Press.

Mitchell, Ronald B. 1994b. "Regime Design Matters: Intentional Oil Pollution and Treaty Compliance." *International Organization* 48 (3): 425–458.

Molina, Mario J., and Sherwood F. Rowland. 1974. "Stratospheric Sink for Chlorofluoromethans: Chlorine Atom Catalyzed Destruction of Ozone." *Nature* 249:210–12.

Moore, Gerald. 1993. "Compliance without Force: New Techniques in Compliance Control for Foreign Fishing Based on Regional Cooperation." *Ocean Development and International Law* 24:197–204.

Moravcsik, Andrew. 1993. "Introduction: Integrating International and Domestic Theories of International Bargaining." In *Double-Edged Diplomacy: International Bargaining and Domestic Politics*, edited by P. B. Evans, H. K. Jacobson, and R. D. Putnam. Berkeley: University of California Press, pp. 3–42.

Morgenthau, Hans J. 1978. *Politics among Nations: The Struggle for Power and Peace.* 5th edition. New York: Knopf.

Morrisette, Peter M. 1989. "The Evolution of Policy Responses to Stratospheric Ozone Depletion." *Natural Resources Journal* 29 (2):793–820.

Morrow, James D. 1994. "The Forms of International Cooperation." *International Organization* 48: 387–423.

MOU. See Memorandum of Undertstanding.

Mosley, Paul, Jane Harrigan, and John Toye. 1991. *Aid and Power: The World Bank and Policy-Based Lending.* London: Routledge.

Multilateral Investment Guarantee Agency. 1990. *Articles of Agreement.* Washington, D.C.: World Bank.

Murphy, Craig. 1994. *International Organization and Industrial Change: Global Governance since 1850.* New York: Oxford University Press.

Nagel, Ernest. 1961. *The Structure of Science: Problems in the Logic of Scientific Explanation.* New York: Harcourt, Brace, and World.

National Research Council of the United States and Royal Society of Canada. 1985. *The Great Lakes Water Quality Agreement: An Evolving Instrument for Ecosystem Management.* Washington, D.C.: National Academy of Sciences.

Nau, Henry R. 1979. "From Integration to Interdependence: Gains, Losses, and Continuing Gaps." *International Organization* 33 (1):119–147.

Ness, Gayle D., and Steven R. Brechlin. 1988. "Bridging the Gap: International Organizations as Organizations." *International Organization* 42:245–273.

North, Douglass C. 1990. *Institutions, Institutional Change, and Economic Performance.* Cambridge: Cambridge University Press.

Nye, Joseph S. 1990. *Bound to Lead: The Changing Nature of American Power.* New York: Basic Books.

Odell, John S. 1982. *U.S. International Monetary Policy: Markets, Power, and Ideas as Sources of Change.* Princeton: Princeton University Press.

Olson, Mancur, Jr. 1965. *The Logic of Collective Action.* Cambridge: Harvard University Press.

Ontario Ministry of Environment and Energy. 1993. *Candidate List of Substances for Bans and Phase-Outs.*

Ontario Ministry of the Environment. 1986. *A Policy and Program Statement of the Government of Ontario on Controlling Municipal and Industrial Discharges into Surface Waters*, June.

Onuf, Nicholas Greenwood. 1989. *World of Our Making: Rules and Rule in Social Theory and International Relations*. Columbia: University of South Carolina Press.

Osherenko, Gail, and Oran R. Young. 1993. "The Formation of International Regimes: Hypotheses and Cases." In *Polar Politics: Creating International Environmental Regimes*, edited by Oran R. Young and Gail Osherenko. Ithaca, N.Y.: Cornell University Press, pp. 1–21.

Ostrom, Elinor. 1990. *Governing the Commons: The Evolution of Institutions for Collective Action*. Cambridge: Cambridge University Press.

Ostrom, Elinor. 1992. "Community and the Endogenous Solution of Commons Problems." *Journal of Theoretical Politics* 4:343–351.

Outer Space Treaty. 1967. "Treaty on Principles Governing the Activities of States in the Exploration and Use of Outer Space, Including the Moon and Other Celestial Bodies." 610 *United Nations Treaty Series* (UNTS) at 205.

Oye, Kenneth, ed. 1986. *Cooperation under Anarchy*. Princeton, N.J.: Princeton University Press.

Oye, Kenneth A., and James H. Maxwell. 1994. "Self-Interest and Environmental Management." *Journal of Theoretical Politics* 6:593–624.

Parson, Edward A. 1993. "Protecting the Ozone Layer." In *Institutions for the Earth: Sources of Effective International Environmental Protection* edited by Peter M. Haas, Robert O. Keohane, and Marc A. Levy. Cambridge: MIT Press, pp. 27–73.

Parsons, Talcott. 1971. *The System of Modern Societies*. Englewood Cliffs, N.J.: Prentice-Hall.

Pateman, Carole. 1988. "Feminist Critiques of the Public/Private Dichotomy." In *Public and Private in Social Life*, edited by S. Benn and G. Gauss. Canberra and London: Croom Helm.

Perez-Diaz, Victor. 1995. "The Possibility of Civil Society." In *Civil Society: Theory, History, Comparison* edited by John A. Hall. Cambridge: Polity Press, pp. 80–109.

Peterson, M. J. 1988. *Managing the Frozen South*. Berkeley: University of California Press.

Peterson, M. J. 1992. "Whalers, Cetologists, and the International Management of Whaling." *International Organization* 46:147–186.

Peterson, M. J. 1993. "International Fisheries Management." In *Institutions for the Earth: Sources of Effective International Environmental Protection*, edited by Peter M. Haas, Robert O. Keohane, and Marc A. Levy. Cambridge, Mass.: MIT Press, pp. 249–305.

Pistorius, Robin. 1995. "Forum Shopping: Issue Linkages in the Genetic Resources Issue." In *International Organizations and Environmental Policy*, edited by Robert V. Bartlett, Priya Kurian, and Madhu Malik. Westport, Conn.: Greenwood Press, pp. 209–222.

Princen, Thomas. 1995. "From Property Regime to International Regime: An Ecosystem Perspective." Paper prepared for the 1996 annual convention of the International Studies Association.

Princen, Thomas, and Matthias Finger. 1994. *Environmental NGOs in World Politics: Linking the Local and the Global*. London: Routledge.

Public Land Law Review Commission. 1970. *One Third of the Nation's Land*. Washington, D.C.: U.S. Government Printing Office.

Putnam, Robert D. 1988. "Diplomacy and Domestic Politics: The Logic of Two-Level Games." *International Organization* 42 (3):427–460.

Ramakrishna, Kilaparti, and Oran R. Young. 1992. "International Organizations in a warming world." *Confronting Climate Change: Risks, Implications, and Responses*, edited by Irving M. Mintzer. Cambridge: Cambridge University Press, 253–264.

Raul, Alan Charles, and Paul E. Hagen. 1993. The Convergence of Trade and Environmental Law." *Natural Resources and Environment* 8 (2):3–6 and 50–53.

Redclift, Michael. 1987. *Sustainable Development: Exploring the Contradictions*. New York: Methuen.

Reed, David, ed. 1996. *Structural Adjustment, the Environment, and Sustainable Development*. London: Earthscan Publications.

Registration Convention. 1974. "Convention on the Registration of Objects Launched into Outer Space." *United Nations Treaty Series* 1023:15–19.

Richardson, Elliot. 1988. "Jan Mayen in Perspective." *American Journal of International Law* 82:443–458.

"Rio Declaration on the Environment." 1992. UN Document A/CONF.151/26/Rev.1. Volume 1, Annex I.

Rittberger, Volker, ed. 1990. *International Regimes in East-West Politics*. London: Pinter.

Rittberger, Volker. 1994. *Internationale Organisationen: Politik und Geschichte*. Leske-Budrich: Opladen.

Rittberger, Volker, and Peter Mayer, eds. 1993. *Regime Theory and International Relations*. Oxford: Clarendon Press.

Rittberger, Volker, and Michael Zürn. 1991. "Regime Theory: Findings from the Study of 'East-West' Regimes." *Cooperation and Conflict* 26:165–183.

Roan, Sharon. 1989. *Ozone Crisis: The Fifteen-Year Evolution of a Sudden Global Emergency*. New York: Wiley & Sons.

Rochester, J. Martin. 1986. "The Rise and Fall of International Organizations as a Field of Study." *International Organization* 40:777–813.

Rodenberg, Eric. 1991. *Eyeless in Gaia: The State of Global Environmental Monitoring.* Washington, D.C.: World Resources Institute.

Rogers, Peter. 1992. "Economic and Institutional Issues: International River Basins." In *Country Experiences with Water Resources Management. Economic, Institutional, Technological and Environmental Issues,* edited by Guy Le Moigne, Shawki Barhouti, Gershon Feder, Lisa Garbus, and Mei Xie Le. Washington, D.C.: The World Bank. World Bank Technical Paper No. 175, pp. 63–69.

Romy, Isabelle. 1990. *Les pollutions transfrontières des eaux: L'Exemple du Rhin. Mozens d'action des lésés.* Lausanne: Payot.

Rosenau, James N. 1986. "Before Cooperation: Hegemons, Regimes, and Habit-Driven Actors in World Politics." *International Organization* 40 (4):850–894.

Rosenau, James N. 1990. *Turbulence in World Politics: A Theory of Change and Continuity.* Princeton, N.J.: Princeton University Press.

Rosenu, James N. 1992. "Governance, Order, and Change in World Politics." In *Governance without Government: Order and Change in World Politics,* edited by James N. Rosenau and Ernst-Otto Czempiel. Cambridge: Cambridge University Press, pp. 1–29.

Rosenau, James N. 1995. "Governance in the Twenty-First Century." *Global Governance* (1):13–43.

Rosenau, James, and Ernst-Otto Czempiel, eds. 1992. *Governance without Government: Order and Chnge in World Politics,* Cambridge: Cambridge University Press.

Ross, Charles E. 1974. "National Sovereignty in International Environmental Decisions." in *Protecting the Environment: Issues and Perspectives,* edited by O. P. Dwivedi. Toronto: Copp Clark.

Rowlands, Ian. 1995. *The Politics of Global Atmospheric Change.* Manchester: Manchester University Press.

Ruggie, John Gerard. 1975. "International Responses to Technology: Concepts and Trends." *International Organization* 29 (3): 557–583.

Ruggie, John Gerard. 1982. "International Regimes, Transactions, and Change: Embedded Liberalism in the Postwar Economic Order." *International Organization* 36 (2):379–415.

Ruggie, John Gerard. 1983. "International Regimes, Transactions, and Change: Embedded Liberalism in the Postwar Economic Order." In *International Regimes,* edited by Stephen D. Krasner. Ithaca, N.Y.: Cornell University Press, pp. 195–232.

Ruggie, John Gerard. 1991. "Embedded Liberalism Revisited: Institutions and Progress in International Economic Relations." In *Progress in Postwar International Relations,* edited by Emanuel Adler and Beverly Crawford. New York: Columbia University Press, pp. 201–234.

Ruggie, John Gerard. 1992. "Multilateralism: The Anatomy of an Institution." *International Organization* 46 (3):561–598.

Ruggie, John Gerard, ed. 1993a. *Multilateralism Matters: The Theory and Praxis of an Institutional Form.* New York: Columbia University Press.

Ruggie, John Gerard. 1993b. "Territoriality and Beyond: Problematizing Modernity in International Relations." *International Organization* 47 (1):139–174.

Rummel-Bulska, Iwona. 1986. "The Protection of the Ozone Layer under the Global Framework Convention." In *Transboundary Air Pollution: International Legal Aspects of the Cooperation of States,* edited by Cees Flinterman, Barbara Kwiatkowska, and Johan G. Lamers. Dordrecht, Netherlands: Martinus Nijhoff, pp. 281–297.

Rutherford, Malcolm. 1994. *Institutions in Economics: The Old and the New Institutionalism.* Cambridge: Cambridge University Press.

Sabatier, Paul. 1988. "An Advocacy Coalition Approach Framework of Policy Change and the Role of Policy-Oriented Learning Therein." *Policy Sciences* 21:129–68.

Sabella, Susan J. 1993. "Upon Closer Inspection..." *Marine Pollution Bulletin* 25,

Saguirian, Artemy A. 1992. "Russia and Some Pending Law of the Sea Issues in the North Pacific." *Ocean Development and International Law* 23:1–16.

Sand, Peter H. 1991. "Lessons Learned in Global Environmental Governance." *Environmental Affairs Law Review* 18:213–277.

Sand, Peter H., ed. 1992. *The Effectiveness of International Environmental Agreements.* Cambridge, U.K.: Grotius Publications.

Sandford, Rosemary. 1994. "International Environmental Treaty Secretariats: Stage-Hands or Actors?" In *Green Globe Yearbook of International Co-operation and Development 1994,* edited by Helge Ole Bergesen and Georg Parman. Oxford: Oxford University Press, pp. 17–29.

Sandler, Todd. 1992. *Collective Action: Theory and Applications.* Ann Arbor: University of Michigan Press.

Sands, Phillipe. 1995. *Principles of International Environmental Law, vol. 1: Frameworks, Standards and Implementation.* Manchester: Manchester University Press.

Scheiber, Harry N. 1986. "Pacific Ocean Resources, Science, and the Law of the Sea: Wilbert M. Chapman and the Pacific Fisheries." *Ecology Law Quarterly* 13:381–534.

Schelling, Thomas C. 1978. *Micromotives and Macrobehavior.* New York: W. W. Norton.

Scott, Anthony. 1980. "International Environmental and Fisheries Pacts." In *The Theory and Structure of International Political Economy,* edited by Todd Sandler. Boulder, Colo.: Westview, 59–95.

Scudder, Thayer. 1989. "River Basin Projects in Africa." *Environment* 31 (2):4–9 and 27–32.

Sebenius, James K. 1983. "Negotiation Arithmetic: Adding and Subtracting Issues and Parties." *International Organization* 37 (2):281–316.

Sebenius, James K. 1984. *Negotiating the Law of the Sea*. Cambridge, Mass.: Harvard University Press.

Sebenius, James K. 1991. "Designing Negotiations toward a New Regime: The Case of Global Warming." *International Security* 15 (4):110–148.

Sebenius, James K. 1992. "Challenging Conventional Explnations of International Cooperation: Negotiation Analysis and the Case of Epistemic Communities." *International Organization* 46 (1):323–365.

Seligman, Adam B. 1992. *The Idea of Civil Society*. New York: The Free Press.

Shibata, Akiho. 1993. "International Law-Making Processes in the United Nations: Comparative Analysis of UNCED and UNCLOS III." *California Western International Law Journal* 24:17–53.

Shih, Chih-yu. 1989. "A Cognitive Approach to International Organization." *Behavioral Science* 34:176–198.

Sikkink, Kathryn. 1992. *Ideas and Institutions: Developmentalism in Brazil and Argentina*. Ithaca, N.Y.: Cornell University Press.

Sikkink, Kathryn. 1993. "Human Rights Issue–Networks in Latin America." *International Organization* 47 (3):411–441.

Sinclair, Margaret. 1974. *The International Joint Commission and Its Involvement with the Public*. Windsor, Ont.: International Joint Commission.

Singerman, Diane. 1996. "Civil Society in the Shadow of the Egyptian State: The Role of Informal Networks and the Construction of Public Life." Paper presented at the G. E. von Grunebaum Center for Near Eastern Studies, University of California at Los Angeles, 29 January.

Singleton, Sara, and Michael Taylor. 1992. "Common Property, Collective Action, and Community." *Journal of Theoretical Politics* 4:309–324.

Sjöberg, Helen. 1994. *The Creation of the Global Environment Facility*. Washington, D.C.: The Global Environment Facility.

Snidal, Duncan. 1985a. "Coordination versus Prisoners' Dilemma: Implications for International Cooperation and Regimes." *American Political Science Review* 79:923–942.

Snidal, Duncan. 1985b. "The Limits of Hegemonic Stability Theory." *International Organization* 39:579–614.

Soroos, Marvin S. 1986. *Beyond Sovereignty: The Challenge of Global Policy*. Columbia: University of South Carolina Press.

Spector, Bertram, Gunnar Sjöstedt, and I. William Zartman eds. 1994. *Negotiating Internationl Regimes: Lessons Learned from the United Nations Conference on Environment and Development (UNCED)*. London: Graham & Trotman/ Martinus Nijhoff.

Spector, Bertram, and Anna Korula. 1992. "The Post-Agreement Negotiation Process: The Problems of Ratifying International Environmental Agreements." IIASA Working Paper WP-92-90.

Squires, Dale. 1994. "Sources of Growth in Marine Fishing Industries." *Marine Policy 18(1):5–18*.

Stairs, Keven, and Peter Taylor. 1992. "Nongovernmental Organizations and the Legal Protection of the Oceans: A Case Study." In *The International Politics of the Environment*, eds. Andrew Hurrell and Benedict Kingsbury. Oxford: Clarendon Press, pp. 110–141.

Stedman, Pamela. 1995. *Setting a New Mandate for the Bretton Woods Institutions*. Washington, D.C.: World Wide Fund for Nature-International.

Stein, Arthur. 1982. "Coordination and Collaboration: Regimes in an Anarchic World." *International Organization 36:299–324*.

Stein, Arthur A. 1990. *Why Nations Cooperate: Circumstances and Choice in International Relations*. Ithaca, N.Y.: Cornell University Press.

Stein, Janice Gross, ed. 1989. *Getting to the Table: The Processes of International Prenegotiation*. Baltimore, Md.: Johns Hopkins University Press.

Stoett, Peter J. 1995. "The International Whaling Commission: From Traditional Concerns to an Expanding Agenda." *Environmental Politics 4:130–135*.

Stokke, Olav Schram. 1990. "The Northern Environment: Is Cooperation Coming?" *Annals of the American Academy for Political and Social Science 512:58–69*.

Stokke, Olav Schram. 1991. *Western Environmental Interests in the Arctic*. *Centrepiece 21:1–42*. Aberdeen: Centre for Defense Studies.

Stokke, Olav Schram. 1994. "Environmental Cooperation as a Driving Force in the Barents Region." *The Barents Region: Cooperation in Arctic Europe*, edited by Olav Schram Stokke and Ola Tunander. London: Sage Publications, pp. 145–159.

Stokke, Olav Schram. 1995a. *Fisheries Management under Pressure: Changing Russia and the Effectiveness of the Barents Sea Regime*. Lysaker: The Fridtjof Nansen Institute. Report No. 1.

Stokke, Olav Schram. 1995b. "Understanding the Formation of International Regimes: The Discursive Challenge." In *The International Politics of Environmental Management*, edited by A. Underdal. Dordrecht, Netherlands: Kluwer, pp. 133–155.

Stokke, Olav Schram. 1996. "The Effectiveness of CCAMLR." In *Governing the Antarctic: The Effectiveness and Legitimacy of the Antarctic Treaty System*, edited by Olav Schram Stokke and Davor Vidas. Cambridge: Cambridge University Press, pp. 120–151.

Stokke, Olav Schram, and Ola Tunander, eds. 1994. *The Barents Region: Cooperation in Arctic Europe*. London: Sage Publications.

Stokke, Olav Schram and Davor Vidas. 1996a. "Conclusions." *Governing the Antarctic: The Effectiveness and Legitimacy of the Antarctic Treaty System*, edited by Olav Schram Stokke and Davor Vidas. Cambridge: Cambridge University Press, pp. 432–456.

Stokke, Olav Schram, and Davor Vidas. 1996b. "The Effectiveness and Legitimacy of International Regimes." *Governing the Antarctic: The Effectiveness and Legitimacy of the Antarctic Treaty System*, edited by Olav Schram Stokke and Davor Vidas. Cambridge: Cambridge University Press, pp. 13–31.

Stokke, Olav Schram, Lee G. Anderson, and Natalia Mirovitskaya. 1996. "The Barents Sea Fishieries Regime." In *The Effectiveness of International Regimes*, edited by Marc A. Levy and Oran R. Young. Ithaca, N.Y.: Cornell University Press, forthcoming.

Straddling and Highly Migratory Fish Stocks Agreement. 1995. "Agreement for the Implementation of the Provisions of the UN Convention of the Law of the Sea of 10 December 1982 Relating to Straddling Fish Stocks and Highly Migratory Fish Stocks." UN Doc. A/CONF.164/33. 3 August 1995.

Strange, Susan. 1983. "Cave! Hic Dragones: A Critique of Regime Analysis." In *International Regimes*, edited by Stephen D. Krasner. Ithaca, N.Y.: Cornell University Press, pp. 337–354.

Suganami, Hidemi. 1989. *The Domestic Analogy and World Order Proposals*. Cambridge: Cambridge University Press.

Susskind, Lawrence E. 1994. *Environmental Diplomacy: Negotiating More Effective Global Agreements*. Oxford: Oxford University Press.

Swinehart, Carol Y. 1988. "A Review of Public Participation in the Great Lakes Water Quality Agreement." In *The Great Lakes: Living with North America's Inland Waters*. American Water Resources Association Symposium Proceedings. Bethesda, Md.: AWRA.

Taylor, Michael. 1992. "The Economics and Politics of Property Rights and Common Pool Resources." *Natural Resources Journal* 32:640.

Tesh, Sylvia N., and Bruce Williams. 1996. "Identity Politics, Disinterested Politics, and Environmental Justice." *Polity* 28:285–305.

Thacher, Peter. 1992. "The Role of the United Nations." In *The International Politics of the Environment: Actors, Interests, and Institutions,* edited by Andrew Hurrell and Benedict Kingsbury. Oxford: Clarendon Press, pp. 183–211.

Thelen, Kathleen, and Sven Steinmo. 1992. "Historical Institutionalism in Comparative Politics." In *Structuring Politics: Historical Institutionalism in Comparative Analysis*, edited by S. Steinmo, K. Thelen, and F. Longstreth. Cambridge: Cambridge University Press, pp. 1–32.

Thomas, Caroline. 1992. *The Environment in International Relations*. London: Earthscan.

Thompson, E. P. 1990. "E.N.D. and the Beginning: History Turns on a New Hinge." *The Nation* 250 (4):117–122.

Thompson, William R., ed. 1983. *Contending Approaches to World System Analysis*. Beverly Hills: Sage Publications.

Thomson, Janice E., and Stephen D. Krasner. 1989. "Global Transactions and the Consolidation of Sovereignty." In *Global Changes and Theoretical Challenges: Approaches to World Politics for the 1990s*, edited by Ernst-Otto Czempiel and James Rosenau. Lexington, Mass.: Lexington Books, pp. 195–219.

Trask, Jeff. 1992. "Montreal Protocol Noncompliance Procedure: The Best Approach to Resolving International Environmental Disputes." *Georgetown Law Journal* 80:1973–2001.

Underdal, Arild. 1980. *The Politics of International Fisheries Management: The Case of the Northeast Atlantic*. Oslo: Universitetsforlaget.

Underdal, Arild. 1983. "Causes of Negotiation 'Failure.'" *European Journal of Political Research* 11:183–195.

Underdal, Arild. 1987. "International Cooperation: Transforming 'Needs' into 'Deeds.'" *Journal of Peace Research* 24 (2):167–183.

Underdal, Arild. 1990. *Negotiating Effective Solutions: The Art and Science of Political Engineering*. Oslo: University of Oslo.

Underdal, Arild. 1991. "International Cooperation and Political Engineering." *Global Policy Studies: International Interaction toward Improving Public Policy*, edited by S. S. Nagel. Houndsmills and London: MacMillan in association with Policy Studies Organization, pp. 98–120.

Underdal, Arild. 1992. "The Concept of Regime 'Effectiveness.'" *Cooperation and Conflict* 27 (3):227–240.

Underdal, Arild. 1995. "The Study of International Regimes." *Journal of Peace Research* (1): 113–121.

UNEP. See United Nations Environmental Program.

United Nations (ECOSOC). 1972. *Developments in the Field of Natural Resources — Water, Energy, and Minerals: Technical and Economic Aspects of International River Basin Development*. New York: United Nations, Committee on Natural Resources, Third Session, 12–23 February. (E/C. 7/35).

United Nations. 1992. *Report of the United Nations Conference on Environment and Development, Rio de Janeiro, 3–14 June 1992*. New York: United Nations.

United Nations. 1988. *Institutional Issues in the Management of International River Basins: Financial and Contractual Considerations*. New York: United Nations.

United Nations. 1963. *Legal Problems Relating to the Utilization and Use of International Rivers*, vol. 1–3. New York: United Nations, Report of the UN Secretary General, A/5409, 15 April.

United Nations. 1978. *Register of International Rivers*. Oxford: Pergamon Press.

United Nations Environment Program. (UNEP) 1989. *Action on Ozone.* Nairobi: UNEP.

U.S. General Accounting Office. 1992. *International Environment: International Agreements Are not Well Monitored.* Publication GOA/RCED-92-43. Washington, D.C.: U.S. Government Printing Office.

U.S. Marine Mammals Commission. 1991. *Annual Report to Congress.* Washington, D.C.: U.S. Marine Mammals Commission.

U.S. Marine Mammals Commission. 1992. *Annual Report to Congress.* Washington, D.C.: U.S. Marine Mammals Commission.

U.S. Marine Mammals Commission. 1993. *Annual Report to Congress.* Washington, D.C.: U.S. Marine Mammals Commission.

Veggeland, Noralv. 1994. "The Barents Region as a European Frontier Region." In Olav Schram Stokke and Ola Tunander, eds. *The Barents Region: Cooperation in Arctic Europe.* London: Sage Publications, 201–212.

Victor, David G., and Julian E. Salt. 1994. "From Rio to Berlin: Managing Climate Change." *Environment* 36:6–15 and 25–32.

Vlachos, Evan, Anne C. Webb, and Irene L. Murphy, eds. 1986. *The Management of International River Basin Conflicts.* Laxenburg: International Institute of Applied Systems Analysis. Working paper.

Vogel, David. 1995. *Trading Up.* Cambridge: Harvard University Press.

Von Moltke, Konrad. 1992. "International Trade, Technology Transfer, and Climate Change." In *Negotiating Climate Change: The Inside Story of the Rio Convention*, edited by Irvin Mintzer and J. Amber Leonard. Cambridge: Cambridge University Press, pp. 295–304.

Von Moltke, Konrad. 1996. *International Environmental Management, Trade Regimes, and Sustainability.* Winnipeg: International Institute for Sustainable Development.

Walker, K. J. 1989. "The State in Environmental Management: The Ecological Dimension." *Political Studies* 37:25–38.

Walker, R. B. J. 1988. *One World/Many Words.* Boulder, Colo.: Lynne Rienner Publishers.

Waltz, Kenneth N. 1979. *Theory of International Politics.* Berkeley: University of California.

Wank, David L. 1995. "Civil Society in Communist China? Private Business and Political Alliance, 1989." In *Civil Society: Theory, History, Comparison*, edited by John A. Hall. Cambridge: Polity Press, pp. 56–79.

Wapner, Paul. 1995a. "Politics beyond the State: Environmental Activism and World Civic Politics." *World Politics* 47:311–340.

Wapner, Paul. 1995b "In Defense of Banner Hangers: The Dark Green Politics of Greenpeace." In *Ecological Resistance Movements: The Global Emergence of Radical and Popular Environmentalism*, edited by Bron Taylor. Albany: State University of New York Press, pp. 300–314.

Wapner, Paul. 1996. *Environmental Activism and World Civic Politics*. Albany: State University of New York Press.

Watson, Adam. 1991. *Diplomacy: The Dialogue between States*. London: Routledge.

Weale, Albert. 1992. *The New Politics of Pollution*. Manchester and New York: Manchester University Press.

Weiss, Thomas G., David P. Forsythe, and Roger A. Coate. 1994. *The United Nations and Changing World Politics*. Boulder: Westview Press.

Weller, Phil. 1990. *Fresh Water Seas: Saving the Great Lakes*. Toronto: Between the Lines.

Wendt, Alexander. 1987. "The Agent-Structure Problem in International Relations Theory." *International Organization* 41:335–370.

Wendt, Alexander. 1992. "Anarchy Is What States Make of It: The Social Construction of Power Politics." *International Organization* 46:391–425.

Wendt, Alexander. 1994. "Collective Identity Formation and the International State." *American Political Science Review* 88:384–396.

Wendt, Alexander. 1995. "Constructing International Politics." *International Security* 20 (1):71–81.

Wendt, Alexander, and Raymond Duvall. 1989. "Institutions and International Order." In *Global Changes and Theoretical Challenges: Appproaches to World Politics for the 1990s*, edited by Ernst-Otto Czempiel and James N. Rosenau. Lexington, Mass.: Lexington Books, pp. 51–73.

Werksman, Jacob. 1996. "Designing a Compliance System for the UN Framework Convention on Climate Change." In *Improving Compliance with International Environmental Law*, edited by James Cameron, Jacob Werksman, and Peter Roderick. London: Earthscan Publications, pp. 85–147.

Wessel, J. 1993. "Institutional Arrangements Which May Promote Ecosystems Water Management." *Journal of Aquatic Ecosystems Health* 2:15–19.

Westing, Arthur H, ed. 1990. *Environmental Hazards of War: Releasing Dangerous Forces in an Industrialized World*. London: SAGE.

Wettestad, Jorgen. 1995. *Nuts and Bolts for Environmental Negotiators? Designing Effective International Regimes: A Conceptual Framework*. Lysaker, Norway: The Fridtjof Nansen Institute. Working paper.

Willoughby, William R. 1979. *The Joint Organizations of Canada and the United States*. Toronto: University of Toronto Press.

WMO. See World Meteorological Organization.

Wolf, Klaus-Dieter. 1991. *Internationale Regime zur Verteilung Globaler Ressourcen: Eine vergleichende Analyse der Grundlagen ihrer Entstehung am Beispiel der Regelung des Zugangs zur wirtschaftlichen Nutzung des Meeresbodens, des geostationren Orbits, der Antarktis und zu Wissenschaft und Technologie.* Baden-Baden: Nomos.

World Bank. 1993. *The World Bank and the Environment, Fiscal Year 1993.* Washington, D.C.: World Bank.

World Bank. 1994. *The World Bank and the Environment, Fiscal Year 1994.* Washington, D.C.: World Bank.

World Bank. 1995. *Toward Sustainable Management of Water Resources.* Washington, D.C.: The World Bank.

World Bank. *Mainstreaming the Environment: The World Bank Group and the Environment since Rio.* Washington, D.C.: World Bank.

World Meteorlogical Organization (WMO). 1979. *Proceedings of the World Climate Conference: A Conference of Experts on Climate and Mankind, Geneva 12–23 February 1979,* WMO No. 537, Geneva.

World Meteorological Organization (WMO). 1989. *Scientific Assessment of Stratospheric Ozone* vol. 1. WMO, Geneva.

World Meteorological Organization (WMO). 1990. *The WMO Achievement: Forty Years in the Service of International Meteorology and Hydrology.* WMO No. 729, Geneva.

World Meteorological Organization (WMO) and the United Nations Environment Program (UNEP). 1988a. *Developing Policies for Responding to Climatic Change: A Summary of the Discussions and Recommendations of the Workshop held in Villach, 28 September–2 October 1987 and Bellagio, 9–13 November 1987, under the Auspices of the Beijer Institute.* WMO/TD No. 225, Geneva.

World Meteorological Organization (WMO) and the United Nations Environmental Program (UNEP). 1988b.*The Changing Atmosphere: Implications for Global Security. Toronto, Canada, 27–30 June 1988.* WMO No. 710, Geneva.

World Meteorological Organization (WMO) and the United Nations Environment Program (UNEP). 1988c. *WMO/UNEP Inter-governmental Panel on Climate Change: Report of the First Session, Geneva, 9–11 November 1988.* IPCC-1, TD No. 267, Geneva.

World Resources Institute. 1992. *World Resources 1992–93.* New York: Oxford University Press.

World Resources Institute. 1994. *World Resources 1994–95.* Oxford: Oxford University Press.

Yarbrough, Beth V., and Robert M. Yarbrough. 1990. "International Institutions and the New Economics of Organization." *International Organization* 44 (2):235–260.

Yearbook of International Organizations, 1. 1995–96. München: K. G. Saur.

Yin, Robert K. 1989. *Case Study Research: Design and Methods. Applied Social Research Methods Series,* vol. 5. London: Sage Publications.

Young, Andrew J. 1986. "A Decennial Review of the Registration Convention." *Annals of Air and Space Law* 11:287–308.

Young, Oran R. 1979. *Compliance and Public Authority.* Washington, D.C.: Resources for the Future.

Young, Oran, R. 1980. "International Regimes: Problems of Concept Formation." *World Politics* 32:331–356.

Young, Oran R. 1982. "Regime Dynamics: The Rise and Fall of International Regimes." *International Organization* 36:277–297.

Young, Oran R. 1983. "Regime Dynamics: The Rise and Fall of International Regimes." In *International Regimes,* edited by Stephen D. Krasner. Ithaca, N.Y.: Cornell University Press, pp. 93–113.

Young, Oran R. 1989a. *International Cooperation: Building Regimes for Natural Resources and the Environment.* Ithaca: Cornell University Press.

Young, Oran R. 1989b. "The Politics of Regime Formation" *International Organization* 43 (3):349–376.

Young, Oran R. 1991a. "Political Leadership and Regime Formation: On the Development of Institutions in International Society." *International Organization* 45:281–309.

Young, Oran R. 1991b. *Report on the "Regime Summit,"* Held at Dartmouth College in November 1991. Hanover, N.H.: Institute of Arctic Studies.

Young, Oran R. 1992. "The Effectiveness of International Institutions: Hard Cases and Critical Variables." In *Governance without Government: Order and Change in World Politics,* edited by James N. Rosenau and Ernst-Otto Czempiel. Cambridge: Cambridge University Press, pp. 160–192.

Young, Oran R. 1994a. *International Governance: Protecting the Environment in a Stateless Society.* Ithaca: Cornell University Press.

Young, Oran R. 1994b. "The Problem of Scale in Human/Environment Relationships." *Journal of Theoretical Politics* 6:429–447.

Young, Oran R. 1995a. "The Problem of Scale in Human/Environment Relationships." In *Local Commons and Global Interdependence: Heterogeneity and Cooperation in Two Domains,* edited by Robert O. Keohane and Elinor Ostrom. London: Sage Publications, pp. 27–45.

Young, Oran R. 1995b. "System and Society in World Affairs: Implications for International Organizations. *International Social Science Journal* 47:197–212.

Young, Oran R. 1996. "Institutional Linkages in International Society: Polar Perspectives." *Global Governance* 2:1–23.

Young, Oran R. Forthcoming. *Creating International Regimes: Arctic Cases, General Processes.* Ithaca: Cornell University Press.

Young, Oran R., and Marc A. Levy (with Gail Osherenko). 1996. "The Effectiveness of International Regimes." In *The Effectiveness of International Regimes*, edited by Marc A. Levy and Oran R. Young. Ithaca, N.Y.: Cornell University Press, forthcoming.

Young, Oran R., and Gail Osherenko, eds. 1993a. *Polar Politics: Creating International Environmental Regimes*. Ithaca: Cornell University Press.

Young, Oran R., and Gail Osherenko. 1993b. "Testing Theories of Regime Formation: Findings from a Large Collaborative Research Project." In *Regime Theory and International Relations*, edited by Volker Rittberger and Peter Mayer. Oxford: Clarendon Press, pp. 223–251.

Young, Oran R., and Konrad von Moltke. 1994. "The Consequences of International Environmental Regimes: Report from the Barcelona Workshop." *International Environmental Affairs* 6:348–370.

Zamora, Stephen. 1980. "Voting in International Economic Organizations." *American Journal of International Law* 74:566–608.

Zürn, Michael. 1993. "Bringing the Second Image (Back) in: About the Domestic Sources of Regime Formation." In *Regime Theory and International Relations*, edited by Volker Rittberger and Peter Mayer. Oxford: Clarendon Press, pp. 282–311.

Index